Reflections in Bullough's Pond

Revisiting New England: The New Regionalism

Nancy L. Gallagher, *Breeding Better Vermonters: The Eugenics Project in Vermont*

Sidney V. James, *The Colonial Metamorphoses in Rhode Island: A Study of Institutions in Change*

Diana Muir, *Reflections in Bullough's Pond: Economy and Ecosystem in New England*

Reflections in Bullough's Pond

Economy and Ecosystem

in New England

❧

Diana Muir

University Press of New England

Hanover and London

University Press of New England, Hanover, NH 03755
Printed in the United States of America
5 4 3 2 1

LIBRARY OF CONGRESS CATALOGING-IN-PUBLICATION DATA

Muir, Diana.

    Reflections in Bullough's Pond: economy and ecosystem in New England / Diana Muir.

      p.   cm.

    Includes bibliographical references and index.

    ISBN 0–87451–909–8

    1. Industrial revolution—New England—History.   2. New England—Industries—History.

I. Title.

HC107.A11 M84   2000

330.974—dc21   99–58013

This book is dedicated to

Binyamin Chaim,

Yonatan Asher, and

Avigail Fruma,

who inherit the world we have made.

CONTENTS

INTRODUCTION

New England is rich despite the fact that it was born poor. These six states were not blessed with the fabulously fertile soils of the Nile Valley, the benign climate of France, or the fabled silver mines of Potosi. Yankee wealth is the creation of human hands, not of nature. Our soil is thin, our weather cold, and the mineral resources that lie under our mountains are negligible. Yet the people who live here are and have long been prosperous. *Reflections in Bullough's Pond* asks why this should be so, and what it means for the planet.

Any book with the word "Ecosystem" in the subtitle is under suspicion of being a jeremiad: an unpleasant, guilt-inducing scold about our reprehensible environmental profligacy admonishing us to mend our ways or else. *Reflections in Bullough's Pond* is no jeremiad, it is a paean to the human ability to overcome daunting odds. Over and over again people in this small corner of the planet have faced disaster in the forms of economic collapse or resource dearth and overcome the odds. The most remarkable tale among the series of such triumphs that I recount in this book is the story of the Industrial Revolution.

New England experienced an industrial revolution second in point of time only to England itself. The most interesting aspect of Yankee industrial history is the fact that this industrial revolution, unlike all the others, was not a mere sequel to British industrialization. Yankees, like everybody else, watched what was going on in Lancashire and copied what they could. But industrialization in New England also had indigenous roots, wellsprings of change that flowed independently of and simultaneous with the revolution underway on the far side of the north Atlantic. *Reflections in Bullough's Pond* is an inquiry into why the Industrial Revolution happened, why it happened here, and what the implications of that revolution are.

Although the Industrial Revolution is at the heart of this book, it is not the only story in *Bullough's Pond*. Economic history in New England begins with the food crisis in prehistory, a crisis that was resolved by the adaptation of agriculture. Later economic crises came about when the flow of Puritan immigration was cut off by the English Civil War; when eighteenth-century population growth outran the supply of arable land; when American independence led to economic collapse; and when the shoe and textile industries moved south in the middle years of the twentieth century, leaving derelict mills and unemployed factory workers in their wake. In each case, economic collapse was avoided by the inventive capacity of the human mind.

New England lacks such desirable raw materials as oil, coal, and iron. No New England state leads the nation in any kind of agricultural production, not even maple syrup. There is, however, one resource that we do have in abundance. More scholarly effort has gone into the study of these six, small states than has been devoted to any similar region of the globe. This wealth of research makes a broad picture discussion of the economic and ecological history of New England possible. To the scholars upon whose work I have drawn, I am grateful.

Reflections in Bullough's Pond

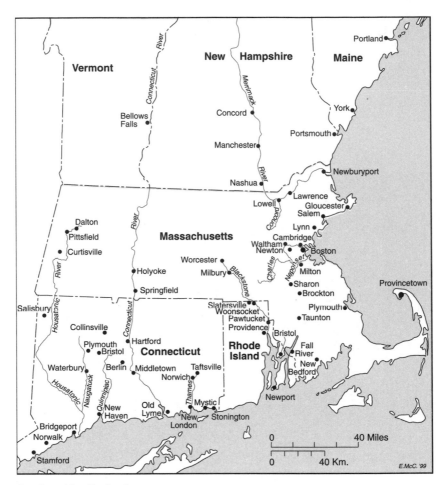

Southern New England. *Eliza McClennan, Mapworks.*

Chapter 1

From Time Immemorial

❧

No Hunter of the Age of Fable

Had need to buckle in his belt.

More game than ever he was able

To take ran wild upon the veldt:

Each night with roast he stocked his table,

Then procreated on the pelt,

 And that is how, of course, there came,

At last to be more men than game.[1]

—A. D. Hope

W E CAME TO THE POND IN FEBRUARY, THOUGH I hardly noticed it at the time. The pressing fact was that we needed a house. So many bedrooms, so many baths. It had to be located in a certain neighborhood, empty by a certain date, available at a certain price and, having found it, I didn't much care that there was a pond not twenty yards from the front door—only that the plumbing worked and the roof was sound.

But the pond was there. And when I tucked my children into bed that first night I could see geese gliding on black water, and I was glad.

It is a small pond. Three hundred yards from the point where the water flows in through a culvert under Commonwealth Avenue to the point where it flows out through the dam under Dexter Road—and not half so wide as it is long. Yet people are drawn to it for the same reasons that draw us to nature on a grand scale, to mountains, and oceans, and rivers: we like to stand in the presence of something larger than ourselves. This pool of silent water was here before any of us was born, and it will be here after we are forgotten. Knowing that, yet not thinking of it, walking along the pond not pondering questions of eternity and mortality, only thinking about how perfectly the orange and gold leaves of overhanging maple are reflected in blue water on this October morning, is to feel a kind of peace.

I know, of course, that the pond that shimmers so enticingly outside my window is not what it seems. It is possible, if you stand at a carefully chosen angle at a time of year when the trees are in leaf, to shut out all signs of civilization; to exclude electric wires, roads, fences, dam, and houses from view, and pretend that Bullough's Pond floats in rural solitude with only a few black ducks for company. This is an illusion. At one end of the pond, up a steep bank, is Commonwealth Avenue. Follow Commonwealth for seven miles and you arrive at the golden dome of the State House on Beacon Hill. Ours is an urban pond; it lies in a busy neighborhood near the heart of a city of eighty thousand, bordered by highways and houses in every direction. But the illusion of rural setting is too pleasing to relinquish. So too the illusion of permanence, of a body of water that has been here and will be here. That does not care if humans come or go or build their dwellings along its shore. It is illusion because Bullough's Pond, like the rest of the familiar New England landscape, is as much a creature of civilization as Commonwealth Avenue or the State House itself.

About a mile south west of our house a spring of fresh water seeps out of the ground in a place that was called Alcock's swamp before Newton grew pretentious enough to rename it Cold Spring Park. Water from that spring, which flows year round, meanders through town for three or four miles, then joins the Charles River. For the first fifteen millennia or so after the last glacier retreated, the brook was content to rise and flow into the Charles without stopping, only hesitating long enough to dampen a wide, low field sufficiently to turn it into a marsh in wet seasons, before darting between two glacial drumlins and continuing its progress to the river. I see those drumlins from my window, one north, the other west of my desk. They are wooded with oak and maple that almost hide the houses from view. I know that elevation and proximity to a rail station prompted Victorian businessmen to erect suburban villas on their crests, but that came later. At first there was only the wet meadow, two drumlins, and the little stream rushing to the sea.

We came to this place toward the end of a strange winter. There are no ordinary seasons in New England, only years that are unusually rainy, or abnormally hot, or remarkably cold. But that winter was especially strange. The temperature dropped at Thanksgiving and never went above freezing again through the entire month of December. The coldest December on record. It was brilliantly, bitingly cold, and in the full moon of early winter, we went ice skating every evening on a little pond in the woods not far from the house in Sharon where we lived. Then, on New Year's Eve, it started to rain, and the entire month of January was wet, grey, and mild. The warmest January in forty years. We moved to the pond on a bright, clear morning in early February when the thermometer stood at sixty degrees and ice on the pond was so far melted that there was open water from the inlet to the warming house. Through the lengthening days of February and early March, I watched the sheet of ice that covers Bullough's Pond advance and retreat, advance and retreat, like the great glacier at Mer de Glace, like the immense glaciers that once advanced and retreated across the New England landscape, until, on the evening of March 9, the pond was free of ice for the season.

It was glaciers advancing inexorably from the north that sculpted the face of New England. Sweeping everything before them they set the long arm of Cape Cod to shelter Massachusetts Bay and raised Long Island to shield the quiet waters of the Sound. Glaciers smoothed the rough edges off our mountains, flung stones and boulders to try the patience of Yankee farmers, scattered sandy ridges over the countryside, dished out lakes, ponds, bogs—then melted, leaving nature's warmer face to cover the barren, gouged-out valleys and hills with a blanket of green. The long work of replanting an ice-scoured landscape was still underway when the first humans appeared, chasing bison and caribou, musk-oxen and woolly mammoths over vast meadows; changing the face of the land forever.

Man cannot enter a landscape without changing it. Even those ancient hunters living on the receding edge of the ice age, their technological achievement confined to the manufacture of spears whose sharply chiseled points struck at the hearts of great mammoths and bled the life out of them, changed the land they lived on. They worked in unknowing collusion with the great climatic dislocations that followed the ice age to harry their prey to extinction. The people were few in number at first, their prey was abundant, and spearheads chiseled from flint enabled them to kill enough animals to sate their appetite on caribou and mammoth.

It was a living. Not a bad living at all. Tracking herds of fur-bearing beasts, spearing, butchering, and skinning them provided these hunters with a year-round diet of fresh meat in such abundance that the population grew. Bands of hunters came in from warmer lands to the south, and the natural increase of a prosperous people showed itself in numbers that increased generation by generation until humans lived in every part of the land. There were mastodon to hunt, horses, bison, and four species of mammoth ranging in size up to the aptly named imperial mammoths, behemoths that stood four meters high at the shoulder, yet were brought down by men of ordinary size wielding three-inch points of chert hafted to wooden sticks. They did not lack courage, these paleo-Indian hunters of twelve thousand years ago.[2]

The land they hunted extended far to the east of Cape Cod and south of Long Island, for the coastline was not yet where we know it today. Much of the coast of Maine was under water, and an arm of the ocean called the Champlain

Sea washed western Vermont with salt waves. The continent, sunken under the weight of mile-thick sheets of ice, was gradually rising. Ocean levels also rose as glaciers shrank, meltwater rushing seaward in mighty torrents.

The first humans to reach New England knew it as a chilly tundra; then a vast sea of grass grew up, transforming the hills of Massachusetts into prairie. Hunters could stand—we know from arrowheads left behind that they did—on a hill above Lake Assawompsett near Middleborough and look across mile after mile of blowing grass, scanning the landscape for herds of game.[3]

Slowly, the land was warming. Spring came across a period not of weeks but of centuries. Seedlings, then forests began to grow on what had been grassland. Spruce trees at first, followed by white pine and birch, and, finally, hickory, oak, chestnut, maple, and beech.[4]

Those first stands of spruce, appearing in Connecticut twelve thousand years ago, three thousand years after the last glacier retreated, heralded the end of a grassy Eden for vast herds of Pleistocene grazing animals. Caribou and bison ranged New England's grassy hills and river valleys when the first bands of paleo-Indian hunters came in pursuit of meat. So did many animals unknown today except to paleontology: American horses, woolly mammoths, mastodon, giant bears, and beaver twice the size of the modern kind.[5]

The warming climate that melted the ice and made grass grow over the rocky soil of glacial deposits now encouraged forest to replace prairie, forcing the animals living here to migrate, find new food sources, or face extinction. Elk and moose stayed, nibbling the tender spring leaves of the new trees and browsing grassy clearings in reduced numbers. Bison moved off, a little to the west, where conditions were more congenial. But mastodon, mammoth, giant bear, giant beaver, and a native species of horse disappeared forever. Were they fated to extinction by a changing climate? Or were they driven to extinction by skilled hunters? Perhaps the survivors offer a clue.

The musk-ox is a large Pleistocene game animal that thrives today in the Arctic—not in New England. Faced with a predator, musk-oxen back into a circle, lower their horns, and glower until the attacker gives up. This is a perfect defense against wolves or saber-toothed cats, but if a herd of musk-oxen backed up and stood glowering at spear-throwing paleo-hunters, it would not be an effective defense. It would be more like an invitation to dinner.

Survival strategies of the large game animals that ranged New England at the twilight of the ice age were evolved for defense against wolves and saber-toothed cats. Humans entered the picture very late, crossing the land bridge from Asia about twenty-seven thousand years ago—although archeologists debate the precise millennium of their crossing.

African game species grew up with humans around, evolving strategies of flight and wariness over the ages it took men to evolve the strategies of stalking and spear throwing. On this continent, bands of spear-throwing hunters were a newly introduced threat coming on the scene just when game species were forced to adapt to major changes in climate and vegetation. Musk-oxen retreated to a northern land where humans did not venture until a mere four thousand years ago. Elk, moose, bear, and caribou still inhabited the New England woods when the Mayflower landed its passengers. But for other species, the advent of paleo-hunters may have tipped the balance toward extinction.

Perhaps woolly mammoths and giant beavers were doomed by environmental changes even had humans never crossed the land bridge from Siberia to Alaska, but it's hard not to wonder about horses. Horses have no trouble living in New England today; two great breeds, the Narragansett Pacer and the Morgan, began here. Horses seem to thrive everywhere in North America; small numbers of escaped domestic animals grew rapidly into great wild herds on the barrier islands of the Atlantic coast and in the great basin, though these are hardly the most favorable environments America has to offer. Yet when the last ice age ended twelve thousand years ago, human hunters spread across the continent, and a species of horse that had flourished during the Pleistocene became extinct.

Perhaps the horses' fates depend on how humans regard them. Three hundred years ago, American Indians regarded the mustang and the Appaloosa as valuable assets, and protected and bred them accordingly. Twelve thousand years ago, paleo-hunters, like their European and Asian contemporaries, saw horses as one of several available types of meaty game animal, and hunted them. The only difference was that in the Old World, they did not happen to hunt them to extinction.

It is also possible that paleo-hunters spreading across this continent in pursuit of game killed the species they hunted quite inadvertently. Crossing the Bering Strait with their deadly hunting spears and mastery of fire, they may have carried stowaways, lethal pathogens to which the denizens of the virgin world they entered had never been exposed. It would be more flattering to imagine that the hunting prowess of our species slew the Pleistocene megafauna, but it is equally possible that diseases carried by human vectors exterminated the woolly mammoth and the saber-toothed cat, or that hunters merely finished off populations already decimated by disease.[6]

What we do know with certainty is that the human population increased steadily, that humans hunted these animals, and that several species of animals favored by hunters became extinct. And we know that the human population continued to increase. There were perhaps 25,000 paleo-hunters in New England 10,000 years ago, eating caribou steaks and wrapping themselves in the skins of giant bears. There were 120,000 Native Americans here when the first Europeans came; 104,000 of them lived below the Kennebec, eating succotash.[7]

The question of how a population of meat-eating paleo-hunters evolved into a much larger population of corn-eating farmers is one of the great chicken-or-the-egg questions of history. Two things certainly happened between 8000 B.C.E. and the year 1600 C.E.: (1) the population of New England expanded tremendously, going from densities of 5–12 people per hundred square kilometers, to densities as high as 266 in the Thames River valley of eastern Connecticut; (2) New England Indians adopted agriculture.[8] Did prehistoric peoples plant corn and beans in order to enable themselves to live in large semipermanent settlements? Or did population growth force meateaters to make do with succotash because there were too many people to be fed by hunting?

The pond outside my window teems with food. No wild furred animal larger than a raccoon comes to drink from it, though there are opossums and muskrats in plenty. There are also fat geese and ducks, snapping turtles and painted turtles, smallmouth bass, blue-gilled sunfish, crayfish, and snails. And there are cattail roots and acorns. All are edible, though no one would eat a muskrat who could have a goose. And no one would gather red oak acorns, boil them with ashes of rotten maple wood to leach the tannic acid, dry them, grind them in a stone mortar with a stone pestle—having laboriously fashioned mortar and pestle for the purpose—and bake the acorn meal into a sort of cake, if he could spear a mastodon.

The answer to the question of what our earliest precursors on this land did when the mastodon became extinct and other large game animals became scarce is fairly clear. The extinctions did not happen overnight, after all, but over the course of decades and centuries. And they did not happen to hunters casually passing through the area, but to groups of hunting people long established in particular territories. These people were familiar with the land they lived on; they knew where fish ran upstream in spring, where blueberries grew in summer. They would not have been reduced to eating muskrats. And they would not have succumbed to the starvation that claimed so many of the early English settlers on this coast. A people of small population and ordinary intelligence who are familiar with the land they live on can easily do better than that.

As large game animals became scarce 10,000 years ago, New Englanders adapted a more varied diet by exploiting other sources of food. There were still deer and bear, beaver and moose; Indians may have missed the giant Pleistocene species, but they hunted and enjoyed the smaller, modern varieties. There were geese and ducks, turkeys and heath hens. There were berries in summer, nuts in the autumn, and, above all, there were the abundant resources of the sea. Prehistoric settlements were made along the coast, or, less desirably, along rivers and lake shores. The sea has been an unfailing source of food to New Englanders for thousands of years.

Some offerings of the sea came almost like gifts. Salmon ran up the rivers in spring in such numbers that a man had only to stand on a rock and spear them. Shad and alewives swam upstream to spawn in runs so vast that early settlers fancied they could walk across the rivers dry-shod, if the fish would only stand still. Eels slipped downstream in the fall to spawn in the ocean. And sometimes a whale would beach itself and await the knives of Indian butchers. With more effort, a great variety of seafood could be caught. Weirs built across rivers caught fish year round, except when the rivers froze; but hook and line dropped through a hole in the ice could procure a meal even in winter. Fishing from a canoe, it was possible to catch wonderful things.

Indians in northern New England fashioned lightweight canoes of birchbark that could be easily carried around a portage; they were the best form of transportation in that country of rivers and lakes. They fished in lakes and shallow bays, just as Indians in southern New England—where great silver birch trees do not grow—fished near shore from dugout canoes of similar size. But serious, deep-sea fishing was done in vessels built on a different scale. New England's native white pines grow to be five feet across. Indian fishermen felled them by burning brush around the bases until the great trees toppled to the ground.

When a massive tree, five feet wide and three hundred feet tall, lay on the forest floor, the patient labor of turning it into a canoe began. Fires were set, and mounds of hot coals were placed where they would burn a section of wood. The Indians scooped the resulting charcoal from the trunk with clamshell or stone scraper, enlarging a cavity that would, when finished, seat forty men. A dugout canoe that size, or even one somewhat smaller, large enough to seat fifteen or twenty fishermen, could take its makers into deep water and bring them safely home with a fifteen-foot swordfish in tow.[9]

Fresh swordfish steak is a pretty reasonable substitute for woolly mammoth and we know from archeological remains that New England fishermen were bringing home swordfish six thousand years ago.[10] But, succulent as the steaks are, would anyone topple a three-hundred-foot tree and scrape the insides out of its five-foot-wide trunk with a clamshell—to say nothing of putting to sea off a coast legendary for the treachery of sudden storms and fog—if he could spear a moose? Moose meat is savory and stalking one is a whale of a lot easier than making a canoe, but by the year 4000 B.C.E., when New Englanders were putting to sea after swordfish, preferred game animals were too scarce to meet the demand. Or, put another way, there were lots of moose and bear in New England, but there were too many people.

Swordfish and salmon are a far cry from dietary deprivation, but as the population grew, people broadened the range of foods they ate to include dishes that do not taste as good as salmon, and foods that required hard, tedious work to produce.

Evidence of vegetable food does not show up in archeological digs as dramatically as the fiercely toothed upper jaw of a swordfish, but we know from the food grinding implements they left behind that New Englanders were gathering and processing acorns for food six thousand years ago.[11] These ancient dwellers on New England's shore also caught small fish in weirs and mined the tidal flats for clams and oysters. We can compile a fairly lengthy inventory of the foods people ate and the tools they fashioned; we know nothing of the stories they told or the jokes that made them laugh. We do know that their numbers increased, and that sometime between eight hundred and twenty-five hundred years ago, the people of southern New England began to plant corn and beans.[12]

The beginning of agriculture was not so much a discovery as a decision. Indians had long known that from little acorns, mighty oaks grow; just as they knew that the yield of a patch of wild rice could be improved by weeding, and that harvesters must allow some grain to fall back into the marsh to seed next year's crop. They knew under what conditions tuberous groundnuts and Jerusalem artichokes grew best. They could have planted them, cultivated them, weeded them—perhaps they did. They certainly ate more wild plants of every kind as the population increased.[13] And then, while the Caesars ruled in Rome, New England Indians began to plant, harvest, and store corn, beans, and squash—plants that had been domesticated in Mexico, knowledge of which spread gradually across the continent.

Writing about corn is a lot easier than growing it. Fields had to be cleared by building brush fires around the bases of trees, and the fires had to be tended so that they killed the trees without killing the forest. Soil had to be carefully hoed into hills using a clamshell bound to a notched stick with deer sinew, or a shovel made from the shoulder blade of a deer or a moose, or from a flat piece of stone. Corn, beans, and squash had to be planted with digging sticks. But the most tedious labor, as every gardener knows, is weeding. Indian farmers spent weary hours on their knees weeding corn hills with sharp-edged clamshells and pointed sticks, painstakingly tending each food-producing hill until the crops grew tall and strong enough that the weeds growing up around the hills could be left to hold the soil through the autumn rains that follow the harvest. When ears of corn began to ripen in the summer sun, fields had to be protected from thieving blackbirds, and in the fall the corn had to be picked and carried to the village in baskets. Then it was shucked, and the kernels were pried from the cob and dried for winter food.

The annual round of hoeing and planting, weeding and harvesting was such hard work that New England Indians left it to women, who worked the fields with some assistance from their children, producing more that half the village's food supply by their labor. Indian men hunted and fished, which the early English settlers did not perceive as work at all. "Their wives are their slaves," one Englishman observed, "and do all the work; the men will do nothing but kill beasts, fish, etc."[14]

The hunting and fishing brought meat into the village, food that was particularly crucial in spring, when the stores of corn and beans were running low.

Beyond meat, hunting furnished leather and bone from which clothing and tools were made. But while the colonial observer who charged Indian men with making their wives do all the work overlooked the crucial role of fish and game in the Indian economy, he had a canny view of the nature of work. A morning spent on your knees grubbing weeds out of a corn patch under a hot, July sun is work—no two ways about it. But a morning spent tracking a buck through the December woods can be many things besides work. Even if the hunter grows tired, hungry, wet, and cold—or comes home empty-handed—he may think of his morning as sport, adventure, or a test of manhood, none of which describes a morning grubbing weeds.

The first people to attempt agriculture on New England soil understood the difference between the work of hoeing corn and the work of hunting deer, just as they understood the difference between a mush of boiled cornmeal and a haunch of roast venison.

One fact alone marks the decision to clear fields, hoe corn, and husband seed for next year's sowing as a clear advance over a life of hunting and gathering: it is the road our own ancestors took. Many centuries ago—longer ago if your ancestors come from the plateaus of Central Mexico, much more recently if they lived on the Scandinavian coast—our hunting-and-gathering forbearers took up farming, a change in economic strategy we call the Neolithic Revolution. They did it for the same reasons that compelled early New Englanders to switch from venison and salmon to corn and beans: too many people, too little land. They did not make the switch because farming offered a higher standard of living. The beginnings of agriculture offered an inferior diet at the cost of distasteful labor. Opera, scientific medicine, cordless telephones, and the other advantages an agricultural surplus eventually made possible came much, much later.

For a hunting-and-gathering people, conversion to farming meant eating porridge instead of meat and grubbing weeds instead of stalking deer, gathering wild rice, or picking blackberries. Hunting-and-gathering people ate better and enjoyed more leisure than premodern farmers. New Englanders made the switch because hunger forced them to it. The pain of that transition, from Paleolithic hunting and gathering strategies to the early agricultural societies we call Neolithic, is nowhere more poignantly voiced than in the book of Genesis.

The Garden of Eden was a paradise so perfect that it never rained. God sent up "a mist from the earth, and watered the whole face of the ground. . . . And out of the ground made the Lord God to grow every tree that is pleasant to the sight, and good for food." (Gen. 2:69) Adam and Eve, we are told, spent their days admiring the trees, thinking up names for the animals, and making love. When they were hungry, they picked a fig or a pomegranate.

Disobedience brought expulsion from this paradise and the necessity of earning a living. Adam, who had lain under a leafy tree and eaten fruit that grew in ground he never tilled, now sweated and cursed the thorns and thistles that sprang up in his fields. Instead of figs and pomegranates, he ate bread. Adam and Eve might have longed for the Garden of Eden, but they could not go back because an angel with a flaming sword barred the way.

The angel with the flaming sword, the last dramatic flourish before the story of creation ends and the narration turns to Cain and Abel, is a knowing detail. Innocence once lost cannot be regained. A people who have experienced the Industrial Revolution cannot go back to agricultural simplicity. India could not do it no matter how many skeins of cotton Mahatma Gandhi spun on his wheel; America could not do it no matter how many college graduates moved back to the land on small Vermont farms. No people who experienced the Neolithic Revolution could go back to a hunting and gathering existence, but, in New England at least, there was a struggle to avert the inevitable exit from paradise.

We know that before New Englanders turned irrevocably to farming, they tried to address the problem of feeding a growing population with static resources by eating further down the food chain, harvesting acorns and oysters when moose and salmon were scarce. If oysters do not sound like hardship food, consider the difference between oysters as a delicacy and oysters as a dietary staple. An oyster on the half shell makes an appealing tidbit, but someone using oysters as a dietary mainstay would have to collect, shuck, and cook a hundred of them to feed a grown man for a single day. A glance at the immense shell middens that dot the New England coast confirms that Indians ate shellfish. A hot August day spent collecting oysters or digging clams will persuade any sensible person to think of them as the Indians did, and as generations of Yankees did: more trouble than they're worth—unless you are too poor to afford something better.

Remember that it takes four or five hundred oysters or quahogs to feed a family for a day, and that thousands more had to be gathered and dried over smoky fires in the hot summer sun for winter food. Stoop-labor. Sweaty, muddy, back-breaking, and often plagued by horseflies. Women's work. Work that even women avoided as long as there were better things to eat; when there weren't, New Englanders ate oysters. Around two thousand years ago—the period that saw the introduction of agriculture—they began eating shellfish not just during famine years, but every year, as a regular and important part of the diet.[15]

We know what prehistoric New Englanders thought of stooping over to pick up oysters by the shells they left; great heaps of shells two or three feet deep covering ten or twenty acres that once lined the New England coast, though vast heaps have disappeared, quarried for lime. The shells at the bottom of heaps such as the great shell midden at Damariscotta, Maine, are immense, ten and

Clam Diggers, Fred Quimby, c. 1890s. Digging clams is hot, dirty, tedious, back-straining labor. In New England, it was a way for the poor to make ends meet. Courtesy of the Society for the Preservation of New England Antiquities (neg. #4322–B).

twenty inches across, the remains of forty-year-old oysters—the remains, that is, of oysters that lived to the age of forty before somebody ate them.[16]

Then a bad year came, a year when drought made the deer scarce or warfare kept a tribe from the river during the spring fish run, and people were forced to eat oysters. They ate them, left the twenty-inch shells on the beach, and when times were good again went back to eating venison. But gradually, with increasing population, people turned to oysters more regularly, and the shells they left shrank to the familiar five- to seven-inch size, and the shell heaps grew as clams and oysters were gathered in great numbers, eaten fresh, dried for the winter, and stewed. At that point the people of New England, already eating acorns and oysters and everything else the land provided without husbandry, turned to agriculture.[17]

The change from hunting and gathering to depending on crops for half the annual food supply was made not suddenly or even in a single generation, but over the course of decades and centuries. It was a choice that redounded to enforce the original decision. A population growing too large to sustain itself by gathering the bounty of nature chooses to cultivate and store crops for the lean season. The surplus thus produced enables the population to grow, which compels a more intensive agriculture, which results in population growth, which compels more intensive cultivation, which results in ...

Of course, the cycle of increasingly distasteful labor in exchange for a diet of ever lessening quality could have been stopped at any time by controlling population growth. It is a fact of nature that people are fruitful and do multiply. Any group that takes no active steps to stem growth will increase, gradually but certainly, until the number of people overwhelms the available resources. "Nature" will check this fatal course only after the crisis is joined and people in an overpopulated area die of famine, disease, or at war over scarce resources—all tragedies that can be averted by foresighted use of population control. Late marriage and infanticide are the low-technology techniques most commonly used to limit growth.

Infanticide is horrible, so horrible that polite people don't speak about such a thing as a method of population control. Yet we know that, compelled by the survival of the group, people in many cultures kill their infants. The practice was not uncommon in early modern Europe, and it is not unfamiliar in China and India today. Moral ideals influence the way human beings behave, but circumstance molds morality. People facing a chronic food shortage may reason that allowing only as many infants to live as the group can hope to feed is a moral act. Late marriage, though not so conspicuously objectionable on moral grounds, also limits the freedom of the individual in deference to the needs of the group. By either method, control of population growth was available to New England Indians—yet they apparently chose to employ neither with sufficient rigor.

The small ravine where Smelt Brook flows out of Bullough's Pond is, on warm evenings, a kind of lover's lane. It is dark, screened by trees and brush, and if two seventeen-year-olds seek a little privacy there on a June night, who's to stop or even see them? Try then to imagine the difficulty of a council of Indian elders attempting to dissuade two seventeen-year-olds from pairing off. "Listen, kids, it's not that we don't understand, we were young once too, you know. All we're asking is that you wait a little while—say, eight or ten years—so that this overpopulation thing doesn't get out of hand. Okay?"

Families, tribes, social groups, sometimes entire societies have done it, have persuaded their young people to defer marriage and sexual intercourse into their late twenties; but such an effort requires tremendous strength of purpose. It is easier and far more pleasant to make a wedding; or to wink at the pairing off and make the wedding when the girl starts to show. Most human societies have done one or the other. So it may have been partly due to their own failure to make the hard decisions necessary to control population growth that New Englanders turned to agriculture. But farming was also forced upon them.

New England peoples on the verge of the switch to agriculture lived in clusters of family groups, each centered on a particular river valley or estuary, occasionally trading, meeting, and intermarrying with groups in neighboring valleys. Each valley already held about as many people as the plants and animals that lived in it could support. The option of cultivating such native crops as groundnuts and Jerusalem artichokes was available to all of these groups, and they would have had access to the beans, corn, and squash, knowledge of whose cultivation had spread slowly north and east from Mexico.

Now suppose that the people of every river valley in New England decided to reject agriculture, limit population growth, and live within their resources—with one exception. The people of a single river valley plant corn, beans, and squash, and store the harvest for the winter. Weak individuals in that valley are far more likely to live through the winter months when hunting is poor and vegetable foods unavailable. Some of the sick recover health with the coming of spring. Young people enjoy the newfound abundance by marrying and bearing children as young as they please. Women are more likely to bear healthy children and nurslings are more likely to survive. Couples space their children more closely, since mothers in sedentary tribal groups are freed of the necessity hunters and gatherers face of carrying their young children across the land, a necessity that requires a three-to-four-year pause between surviving children in a family. With larger families, the population of the group that chose agriculture rapidly expands to the point that the deer grazing in upland forests separating their river basin from the next valley look very tempting—even though deer on these lands have been hunted by the people of a neighboring valley from time out of mind. Suddenly, however, our hypothetical agricultural tribe outnumbers its hunting-and-gathering neighbors two to one, and taking over neighboring territory is easy. Because a larger population provides a larger army, once any group in a region decides to adopt agriculture, no neighboring group can afford not to.

Maps of Indian settlement before Columbus show Algonquin-speaking peoples spread across the Northeast in a broad arch that extends inland to include the Great Lakes. Thrust into the center of this wide, culturally homogenous region is the Iroquois nation, platted on the map like an arrowhead pointing north. The Iroquois, moving north with agricultural skills, an ever expanding population, and a warlike culture, brushed the hunting-and-gathering Algonquin out of their path. This trend slowed only when people indigenous to the Northeast began to plant beans, corn, and squash, and let their populations grow until they gained the strength to check the Iroquois advance.[18]

Shifts in population as farmers wrested hunting grounds from hunter-gatherers were still going on when white settlement began. The only emplaced fortifications that English explorers found in New England were along the upper Merrimack, where the Western Abenaki had built palisaded villages on defensible bluffs to protect their hunting grounds from the corn-growing, expansionist Massachusett tribes.[19] That line of wooded forts marked a dividing line between people who kept their population low enough to live off the bounty of the land, and people who altered the face of the land to produce food for an expanding population.

Chapter 2

Improving Nature

ᗒᗕ

Though it bee here somewhat cold in the winter, yet here we have plenty of Fire to warme us, and that a great deale cheaper then they sel Billets and Faggots in London: nay, all Europe is not able to afford so great Fires as New-England. A poor servant here that is to possesse but 50 acres of land, may afford to give more wood for Timber and Fire as good as the world yeelds, then many Noble men in England can afford to do. Here is good living for those that love good fires.[1]

—Francis Higginson, 1630

HARRIED TO DISTRACTION BY THE MYRIAD demands of civilized life, a seventeenth-century European could sit on a mahogany chair, sip dark, sugar-sweetened chocolate from a porcelain cup, take a pinch of snuff, and dream of a better life. He could dream of a place where the lithe, bronze bodies of carefree savages frolicked in perpetual sunshine. A place where happy natives plucked succulent, exotic fruits from trees when they thirsted and, when they hungered, reveled in the thrill of the chase in primeval forests teeming with game. To an Old World weary with care, America was the stuff of dreams.

Not all Native Americans were young, beautiful, and happy, but disease was scarce and, where population was sparse, they lived in a land that offered its fruits in abundance. North of the Kennebec, where corn was not grown, they lived as Europeans could live only in dreams: by plucking fruit and chasing the wild buck in the greenwood.[2] It was that rare case of reality approaching idyll.

Nature's generous hand opened in the warming days of March. No sooner had the ice broken up in northern New England, then smelt flashed upstream to spawn, so many fish that a man could not reach his "hand into the water, without encountering them." Villages were still feasting on smelt when alewives arrived, filling river and stream with their silver bodies. Delicious and tender when the fish were taken on their way upstream; nasty as rotten offal if a man were foolish enough to catch and eat one as it headed back to the open sea. But no one had to eat alewives as they ran downstream, for by then ducks and geese were passing overhead in great, northering wedges, stopping to rest in tidal marshes where Indian women harvested them with snares and clubs. By the time waterfowl had begun to nest, giant sturgeon and salmon were swimming upstream to spawn and fishermen stood on rocks at the water's edge, easily spearing enough to sate the appetite of the village.

Summer was as bountiful as spring. Scallops, crabs, clams, and oysters could be gathered in the shallows, while brook trout and bass, flounder, and cod were plentiful. And in grassy meadows sloping toward the sun, it was strawberry time. Strawberries, raspberries, and blueberries delighted the palate and at- tracted great flocks of passenger pigeons for people to snare and enjoy.

August and September were the only months when northern Indians had vegetable food in abundance. Grapes hung ripe in the rich clusters that in- spired thirsty Vikings to call this western shore Vineland. Groundnuts and Je- rusalem artichokes were dug up in damp meadows, and the sweet, gelatinous roots of yellow pond lilies were harvested at the water's edge. Canoeists push- ing into the marshes bent stalks of wild rice over the gunwales to thresh the succulent grain, and as the season advanced, beechnut and acorn were gath- ered in the wood.

Autumn brought a move inland, to upland woods where beaver and cari- bou, moose and bear were hunted. The tooth of the walrus, the shell of the tur- tle, the antler of deer all had their assigned place as hand tools, and the animals from which they came provided sustenance until spring brought fish running upstream. Of course, if drought made game animals scarce and lean, or if snow didn't fall to help hunters track deer through the woods, winter was a starving time.

Northern Indians knew that February and March, when deer were lean and the land offered little else, would be hungry even in the best of years. Early En- glish visitors to this coast scoffed at the natives' lack of foresight. If they weren't so lazy, the Englishmen said, they could easily smoke enough fish and meat in the warm months to supply their want in late winter. But perhaps the Ameri- cans were wiser than the English knew. Their hunting-and-gathering life could be sustained only by low population density. Storing enough dried meat and fish to make winter a time of plenty might have encouraged population growth to exceed the capacity of the land to provide food. If the enforced fasting of late winter helped keep the population low, it was sound policy—deliberate or not.[3]

South of the Kennebec, where population far exceeded the ability of the land to sustain life without resorting to agriculture, the rhythm of the year was very different. Indians there also waited for the fish runs and stalked deer in the win- ter forest, but life depended on the success of corn and beans growing in wood- land clearings. Grain, carefully nurtured, harvested, and stored, comprised the bulk of their diet. Smelt and salmon, goose, whale, oyster, beaver, and venison, all relished in season, were the spice, not the staff, of life.

The notable aspect of Indian cornfields is not that they nourished the population, but that they did it with so little impact on the ecosystem. An Indian field was cleared, cultivated for a few years, then given back to the forest. In a short time the site would have grown up so well that no one would suspect it had recently been a cornfield, unless he or she walked among the trees and noticed the regular rows of old corn hills, earth mounds rounded down by weather but still visible on the forest floor in some New England woodlands three centuries after the last Indian hoed corn.[4] The growing corn, beans, and squash of an Indian field drew on the fertility of land nourished by forest growth until the nutrients were exhausted and the field abandoned, but—and this is the key—the use of a patch of land as a cornfield did not disrupt the life of the surrounding forest. Around the cornfield, trees grew, squirrels buried acorns, ancient trees rotted back into the soil, and seedlings took root. When a field was abandoned, the forest was there to take it back. In Indian agriculture, the round of the seasons was permanent; the fields, transient.

An Indian field was a plot of land briefly used for growing corn, then used for growing trees—a marvelous crop that seeds itself and does not want weeding or protecting from crows. Yet a forest is, in its way, as productive as a cornfield. Deer will browse on the leaves and twigs of birch, maple, and hemlock; both they and the black bear eat nuts that fall to the forest floor; woodcock, turkey, and grouse eat them too. From the rabbit making breakfast of an oak seedling to the nuthatch spiraling down a snag, trees support wildlife in all its abundant variety and provide for the needs of human settlements in more direct ways as well.

Indians wanted many things from the forest. They wanted wood to build everything from fish weirs to lodges; they wanted nuts for food, roots of cedar and tamarack to use as thread, pine pitch for caulk, and the bark of birch and dogwood for medicine. Above all they wanted fat game and firewood.

Indians used firewood in immense quantities to cook, cure food, and heat wigwams. Especially to heat wigwams. Thin-walled structures framed of bent saplings and covered with bark mats, wigwams were kept warm by large, constantly burning fires, and were designed to be moved to a new site when nearby supplies of wood gave out. The need for firewood convenient to the village kept Indians moving through the year and changing village sites from year to year. The trick was to move house often enough that a fresh supply of firewood was always close at hand.

The life of any particular group of Indians was absolutely confined within a territory whose bounds were rigidly defined by the neighborhood of other groups. Every woodland, every pond, every stream—or, more accurately, the right to hunt, fish, or gather food from every meadow, river, and beach, belonged to some specific group or family. Such a system is wonderfully embodied in the name of a lake near Worcester called Chabanakongkomuk, or, "You fish on your side, I fish on my side, nobody fish in the middle—no trouble."[5] Within these defined territories, Indian families and villages moved constantly. I am not so vain as to suppose that they often came to Bullough's Pond.

A poet has published a book called *Once Around Bullough's Pond*; the title comes from his habitual daily run "up Grove Hill, onto Prospect, down the hill, across Walnut, and once around Bullough's Pond."[6] Douglas Worth's poem imagines an Indian family living in this place. His imagined Indians lived in harmony with nature, hunted, loved, and tried to make sense of the coming of the English. The Indians I imagine were just trying to make a living, and although smelt ran up the brook here every spring, a better living was to be had closer to large bodies of water. Pleasing as it would be to imagine Indians living here, I accept the probability that they merely passed through en route to more bountiful locales.

Food, like firewood, was plentiful—provided the village moved regularly to be near the places where it was found, and altered the condition of the land to encourage food to thrive and multiply. In other areas, the Indians' role in encouraging the growth of wild plant foods was more passive. Blackberry and raspberry seed themselves wherever the forest ends. They grow unbidden at the edges of cultivated fields throughout New England today.

Old fields could be burned, and the depleted, hot, dry, treeless land would produce wonderful crops of blueberries. Other abandoned fields, kept free of brush by regular burning, produced strawberries, acre on acre of strawberries, which English colonists marveled to find growing wild. Settlers coming to the mouth of the Piscatuqua found open land, clear of trees and brush, covered with such an abundance of low, fruiting plants that they called their town Strawberry Banke, and blessed a land where nature was so bountiful.

Nature left to itself plants but an occasional strawberry. It was Indians who cleared acres of sunny ground and kept them open for strawberries, encouraging nature to produce fruit in juicy red profusion.

Further north, Frenchmen exploring the coast of Maine were delighted to find vineyards in the wilderness, "black grapes marvelously faire . . . plummes growing on trunks as big as a man's fist."[7] Vines lined the banks of river and stream, trailed over branches of riverside oak and maple, and flourished in the sunshine. Some visitors marveled at the richness of a land where such desirable fruit grew wild; more astute observers recognized the grapes for what they were: Indian vineyards, the grapes fed and watered by the stream, the competing branches of oak and maple trees that served as trellises pruned by Indian arborists to let sunlight reach the vines.[8] They grew at the edges of cornfields cleared by Indian women. But the most important wild crop whose production was enhanced by Indian management was venison.

The number and fatness of deer in New England astonished English set-tlers as fully as the quantity and richness of the wild strawberry crop. What they failed to realize was that the deer were no more wild than the strawber-ries. Indians built no cattle barns, fenced no pastures, mowed no hay; but they raised venison as surely as the English raised sheep. Twice a year the people of southern New England burned vast tracts of forest. Because large fallen branches were gathered regularly for firewood, and because the land was burned too often to allow much brush to grow, the fires moved rapidly through the dead leaves and new growth of the forest floor, leaving mature trees unscathed. The result was a forest that Englishmen could only marvel at: a forest of great, lofty trees filtering sunlight onto an open, grassy floor abounding with white-tailed deer.

The deer were not there by chance. Burning kept down brush, opened the canopy, and let far more light reach the floor than nature would have allowed. On the dry, well-lit forest floor, New England's native little bluestem grass grew rampant, nourishing much larger populations of deer than a natural woodland could feed. Between stretches of carefully burned upland forests were low-lying swampy thickets where the deer retreated in winter to feed on the new growth of swamp maple and hemlock.

Repeated burning changed the mix of species in a forest. Hemlock, pine, beech, sugar maple, black and yellow birch could not survive fires, while oak, hickory, and chestnut not only thrived, but could also resprout strongly from roots if a fire got out of hand and killed the parent tree. Oak, hickory, and chestnut all produced nuts in quantity, nuts that were not only gathered and enjoyed by Indians, but that fed deer, turkey, geese, bear, porcupine, elk, grouse, and other game animals. Some of these species—and others, such as rabbit and pigeon—also ate the blueberries, blackberries, pin cherries, huckleberries, and raspberries that grew well in burned-over land when light penetrated the forest. By the moderate labor of setting fire to selected parts of the forest, hunters greatly increased their supply of good things to eat.

Hunting lands belonging to particular village groups were not necessarily adjacent to the lake or ocean shore where they made their summer camps. Southern New Englanders depended on farming—and no farmer in her right mind encourages deer to multiply near unfenced cornfields, or bear to breed near household berry patches. Indian farmers very sensibly kept things separ-ate, like the Pocumtucks of Deerfield, who kept the Ware River valley, twenty miles distant, in grasses to fatten the deer. It was easier to walk twenty miles to go hunting than to keep deer out of the corn.[9]

Connecticut, Rhode Island, and Massachusetts were a cultivated wilderness, a countryside of small fields, berry patches, and managed forests. North of the Kennebec the land was as wild as a European could imagine it. Except for tend-ing riverbank vineyards, and perhaps a few blueberry and strawberry patches,

Indians of the northern forest did not farm the land. Northern Indians knew about agriculture, but any Maine gardener will sympathize with the reasoning that kept them from adopting it, especially when reminded that until about 1850 the climate was considerably colder than it is today. A single late-spring frost, or one coming too early in fall, would have spelled hunger. Better to depend on what nature provides than to stake survival on a crop that is likely to fail every few years. So northern Indians did not plant corn. And they did not burn the forest to improve forage for caribou and elk for the simple reason that the southern method of burning would not have worked. Northern forests are largely made up of evergreen trees that drop many highly combustible dead branches to the forest floor, burn easily, and will not resprout from roots after a fire. The hickory, chestnut, and white oak that survived regular burning to produce copious nut crops for the foraging animals of the southern New England forests reach the northern limit of their range near the Kennebec. Fire here would have consumed the forest, not improved it for hunting.

When the first Englishmen explored these shores, the coastal islands south of the Kennebec, the land sloping down to coastal bays and inlets, the land at the mouths of rivers, and the entire mainland shore of Massachusetts Bay, was planted with corn or made up of old cornfields growing blueberries and strawberries. Forests had been cut back until they began some distance from the shore. This situation, perfect for European settlers who could plant on land the Indians had cleared without the labor of clearing forests, was a portent of disaster to a people who lacked draft animals and wheeled vehicles.[10]

Indian agriculture depended on the fertility of the forest. Generations of trees growing, losing their leaves, and rotting back into the soil produced a rich humus, which Indians exploited to grow crops that depleted the fertility of soil after a few years use. Soil fertility can be mended with dung. Cartloads of manure, seaweed, or dead fish, plowed into the ground, enabled nineteenth-century farmers to enjoy good yields on old fields. The Indians didn't have carts, they didn't have ploughs, and, by the sixteenth century, they were running out of forested land near the coast to clear for cornfields.

Forested land on the coast was a crucial part of Indian subsistence strategy. Oysters, clams, and fish had to be smoked in great volume to preserve them for winter use. Without wheeled vehicles, the burden of dragging firewood to coastal fish-smoking stations was very heavy. It is difficult to say how far it was worthwhile to transport wood for smoking fish, but there must come a point when the labor of moving wood is greater than the value of the smoked clams. Canoes could have been used to transport wood from upriver, provided that there was standing timber on the riverbank and that the group desiring to smoke fish had the right to cut timber. Cutting timber was another difficulty. Chopping wood is hard work with a stone ax, which is why Indian fires were fueled with whole branches pushed into the fire little by little as they burned.

The method saved a vast amount of labor. But wood must be cut into short lengths if it is to be transported by canoe, and the labor cost of doing so with a stone ax is prohibitive.[11]

Populous Indian villages along the shore of southern Maine, New Hampshire, Massachusetts, Rhode Island, and Connecticut faced increasing conflict between the need to stay on the coast for fishing, and the imperative to move inland and open up new cornfields. We cannot know what they would have done as deforestation progressed, forests receded farther from the coast, and old fields lost their fertility, although there is evidence that Indians on Cape Cod used fish to fertilize their depleted cornfields.[12]

Cape Cod is blessed with numerous small streams that once teemed with alewives, so the distances over which fish had to be hauled from weir to field were short. Not all territories were so well supplied with herring runs. We can fancifully imagine Indian farmers domesticating the moose, inventing the wheel, and training the big animals to pull cartloads of firewood to coastal fishing stations and cartloads of seaweed and fish heads inland to dung cornfields. More realistically, we can guess that a population already depending on corn and beans for more than half of its caloric intake would have moved its planting fields inland where virgin soil was available, and eaten more corn and beans. People would have missed the oysters and codfish that now came less frequently into their diet, and they would have had to spend more time grubbing weeds and less time fishing, but people who allow population to outgrow the natural resources that support their lifestyle must accept some deterioration in the conditions of life. The Indians of southern New England depended heavily on the bounty of the forest. When they had cut all of the trees near the shore, they would have been forced to alter their lifestyle, even if that alteration was for the worse.

At the time of first contact with Europeans, the crisis of coastal deforestation was not yet joined. From the treeless land European explorers saw all along the coast, however, we can predict that, like the shift from hunting to harvesting shellfish that occurred when the population outgrew the supply of game animals, that crisis would have come. Instead, a disaster far worse than deforestation struck the Indian peoples of New England.

Chapter 3

The Economics of Extermination

❧

The Beaver was a small animal weighing from twenty to forty pounds and re-
sembling the bear.[1]

—W. R. Cochrane, 1880

W E DON'T KNOW THE NAMES OF THE FIRST
Europeans to visit the coast of New England; we don't even know
what year they came. Viking sailors, who certainly landed in Newfoundland, may have visited the coast as far south as Maine—or it may have
been Nova Scotia that they referred to as Vineland.

We do know that in the mid-1400s, European fishing boats met the demands of a growing population by venturing farther and farther into the Atlantic, and we know that by 1480 or 1481, boats from Bristol, England, were
catching fish off the shore of Newfoundland. Within a few years French, English, and Basque fishermen were coming regularly to fish the Grand Banks. At
some point, one of these fishing boats made landfall in the New World; we
don't know where, only that the captain wasn't named Columbus, and that
those anonymous, fifteenth-century fishermen had a reason for keeping mum
that anglers of any era will understand: having found a good place to fish, they
wanted to keep it to themselves.[2]

These men had not come to trade, settle, or explore; they had come only to
fish. If they visited the nearby coast, it was to get fresh water or firewood. Once
on shore, they met the indigenous people, and a little trading went on, and reports of the land they had visited filtered back to Europe. But it was not anything the fishermen found on this coast that inspired Henry VII of England to
back John Cabot's voyages of exploration; that decision was prompted by news
of Columbus's voyages to the Caribbean, and by the fear that new Spanish trading posts on islands then thought to be located off the coast of Japan would cut
England out of a potentially profitable trade sailing west to bring Oriental
spices to Europe.

It soon became clear that neither the lands Cabot explored in the North Atlantic, nor Columbus's Caribbean islands were anywhere near Japan, China, or the spice islands of the East Indies, but the news was worse for England than for Spain: natives in the Spanish islands wore necklaces and earrings wrought of gold, natives in New England wore seashells. The fishing was good, but the long-anticipated northwest passage eluded discovery and there seemed very little reason to bother with the northern islands, or continents, or whatever they were. The new land had lumber; England had lumber. It seemed likely that grain would grow here; grain grew in England. If spices, jewels, or precious metals had been found in New England it would have been a different story; they were not. For over a century the unpromising, new-found land was left to fishermen and the native peoples.

No cities of gold were discovered in Maine between John Cabot's voyage of 1496, and Elizabeth I's interest in colonization in the late 1500s; no mountains of emeralds were found in Connecticut. New England was the same country of forest and hill—but old England was by no means the land it had been a hundred years before. The England of 1496 was a poor, undeveloped backwater; a country that exported such unprocessed raw materials as cordwood to wealthier lands and imported the few cannon its meager navy possessed from Antwerp, for lack of English iron foundries. By the end of Elizabeth's reign, England not only produced but exported iron, glass, copper, and finished woolens. A century of cutting forests, of burning timber to manufacture everything from salt to ale to the cannon that defeated the Spanish Armada, and of expanding farming into recently cleared forest lands, had made England rich and powerful. That same century of industrial development saw a doubling of England's population, a scarcity of arable land, and widespread deforestation that raised the threat of famine and caused the poor to shiver for want of fuel. The wooded farmland of New England took on a new allure.

Colonization was vaunted as the answer to many problems. Perhaps the landless poor could be resettled abroad. Perhaps the native people would buy the surplus woolens England produced. Perhaps a short, profitable trade route to the Indies would yet be found in some deep bay or river leading west. Perhaps southern colonies could produce the olive oil, currants, wine, and sugar England imported from the Mediterranean at great expense. Perhaps northern colonies could produce the ship timber, tar, and cordage England was forced to import from the Baltic now that British forests had been cut down. And perhaps—oh, most wonderful possibility of all!—perhaps English colonists would discover mountains of silver, emeralds, and gold.

England was not alone in its dreams of gold and glory. Holland, Sweden, and France envied the Spanish and Portuguese empires; all four nations sent expeditions to explore the North American continent, planted or attempted to plant colonies, and brought Native Americans into close contact with large groups of Europeans for the first time.

Fishermen had continued to cross the Atlantic in such numbers that the occasional explorer was likely to be greeted by Indians able to conduct trade in rudimentary English or French. English explorer Sir Humphrey Gilbert, sailing into the harbor at St. John's, Newfoundland, in 1583, found thirty fishing boats from various European nations lying at anchor. Unperturbed, Gilbert exercised the explorer's perogative in newly discovered lands by setting up a pillar claiming the island in the name of Her Majesty, Queen Elizabeth.

From the Native American perspective, early explorers must have seemed to differ little from fishermen. Both groups traded kettles, glass beads, and woven cloth for beaver and other furs; both were liable to kidnap unwary individuals or turn a trading meet into a battle with their lethal guns. A century of such contact had relatively little impact on life in New England beyond teaching Americans to approach European visitors with caution. The effects of the large exploring expeditions of the early 1600s were different, not only because they were harbingers of colonization, but because their crews harbored the diseases that killed the native people.

Death rates from the epidemics that swept New England in the seventeenth century were almost unimaginably high: 80 percent, 90 percent, 95 percent. Where twenty people had lived in 1600, one would survive. In a countryside where 120,000 native people had lived when the first Europeans came, a mere 16,000 would survive a century of fatal epidemics and wasting disease.[3]

When small groups of big game hunters crossed the Bering Strait to populate this continent twenty-eight millennia ago, they traveled in small bands; too small to harbor diseases like smallpox, chicken pox, and measles that must be transmitted directly from one infected individual to the next. Disease-free themselves, they conferred freedom from contagious Old World diseases on their children. Domestic livestock are reservoirs of disease organisms that occasionaly mutate and spread from chickens or pigs to human hosts. Flu, measles, cholera, smallpox, malaria, plague, and tuberculosis are epidemic human diseases that evolved from diseases of domestic livestock. The Americas knew only a handful of species of domestic livestock, guinea pigs, muscovy ducks, and llamas in the Andes, turkeys in Mexico; dogs were the only domestic animals kept north of Mexico. With such a meager array of livestock, there was little opportunity for diseases to arrive in domestic animal populations and be transmitted to humans, and little chance that uniquely American epidemic diseases could arise that would slay immigrants to these shores with the efficiency with which Old World diseases mowed down New World people.

The New World's freedom from disease would one day turn and kill its children in a macabre epidemiological paradox. For twenty-eight thousand years, no American child suffered from chicken pox—and no American girl grew to adulthood with an immunity to the disease that she could pass on to her children. When European exploring and fur-trading expeditions brought infections across the ocean, virulent microbes attacked a people with no natural immunities, none of the inherited and acquired antibodies that enable Europeans to survive contact with infectious diseases.

An unknown European sailor landed on the New England coast in 1615 with a case of shingles from childhood chicken pox, or perhaps it was an active case of smallpox, or of measles. We cannot be certain which disease it was, only that it spread with a consuming intensity, devastating communities from Narragansett Bay to the Merrimack and as far as thirty miles inland. Within a year the Massachusetts coast was empty; entire villages lay dead with no one to bury the victims or even remember their names. The Pilgrims, arriving four years later, found meadows strewn with bleached bones and human skulls.

Because the crews of early transatlantic voyages were small and their contact with the natives slight, more than a century elapsed between the arrival of the first European fishing boats on these shores and the first of the lethal epidemics that nearly exterminated New England's aboriginal people. The size of the crews is important. Fewer than a dozen sailors manned a Breton cod-fishing boat, and even John Cabot's *Matthew*, voyaging to discover new worlds under the sponsorship of the king of England, shipped a mere eighteen souls. The incubation period for measles is eight to twenty-one days; for smallpox it is eight to ten, and you can only become infected by coming in contact with someone who has the disease. The crew of a sixteenth-century fishing boat, even if every hand had come down with the pox, would have all been convalescing, or dead, before landfall in the Gulf of Maine.

Seventeenth-century voyages of exploration were on an altogether different scale. When he explored the coast in 1604, Champlain had a hundred men with him, men who went ashore for the purpose of meeting the indigenous inhabitants. And, even earlier, by the late 1500s, fishermen and entrepreneurs were actively trading with native Americans for furs.[4] With so many Europeans in contact with so many Americans, the transmission of the disease became inevitable. It required only a single European sailor who had once had chicken pox and was now suffering from shingles to shake hands with a single American on the densely populated Massachusetts coast for an epidemic to start that would consume tens of thousands of lives.

Measles, smallpox, influenza, venereal disease, scarlet fever, plague, yellow fever, malaria, chicken pox and more; Americans died from Old World diseases to which they had no immunity. We are mistaken if we think our ancestors slew the Indians to win this land. They didn't have to. They had only to watch them die. There were no cures for scarlet fever or measles, no inoculations against smallpox, no quinine to treat malaria. There was nothing but death.[5]

London and Bristol were full of men talking about colonization in 1620, the year the Pilgrims set sail for America. In 1614, the London Company had sent the redoubtable John Smith to explore the New England coast with an eye to commercial possibilities and colonization. Sir Ferdinando Gorges, undeterred by a failed attempt to plant a colony in Maine, sent Richard Vines and Thomas Dermer to scout New England for likely spots to establish trading posts and colonies. Dermer, returning to England in 1619, was able to inform his employer that the thousands of warriors who had been expected to fiercely defend the Massachusetts coast from foreign incursion were dead.[6] To Pilgrim colonists stepping ashore from a harbor recommended by John Smith onto a well-watered land of cleared fields and fair prospects, it seemed as though the hand of God had reached out and made a place for them in the wilderness just as surely as He once opened the Red Sea for Moses to lead the children of Israel to the Promised Land.

The Plymouth colonists could have lived well on venison, goose, salmon, and corn, with plenty of clear water to drink. A village site that had supported two thousand Pawtuxet could amply provide for the needs of fifty English; but the Pilgrims were not satisfied with so simple a life. Partly because they were deeply in debt to the London merchants who underwrote their voyage, but mostly because they were European, they wanted more than to live in warm houses and eat well. They wanted to make money.

Gold, everybody's first-choice road to wealth, has never been found in New England in any quantity, but in the mid-1500s, a new trend in millinery fashion created a very reasonable alternative. The soft hats of the Renaissance—those large, velvet berets of gathered brim and elegant plume familiar from Holbein's portrait of Henry VIII—went out of style, and hats made of felt came in. These were the wide-brimmed, round-crowned hat of the Quaker merchant and the rakishly upswept and befeathered chapeau of the Restoration cavalier, the plumed hats of the Three Musketeers and the sober, high-crowned buckled hats of the Pilgrim fathers. Sober or extravagant, pious or worldly, modest shop-keeper or wealthy merchant: for nearly three centuries every European man who could afford a hat at all had one made of felt. Very often the women did too.

The finest felt is made by skilled furriers from beaver pelts. Specifically, from the thickly grown underhair of beaver trapped in the winter months in a cold climate. Beaver, once as common in the Old World as the New, had been eradicated everywhere in Europe except for eastern Russia and the steep valleys of the Pyrenees, a region far too small to supply the fashion needs of a prosperous continent. North America had millions of beaver, a flat-tailed, buck-toothed rodent that will live happily in a riverbank or natural pond, but is famous for its ability to dam streams and create ponds—and make a mess in the process.

The unwary hiker happening upon a beaver pond for the first time stumbles into a scene of ugly devastation. Approached from downstream, the ground underfoot becomes boggy as mud flats flank rivulets of clear water running between trees whose thin crowns and yellow leaves betray roots rotting in slow death. Upstream, the destruction is even worse. On the muddy shore, marsh grass and cattails grow between the stumps of felled alder and birch, while the bleached bones of maple and oak stand in a watery grave. A blue heron rising to croak ugly imprecations at the interloper adds to the weird ghostliness of the scene; taking wing at close range the great bird resembles nothing so much as some unwieldy pterodactyl improbably reincarnated to preside over the drowning of a forest.

The guilty authors of this sylvan destruction are asleep.

As industrious in life as in fable, the beavers' workday runs dusk to dawn. While humans sleep, beaver fell timber, store provisions, dig canals, construct lodges, excavate tunnels . . . and build dams. Those dams, messy heaps of gnawed-off sticks that hold back water with admirable efficiency, shape the face of the land more dramatically than the activities of any other nonhuman species.

One hardly supposes that the beaver care. Like the rest of us, they're just trying to make a living for the family. Picking a good spot, a stream with plenty of tasty aspen, alder, willow, and birch along the bank, the beaver dam it, build a safe home for the kids, and venture out on dry ground only as often as they need to bring home fresh sticks for supper or cut timber to maintain the dam—no point in risking encounters with wolves, bobcats, or mountain lions. Beaver are remarkably savvy at picking real estate, unerringly selecting optimal pond sites first, settling more marginal neighborhoods only when the prime locations are all taken. Prime, in this context, means a stream of a certain size—big enough to fill a pond, not so big that it might wash a dam away in the spring floods—flanked by acres of hardwood forest. Having found a likely spot, the beaver begin a process that only looks like destruction; in reality it is a thousand new beginnings.

Life in a pond begins with death: the death of leaves, branches, or whole trees that fall through the water and cover the pond floor to become food for aquatic fungi and bacteria—immense hordes of bacteria so small that a million of the tiny beings may inhabit a cubic centimeter of pond mud, eating dead leaves and releasing phosphorous and carbon dioxide into the water. The dead leaves, and the bacteria and fungi that feed on them, lie at the dark bottom of a pond; currents carry the gases they release to the surface where sunlight penetrating the water begets algae.

Green, brown, or red-brown, algae is slimy; when great masses bloom simultaneously, deplete the nutrient supply, and suddenly die, it smells bad. Slimy, unsightly, malodorous—algae is the very stuff of life. Tiny leaves of algae, drawing carbon dioxide from decomposing matter in the water, turn their faces to the sun and create matter. It is a miracle no member of the animal kingdom can perform. Photosynthesis, from the Latin for light and putting together. This is what algae does, it takes energy from sunlight to put together carbon dioxide and water into a living, growing plant; a tiny miracle of creation replicated with such wonderful regularity that we fail to notice the marvel of it. The black fly larvae that feed on the algae surely fail to recognize its abundant growth as a miracle of creation. The trout that feed on black fly larvae notice only that they have had a good meal, not the fact that neither fish nor black fly are able to synthesize, to create green food from sunlight.

Yet there it is, the lowly algae, competently producing food for the tiny creatures that feed the small fish that feed big fish that feed the majestic osprey, plunging out of the sky to catch an unfortunate perch. The pond and its marshy edge are dense nurseries of life fostering animals large and small. Tiny, round leaves of duckweed, their delicate roots hanging unanchored, float in rafts on the open water, while far up on the banks where the land is only slightly damp, the feathery fronds of ostrich ferns wave. Wild turkey favor the winter stalks of ostrich ferns; humans eat the furled tops in spring and call them fiddleheads. Sedge, moss, arrowhead, pickerelweed, water milfoil—every plant between the ferns far up the bank and the duckweed floating on open water is home to some animal or its young, a necessary food for some growing thing. Like the beautiful water lily.

Snails, water mites, and freshwater sponges make their homes on the underside of green lily pads. Dragonflies and frogs rest on them. The lily leaf caterpillar neatly cuts out two pieces of leaf and joins them to make a tidy cocoon where it retreats to turn into a moth. Even as the dragonflies rest and moth larvae swim among the lily pads waiting to grow big enough to learn to fly, a twelve-hundred-pound bull moose may wade into the beaver pond, submerge himself up to the nostrils to escape the pestilential black flies, and, while there, munch lily pads by the mouthful; the succulent green leaves are a moose's favorite food.

Even the hulks of dead trees killed by rising waters are a life-giving part of the ecosystem, as perfect homes for wood ducks. These beautiful waterfowl nest in the cavities of dead trees, but the young must tumble from the nest and spend their childhood on the water. Whole forests of dead trees without ponds cannot produce wood ducks any more than can oceans of water without dead trees; the ducklings need both, dead tree and pond together. Beaver ponds are so perfect a place for raising wood ducklings that populations of the handsomely colored birds rise and fall with fluctuations in the beaver population. From the kingfisher devouring a polliwog to the fingerling bass in the shallows, the beaver dam has created a nursery of life. Yet the invisible effects of the beaver's work are even more subtle and more profound than the lives of the animals moving in and about the water.

A beaver dam is a bursar, not a gaoler. The waters it impounds are not prisoned behind an impermeable wall; they are doled out, slowly, as the land needs them. Rain, falling unevenly through the year, overfills the stream beds of April, leaving August dusty and dry. Beaver dams moderate the seasonal extremes of rainfall, trapping the rains of April to release them in slow, even seepage through the hot, dry days of summer and early fall. A single beaver dam releases only a small flow of water into an August stream bed, but when settlers arrived in New England there was not just a single beaver pond—there were tens of thousands. Dozens of dams on a single stream. A new dam each time the water ran downhill into new acres of forest. Hundreds of dams on each tributary, thousands in every river valley—all releasing the waters of spring in an even, life-giving flow.[7]

Water that failed to go over the dam was equally important, because it seeped into the soil and, depending on the underlying geology of the site, replenished the groundwater. Abundance of every kind impressed the first Europeans to reach these shores, abundance of strawberries in the fields and of deer in the woods, abundance of trees, and an astonishing abundance of fresh, clear water. "The country, it is as well watered as any land under the sun, every family or every two families having a spring of sweet water betwixt them. No man hath been constrained to dig deep for his water, nor to fetch it far." The groundwater was so abundant, any man could reach it by digging a shallow well, if he lacked a spring, but springs were abundant. Springs pure, ever flowing, and plentiful, springs that bubbled out of the ground everywhere, even bringing fresh water to the surface on sandy beaches, "where the tides overflow them, which is accounted rare in England."[8]

It is accounted rare in twentieth-century New England as well. A reservoir of groundwater so abundant that it burst forth in ever-flowing springs on the beach could be created only in a forested land with myriad marshes and tens of thousands of ponds. Forested, because the forest absorbs water that would run off if it fell on a plowed field or open meadow. Dammed with tens of thousands of ponds, because that is how many there were; each beaver dam holding back a few acres of rainwater that seeped slowly into the earth, producing the vast reservoir that amazed the first settlers by bubbling up in springs on every farm and even on the beach.[9]

In holding back water, the dams also stopped the downstream flow of silt. A beaver dam, or a series of beaver dams on a forest stream, is a filtration system, each dam catching and holding silt washed downhill by a heavy March downpour before it can saturate the water and bury and suffocate fish eggs, or suffocate the adults by clogging their gills with fine particles of water-born soil. Safely trapped behind an untidy wall of gnawed sticks, the waterborne particles settle peacefully to the bottom where they begin the slow process of killing the beaver pond.

Slowly, silently, every pond is dying from the minute it is born. Even as a beaver pond grows and deepens with the building up of a dam, it is sowing the seeds of its own death. Behind the dam, the layer of silt thickens until it fills the low spot the first beaver selected as his home and the dam, no longer at the edge of a small valley, can no longer hold back the waters.

All around the pond, even when the edges are new and the water still rising, plants begin to grow that will fill the pond and choke it to death. Sedges and water lilies, which give life to the pond and its inhabitants, add to the layer of organic matter gradually accumulating on the pond bottom. Leaf by leaf, year by year, the decayed matter accumulates, silt and leaf litter filling the valley floor, where water once stood, held back from washing downstream by the dam, decay giving birth to new life, decaying and accumulating until the valley that became a pond is full, and a damp meadow stands where beaver once built and wood ducks swam.

This meadow, too, is a fertile gift of life from the beaver. The process of damming a stream, filling a valley with silt and pond muck until it becomes a meadow with a stream running through it may take decades or millennia, but when it is over the beaver leave behind land richer than the land they came to, for a beaver dam traps the promise of new life behind its wooden wall. Soil, minerals, and organic debris that might have washed out to sea stay in the forest where they were born, stopped from running away by the dam. In a final gift to the forest that supported them, generations of beaver who lived in the meadow when it was a pond left an immensely fertile soil into which a new forest can sink its roots and grow.

Outside my window, at the foot of a great oak where a pair of Baltimore orioles perch this May morning, Bullough's Pond is turning rapidly into a marsh. It has to happen someday; it happens to all ponds—quicker, if they are shallow and fed by slow-running streams, and over a much, much longer period of time if torrents of water sweep through in spring, scouring the bottom and carrying silt and debris seaward. Bullough's Pond is slated for a rapid conversion from pond to marsh. The dam at Dexter Road insures that almost nothing washes out, however heavy the rain, while warm, shallow water encourages luxuriant blooms of algae, duckweed, and the beautiful, yellow iris that ring the pond in spring—all of which drop their leaves to the bottom where bacteria turn them into the muck that is rapidly making this pond into a marsh, and, someday, a meadow. In Bullough's Pond, there is an additional factor at work, a man-made factor that condenses a process of decades or centuries into a few years.

Every winter it snows in Newton, and when it snows the highway department sprinkles the streets with sand. Then it rains, and the sand is washed into storm drains. In spring, the whirly-gig seed pods of maples and the tasseled green blossoms of oaks fall to the pavement and are washed into the drains. These are seeds and flowers that, when this land was a forest, stayed to fertilize the forest floor. Leaves, acorns, mud washed from construction sites, dirt, debris of all description—for a radius of five square miles, whatever falls onto the pavement and washes into a storm drain ends up in Bullough's Pond, depositing a layer of silt so thick that mallards can stand up to feed in the shallow water.

The first English settler arrived in Newton in 1636. If he walked through the woods to the spot where my house stands today—though I doubt he did; the first settlers were too busy getting a crop into the ground and a roof over their heads to stroll about—he would most probably have found an open meadow in which a few alder or red maple seedlings were starting to grow, and, about where Dexter Road runs today, the remains of an abandoned beaver dam. I am as persuaded that a beaver colony once lived on Bullough's Pond as I am convinced that an aboriginal village did not, for the simple reason that it was a perfect spot for beaver but not anything special for native people. Algonquin summer camps were always near a body of water large enough to provide an abundance of fish, such as the Charles River or Boston Harbor, not the small stream that feeds Bullough's Pond. Beaver, on the other hand, want very much what a colonial miller wanted: running water in a place that can be damned to make a pond. Ours would have made a very nice beaver pond, with two glacial moraines to keep the water in and flat woodland spreading to the south. From the favorable lay of the land we can be almost certain that beaver were here—they built ponds on virtually every favorable site in the country—and from what we know of the fur trade we can almost pin down the year when the last beaver on Bullough's Pond died. It happened in 1631 or 1632; they were killed by Native Americans, probably by a hunter from Chief Waban's band on the slope of Nonomtum Hill, and their demise was profitable to somebody, probably to Mr. William Pynchon of Essex, England, and Roxbury, Massachusetts.[10]

Pynchon was the leading fur merchant among the Puritan settlers who arrived in 1630 to establish the colony of Massachusetts Bay. A gentleman of some wealth, Pynchon speculated that his fortune, modest by the standards of England's upper classes, could be increased by coming to Massachusetts and engaging in the fur trade. He was correct. In 1632 and 1633, Pynchon shipped 400 of the 622 pounds of beaver fur exported from Massachusetts Bay.[11] While those 400 pounds of fur represented the lives of 250 or 300 animals, the last beaver to live on Bullough's Pond very likely among them, it was a drop in the bucket compared to the 10,000 pounds a year the Dutch were exporting annually from trading posts on the Hudson and Connecticut Rivers, or even the 3,738 pounds sent to London in 1634 by the Plymouth Colony from trading posts on Narragansett Bay and on the Kennebec and Penobscot rivers. Yet that 622 pounds of fur probably represented a good share of the skins of the beaver living on tributaries of the Neponset, Mystic, and Charles rivers.[12]

William Pynchon could see that there was little future in being a fur trader in Roxbury. In 1636, he moved to a site on the Connecticut River that would become Springfield, Massachusetts, and built a warehouse at Enfield Falls, the head of navigation on the river. This location—along with wealth, social standing, political savvy, business acumen, and close connections with the ruling oligarchies of the Connecticut and Massachusetts Bay colonies—put Pynchon in a position to control the fur trade of central New England. At the height of that trade, between 1636 and 1652, Pynchon exported 4,000 to 6,000 pounds of beaver pelts a year.

Pynchon was the most successful of a small army of fur traders who spread through seventeenth-century New England, the only one successful enough to retire to England a wealthy man. But, from the fishermen who bought a few furs on the Maine coast, to the Puritan merchants who settled New Haven, Connecticut, in hopes that fleets of native canoes carrying beaver skins would float down the Quinnipiac River to their trading post, every trader dreamed of wealth. It was not a foolish dream when every barrel of fur sold in London brought a small fortune; the difficulty lay in filling the barrels. Englishmen could not trap the furry animals, though some tried. Superlative swimmers that come out mostly at night, beaver were "too cunning" for English hunters.[13] Indians would have to hunt beaver and bring the skins to trade; there were fortunes to be made by English fur traders in such an arrangement. It was not, however, immediately apparent that there was anything in it for the Indians.

Here was a people who stalked, or picked, or raised everything they needed. Indians lived secure in the knowledge that so long as rivers flowed to the sea and trees grew in the forest, they and their children would have warm lodges to live in, warm skins to wrap themselves against the cold, and plenty to eat. Accumulating more coats than a family could wear or more pots than were needed for cooking was worse than pointless: it was burdensome. Real prosperity depended on moving frequently from fishing camp to hunting camp; somebody would have had to lug all those brass kettles the English wanted to trade.[14]

Englishmen viewed the world in quite a different light. Against life's vicissitudes, with the ever pressing need to provide for one's children, the constant striving for social position, the always threatening possibilities of financial loss, a bad harvest, or an investment gone sour, one could never pile up too many goods. Wealth was the shining prospect that beckoned every man forward; sufficiency, a thing no Englishman could attain. The Indians not only had sufficiency, they had the assurance that their children would have it too. Living in a land that supplied all a family could want, with no desire to pile up heavy, hard-to-transport goods, Indian hunters would have had little incentive to trade furs with the English, had vanity and ambition not been as common on the Penobscot as on the Mersey.

The English, not knowing what would induce the Native Americans to trade, offered brightly colored cloth, glass beads, brass and copper kettles, shiny mirrors. The Indians, after an initial flurry of enthusiasm for the curious goods, lost interest. They noticed that steel knives could hold an edge better than flint, and that was worth something. So were hatchets, iron hoes, and woolen cloth. But Indian desire for even these useful goods was finite. When Plymouth colonists brought shiploads of Massachusetts-grown corn to northern Maine, the Indians traded enthusiastically—if the hunting had been poor. When hunting was good, they were less eager to trade, and the Pilgrims sailed back to Plymouth discouraged. In the 1620s, trade languished for lack of a commodity Indians wanted in the same unlimited way Europeans wanted fur. Then, in 1622, a greedily incompetent Dutch trader named Jacques Elekens seized a Pequot sachem and threatened to behead him if the natives did not produce a "heavy ransom." The sachem's kin handed over 140 fathoms of wampum. Horrified company officials denounced and withdrew Elekens, but the shell beads he had collected revolutionized the fur trade.[15]

Wampum was made by drilling the purple-white shells of whelks and quahogs to form cylindrical beads. The right kind of shellfish for making wampum live only in the eastern waters of Long Island Sound. The necklaces and belts were worn by powerful sachems as emblems of rank and power, and sometimes given by one sachem to another in a symbolic exchange of gifts on important ceremonial occasions.[16]

When the Plymouth colonists got some wampum from Dutch traders and tried to buy furs with it on the coast of Maine, the hunters they dealt with were uninterested: either wampum was unheard of so far north, or it was known and reserved for the use of high-ranking chiefs.[17] Whatever the cause of this initial resistance, it was soon overcome. Hunters who had brought a modest number of beaver pelts to trade for corn and brass kettles became willing to empty the streams of beaver to trade for strings of shell beads that proclaimed their prowess. But wampum could buy something more desirable than prestige; it could buy power. In the political turmoil of native life destabilized by high death rates from European disease, alliances shifted and leadership vacuums were created. A brave display of wampum helped ambitious men climb into leadership positions. An aspiring chief could never have too much of it.

Every Indian who took beaver in the seventeenth-century New England woods knew that the animals were being hunted to extermination, yet they kept on hunting. Although beaver tail was considered to be good eating, beaver were not a vital food source. It was not as though the English wanted hunters to kill all the deer or all the salmon; beaver were expendable. But the Indians did not kill beaver in a conscious decision that they were expendable in a way that deer would not have been; they hunted because they were swept up by economic forces too overwhelming to resist.

No individual hunter had the choice of trapping only a few animals while others were left to breed. If the man who first came upon a beaver colony did not slaughter every animal present, another hunter would soon finish the job.

The choice was not kill or conserve, it was take the wampum or let somebody else have it; a brutal crash course in market economics.

Larger power networks of the aboriginal community, those channels of authority that regulated fishing rights at major waterfalls and the rights to hunting territories, could have stepped in to conserve the beaver—if they had not been destroyed by the epidemics of European disease that ravaged populations. Instead, the striving of ambitious individuals to fill power vacuums encouraged the rapid killing of beaver to obtain wampum. Only in northern Maine, where sparce population and less regular contact with Europeans slowed the spread of disease, were native communities able to regulate hunting in order to conserve beaver as an economic resource.

These northerners limited the beaver kill not because the beaver were a totem animal or because they attached any particular value to conserving every part of the ecosystem, but because killing only a few animals every year ensured a perpetual supply of wampum, corn, steel knives, woolen blankets, and muskets.[18] Beaver conservation also allowed Indians in the Penobscot drainage and further north to become farmers. Relying on corn for winter food is foolhardy in regions with fewer than 150 frost-free days in the growing season, as Indians certainly knew. Bangor and Oldtown have 120 to 140 days without frost, enough to grow corn with the expectation that in some years the crop will be lost to an early frost, or have to be planted a second time after a late one.[19] Before contact, Indians in the region were too wise to rely on a food crop that was guaranteed to fail every few years. Once the beaver trade was established, they could plant corn secure in the knowledge that in years when the crop failed they could buy grain with beaver pelts.[20] Elsewhere in the region, the beaver were extirpated.

By 1675 it was over. English, French, and Dutch fur traders had paid for, packed into white oak barrels, and shipped to Europe the skin of virtually every beaver that once lived in New England. On the St. John, the Hudson, and the St. Lawrence, the fur trade would continue for two profitable centuries, pushing inexorably north and west until the North American beaver was driven to the brink of extinction.

Chapter 4

Salt-Watered Prosperity

❧

The aim of the farmers in this country is, not to make the most from the land, which is or has been cheap, but the most of the labor, which is dear.[1]
                                                                    —George Washington, 1791

T HE GREAT WAVE OF PURITAN SETTLEMENT THAT swept eleven thousand English men, women, and children across the Atlantic in the 1630s was not a harried flight of desperate refugees forced to extreme measures to save their lives. Nor was it a movement of hardy pioneers inured to the deprivations of frontier life. These were English farmers, tradesmen, and gentry, who fully expected, after initial hardships were overcome, to live as they had lived in England—or better. If they had not expected to live well, they would not have come. They did come because Charles I, who ascended the throne in 1625, was even less friendly toward Puritanism than his father had been; because the teaching of predestination was prohibited at Cambridge and at Oxford; because Archbishop Laud blocked Puritan preachers from occupying English pulpits; because in a hundred ways petty and profound the position of Puritans in England was becoming untenable. They came because they believed that they could bring their children to Christ only by bringing them out of England. And, finally, they came because times in England were hard.

The economic expansion of the Tudor reigns—years when an enterprising and rapidly increasing population had made forests into fields and appropriated the holdings of monasteries for private profit—was over. There were no empty acres left in England. Land prices rose steadily under pressure from a population that doubled between 1530 and 1630. England was still a nation of farmers, yet there was no land to be had. Reverend John Cotton explained in his sermon to the vanguard of settlers departing Southampton on April 8, 1630, "Nature teaches bees . . . when the hive is too full, they seek abroad for new dwellings."[2]

The first wave of Puritan migrants overwhelmed the meager resources of the scattering of English agriculturists on the New England coast with its sudden demand for seed corn and livestock. The next year the colonists planted much more corn and slaughtered few cattle for food; it was infinitely more profitable to save the heifers as breeding stock and geld the steers as oxen for sale to English farmers arriving by the thousand at Boston harbor.

In England, Puritan families sold barns, fields, workshops, and homes, then crossed the ocean with their fortunes sewn up in small bags of gold pieces. Once on the ground, they sought an allocation of land, bought a heifer, a pig, and a sack of seed corn.

Immigrants who had been settled for a year or two found a ready market for every animal and bushel of corn they could produce; the gold they earned went directly back to England to pay for the things they could not produce—iron pots, guns, gunpowder, salt, wool and linen cloth, knives, nails, saws, hammers, and axes. So long as the flow of migration continued, there was gold to send back to England for the things the colonists needed. Until the Long Parliament sat down in 1640. Then English Puritans began to hope for better times at home, and ceased to migrate.

Roundheads and Cavaliers fought out their differences on religious and political questions in a bloody civil war. On this side of the Atlantic, the crisis was economic. With no immigrant ships arriving, New England had no means to pay for the goods it needed to import. The lone commodity New England produced that could be packed in a barrel, shipped to London, and sold at a profit was fur, and there were not enough beaver in all New England to keep its settlers in kettles and axes.

The obvious solution was to make what New England could no longer afford to buy. John Winthrop, Jr., set up an ironworks on the Saugus River. Bounties were offered for the weaving of linen and woolen cloth. Salt pans, a graphite mine, and a glass works were all attempted. All failed. Some pigs of iron were smelted, some yards of linen and woolen cloth woven, but the settlements lacked the financial resources to fund industrial enterprises through the early years before they could turn a profit. Even if the start-up money had been there, the colonial markets for goods like glass, iron, and gunpowder were too small to make manufacturing profitable. The only successful industrial enterprise in the Puritan colonies was Emmanuel Dowling's Salem distillery. Having failed in the attempt to produce the manufactured goods it craved, New England searched for an export commodity to pay for what it bought—and here a glimmer of hope flickered as the 1640s began.[3]

Ever since the bold sailors of Bristol and Brittany discovered the Grand Banks, Englishmen had been coming to the New World to fish for cod. In the 1630s, English fishing boats did a little side business selling salt cod to Puritan colonists in exchange for fresh meat and vegetables, though the bulk of the catch was shipped to the wine islands—the Azores, Canaries, and Madeira—and to the Catholic countries of southern Europe. But during the English Civil War, control of Bristol switched back and forth between Parliamentary and Royalist armies, while sailors and ships alike were impressed for naval service: the Bristol fishing fleet failed to sail. Its absence meant no codfish balls for New England breakfast tables; in the long run it was to mean much, much more.

Take a fresh fillet of flounder, salt it, set it in the sun, and you will soon have a stinking mess. Salt a herring, and you have a savory treat in store, so long as you do not wait too long to enjoy it—herring salted down in summer will reek before summer comes again. Salt down almost any fish you catch, and you will have a rotten fish sooner or later, usually sooner; but salt a cod, and, because the flesh contains far less fat than that of most species, you have a meal to look forward to a year or even two years after the fish was caught. Codfish keeps. Until canning and artificial freezing made preserving all things possible, fish that would keep was as bankable as gold and codfish was king of the sea.

When the large and profitable cod fishery long monopolized by Bristol suddenly opened to all comers, New Englanders leapt into the breach. Men from settlements up and down the coast went to sea in boats equipped by London merchant-capitalists, salted down the catch, and brought it to Boston, where English shipmasters waited to carry the barreled cod to Mediterranean ports. There it was exchanged for salt, wine, gold, Malaga grapes, and Valencia oranges, which went to London to pay for the manufactured goods New England so desperately needed.

Codfish was the first step in a maritime enterprise that would bring two centuries of prosperity to New England. Almost from the start, Boston merchants realized that fish carried in Massachusetts-built, Massachusetts-owned ships would bring more profit than the same fish shipped in London bottoms; and the Massachusetts captains who carried Grand Banks cod to the wine islands and Mediterranean ports quickly realized that countries that had long since cleared their own hillsides of forests were a natural market for New England's white-oak barrel staves. In 1643, five New England-owned and built ships carried pipe staves and cod to Iberia and the wine islands: hulls, rigging, crew, and cargo hailed from New England; only the letters of credit that made possible the triangular exchange of American fish and barrels for Iberian and Madeiran wine and then for English manufactures, came from London.[4]

The quest for economic opportunity that bolstered Puritan resolve to leave England sent other English settlers to the West Indies. By 1640 there were about forty thousand English living in New England, and eighty thousand English on St. Kitts, Barbados, Nevis, and Guadeloupe. (Virginia and Maryland, that year, had nine thousand Europeans between them, while all of Quebec had three hundred.)

Like New Englanders, settlers in the islands had crossed the Atlantic with English livestock and seeds, planning to found self-supporting, crop-growing colonies in a land about whose climate, soil, and weather they knew almost nothing. The choice of Barbados or Massachusetts may have been almost random for many settlers, but the choice was fatal: Literally, for the thousands of immigrants who died of yellow fever or malaria, figuratively, for those who saw their hopes die.

The first English West Indians were small farmers, planting grain and keeping cattle and chickens, but turning to cotton and tobacco for cash crops, and prospering moderately despite the difficulty of transferring English agriculture to the tropics. But by the 1640s it was apparent to everyone that the most profitable use for island land was growing sugar. Sugar required the investment of large amounts of capital in mills, but the potential for profit was so great that a few settlers aggressively consolidated the small farms into large plantations worked by slaves. Those few made themselves into sugar magnates; the rest took ship for North American colonies, leaving behind islands where enslaved Africans toiled ceaselessly for the benefit of a handful of wealthy Europeans.

The seventeenth-century world took little notice of the northern colonies, where dirt farmers wrested a modest living from the reluctant earth. It was the sugar islands that commanded the attention of Europe; that was the place where vast fortunes were made. New England was only an unimportant cluster of colonies too far north to grow sugar, tobacco, or anything else of special importance to the world economy.

By 1647 Boston heard that these West Indian islands were "so intent on planting sugar that they had rather buy foode at very deare rates than produce it by labour, soe infinite is the profitt of sugar."[5] So infinite were those profits that it paid to plant every inch of island soil to sugar; importing meat, vegetables, wheat, even the horses that pulled loads of sugar to the docks. New England had what the planters needed, and New England was eager to sell. Pipe staves to pack sugar and molasses for export, lumber to build sugar mills, even the wooden frames of complete houses—sawn, numbered, and carefully packed—went to the sugar islands. Here were markets for the cheapest grade of salt fish (to feed enslaved Africans) and the finest grade of fresh butter (for the owner's table). Barrels of salt pork and beef went south, along with crates of turkeys and deckloads of sheep and steers for West Indian dinner tables. The islanders bought elegant Narragansett pacers, bred for the saddle with prices as fancy as their gait, and stolid workhorses to walk out their lives in endless circles turning the great wooden screws of the sugar mills. Apples and wheat, hay and eggs, brooms and onions, beeswax, bacon, and cheese—everything New England farms produced found a market in the sugar islands. In exchange, the West Indians sent money, in the form of letters of credit, and something even better than money: molasses.

Average Annual Value and Destination of Commodity Exports from New England, 1768–1772 (in pounds sterling)

Commodity	Great Britain	Ireland	Southern Europe	West Indies	Africa	Total
Fish	206		57,195	94,754		152,155
Livestock, beef, pork	374		461	89,118		89,953
Wood products	5,983	167	1,352	57,769		65,271
Whale products	40,443		804	20,416	440	62,103
Potash	22,390	9				22,399
Grains, grain products	117	23	3,998	15,764		19,902
Rum	471	44	1,497		16,754	18,776
Other	6,991	1,018	296	247		8,552
Total	76,975	1,261	65,603	278,068	17,194	439,101

Source: John J. McCusker and Russell R. Menard, *The Economy of British America, 1607–1789* (Chapel Hill: University of North Carolina Press, 1985), 108.

The table somewhat overstates the centrality of provisioning the sugar islands in the colonial New England economy. Some commodities, such as spermaceti candles, fish, and rum, found important markets in the southern colonies not reflected in export tables. More significantly, a table of commodity exports omits two of the most important exports: ships and shipping services.

Yankee commerce sailed on a bottom of salt cod, but it was fueled with molasses. It was no accident that New England's first going industrial concern was a distillery that turned molasses into rum. Rum could be sold, along with apples, beef, and bread, to Newfoundland fishermen for more codfish. Rum could be traded for Pennsylvania wheat and Chesapeake tobacco. Rum could be exchanged in Mediterranean markets for olive oil and wine, oranges, raisins, silk, and gold. Rum could be sold on the Guinea coast for black-skinned human beings to plant the sugar cane and work the mills that would produce more molasses.

New England sought its fortune in the shipping lanes of the Atlantic, and each boat that departed Portsmouth or New London or Newport represented a double opportunity for the farmer. Merchant shippers sent the farmer's apples to Newfoundland, the farmwife's butter and eggs to the West Indies, and barrel staves from the farm woodlot to the wine islands. But each sailing also called for provisions: salt beef and pork, wheat flour and cornmeal, cider, dried apples, beans, butter, and a crate of live chickens. Everything captain and crew ate at sea was purchased from New England farmers. If a vessel carried live horses, hogs, cattle, sheep, or poultry, then the hay, oats, and corn they would eat was also purchased on Yankee wharves.

Whether a New England farmer tilled the Berkshire hills or the shores of Narragansett Bay, from 1640 onward his profits grew in salt water. Not that most of what New England farmers grew was sold in the seaports. Far from it: seventeenth- and eighteenth-century farms produced very little surplus; most

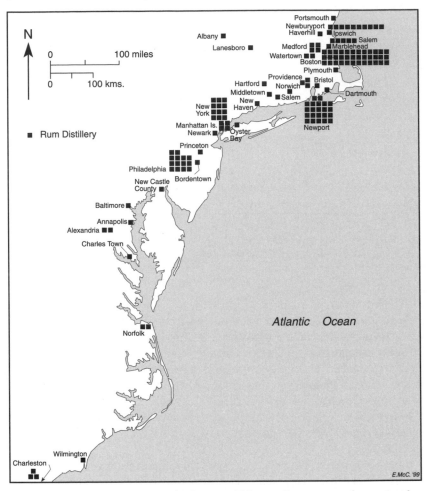

Rum distilleries in the American colonies, 1770. This map demonstrates the contrast between the intense commercial activity of New England and the commercial agriculture
that dominated the southern colonies. From *The Economy of British America, 1607–1789* by John J. Mc-
Cusker and Russell R. Menard. Copyright © 1985 by the University of North Carolina Press. Used by permission
of the author and publisher.

of what grew in New England fields was consumed on the farm or in the township where it grew. But it is the surplus we are discussing here because, however
small, it was the surplus that made the system work.[6]

A few bushels of corn, a pig, some butter, a few bundles of shingles—these
market commodities made the farm viable because they made it possible
for the farmer to buy the few goods—principally salt and iron—that a New

England farm needed but could not produce. Moreover, if the surplus of any single farm was small, the number of farms was large. Thousands of Yankee farms all shipping their surplus to a handful of seaports amply supported a thriving maritime enterprise, just as the shipping industry supported the farms.

Profitable sales of farm produce in the market created by shipping made it possible for farm families to buy not only the iron and salt they needed, but also the glass, molasses, spices, and imported fabrics that made life pleasant. They enabled farm families to set money aside to buy farms for grown children, to support the minister, the schoolteacher, and the college, to buy a book of sermons or hymns, indulge the wish for a beaver hat, a silk ribbon, or a cone of white sugar. The intricate triangles and quadrangles of the seventeenth- and eighteenth-century colonial trade: Newport, to Guinea, to Barbados; Boston, to Madeira, to London; Boston, to Newfoundland, to Port Royal, to Marseilles, to London, to home—the hundreds of Yankee ships at sea were what made it profitable to clear the hillsides and plow the fields.

The immigrant farmers of 1630 were, of course, in no position to send apples to Newfoundland or corned beef to the West Indies. Their need was to clear a field, get a crop into the ground, and feed their cattle through the winter. The fine breeds of horses, cattle, and sheep that New England farmers would one day take pride in were undreamed of in the early decades of settlement. When Massachusetts was settled, few breeds worth speaking of existed, and agriculture shared more with the habits of the Middle Ages than with the improving scientific methods of the Enlightenment. Seventeenth-century cattle were smallish, shaggy, and tough. Yet not even the scruffy stock of a pre-modern English farm could survive in New England without some sort of crude barn, cut hay for winter feed, and protection from wolves, bears, and mountain lions. Cows would come into their own as towns became more settled; the hero of the pioneer hour was the pig.

A healthy sow and a boar could be turned into the woods to fend for themselves. If his tusks were allowed to grow, a boar could fight off most attacks by wild predators, while each sow produced one, or, with luck, two litters a season. And feeding them cost nothing at all. Loosed in the woods, swine fattened all summer on the chestnuts, acorns, and hickory nuts made plentiful by Indian forest management; in November, the farmer could gather bushels of nuts for winter feed; and when snow began to fall, the old boar led the whole herd back to the barn. Most pigs were slaughtered when the weather got cold—either eaten, salted down for family use, or packed in barrels and carted to the local store, where salt pork was as good as money.

Feeding cattle was a more complex affair. Cows and oxen could not survive the winter without hay, but no settler with two oxen and a cow could fell enough trees to clear enough land to plant enough grass in time to cut enough hay to see his stock through the first winter. The earliest English settlements had to be built where there was enough wild grass to get through the first years. Fortuitously, tall stands of grass grew wild in three New England environments: the salt marshes of the New England coast, the fresh marshes, which grow where river valleys are too wet to support trees (the Great Meadows of Concord, Massachusetts, are a prime example), and the meadows left behind where beaver dams were abandoned and breached.

Here was a resource the English incursion inadvertently created for English farmers to exploit. The beaver themselves were killed by Indian fur hunters at sites well inland from the vanguard of settlement. For a year or two, the dam might hold. Even when it was breached, more years might pass before the soggy marsh became a fertile meadow. Not every beaver pond became a meadow— some became semi-permanent swampy marshes; some passed through the marsh stage to become young forests that had to be chopped down before they could be farmed—but, very often, just as English settlers pushed into a new area, an old beaver pond reached the point where it was a meadow able to produce four tons of hay from a single acre.[7] That was wealth. That was verdant riches, fat meat, and easy living.

Where marshes, salt or fresh, or beaver meadows stood beside abandoned Indian fields, cleared of trees and ready for the plow, English farmers settled. Marshfield, Concord, Fairfield, Springfield, Wethersfield, Portsmouth, Saco, and more: the first settlements were made where Indians had cleared fields and nature had planted hay.[8]

Beyond the thin fringe of settlement, wolves howled, owls screamed, lions roared, and the mythical pilhannaw bird swooped from the skies to bear off whole jackals in its fearsome clutches.[9] Underlying the fear of townsfolk for untamed land and mythical beasts were very real bogs, mountains, swamps, forests, and impenetrable thickets of greenbriar, which had sprung up where Indians slain by European disease had ceased to burn the undergrowth. Remote, unknown, thorny, inhabited by fierce creature, the land still beckoned; for on it, a family could raise cattle, "And no man now thought he could live, except he had catle and a great deale of ground to keep them."[10] It was the quest for land on which to grow hay and fatten cattle that pushed back the frontier in New England.

The prime imperative in settling a frontier farm was to clear enough land to get a crop into the ground. The first English immigrants insisted not only on cutting every tree, but on pulling every stump, so to ready a field for the plow before planting it. With back-breaking tenacity, they created tidy fields that looked something like England. The next generation found such fastidiousness to be so much labor lost. Like Algonquin and Narragansett farmers before them, English settlers learned that trees did not have to be dug out by the roots to allow crops to grow; it was necessary only to prevent them from leafing out.[11]

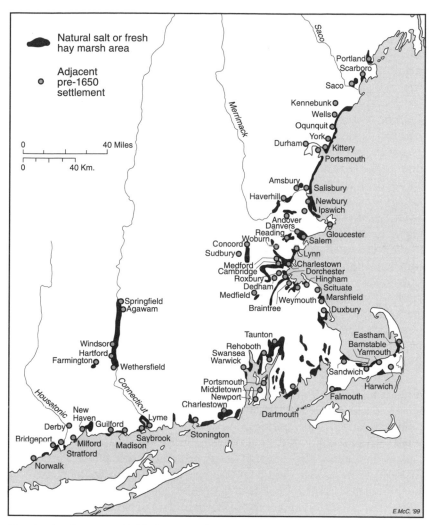

New England towns settled before 1650 that were situated on large natural fresh or salt marshes. Virtually every early settlement was situated alongside a highly prized natural hay marsh. Plymouth is the conspicuous exception, but the Pilgrims did not bring cattle on the Mayflower. They were attracted by a good harbor and the cleared fields left abandoned when an epidemic killed the local Indians. Families soon left the original settlement to raise cattle alongside Duxbury's natural marshes. Russell also includes a map of pre-1650 towns situated on Indian-cleared fields. Howard S. Russell, *A Long, Deep Furrow: Three Centuries of Farming in New England* (Hanover, N.H.: University Press of New England, 1976), 55.

Some farmers did as the Indians had done, girdling trees and allowing them to stand leafless until they fell. Others chopped them down, burned trunks and branches, but allowed the stumps to stand where they were until the roots rotted, making the stumps easy to pull. Rows of such stumps, pulled by teams of oxen and lined up along the edge of a field with their projecting root stubs intertwined, made a cheap, ugly, rot-resistant, and virtually impenetrable fence.

Cut-and-burn land clearing wasted incalculable millions of board feet of chestnut, hickory, and oak, and Yankee farmers are the farthest thing from wasteful by nature. Where there was a market close enough to make it pay, they converted standing timber into lumber, shingles, charcoal, or potash. But with so much wood, so little plow land, and such high transportation costs, it generally paid only to chop and burn the stuff as quickly as possible. Besides, as the farmers knew, burning was far from wasting.

The virgin soil of New England was the product of thousands of years of forest growth, thousands of years of trees falling to earth, leaf, branch, and bole, rotting, leaving a thick layer of humus decomposing into soil rich in the nitrogen, sulfur, and phosphorus without which nothing can grow. Burning the timber made the soil even richer by releasing mineral nutrients bound up in wood and pouring them onto the ground. Indian corn, field peas, pumpkins, beans, or potatoes hoed in among stumps and half-burned logs produced bountiful crops without plowing. In a few years, after the last logs were piled and burned, the last stubborn stump uprooted and turned into part of a fence, the plowed field could be planted to rye, field peas, flax, or wheat. Most often, it was planted to corn.

Corn was easily grown, even by farmers who lacked the plow and oxen needed for growing wheat, rye, and flax. It produced larger yields than other grains and was excellent food for the farm family, in addition to which, any surplus could be used to fatten livestock. The only drawback was that corn exhausted the land. Unlike European grains that cover a field thickly, corn grows on widely spaced stalks, and English farmers planted no companion crop like the thick mats of squash leaves that covered the ground between cornstalks in Indian fields. The ground of a colonial cornfield was exposed to summer rainstorms that carried off valuable topsoil. This erosion did heavy damage, though not so heavy as the damage done by healthy cornstalks simply growing, for few crops deplete soil as rapidly as corn.

To Indian farmers, it mattered little that corn virtually siphoned nitrogen and other nutrients from the soil, since corn was always planted in a hill with beans whose roots were busy infusing the soil with new supplies of nitrogen, and, even more to the point, since the forest around an Indian cornfield was constantly producing fresh, nitrogen-rich humus. When an Indian field wore out, it was time to clear a new one.

For the first century of settlement, New England's English farmers thought

Stump fence edges a field in Maine, in a photo probably taken in Aroostook County in the 1890s. A horse and buggy can be seen between the fence and the woods. The size of the stumps, which dwarf the buggy, give some idea of the size of trees felled by farmers. Stump fences, nearly impentrable and highly resistant to decay, were commonly the first fences built when forests were cleared. They required no labor beyond pulling the stumps—which the farmer was in any case obliged to do before he could plow the field. New England's famous stone fences came generations later, at a time when labor was cheap and land was dear. Maine Historical Society.

the same way. Land was plentiful, newly cleared land remarkably fertile, so the sensible thing for a farmer to do was to clear new fields for corn and cut old fields for hay or, if they were too worn out even to produce a good crop of hay, use them for pasture. In an economy of plentiful land and scarce labor, cattle were more profitable than grain in any case.

Wheat, rye, corn, and peas were wonderful crops. They grew bountifully. They tasted good. Storekeepers welcomed them by the bushel basket as readily as cash. The only problem was that somebody had to plow the field and harrow it, then plow again between the growing rows to keep weeds down. Somebody had to harvest the grain, stack it to dry, then thresh it. Then somebody had to cart it to the mill and pay the miller. A cow, on the other hand, had only to be led to pasture and invited to dine; come spring, she would double her worth by producing a calf. All summer long the cow produced milk the family could drink or turn into cheese. If she had some pumpkins, turnips, or corn along with her hay in the winter, she would produce milk that could be churned into sweet yellow butter. Old cows were readily converted into salt beef and raw-hide. Yearling steers could be butchered too, or turned into the oxen New England needed to haul loads to the docks and grub the stumps from newly cleared fields, or sold to a drover who would herd them to market in a seaport. And unlike wheat or flax seed which had to be carted to market, steers provided their own transportation. Steers, oxen, leather, salt beef, cheese, butter, and even cow horn to be shaped into combs and buttons, were as good as money, and much easier to grow. For two centuries old fields were turned into pastures, and when a field ceased to produce adequate pasture, it was simply abandoned, left to whatever weeds, scrub, or trees might choose to grow there. It was easier and more profitable to clear a new field from the forest than to revive an old pasture by collecting and carting dung, plowing, and seeding clover or timothy.

This system demanded a great deal of land, but land was something New England had to spare. Early settlers were granted land of varying amounts according to their wealth and rank in society, but farms of 140 to 150 acres were not unusual.[12] A husband and wife working alone—and with land plentiful and hired labor scarce there was little choice but to work alone—could manage a farm with four to ten acres planted to corn and rye, ten acres of mowing land for hay, another ten acres in pasture, a one-acre vegetable garden, and a wood-lot for fuel.[13] A farm this size could provide corn, apples, vegetables, and a few cows and pigs—enough to supply meat and milk for family use, and allow the couple who farmed it to feed and clothe three or four small children. A farm couple working alone with young children to feed were unlikely to produce much of a surplus, but few families stopped after the third or fourth child. Children were economic assets. With half-grown sons and daughters working alongside them, the couple who had once just gotten by could clear new land, plant more crops, raise more stock, weave cloth, press cider, salt down beef, make cheese, butter, candles—and money.

Land ownership and financial success followed the life cycle. A young couple would clear the few acres needed to keep themselves and their small children. As the children neared their teens, they helped clear and farm enough land to produce a surplus that enabled the parents to acquire additional acreage and lay money by. Then, when the children were in their twenties, the acquired acres were given to the sons to enable them to start farms and families, while accumulated wealth provided household goods and furnishings to daughters as they married.[14]

The land I live on was granted to Jonathan Hyde in 1647 when he was twenty-one years old. Hyde lived into his eighty-fourth year and eventually acquired 350 acres, a comfortable, though by no means unusual, estate for a settler of the first generation. With his wife, Mary French Hyde, he was blessed with fourteen children. When the first Mrs. Hyde died, Jonathan married again, and Mary Rediat Hyde bore seven more children. Eleven of those twenty-one children lived to adulthood. Long before his own death, Hyde provided marriage portions for his daughters and divided the family land into farms for his sons, whose own sons and grandsons continued to farm this land into the early 1800s.[15]

The houses they lived in were modest affairs, sheathed in unpainted clapboards and crammed in winter with onions looping from the rafters, spinning wheels crowding against beds, and skeins of wool heaped atop storage chests. The work of the farm spilled out of the house and sprawled through corn cribs, woodshed, dairy, sheep barns, cow barns, and grain barns. Surrounding the buildings, productive fields and orchards presented a picture of prosperity that appalled European observers by its slovenly raggedness.

Why, the Europeans wanted to know, could Americans not plant neat hedgerows, build tidy stone walls, cut down the shrubs that grew on old pastures, keep their cattle fenced in, or, at the very least, make their fences run in straight lines? Americans could have, of course; they didn't because it wouldn't pay.

Careful European plowing and planting of pastures, penning of animals to collect dung, and neat, straight fences, made sense where scarce land must be made to produce high yields by abundant labor. In a country where land was cheap, wood was abundant, and only labor was scarce, it made sense to pile rails one atop the other in the endless zig-zag of wooden fencing that surrounded cornfields—a system profligate of wood and land, ugly to the European eye, and admirably efficient for the colonial farmer who could easily take the fence apart and use it to surround a new cornfield when this one wore out, saving even the labor of splitting new rails. As for penning animals at night or carting their dung, who had time? Decades would pass before Yankee farmers found it worth their while even to fence their pastures; in the early years only cornfields and gardens were fenced, to keep out the cattle who otherwise walked where they wished and ate what they liked. It was not slovenliness that gave early New England its unkempt aspect of scruffy pasture and scraggly fencing, it was efficient application of scarce labor and capital to the region's only abundant resource: land. Stone fences, pens, dung heaps—all the paraphernalia of an improving agriculture in which nineteenth-century Yankee farmers would take such pride—were neglected by colonial farmers in favor of turning the rich virgin soil into cash, or its near equivalents, corn and beef.

For several generations of Hydes and for their neighbors, Massachusetts was a land of plenty. They lived well, married young if they pleased, and reared large families in the full confidence that their children would enjoy a life as comfortable as their own. The constant necessity of clearing new land presented no serious limitation. Newton and other early-settled towns might

"Southwest view of the seat of the Honorable Henry Marchant, Esq. in South Kingston." Anonymous pencil sketch, c. 1785. The country seat of a wealthy Newport attorney is surrounded by post-and-rail fencing and tidy stone walls. A zig-zag fence, also known as "worm" or "Virginia rail" snakes along the side of the road. Zig-zag was the easiest style of fence to build and was widely used after the first generation of stump fences finally rotted. There was no need to painstakingly notch posts or laboriously dig post holes; the zig-zag course and buttressing rails gave stability without posts. With close-set rails occupying a space five feet wide, zig-zag fencing wasted land and wood, but land and wood were plentiful. Courtesy The Rhode Island Historical Society, RHi(x3)3019.

not have had enough space for every young couple to settle on, but there was land enough elsewhere to allow the surplus young people of each generation to pioneer farms of their own.

Edward Sanderson, a slightly older contemporary of Jonathan Hyde, emigrated from England to become one of the founders of Watertown, Massachusetts, the town just across the river from the point where Smelt Brook empties into the Charles. He accumulated enough property to enable one of his sons, Deacon Jonathan Sanderson, to live comfortably in Watertown and acquire land in the frontier settlement of Leicester, Massachusetts, on which one of Jonathan's sons, John, reared a family. One of John's sons, Benjamin, realizing that he could never acquire enough land in Leicester to provide a Massachusetts farm for each of his sons, sold out, moving with his grown children to be among the founders of Woodstock, Vermont. Benjamin's son Rufus, a Revolutionary War veteran, settled land along the Sandy River in the frontier town of New Sharon, Maine, and one of Rufus's sons, Beriah, cleared a hill farm in

Vienna, Maine. The Sanderson family had been living in New England for eight generations when Beriah Sanderson began clearing that hill farm in Vienna; seven generations of chopping farms out of the forest.[16]

Far from being the quirk of a restless family, constant expansion of the frontier was an economic imperative. Emigration to New England was negligible after the Puritan migration of the 1630s ended, but early marriage, large families, and the excellent health of a prosperous, rural society meant that the population doubled every twenty-five years.[17] The amount of land in cultivation also had to double every twenty-five years. Unfortunately, the size of New England could not double every twenty-five years.

The first solution to land shortage was dietary reform. Seventeenth-century New Englanders drank ale brewed from barley and ate a monotonous diet of field peas, corn meal, and salt pork. Eighteenth-century New Englanders, running out of land to devote to barley, planted apple orchards and drank cider, producing an equal degree of inhebriation from a significantly reduced acreage. They replaced field peas in the diet with potatoes, turnips, parsnips, and pumpkins. Kitchen gardens expanded, but still represented far less acreage than had been devoted to field peas, while the new vegetables provided a diet that was both more varied and more nourishing. Production shifts actually enabled farm families to improve their diet while working smaller farms, but there was a limit to the new strategy, a limit to how much land a family could save by switching from field peas to garden vegetables and planting apple trees along the fence rows. Sooner or later, they simply ran out of land.

The vast country that confronted the Puritan emigrants of 1630 shrank before each rising generation. By the late eighteenth century, the only land left was on hill slopes way up north, fields even steeper and higher than the land in New Sharon, Maine, where Rufus Sanderson cleared a farm. The soil of those hill farms was so thin that it was sometimes exhausted by a single year's corn crop. It wouldn't have been worth settling at all, except for the money a man could earn cutting wood. Lumber was the only cash crop the hill farms of Maine ever produced; once it was cut, the land was nearly worthless. The next generation had to look elsewhere. Rufus Sanderson's grandson Rufus did, moving west to pioneer a farm in Iowa.

In the 1770s, however, Iowa was not an option. Nor were Michigan, Ohio, western Pennsylvania, or even upstate New York. At the conclusion of the French and Indian Wars, Lord Shelburne's ministry, fearful that westward settlement would provoke Indian attacks on the difficult-to-defend frontier, and preferring to keep the colonists where British governors could keep an eye on them and British industry profit from their trade, forbade English settlement west of the sources of rivers that flowed into the Atlantic. The ministry hoped that stopping settlement at the Alleghenies would encourage settlement of Canada, Nova Scotia, and Florida. It did.

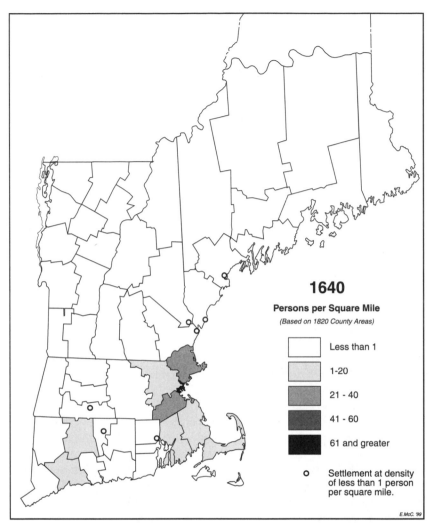

1640

Persons per Square Mile

(Based on 1820 County Areas)

	Less than 1
	1-20
	21 - 40
	41 - 60
	61 and greater
o	Settlement at density of less than 1 person per square mile.

E.McC. '99

Most of New England could support about forty persons per square mile making a living exclusively from farming. Counties with densities much above forty were engaged in fishing, manufacturing, or commerce.

The basic map uses county lines of 1820, as reconstructed by William Thorndale and William Dollarhide, *Map Guide to the U.S. Federal Censuses, 1790–1929* (Baltimore: Genealogical Publishing Co., 1987). 1820 and 1790 densities were calculated from raw census data. Earlier densities were drawn from the censuses, surveys, and estimates collected by Evarts B. Greene and Virginia D. Harrington, *American Population Before the Federal Census of 1790* (N.Y.: Columbia University Press, 1932), in particular: Plymouth County densities for 1640 are based on 1643 "men 16 – 60 able to bear arms," Plymouth Colony Records; Massachusetts, Connecticut, and Rhode Island densities for 1690 are

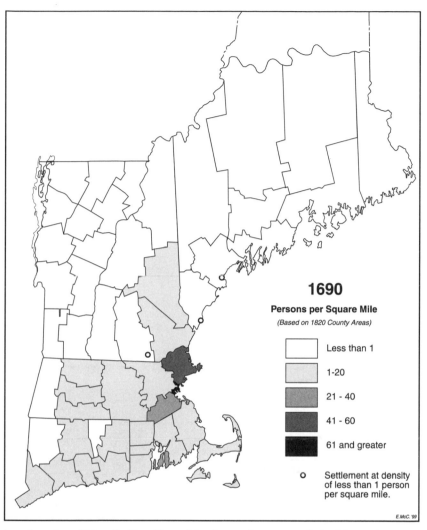

1690

Persons per Square Mile

(Based on 1820 County Areas)

☐	Less than 1
☐	1-20
☐	21 - 40
☐	41 - 60
■	61 and greater
○	Settlement at density of less than 1 person per square mile.

E.McC. '99

based on the militia rolls; New Hampshire figures for 1690 are derived from Lieutenant Governor Usher's letter to the Board of Trade of 1692; New Hampshire census of 1775; Rhode Island census of 1774; Connecticut Census of 1774; Massachusetts Census of 1776; Vermont estimates for 1774–76 are drawn from Governor Moore's letter of July 5, 1768, and local histories cited in Greene and Harrington. Settlements indicated in counties with densities below one person per square mile are drawn from various sources.

In cases where a state was only partially settled, population densities are calculated by dividing the number of settlers by the number of square miles that would in 1820 comprise the county in which they were living, not by the entire volume of vacant land in the state or in the seventeenth- or eighteenth-century county.

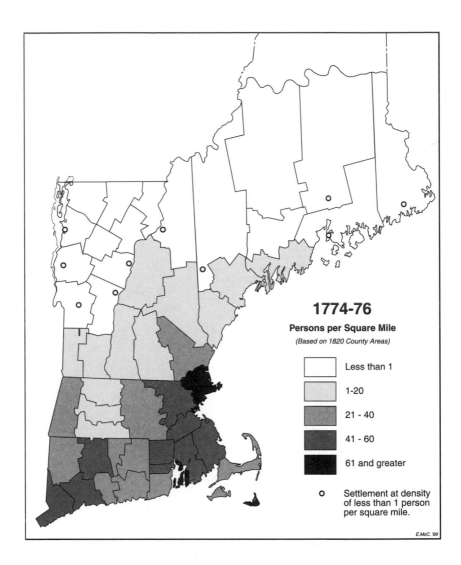

1774-76

Persons per Square Mile

(Based on 1820 County Areas)

☐	Less than 1
☐	1-20
☐	21 - 40
☐	41 - 60
■	61 and greater
○	Settlement at density of less than 1 person per square mile.

E.McC. '99

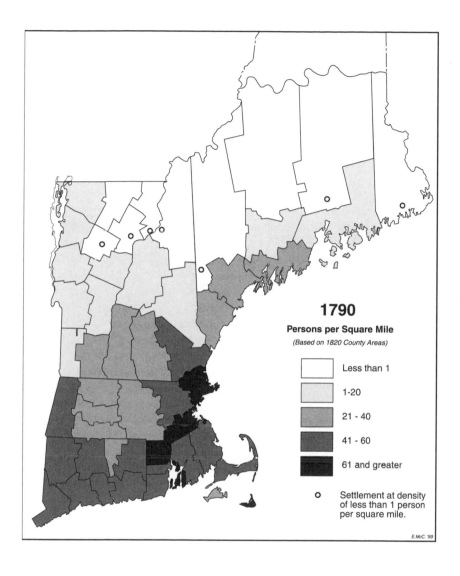

1790

Persons per Square Mile

(Based on 1820 County Areas)

Less than 1

1-20

21 - 40

41 - 60

61 and greater

○ Settlement at density of less than 1 person per square mile.

E.McC. '99

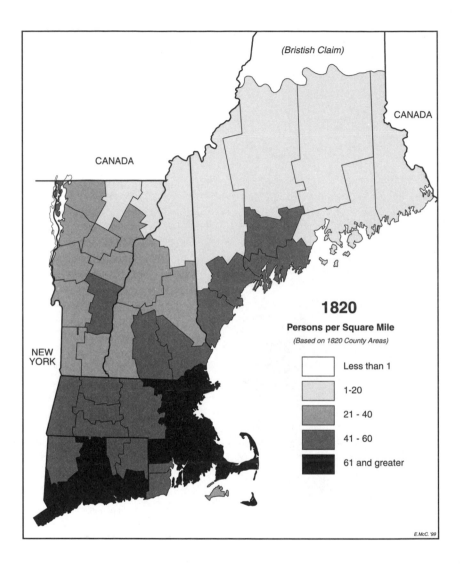

(Bristish Claim)

CANADA

CANADA

NEW
YORK

1820

Persons per Square Mile

(Based on 1820 County Areas)

Less than 1

1-20

21 - 40

41 - 60

61 and greater

E.McC. '99

In June 1761, my own ancestors, John and Mary Whitman of Stowe, Massachusetts, and Michael and Jane Spurr of Stoughton, Massachusetts, boarded the schooner *Charming Molly* out of Boston bound for Annapolis Royal, where they took up farms and reared large families. Would they or the thousands of other New Englanders who emigrated to chilly, thin-soiled, windswept Nova Scotia have gone north if the deep, rich soils of the Ohio Valley had been open to them? I like to think my ancestors were smarter than that.

Ohio would not become an option until America had a federal government willing to send an army to take it from the Indians, and more armies to defend it once it had been taken. But if moving west was not an option, neither was staying home. There could never be enough land in a settled town to make a farm for every young couple who had grown up there, and small-scale colonial industries could employ only a few. So the young people moved north, into Vermont, New Hampshire, Maine, and Nova Scotia. By the end of the eighteenth century, the little land left was poor, far from easy transportation to market, and, often, so far up a mountain that late frosts and early freezes shortened the growing season to the point of penury.

Penury had already come to some settled towns where worn-out fields produced steadily declining yields, marginal land was forced into production, and population was swollen by young people who could not emigrate to the frontier because there was so little frontier left.[18] For young men who inherited only a few acres, or no land at all, the choice was poverty in a long-sttled town, or poverty on a hardscrabble hill farm. Small wonder that resentment over British refusal to push the Indians out of the Ohio country contributed to the movement toward independence.

Chapter 5

This Well-Watered Land

❧

The American farmer despoils his field without the least attempt at method in the process. When it ceases to yield him abundant crops, he simply quits it and, with his seeds and plants, betakes himself to a fresh field.[1]

—Baron Justis von Liebig, 1859

THE STREAM THAT DRAINS BULLOUGH'S POND IS called Smelt Brook, despite the fact that no smelt swim here. Smelt, like the first English settlers, prefer to dwell near the coast. They live in estuaries: river's mouths where fresh water mingles with salt. But once a year, on a night in early spring, they dash up little streams flowing fast over rocks, deposit their eggs on a clump of riverweed, and race back to the sea before dawn. After the larvae hatch, the fast-moving waters that washed oxygen over the eggs carry the young downstream to the estuary.

Smelt Brook enters the Charles River a good nine miles from salt water—a stiff all-night swim for a seven-inch fish. But not so very many years ago tides rose and fell in the Charles as far upstream as Watertown Square, and the nine-mile stretch of water known as the Charles River Basin was a marsh-rimmed estuary where schools of rainbow smelt teemed to the delight of ravening striped bass.

Smelt never spawned in Bullough's Pond. For one thing, they spawn in fast-moving brooks, not in still water. For another, the pond wasn't here. Not until 1664, when a man named John Spring decided that a grist mill on Smelt Brook could turn a profit. He built his mill at a spot where the brook flowed over a rocky bottom to run between two glacial drumlins, just across Dexter Road from the present dam. The smelt favored this spot as a spawning ground because waters flowing rapidly down a rocky slope constantly mixed with oxygen; beaver built here because a dam on this site could create a pond large enough to store spring rains for the dry months. Thinking like a miller, John Spring wanted both what the beaver wanted and what the smelt needed: a site where a dam could back up a large mill pond, then let the water fall several feet. He chose well: a grist mill would operate on this spot for two centuries.

Smelt continued to spawn in the waters below the dam, but they could not swim over the dam itself, or spawn in what had once been a creek but was now a pond, or in the long stretch of creek that still flowed above the pond. Mills like the one at Bullough's Pond were built everywhere in New England in the seventeenth and eighteenth centuries, modest wooden buildings beside wooden wheels turned by waters impounded by dams that were themselves often built of wood.

Oak, pine, hickory, and chestnut; woods were the riches New England offered. English settlers would have preferred gold, or a staple crop valued on the international commodities market, like sugar or tobacco. There was no gold, but there were oak and pine. The difficulty lay in making trees pay. Barrel staves and even sawn lumber could be profitably shipped to the deforested wine and sugar islands, but it was England that supplied the bulk of New England's imports. A forest product that would bear the cost of shipment directly to England was what New England wanted. Planks, barrel staves, and shingles could all be brought so cheaply from Baltic forests that shipping them from New England did not pay. Then, in 1646, a group of London merchants sent a ship captain to Boston with orders "to buy or build a ketch of 40 or 50 tons." New England had found a way to turn oak trees into gold.[2]

The Thames was a great shipbuilding center and the London merchants could have had their ketch built at home; they sent to Boston to have the work done because on this forested coast, wood was so cheap that a finished ship could be built at 40 percent below the British price. England, that wooded island whose vast forests had impressed Caesar, was running out of trees. The gravity of such a situation can be realized only by imagining plastic, steel, and fossil oil nonexistent, and remembering that in 1646, everything was made of wood—even iron.

Producing a single ton of bar iron meant burning 1,920 bushels of charcoal made from 48 cords of wood. Put another way, it was necessary to cut and burn all the wood standing on two acres of forest to produce one ton of iron. More charcoal was needed to work the iron bar into useful objects. The year the Massachusetts Bay Colony was founded, England produced 26,000 tons of iron, which is to say, England cleared or coppiced 52,000 acres of forest a year just to make bar iron.[3] There weren't enough forests in all of the British Isles to maintain production on this scale; imports from Sweden soon began to supplement domestic iron-making.

The bellows, tool handles, carts, buckets, and forge buildings were all wooden too, of course. Everything was, except the furnace, which was made of brick—wood-fired brick. Pottery kilns were fired with wood, glass was produced by melting sand over wood fires, lime was extracted from limestone by fire, leather was tanned with tree bark, gristmills turned on wooden gears, canals flowed

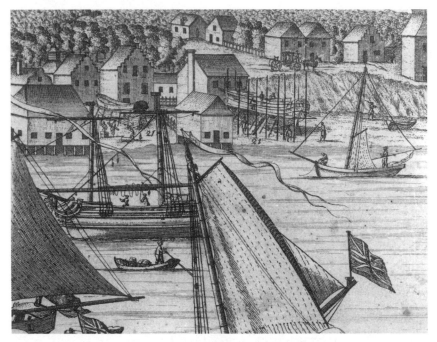

Detail of "A South Prospect of Ye Flourishing City of New York in America," engraving by William Burgis, Thomas Blakewell, London, 1746. The two shipyards pictured were located at the modern intersection of Fulton and Water Streets in lower Manhattan. The forest rising behind the fringe of buildings reminded the British audience, for whom the print was intended, of what made America a good location for a shipyard, although the artist may have drawn trees where field and pasture in fact existed. The vessel to the left is being built on stocks between two slaughterhouses that stand on pilings over the river. This was a sanitary location for a slaughterhouse, since offal could be shoveled or washed directly into the stream.

New York's fleet in the seventeenth and early eighteenth century was dwarfed by the fleet that sailed out of Boston, and the New York shipbuilding industry did not hold a candle to the Yankee industry (see Joseph Goldenberg, *Shipbuilding in Colonial America* [Charlottesville: University Press of Virginia, 1976.]) However, to my knowledge, no image of the colonial shipbuilding industry in New England exists. © Collection of the New-York Historical Society.

through wooden locks, freight rolled in wooden carts on wooden rails. Without wood; England would have been without industry, without so much as a mug of ale—a beverage brewed over wood fires, fermented in wooden vats and flavored with hops, which were grown on wooden poles and cured over charcoal fires.

Yet, even though England was experiencing a severe timber shortage, it did not pay to send lumber across the Atlantic. Processed forest products were worth sending. Pitch, potash, tar, turpentine, and sooty lamp black to make ink were profitably shipped across the ocean. Lumber was not. England could obtain that more cheaply from the forested, impoverished shores of the nearby Baltic and the North Sea. There was only one exception to the rule that lumber was not worth shipping across an ocean; it was a magnificent exception.

Scattered through the forests of New England grew the majestic white pine, a tree taller, straighter, and altogether grander than anything known to the Old World. The English were not connoisseurs of majestic trees, but they were a nation that lived by its fleet, a fleet that needed masts.

A Royal Navy ship of the line required a mast that was 40 inches across at the base, 120 feet tall, and absolutely straight. In the entire continent of Europe there grew not a single tree that could produce such a mast; skilled naval carpenters spliced masts together from lengths of Baltic fir, and British admirals sighed for the strength of masts cut from a single great tree. In a world that had not discovered the towering California redwood or Chilean alerce, the white pine was the only tree big enough and straight enough to make masts for the navy.

For two centuries, mast fleets sailed regularly from New England ports, slow-handling, unwieldy freighters built to carry a cargo that would swamp an ordinary hull. Escorted by frigates in time of war, unnoticed in peacetime except by the more marginal farmers of New Hampshire and Maine, who cut and ox-teamed white pine to the coast for sale to the king's mast agents, the mast fleets made their passage, carrying a vital strategic resource to England and returning gold to the colonies—until April 1775, when Captain Mowatt, in command of His Majesty's mast ship *Minerva* at Falmouth (now Portland), Maine, was briefly imprisoned by the local Committee of Safety while patriots towed the annual supply of masts to a secure backwater several miles from the harbor.[4]

Captain Mowatt got his revenge when he returned to Casco Bay in command of a British force that burned Falmouth to the ground, but the colonists had the last laugh as they forced the Royal Navy to fight a major war while suffering a severe shortage of masts. On the day Washington defeated Cornwallis at Yorktown, His Majesty's fleet was three hundred miles away in New York harbor, having its masts repaired.

From the perspective of the admiralty, nothing was more important than the mast supply—without masts, there could be no Royal Navy. Seen as part of the New England lumber trade, masts were only one segment of a thriving export market. They were profitable, especially for mast agents holding lucrative contracts, but scarcely as important as the market for timber used in constructing ships for sale to Europe. And the profitable business of building boats, an industry that each year produced £140,000 worth of shipping for sale to European buyers (and an even larger number for the colonial merchant fleet), was overshadowed by the very profitable carrying trade of which it was a small but not insignificant part. Not insignificant, because the low cost and high quality of New England's shipyards helped give Yankee merchants their profitable edge.[5]

In a world built of wood, forests meant wealth, moderate wealth for Swedes and Norwegians, who exported their trees as lumber and iron, or constantly widening commercial horizons for New Englanders, who exported their forests in the form of New England-built ships with Yankee owners, Yankee captains, and Yankee crews. It was the merchant fleet that cleared the forested hillsides of New England, turning them into cornfield and pasture. Not directly—not through the export of potash and tar, masts and barrel staves, larch frames and white cedar plank fashioned into seaworthy ships in hundreds of Yankee ship-yards. Not even through the thousands of cords of firewood that Boston and other seafaring towns burned every winter. All of these timber markets to-gether did not use as much wood as was simply chopped and burned by farm-ers clearing land.

The merchant fleet cleared the land through its constant demand for the small surplus of the Yankee farm. Demand for a firkin of butter, a barrel of salt beef, a bushel of corn; demand that created the prosperity that made possible the early marriages, the families of eleven and twelve children, the fertility that appalled Malthus and brought forth generation after generation of Yankee

Morning View of Blue Hill Village. Jonathan Fisher, oil on canvas. When the Republic was young, New England was an open landscape of cleared field and pasture punctuated by the occasional woodlot, as this view of Blue Hill, Maine, in 1824 shows. Courtesy of the William Farnsworth Museum, Rockland, Maine (65.1465.134).

Blue Hill, Maine. Photograph by Ken Woisard. The same view of Blue Hill Village in 1999 shows a wooded landscape. The boulder that stood beside the horse in the earlier picture can be seen in front of the snowbank; the harbor can still be seen to the left of the photograph; the old stump has disappeared. Two church steeples emerge above the trees; the one on the right appears in the 1824 painting. Most of the buildings in the original painting still stand, obscured by the woods that now blanket the New England countryside.

farmers to clear the hillsides, plant corn, and clear more hillsides. Right from the start, New England was part of the Atlantic economy, a place of green fields and family farmsteads as dependent in their way on bills of exchange from London as were the Chesapeake tobacco planters or the sugar islands. The economic system colonial farmers established altered the face of the land as inexorably as the draining of the English fens or the deforestation of the Italian piedmont.

When John Adams left his Braintree farm to assume the presidency in Washington, he left a countryside of fences and plowed fields. Indian New England greeted spring with an exuberant leafing out that covered the hills with every soft shade of green, while salmon and shad, alewife and smelt celebrated by leaping upstream. Leafing out in 1797 was restricted to apple orchards and woodlots; in the fields, pastures, farmyards, and village centers that covered most of the land, spring was known as mud season and the fish runs were rapidly fading into memory.

Fish are notoriously picky about where they spawn. Like finicky home buyers who refuse to look at anything without three bathrooms and a fireplace, the anadromous fish that swim up New England rivers to lay their eggs have exacting standards, which differ for each species. Smelt, for instance, spawn when water temperatures in the fast-flowing streams they favor reach 40 to 42 degrees Fahrenheit. Shad wait until temperatures reach a comparatively balmy 62 degrees, but cease migrating should temperatures exceed 68 degrees. Nor is temperature the only consideration; conditions on the stream bottom are every bit as important.

Atlantic salmon, like their equally delectable cousins, the brook trout, insist on a clean gravel bed in which to dig a nest and deposit their eggs. Sea lamprey seek the muddy bottom of a quiet pool; alewives spawn in ponds or in the deep, sluggish pools of flowing streams; while sea sturgeon—well, we don't actually know where sea sturgeon spawn. When the first English settlers arrived, New England rivers boasted sturgeon eighteen feet long that weighed in at nine hundred pounds. A princely fish. We know that the handful of young Atlantic sturgeon spawning in New England rivers today take up to twenty-eight years to reach sexual maturity, but so few of them are left that we are not sure what kind of spawning conditions they prefer.

Without doubt, New England's smelt, salmon, sturgeon, lamprey, alewife, shad, brook trout, and eel—fish that move from ocean to fresh water as they are born, mature, and spawn—do not like dams. Yet dams, to power mill wheels that ground grain for bread, were as central to the life of a Puritan village as the meeting house itself. Every settlement had a mill. Some had tide mills, set up in places like Boston's Mill Pond, where the ocean rushed through a narrow channel twice daily; a few used windmills; but most dammed small streams like Smelt Brook. The fish runs might have ended with the building of mills; they did not because New Englanders valued the fish and because seventeenth-century mill dams were small.

Nobody in the first century of settlement attempted to dam the Connecticut or the Merrimack. For one thing, the colonists lacked the resources to try; for another, they had no need of that much power. The water power in a small stream like Smelt Brook was ample to grind the rye and cornmeal of a farming village. Connecticut millers dammed the Farmill and the Naugatuck, Beaver Brook, Eight Mile Brook, and Halfway River; the Housatonic was left for the power needs of a later age. Salmon, shad, and sturgeon swam up the main rivers into undammed spawning streams, or they swam past the mill dams through sluice gates opened for their passage. Colonial fish runs were reduced; they were not decimated.

English common law had long recognized the importance of anadromous fish runs by forbidding any subject from obstructing their passage. Colonial American fishermen had a legal right to open fishways or even destroy a dam that blocked a fish run, though such measures were not necessary in practice.[6] In a New England village, every miller was at least a part-time farmer—as was virtually every minister, lawyer, blacksmith, and storekeeper—and the farms they worked produced a very small surplus, when they produced a surplus at

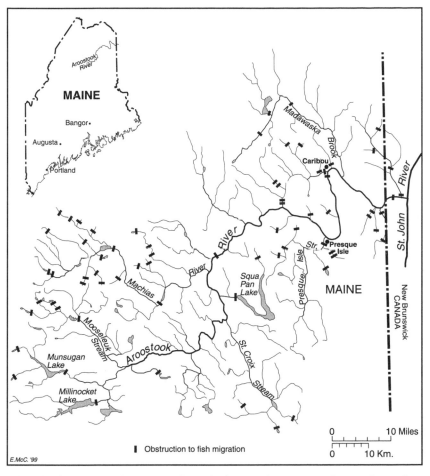

When the first dam on the Aroostook was built at Caribou in 1890, the river boasted an abundant salmon run: fish were caught a hundred miles upstream from the point where the Aroostook joins the St. John. By the middle of the twentieth century, there were seventy-two dams on the river and its tributaries; the weary salmon that managed to ascend the fishways had to contend with untreated domestic sewage, effluent from frozen food, woolen, and potato starch mills, and the effects of clear-cutting (siltation, flooding, and low water in summer). The salmon vanished. Anthony Netboy, *The Atlantic Salmon: A Vanishing Species?* (Boston: Houghton Mifflin, 1968), 341. By permission of the Houghton Mifflin Company.

all. With luck, enough pork and beef were salted in November to last through the winter, enough fish smoked in spring to last until the spring lambs were big enough to butcher. In the words of a Yankee proverb: "We hope meat will last 'till fish comes, and fish will last 'till meat comes." Everyone in town wanted a fishway maintained or a water gate opened to let the fish through. And the practice of opening the dams had little real cost; corn, after all, is ground in fall while fish spawn in spring.

Public sentiment in favor of smoked river herring is not the same, however, as effective protection of suitable spawning habitat, and that was being altered daily by the very farmers who looked forward to spring fish runs. Some changes took waterways that had long harbored one species and made them more suitable for a different kind of fish, as when mill dams destroyed the spawning grounds of smelt, brook trout, and Atlantic salmon, but provided an ideal habitat for spawning alewife and young eel. Silt from plowed fields that washed into rivers and covered graveled bottoms with mud, however, destroyed much prime spawning ground with no benefit to any competing species. And even where graveled bottoms remained unsullied, the cutting of trees to create farmland let the sun shine on what had once been shaded brooks, raising the daytime temperature of trout pools until the water was too warm for the young fish. Even a single pool of warm water can block migrating fish from swimming upstream to a place where conditions may be cool enough for spawning. A pool where trees have been cut can become so warm from the sun that algae chokes the water, using up so much oxygen that no fish can live. It was land clearing, as much as mill dams, that killed the fish runs.

Dams did their part, of course. The twentieth century has yet to design a fishway that shad can ascend with aplomb; with the best will in the world, no eighteenth-century corn miller could get shad or other fish over his dam in the numbers that would have swum upstream had no dam been there. And not every miller tried, especially not saw millers.

The first New England sawmills were built in 1634.[7] They represented an innovation in the replica of old England many settlers were hoping to build: In England, lumber was sawn by thin-bladed, two-handled saws, one sawyer standing in a saw pit, the other atop the log, pulling the saw by turns. Pit-sawing was hard work, but it wasted only one-eighth of the log as saw dust. Saw mills require a thicker blade to withstand the stress of mechanical operation; they waste one-fifth of the wood as dust. England, with plentiful labor and a wood shortage, sawed by hand. New England, awash in forests but short of labor, built sawmills, and dumped the sawdust into the millstream where it sat in great sculpted masses, man-made sandbars sometimes visible fifty years after the mill closed down.[8] Trout and salmon abandoned the turbid waters of sawdust-filled streams, or, if they came, found their graveled spawning grounds buried under a mountain of sawdust, and failed to reproduce.

New England needed lumber for houses, barns, ships, and barrels; the demand was as inexhaustible as the supply seemed. Every town had at least one sawmill, sometimes near the gristmill, sometimes further from the center, near hilly or swampy land less desirable for farming. Sometimes millers opened dams to let fish through; sometimes they did not. The further north the sawmill dam,

Dipnetting alewives at the first falls on the Medomack, Waldoboro, Maine, 1874. A fish-ladder is visible in the center of the photo. Couresty of Maine State Museum.

the less likely it was to open a fishway. Settled farming towns protected their shad and alewife runs by monitoring the millers, but the numerous commercial saw mills in the district of Maine were located far from the watchful eyes of farmers concerned about fish. Besides, so many salmon ran up the Androscoggin and the Kennebec that the few whose spawning was blocked by a mill dam on a tributary near the coast scarcely seemed to matter.

By the late 1700s, the lands of southern New England and the flatter, lower-lying parts of the northern states had long since been cleared for farming. Woodlots remained, along with swamps and an occasional patch of rocky

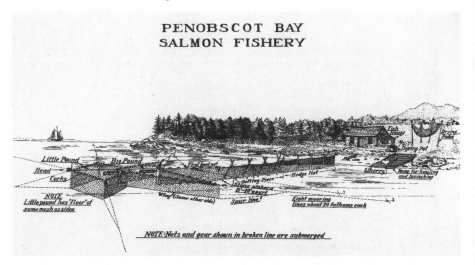

"Penobscot Bay Salmon Fishery." Sketch by John Leavitt. Commercial fishermen set huge nets across the mouth of every major river in the region to catch runs of salmon, shad, and herring. This sketch of the Penobscot salmon fishery in the early years of the twentieth century gives some idea of the scale of such operations. Although intensive fishing did deplete the resource, very large annual catches were sustainable until dams decimated the population. Courtesy of Mystic Seaport Museum (75.338).

hillside too steep to be worth clearing, but mile after mile of open land stretched before the eye, land that had not lain so open to the sky since the glaciers melted back.

When the glaciers retreated, the land they left was rubble, chunks of rock, gravel, sand and boulder strewn barrenly over a surface where lichens, and very little else, could grow. Lichens are the most admirable of plants. Whether coloring the face of an old stone wall in dense mats or clinging in wispy beards from fir branches in our mountain rainforests, lichens are admirable not for their beauty but for their character. A lichen is not one plant but two: millions of individual algae cells live woven in a matrix of fungal filament, the two plants forming that rarest of relationships, a perfect symbiosis. The fungal structure supports the algae and captures moisture for its use; the photosynthetic algae cells produce chlorophyll, which they convert into sugars that nourish the fungus. Not only do two species combine in perfect harmony to form a lichen; the lichen itself makes almost as few demands on its surroundings as each part does on its partner. Lichens live on air—rainwater and fog—and require little nourishment from the rocks or branches that support them. That is how they can live where other plants cannot. That is also how they can position themselves on bare rock and begin the process of manufacturing topsoil by producing acids that break down the surface of the stone. Tiny fragments of lichen mixed with particles of stone can provide sufficient soil to give other simple plants a start in life.

Beautiful, exemplary, hard-working, and able to grow in a cold land devoid of nutrients, lichens cannot, however, support human civilization alone; that requires topsoil and topsoil is created by forests. As the New England forest disappeared, so did the topsoil. Not all at once, of course; drop by drop would be more like it. Some topsoil blew away from plowed fields in dry seasons. Some remained, worthless, depleted of nutrients by too many crops of corn. And some simply washed away; there was nothing to stop it from going.

Forests are agents of moderation. They slow winds, shade the understory from the heat of summer sun, blanket the ground against the worst of winter

THE SAWYER.

"The Sawyer." This time-honored, labor intensive method of sawing was rare in New England, where sawmills were built immediately following settlement. This picture, indeed the entire book, was likely copied from a British work since pit-sawing was as rare in Pennsylvania as it was in New England. *Jack of All Trades* (Philadelphia: William Darton, 1808). Courtesy, American Antiquarian Society.

cold, break up the force of a driving rainstorm before it batters the soil, absorb water in a wet season, and draw moisture from deep underground in a dry one. When forests are cut, conditions on the land become more extreme, hotter and dryer in summer, colder and dryer in winter—dryer, in fact, year-round, except when it is actually raining. In a deforested land, there is nothing to absorb rainwater, and heavy downpours produce roaring freshets that cut gullies through plowed fields, carrying off valuable soil and flooding low-lying areas in their rush seaward.[9]

On July 25, 1990, our first summer on Bullough's Pond, it rained so hard that traffic on Route 128 slowed to a crawl and motorists with a high value for life pulled off the road to wait for the deluge to stop. It didn't. Seven inches fell in four hours. Muddy water boiled at the pond's inlet like an angry cauldron; the water rose eighteen inches, and great sheets of duckweed went sliding over the lip of the dam. Downstream, flood waters tore up a wire screen, designed for peas to clamber on in a vegetable garden, and stuffed it against the open mouth of the concrete culvert that carries Smelt Brook under Hull Street.

There it stayed, a fine mesh of wire covering the mouth of the culvert as masses of duckweed coursed down Smelt Brook and stuck fast. It took only minutes to plug the outlet completely. The rapidly eutrifying pond had been covered with floating mats of duckweed. Flood water rushed in so fast that it seemed to come down the pond in waves. The water had to go somewhere. When it couldn't go through, it went up. Up into the gardens of houses whose lawns slope down to the brook. Up onto Hull Street. Up and over Hull Street onto the high school playing fields and tennis courts.

There were people who thought that the devastated gardens and expensive repairs at the ruined tennis courts were a good reason for dredging the pond and cleaning up the duckweed, a view not shared by city hall, where they had a formula by which storms are calculated in twenty-four-hour intervals. Seven inches of rain fell in four hours. If rain had kept on falling at that rate for twenty-four hours, there would have been forty-two inches of rain. That's a lot of rain. It's the sort of storm that might not happen if you waited half a millennium. No one could recall so much rain ever falling in Newton. No one could recall a rainstorm ever causing Bullough's Pond to overflood its dam. Using this logic, the authorities classified the rain on July 25, 1990, as a five hundred-year storm, and it doesn't pay to plan against a downpour that won't recur for five hundred years.

But August was rainy. Not just rainy, but hot. And not just hot, but humid. Newton felt like Panama City, with dense, hot air that gave way to cloudbursts that gave way to more humidity. Clothing was damp. Furniture was damp. I took a manuscript to the copy store only to find that the paper was so impregnated with moisture that it wouldn't feed into the machine. Duckweed bloomed effusively.

When we woke on Saturday morning, August 11, it was raining steadily. My husband and children left for synagogue; I couldn't find my rain hat. I searched the closets fruitlessly and decided to wait for the rain to let up. It didn't. At about ten o'clock, the steady rain became a downpour that sent water coursing down the almost imperceptible slope of Berkshire Road, crashing against the curb in a torrent four inches deep piling up too fast for the storm drains to carry off.

A streak of Yankee contrariness led me to get the field glasses out when we woke up to raindrops. What if city hall's five-hundred-year storm repeated after only two and a half weeks? But the water was still eight inches below the lip of the dam in the early morning, eight inches above normal, but flowing easily through the spillway and, at that rate, offering little hope of a real flood.

When the rain picked up at ten I got the glasses back out and watched the water rise four inches in an hour before the rain let up a little. By then I was so disgracefully late for services that I headed for the synagogue without a rain hat. A neighbor told me later that in the last moments before the water rushed over the dam, she stood on the bridge and watched it rise an inch in two minutes. I wish I had been there to see the first raft of duckweed go over the top. After all, a woman could live five hundred years and not see a storm like that again.

There was no pea trellis this time. This time it was a lawn chair. And a few dead branches. It took only minutes for duckweed to plug the culvert; then the water began to rise.

When we got home at about four-thirty, it was raining steadily. We stood on the bridge along with a handful of neighbors and a snapping turtle with a twenty-four-inch carapace, watching sheets of duckweed pour over the dam. We crossed Dexter Street and walked down the path where a small stream normally bubbles past stolid boulders. Not today. Today water crashed and eddied past rocks that sit dry above the waterline from one season to the next. It pounded the footings that once supported the old mill. It overtopped banks and swirled among weeds at the edge of the path. It embraced the little island, submerging half of its modest land area. Across Walnut Street, where well-tended lawns sloped down to meet the brook, the most impressive feature of the flood was quiet. Here was no tearing, frothing rush of water like the flood tumbling past the footings of the old mill. Here was a silent brown lake lapping peacefully at the wooden clapboards of a large, white house. Hull Street lay beneath the same broad lagoon, though here it was not so quiet. A rushing, foaming rapids greeted us where flood waters tumbled eagerly onto the playing courts and tennis fields at Newton North High School. A teenager stood atop his stranded, red pickup until two friends arrived to push it free of the hip-deep water. He'd been sure his truck could make it through.

A second bunch of kids emerged from the drowned playing fields. New to the neighborhood, we asked them where the brook normally went after flowing under Hull Street.

To Bullough's Pond.

No, we insisted, that's where it comes from. Where does it usually go now?

They conferred, finally concluding that it doesn't go anywhere. Just goes around in a circle, kind of. City kids.

The culvert, it turns out, goes underground most of the way to the Charles. Once the culvert was blocked, there was no way the water could run back into the brook further downstream.

When the sun came out on Sunday, I went back over to Hull Street, just to step onto the embankment and look at the brook, still running brown but confined now to its bed, and at the maple branches high above my head, festooned with duckweed.

Our second five-hundred-year storm in less than a month was no coincidence, even if local memory is correct in asserting that it had never happened before. The 1980s had seen a building boom. In Newton, as everywhere in New England, trees were cut down, buildings erected, ground paved over for parking lots and driveways. Rain falling on wooded land is caught by leaves, absorbed by the leaf litter on the ground, and enabled to sink into the ground itself. When rain falls on a lawn or garden, some of it is absorbed as it would be by a farm field, though a good deal runs off before it can be absorbed. But nearly every drop of rain that falls on a roof or driveway runs into the gutter and, if it falls in Newton, directly into Bullough's Pond. When you cut trees, whether for farmland or suburban housing, you had better provide good drainage, or there will be floods.

There may have been more floods as New England was deforested to clear land for farming, or there may have simply been more people interested in recording the floods that did occur.[10] People living in the 1700s certainly believed that there were more floods, that the rivers were fuller at spring runoff, that small streams dried up more frequently in the summer, and that useless swamps sometimes appeared when perfectly dry stands of forest were cut for farmland. They probably were right.

Snow, which takes its time melting on the shady floor of a March forest, rushes off a March field on the first sunny day, creating floods downstream. Water, which seeps from forested hills all through the summer, rushes off farm fields while the rain is still falling, leaving little to sink in and replenish underground water courses. Those new swamps appearing where farmers had planned to plow fields were a oddity in an landscape that was mostly made dryer by deforestation, but while forests absorb rainwater and keep it on the land, they also efficiently wick moisture out of the soil and release it into the atmosphere through their leaves. When trees are cut on a low-lying piece of ground, this wicking stops and ground that looked dry when it was wooded may be too marshy to farm.

There is a piece of such land about two blocks from here, on the corner of

Homer Street and Walnut. The land fronts toward city hall and backs up to the cemetery; for years it was empty and uninteresting, except that certain marshy plants grew there and if you walked among them after a rainy spell you were likely to get your shoes wet. The new library stands on that lot today, a handsome, neo-Georgian structure with wide roofs, a spacious entry piazza, and an expansive asphalt parking lot. Between the parking lot and the building, a streamlet trickles across the bottom of a man-made dell that only turns into a pond when it rains hard. In heavy downpours, I have seen ducks swimming there.

The summer of the floods, the library was still under construction. The dell had not yet been excavated and the brown water pouring off the half-finished building and its muddy parking area had nowhere to run but the playing fields of Newton North. There is less likely to be another flood now that the dell beside the library stands ready to hold water running off the roof and parking lot, but there very likely would never have been a flood if that spongy, vacant lot hadn't been filled with a building.

Floods, exciting though they are, were not the crucial change wrought by seventeenth-, eighteenth-, and nineteenth-century deforestation, the change that rendered Yankee agriculture unsustainable. That honor goes to the failure of topsoil replacement.

Forests created the topsoil Yankee farmers depended upon, and it was a long, slow job. The succession of plants that colonized New England as the world warmed in the aftermath of the ice age—lichens followed by mosses, then sedges and grasses, then spruce and pine, and then finally, deciduous forests with the fertile topsoil they produce—did not proceed rapidly. Thousands of years elapsed between the appearance of the first lichens on rocks laid bare by retreating ice, and the creation of topsoil that could support a chestnut tree. The standard estimate is that a foot of topsoil is created by a mature forest in ten thousand years, but New England forests did not have time to create so much. As little as two to four inches of fertile topsoil lay beneath the virgin forests of the region, even less on the steep, spruce-clad northern hills.[11] The soil was fertile, well watered, and capable of yielding generous crops, but there was none to waste.

Waste topsoil was precisely what Yankee farmers did during the first two centuries of English settlement. They wasted by exposing plowed fields to erosion by wind and rain, but mostly they wasted soil by cropping land without feeding the soil. Corn was planted, but not in rotation with nitrogen-fixing clover. Corn shocks were fed to cattle, not plowed under. Cattle were fed, but their dung was not collected to dress the fields.

With the clarity of hindsight, we can charge colonial farmers with destructive husbandry. Not that they were unaware of the problem; students of agriculture in the eighteenth century knew perfectly well that fertilizers could mend "our old land which we have worn out."[12] The problem was that the first careful study of soil chemistry, by Justus Liebig, was not published until 1840. Before that date a farmer with the best of intentions attempting to maintain the fertility of his soil might have been more likely to waste his labor than improve his fields. The difficulty was that although farmers observed that certain soil amendments seemed to work, without an understanding of soil chemistry they could not understand why they worked, or know which would be likely to work on a particular field. The general principle that organic matter, everything from feathers to ashes, would serve as a useful fertilizer was well known, as was the fact that many, inorganic substances, such as lime and marl, were fertilizing agents. But without an understanding of soil chemistry, the eighteenth-century farmer could not know that nitrogen can be obtained from animal manures while potassium is best gotten from ashes, or that the acid soil of humid New England farms especially needs the calcium that lime can supply.

The eighteenth century not only lacked the knowledge of soil chemistry that might have enabled farmers to apply the correct fertilizers to particular fields, it was innocent of the statistical methods that enable contemporary researchers to know when a thing works. Even if modern agricultural researchers lacked all chemical knowledge of soil composition and plant growth, they could apply a traditional soil amendment like seaweed to half of a field and nothing to the other half, repeat the experiment several times, and know empirically which grew better. Or seaweed could be applied to one field, ground oyster shells to another, the experiment repeated, and the results compared. Eighteenth-century farmers couldn't do that; reliable experimental methodology had to await the development of statistics, just as intelligent application of the right soil amendment to a particular field had to await the development of soil chemistry. Eighteenth-century agricultural improvers used a fairly random trial-and-error method, if a thing worked or seemed to work once, they recommended it. A diligent farmer seeking advice from the most respected sources might be told to try a variety of fertilizers that included plowing under the morning dew, spreading seawater over his fields, and burying animal hoofs upright in dry soil to retain moisture.[13] It is amusing to calculate the number of dead horses required for upright hoof burial under an acre of corn, but there can be no doubt that the scheme, like recommendations to collect, compost, and plow under every kind of organic waste (feathers, leather scraps, blood, old thatch, wood chips—the detritus of colonial life) would, on the whole, have helped. The obstacle was that the balance of land resources and labor was wrong. At a time when even such well-understood and relatively easy recourses as penning cattle at night so that their droppings would dung a field were rejected as being not worth the trouble, it was hardly likely that farmers would go to the trouble of carting peat from a bog and plowing it under. Only gentlemen farmers of a scientific bent experimented with fertilizers.

Ordinary farmers were no more intent on preserving the fertility of the soil for future generations than they were on increasing the scientific understanding of field husbandry. The goals they acknowledged were to make a living this year and, in the course of a working lifetime, to set enough by to give their children a start in life. If, in the process, they filled the beds of some trout streams with silt and caused other streams and springs to dry up, if fish runs failed as creeks were dammed and topsoil washed off the land into the estuaries, if topsoil lost nutrients and was therefore able to produce less and less food with every passing year, it wasn't the farmers' fault. They were only trying to make a living.

Chapter 6

To the Farthest Port of the Rich East

❧

Divitis Indiae usque ad ultimum sinum[1]
—Motto of the city of Salem

T HE REVOLUTIONARY WAR WAS BARELY OVER WHEN American merchants went on a buying spree, filling warehouses with laces, latches, satins, shoe buckles, teapots, and tumblers—all the European goods Americans had gone without in wartime. But the world had changed. The newly independent states found themselves unable to pay for goods that as British colonies they had freely imported from the mother country.

The tens of thousands of pounds worth of merchant shipping that colonial New England yards once built every year for English owners had become a foreign product that England did not want. The exchange of codfish, lumber, and produce for molasses, the very lifeblood of colonial New England commerce, was forbidden by a mercantilist British government that saw no advantage in allowing its sugar colonies to trade with foreign nations. Even the narrow range of American commodities British authorities were willing to accept met with discriminatory duties if they were shipped in American bottoms.

Nor was there any easy way to replace British markets with sales to Britain's rivals. Protectionist governments in France, Spain, and Portugal banned our ships from their colonies and levied stiff duties on commodities we might have sold them. Shipyards fell silent. Wharves lay empty. There was no market for the farmers' produce, no employment for craftsmen, nowhere for merchants to sell the goods that crowded their warehouses. Thoughtful New Englanders could see only one solution: become a manufacturing nation.

It was not an entirely new idea. By the 1780s, there was scarcely a village in New England that could not boast a gristmill, a sawmill, a cooper's shop, a tannery, a fulling mill to finish homespun woolen cloth with mechanical beaters, and a smithy capable of fashioning hardware for kitchen and farm. Where there

74

was clay, there was likely to be a pottery; where the fuller was enterprising, there might be a dyehouse beside his mill.

Few of these "industrialists" made a living from their mills. They were farmers first and coopers or fullers only as time allowed and the market demanded—a market defined by a radius that ended halfway to the next mill, tannery, or smithy. It was an efficient system at a time when transportation meant loading an oxcart and plodding at snail's pace over roads that imposed a crawl on even the fastest horses, so pitted were they with mudholes and frost heaves. A village that turned its own hides into shoes and its own fleece into coats saved the expense of carting goods over bad roads, and kept its money at home. A small flow of surplus farm produce, with an occasional barrel of locally made boots or earthenware, moved toward the seaports. A trickle of imported necessities, fancy goods, and a little cash flowed back to the farming villages. Village manufacturing was a microcosm of the mercantile philosophy that made England rich: do the skilled work within your own borders, export a surplus, keep imports to a minimum, and watch the gold pile up. The piles of gold in question were piddling by London standards, but as long as there was a market for village agricultural exports, the piles grew.

A second tier of small factories supplied regional demand for such goods as chocolate, snuff, nails, and paper.[2] And there were colonial industries that supplied an export market: potash making, shipbuilding, rum distilling and the manufacture of spermaceti candles.

Spermaceti burns clean. This fact, of limited interest in an age of electric lights, was once enough to make Nantucket rich. A spermaceti candle, or a lamp burning whale oil, gives off no unpleasant odor and sends no trail of inky smoke to mar the ceiling. In an age when winter meant crowding for warmth into dark, smelly rooms, air foul from the fumes of burning tallow, walls and ceiling blackened by soot from grease lamps, which compounded their unpleasantness by spitting at those who attempted to work by their flickering light, the steady, sweet-smelling flame of a spermaceti candle was a blessing worth paying for—provided you had the cash. Few Americans did, but wealthy Englishmen and West Indian sugar planters indulged themselves in £60,000 worth of candles every year, made from sperm whales caught by Nantucket boats and made into candles at Newport.[3]

Sperm oil was then, and remains today, one of the finest lubricants for precision machinery; ambergris from the animal's intestine was an essential ingredient in superior perfume; and it was well understood that the powerful animals' massive hoard of waxen "sperm" was among the world's most potent aphrodisiacs. A sperm whale made a very profitable package. But if England could not rule Nantucket, she did not want its oil. With the stroke of a pen, Whitehall wiped out hope for recovery in the Newport candle industry. The Nantucket whaling fleet had already been destroyed by war at sea.[5]

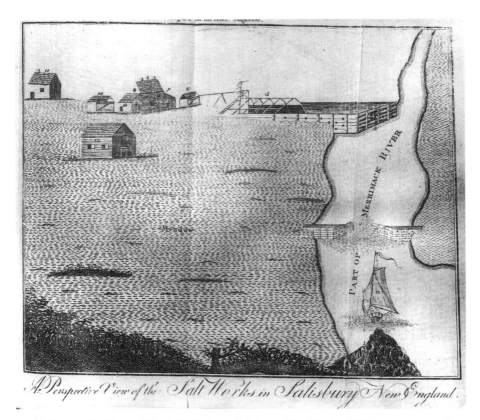

A Perspective View of the Salt Works in Salisbury New England.

"A Perspective View of the Salt Works in Salisbury, New England." Salt was imported from Europe in colonial times. Americans endeavored to produce their own salt as a patriotic exercise in the revolutionary period and as an economic one during the depression that followed. This illustration from the March 1776 *Pennsylvania Magazine* showcases the saltworks of Salisbury, New Hampshire, as an example of American enterprise and patriotism. The text explains, "The water in full tide is received through sluice no. 4 into the reservoir no. 5 (which is a hundred feet long and 40 broad) where it stands in the sun to evaporate to a pickle, thence it is pumped into a refining cistern, there to refine; thence it is drawn into the pans (which are made of plate iron riveted together, about ten feet square, and twelve inches deep) there boiled and skimmed as the salt makes; then carried to the hot house to cure, and from thence to the store."

1. Hook's Rock	6. A refining cistern	11. Dwelling house
2. The dam	7. A boiling house	12. The store
3. The wharf	8. Hot house	13. Salt boat
4. A sluice	9. Boiling house	
5. The reservoir	10. Refining cistern	

All colonial manufacturing put together amounted to very little alongside agriculture. Ours was a nation of farmers, and Thomas Jefferson was not the only American to view "artificers as the panders of vice and the instruments by which the liberties of a country are generally overturned." But severe postwar depression combined with real, if limited, wartime manufacturing success to create an atmosphere in which the "expediency of encouraging manufactures in the United States, which was not long since deemed very questionable, appears at this time to be pretty generally admitted."[5] By 1792, societies for the "encouragement of domestic industry" had been formed in Philadelphia, New York, Baltimore, Wilmington, Morristown, Newark, Burlington (New Jersey), Providence, and Boston; while the legislatures of Massachusetts and New Hampshire voted to exempt manufacturing establishments from taxation.[6]

Enthusiasm ran so high that legislatures in Connecticut, Rhode Island, Massachusetts, and New Hampshire granted privileges, including the right to hold public lotteries to raise capital, to entrepreneurs endeavoring to build glass-making factories. The fate of Mark Leavenworth's New Haven glassworks was typical. The factory, built with considerable fanfare, is not known to have produced any actual glass. In 1792 the Connecticut legislature ordered an investigation into what had become of the four hundred pounds raised from public-spirited citizens. Of the lot, only Robert Hewes's glassworks in Essex Street, Boston, succeeded, producing high-quality window glass starting in 1793.[7] Most glassware continued to be imported.

The enthusiasm for producing cotton textiles was even greater. Americans knew that English manufacturers were spinning cotton by water power. The problem was that the English wouldn't tell how they did it. A regular stream of British artisans arrived in American ports claiming to know how, and several were hired to build spinning jennies. The Massachusetts legislature even paid two brothers named Barr to construct and exhibit power spinning machinery that would-be manufacturers could copy. The hitch was that none of the machines worked—until Moses Brown invited Samuel Slater to Providence.[8]

Even in England, machinery was not built from blueprints—such a thing was hardly possible at a time when machine tools operated to tolerances no greater than the estimations of the naked eye. What Slater brought to America was not a set of plans, but the knowledge of how textile machinery worked. The workmen who preceded him had understood spinning in only a partial way. Factory hands of varying sorts, they had at best understood the construction and workings of the specific machines they operated. Slater was not a hand. He was the son of a friend of the owner-operator of one of the early English cotton mills, where he trained as a management apprentice and worked as a supervisor before seeking opportunity in America.

For a man with Slater's knowledge to leave England was illegal; he dressed as a common workman and arrived in New York to find that American investors had grown wary of workmen who claimed to know how to build cotton mills. But Samuel Slater did know, and when Moses Brown set him up on the Blackstone River, he spun cotton. That left the problem of where to sell the quantities of cotton yarn Mr. Slater's machines could spin.

Americans pointed with pride to the success of native manufacturers, but continued to buy English yard goods for the simple reason that they cost less. They were cheaper because wages in England were low, because sometimes economic conditions left English manufacturers overstocked with goods, which they dumped on the American market below cost, and perhaps—as American manufacturers charged—because British merchants deliberately undersold the Americans in an attempt to kill American manufacturing in its infancy.[9]

Most American families continued the thrifty practice of making some part of the family's cloth at home, and it was in their homes that the fledgling manufactory found its market. Slater's strong cotton yarn was purchased throughout the northern and middle Atlantic states for use as warp on the home looms that produced homespun wool-and-cotton or linen-and-cotton cloth. It was a small niche compared to the market for yard goods being profitably served by English mills, but the little mill on the Blackstone, and a small number of imitators run by men who learned the trade working under Slater, consistently spun profits.

A cluster of yarn mills near Providence and a window-glass factory in Boston were not much to show for the proud industrial independence Alexander Hamilton foresaw as America's future. But in 1804 Hamilton was dead and, from what anyone surveying the American scene could observe, so was his vision. The cause of death was plain. Americans had never been as interested in making yard goods as they were in making money, and while European tariff barriers had made manufacturing appear necessary at the depth of the postwar depression, by 1793 profits could most easily be found where New Englanders had always looked for them—in the sea lanes of the Atlantic.

Some men had never stopped looking for shipping profit, the trick was to find some new route to replace the old West India trade. Not that the West India trade was quite as dead as London wished; as long as planters needed provisions and New England needed markets, traders found ways to tack around Imperial regulations. But slipping schooners laden with clapboards and codfish past the customs officials of small sugar islands was penny ante. American merchants wanted more, and, no longer bound by British law restricting trade beyond the Cape of Good Hope to the East India Company, ambitious Yankees set sail for Chinese tea, silk, and porcelain, Indian cottons, and East Indian spices.

In 1784 a Hingham merchant filled the fifty-five-ton sloop *Harriet* with ginseng and sent her to China. Ginseng was common; the low-growing, five-leafed plant of the forest floor was found throughout the New England woods, particularly under chestnut trees. The branched root of a ginseng plant roughly resembles the lower half of a human torso—hips and two legs. Whether for this reason or some other, China believed that ginseng was a useful medicinal herb and a powerful aphrodisiac. Carefully dug and dried so that it arrived in Canton intact, ginseng brought a good price, a fact of which Americans, who had been selling roots to the East India Company for over a century, were well aware.

At the Cape of Good Hope the *Harriet* met a British East Indiaman eager to trade tea for her cargo of ginseng, saving the Massachusetts men a long voyage and precluding the opening of a direct American trade with China, or so the British captain may have thought. In fact, the *Empress of China*, out of New York with another cargo of ginseng, was also on route to Canton that summer. The China trade, one of the most profitable enterprises Americans ever engaged in, was under way.[10]

Ginseng alone was not enough to sustain a China trade, even if Americans had uprooted every plant in the forest—which they very nearly did. Once as common as wintergreen and clubmoss, ginseng has retreated to remote mountain fastnesses, where it is pursued by collectors eager for the high prices Oriental herbalists still pay for roots dug in the wild. In most of its former habitat it has been so thoroughly eradicated that few contemporary field guides mention the once-common plant.

Western demand for tea and silk was almost unlimited, but the supply of ginseng was finite and the only other commodites China was willing to accept in payment were silver and gold. Americans, unlike the British and Dutch East India Companies, had little specie.

Eager as they were known to be for some medium of trade with China, the shipping magnates of New York and Boston were probably not surprised by the appearance of a Connecticut marine named John Ledyard, who claimed to possess the key that would unlock the riches of the Orient. Ledyard's story was romantic enough. He had sailed under Captain James Cook and, his clothes in tatters after two and a half years at sea, bartered trinkets for furs from the natives of the northwest American coast. By the time Cook's expedition reached China, the furs were considerably the worse for wear, yet the Chinese paid one hundred dollars apiece for them. If the merchants would only pay to outfit a trading expedition to that fur-rich coast, Ledyard claimed, there were fortunes awaiting them all in Canton.[11] It was a tall story. Ledyard was, after all, nobody, and rich men tire of being importuned by poor men who know how to make a fortune if only somebody else will front the money. Small wonder that nothing came of Ledyard's scheme, until publication of Cook's own journals—recounting the same story Ledyard had told—and reports brought by American merchant captains back from Canton combined to persuade a group of Boston men that northwest coast furs might be the trade medium they sought.

The *Columbia* and the *Lady Washington* set sail for Nootka Sound in 1787. They were the first American ships to round Cape Horn, and, on its return voyage around Africa, the *Columbia* became the first American ship to circle the globe—a fact that did not overly impress the Boston merchants who paid for the trip. What impressed Boston was evidence that money could then be made in a triangular trade of iron and brass goods bartered to northwest coast Indian hunters for sea otter pelts, which could then be traded in China for tea.

England had chafed for years under the necessity of buying tea with specie, and London was as quick as Boston to spot a good thing, but the cumbersome regulations of the East India Company hampered English enterprise. Not only did British traders have to pay the East India Company for the privilege of entering the Pacific; when they sold their otter pelts at Canton, they could not buy a return cargo of tea to sell at home for profit. Regulations compelled them merely to freight the tea at rates stipulated by the company.

What's more, northwest coast Indians liked the Americans' style. Whereas British traders anchored well off shore, cautiously sending small boats in to trade, American captains sailed into harbor and invited the Indians on board, brought shipboard blacksmiths to do custom iron work, found out and presented the items high-ranking Indians regarded as handsome gifts: brass-buttoned officer's coats and handsomely tooled hunting rifles. The British had reason for their caution: Indians allowed on board to trade sometimes attempted to overpower the crew and capture the ship. Several vessels had to be defended in bloody hand-to-hand battles and some of the attacks succeeded; in two recorded instances entire ship's companies were killed. By the time a ship brought its profits home to Boston, it had weathered the perilous passage around Cape Horn, avoided or survived armed confrontation with northwest coast trading partners, and evaded or fought off attack by the pirate fleets that scourged the China Sea. It was the ultimate high-profit, high-risk business.[12]

Canny Yankees soon discovered other commodities that could be carried to Canton for tea and profits. Bêche-de-mer, sea cucumbers of the East Indies, were boiled, dried and smoked on tropical beaches, then shipped to China where they were made into soup. Fragrant sandalwood from the islands of Hawaii brought a good price from wealthy Chinese buyers. The pelts of millions of fur seals from islands off the southern Chilean and Argentinean coasts were carried to China on New England ships.

Seal skins did not fetch the kind of fancy prices otter skins brought, but they were easier to come by. Unlike the wary sea otter, which had to be killed by skillful Indian hunters, fur seals were so unaccustomed to predation that they sat on their barren islands waiting to be slaughtered. The work was cold, unpleasant, and bloody as gangs of sailors clubbed the seals to death and skinned them—(a good man could skin sixty in an hour), but money poured into the ports of Stonington and New Haven, which specialized in the seal trade.[13]

"View of the Seal Rookery." Lithograph. Seals, hauled out on remote islands where they faced no natural predators, were easily slaughtered by men walking through the herds armed with clubs. Edmund Fanning, *Voyages Around the World* (New York: Collins and Hannay, 1833). Courtesy Peabody Essex Museum, Salem, Mass.

The seal and sea otter trades ended only when the animals had been hunted to the brink of extinction, at which point there was no profit in scouring the seas in search of lonely survivors to slaughter and sell. Sandalwood was harvested from Hawaiian forests until there was no saleable timber left standing. It was environmentally benign, for New England. The devastation of Hawaiian forests and Chilean seal populations did not perturb the merchants of Boston, Providence, and New Haven, except that when the resources were used up, the profits ended, and they had to find other ways to make money. As long as they could do that, as long as Yankee ships could sail to a foreign coast and find something to sell at a profit on some other foreign coast, few Yankee boys became industrialists. With Yankee enterprise funneled into merchant shipping, New England rivers ran clear and sea captains returned with their profits to comfortable homes on the shady streets of small seaport towns.

Up and down the New England coast in little harbors where nothing larger than a weekend pleasure boat has moored in over a century, streets are lined with the beautiful houses that tourists call colonial and bridling architectural historians call Federal. I am not speaking of once-busy international ports like Salem, Massachusetts, which sent its ships to the far corners of the globe, but of sleepy backwaters like Old Lyme, Connecticut, the town where I grew up, and where, to my certain knowledge, nothing has ever happened. Yet Main Street in Old Lyme, like the main street of every insignificant tidewater anchorage on this coast, is lined with gracious mansions that local lore celebrates as sea captains' houses. Where in creation did they sail to earn that kind of money? Ask, and you may be told whaling, or the China trade, or slaving, all of which are at least partly true for certain ports. But check the dates on the houses. The fortunes that built the beautiful Federal mansions of New England, from High Street in New-buryport to Main Street in Old Lyme, were earned in the neutral trade.

Four years after the Revolution began in Paris, Great Britain declared war on France. Americans grew nearly as heated as Europeans debating where justice lay in the conflict, but as war engulfed the continent, most merchants were willing to lay political questions aside in the quest for profit.

British sea power severed France from her colonies and their supplies of sugar, coffee, cocoa, and pepper. Ships of neutral nations carrying these commodities from French colonies to the mother country were liable to seizure by

Getting Sandalwood from Dula, Timor. Painting by Lucy Hiller Cleveland, c. 1830. Sandalwood, shown being loaded at Dula, Timor, in this painting by the captain's wife, was one of numerous commodities pursued on remote coasts by enterprising Yankee traders.
Courtesy Peabody Essex Museum, Salem, Mass. (M 1346).

Britain. An American captain, however, could sail from the sugar islands to Derby Wharf in Salem, unload his cargo, pay duty on it, reload the cargo, receive a refund or "drawback" of the duty paid, and begin a fresh and perfectly legal voyage to France in the same vessel carrying the same cargo. Under this system, American reexports of foreign goods averaged $35,600,000 annually between 1796 and 1805. In 1805 a British admiralty court sitting under Sir William Scott declared the system illegal. After that, merchants had to go to the trouble of breaking a cargo up and reshipping it in different vessels, or even, just to be sure, of landing a cargo of indigo or coffee at Newburyport and

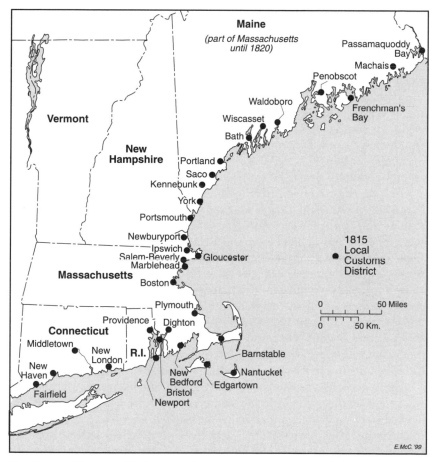

New England Customs Districts, 1815. Boston owned only 137,000 of the 581,700 tons of shipping registered in New England. No other port claimed more than 35,500 tons (Salem) of a fleet whose ownership was spread along the coast from Fairfield to Passamaquoddy.

Eliza McClennan, Mapworks.

transferring the goods to Portsmouth or Salem before shipping them to Bordeaux. In 1792, just before the war started, the United States reexported just over a million pounds of West Indian sugar. In 1807 American merchants carried home and reexported cargo worth £143 million."[14]

The Revolutionary and Napoleonic wars continued for twenty years; every year the war continued, adroit Americans made money. A series of poor harvests combined with the war's drain of farming manpower to produce grain shortages and high prices in France, and therefore to produce a demand that was filled with American wheat. With British seamen tied up blockading France, American ships also carried the trade of Britain's colonies. Other American captains moved into the Mediterranean trade long dominated by Britain. Still more ships carried tropical goods to Germany to obtain specie for use in the Russia trade. Russian goods—hemp for rope, linen for canvas sails, and iron for cannon and ship's fittings, were the sinews of international commerce and naval strength.

Commerce with Russia, like commerce with China, required payment in specie. China insisted on gold because it was too rich and its civilization too highly developed to need anything the West could offer (although in the 1790s a representative of the Perkins family of Boston was established in Smyrna buying opium for the China trade). Russia required specie because it was too poor to buy anything. Sugar, coffee, rice, pepper—the tropical goods Europe craved—were worth nothing on the wharf at Kronstadt (the port of St. Petersburg), because Russian peasants were too poor to consume them. The Russian nobility sipped sugar-sweetened chocolate in imported porcelain cups, but there were too few nobles to conjure a trade route into existence. American ships went to France, Spain, Germany, and England to sell and to trade; they went to Russia only to buy hemp, linen, and iron.

Iron had to be obtained in Russia or Sweden because only those countries possessed ore pure enough to work into iron fittings that would bear weight under pressure. Russian and Swedish ore were so valuable that they could be shipped as far as Canton at a profit. Hemp and linen were not unique Russian productions; they grow anywhere with a temperate climate. The reason they had to be obtained in Russia was that Russia was desperately poor.

A great deal of hemp was grown in Kentucky. After harvest, Kentucky hemp was spread on the ground where over a period of several weeks dew and rain leached away the viscous gum covering the valuable fiber. The process resulted in a weakened fiber that could not be effectively impregnated with tar. Rope not saturated with tar for waterproofing is useless as ship's rigging. Kentucky hemp was good for baling cotton, and that is what it was used for.

In 1791, amid economic depression and enthusiasm for the promotion of American goods, canvas manufactories were started in several New England seaports, including one in Boston that actually produced finished canvas. By

Crowninshield's Wharf, Salem, 1806. Painting by George Ropes, Jr. Salem was never a large city, but at the peak of the neutral trade during the Napoleonic Wars, it was a major international port that fairly hummed with activity. This painting of Crowninshield (India) wharf crowded with shipping in 1806 gives some idea of the source of the Federal-era shipping fortunes that built the cotton mills and railroads of the industrial era. Courtesy, Peabody Essex Museum, Salem, Mass.

1795, all had closed.[15] In the early 1820s, another period of postwar depression and enthusiastic promotion of domestic manufacturing schemes, the navy department was induced by Congressional prodding to try rope made from Kentucky hemp. The cables rotted.[16]

Russian peasants carefully dried their hemp on specially constructed racks. Once dry, it was immersed in clear streams or ponds of clear water to leach away the gum. Then it was dried again on racks, then dried through the winter in hemp kilns. The stalks were then broken in hand mills and peasants unraveled the fibers with wooden combs before storing the finished hemp carefully in dry sheds. The process took two years from planting to sale and was the primary profit center on many Russian estates.

The fact that water-retting hemp killed all the fish in the streams and ponds, as well as any livestock watering there, was probably only a secondary discouragement to Yankee farmers. Some high-quality hemp was produced in Connecticut by the same methods the Russians used. The problem was that the amount of labor involved was too great to make it pay.[17]

Connecticut also experimented with making high-quality flax. Flax, like hemp, could be retted either in open fields, which produced fiber of inferior quality, or by a painstaking process of careful immersion in clear water, which produced fiber that could be woven into first-quality canvas. Yankee labor was too expensive to make the production of sailcloth-quality flax pay. For hemp and linen good enough to rig a seaworthy ship, one had to sail to Russia. To pay for them, one had to carry a valuable cargo to Germany, the low countries, or Scandinavia, exchange it for specie or letters of credit, then sail again for Kronstadt where the coveted naval stores waited in warehouses and agents of the Russian aristocracy waited to convert the labor of their serfs into gold and luxury goods. Customers for Russian hemp, iron, and linen could be found in seaports the world over. The difficulty was in getting through the Baltic in wartime.

Early in the war, the British Navy seized American ships in an attempt to strangle France. John Jay was dispatched to settle the dispute, which he did in a treaty that went into effect in 1796, the terms of which put America and Great Britain on such intimate terms that France took offence and began itself to seize American ships. By June 1797, France had seized over 316 American vessels and we were on the verge of war. Roused to defend its commercial interests, America built a navy, and American shipping began to go around Europe in convoy—sometimes American naval convoy, more often under the protection of British naval convoys or in convoys made up of armed Yankee merchants. Britain was only too glad to convoy American ships carrying Russian naval stores to English ports. When Denmark came into the war on Napoleon's side, however, privateers poured out of harbors in Denmark and the Danish province of Norway to make the Sound nearly impassible for American shipping.[18] Throughout the French Revolution and the Napoleonic wars, American captains had to sail through continually shifting political winds that made legal cargo into contraband overnight, and American ships at sea suddenly and unpredictably liable to capture by the British or the French. Hundreds of American ships were seized by combatants, but the risk was eagerly taken by men who could make 300 and 400 percent profit on a single successful voyage.

The neutral trade ended not because the European war did—that continued off and on until Waterloo in 1815—but because of an ineffectual federal attempt to force Britain and France to respect American rights by imposing a unilateral commercial embargo. On orders from President Jefferson, millions of dollars worth of shipping lay rotting at the wharf, to no purpose New England could discern. And when the fruitless embargo finally ended, Congressmen from land-hungry western districts declared war on England with the goal of opening British and Indian frontier territory to American settlement.

The federal government destroyed a trade that had brought vast profits to farms and ports from Maine to Georgia, then declared war without an army, a fleet, or an arms industry. A war that we were not prepared to win, a war that ended in a kind of draw only because England was too busy fighting France to be bothered. Seaboard exasperation with Jefferson's embargo and Madison's war was so intense that a convention met at Hartford to consider seccession.

Yet on farms in the backcountry of New England, men and women sided with Henry Clay and his war hawks. Land was what they wanted. If war with England was the way to get land, then they were for war. Always and any way they could, they were for getting land.

Chapter 7

Cobbling a Living

❧

Of the advancement of our manufacturers we do not boast, for they only increase . . . where we have more than the average of our population.[1]

—Samuel Blodget, 1801

A MERE CENTURY AFTER THE GREAT MIGRATION, New England, with one of the highest rates of natural increase in recorded history, was careening toward overpopulation. Citizens of younger towns continued to carve new farms out of woodlots and hill pasture, but in old settled communities like Lynn on the Massachusetts coast, there was no more land to carve up.[2]

If only Lynn had a deep-water harbor, like neighboring Salem, the town could have built wharves, sent out ships, and brought home the wealth of the Indies. But there was no anchorage. There were only salt marshes, shelving beach, stony fields, and the road from Boston to Salem. Lynn sent what it could down that road—hay, salt pork, an occasional barrel of handmade shoes, even salt from evaporation pans built in a short-lived attempt to exploit the town's marshy oceanfront—but the export of agricultural surplus could not support a new generation unless there was land to farm, and there was none. It was not possible even to settle a frontier farm while the last of the French and Indian Wars continued, though many a young man without prospect of inheriting land went to that frontier as a soldier.

Two choices people living in overcrowded farm towns had were the same in 1750 as they had been thousands of years earlier, when New Englanders first encountered the problem of too many people and too little land: reduce the rate of population growth or reduce living standards.

Reducing the birth rate may have been the solution for some members of an earlier generation, which, unable to expand settlement in the face of French and Indian opposition between King Phillip's War in 1675 and the Peace of Utrecht in 1713, gave birth to smaller families in the years around 1700.[3] This choice was not made in 1750. Nor did society as a whole choose to reduce its standard of living by dividing farms into smaller and smaller plots until, like Ireland, each household would own only a garden large enough to yield a subsistence of potatoes. Most families kept the farm intact, or divided it into two or three farms each barely large enough to support a family, and made some other provision for giving the landless sons a start in life. The landless pieced marginal livings together from craft work and stints as hired help, tilled the odd field available for rent, and lived less well than their landowning parents and grandparents. There was, however, a third option, an option not available to our hunting-and-gathering forebears: eighteenth-century Yankees had the choice of trying to produce something that people elsewhere would want to buy. Lynn would depend on the sale of manufacturers to bring from distant ports not luxury and exotic goods, but the food on which life itself depended. As its population continued to grow, eastern Massachusetts, uniquely among the mainland colonies, could no longer feed itself. Trade, which once supplied prosperity, had become essential for survival.[4]

The advent of sailing craft capable of carrying staple foods dependably and economically over ocean trade routes made it possible for people in Massachusetts to live on Pennsylvania wheat. But landless youths did not need to know of the development of the stern rudder or the lateen sail. They had only to look around them, like young Ariel Bragg, eighteen years old, penniless and with no prospect of inheriting land. "To labor on a farm was more than he could think of."[5] And well it must have been. A farm worker in a time of labor surplus earns his keep and enough to clothe himself, with no prospect of getting ahead or ever earning enough to marry on. "In the meditation of his thoughts [young Ariel] remembered when at Samuel Griggs in Brookline, the year past, hearing Samuel Slack say that James Tolman had hired a man to work for him at shoemaking, and the man neglected to do so, which was the first intimation he ever had that one shoe maker employed another."

In the rural world of Bragg's experience, a shoemaker was a farmer who made shoes, or, increasingly, a landless sometime shoemaker, sometime field hand, struggling to cobble a living together by making and repairing neighborhood boots. Bragg—desperate, ambitious, and appalled by the prospect of life as a farm hand—walked to Brookline, persuaded Tolman to take him on, and learned to make shoes. Then, while doing the familiar, custom work of a country cobbler, he borrowed money to buy enough leather to make forty pairs of men's ordinary shoes. When the shoes were finished, Bragg borrowed a horse, rode to Providence with the shoes in a sack, sold them to a merchant lading a ship for the southern market, and walked home with a profit that enabled him to buy enough leather to produce an even larger number of shoes.[5]

Up and down the seaboard, men and women turned time into products they could carry to the seaports. Local cow horn was carved into combs, native walnut and cherrywood were made into tables and chairs, tedious yards of thread lace were worked by hand, brass and pewter were poured into button molds and sent by the case to decorate jackets in the south and west.[6] But above all, New England made shoes.

It was not that Yankees preferred cobbling shoes to cutting combs or working lace. It was a case of trying everything and finding that shoes would sell. Especially the rough, cheap "brogans" and "slaps" New England farmers made by their winter firesides and shipped south by the barrel for sale in regions frosty enough to dictate that human chattel be provided with shoes in the cold months. If Lynn made more shoes than other towns, it had circumstances other towns lacked: proximity to the port of Salem; a surplus of landless youth; an even larger surplus of semi-indigent women living in nearby ports from which the men went to sea and to which they often never returned; and John Adams Dagyr, a Welsh cordwainer who set up shop on the Boston-Salem road in 1750.

Every town in New England had a cobbler or two. Large towns had full-time professional shoemakers, though few could turn out shoes as stylish and well made as those shipped from London. Dagyr knew how to make the finest grades of ladies' shoes, and he chose his location cannily. For raw material, he depended not merely on the thick, locally tanned leather with which he soled his shoes, but on fine, imported Moroccan kidskin, and on special grades of satin, linen, and woolen cloth manufactured in Europe. These fancy goods were brought to him by Salem and Boston vessels, which also brought ready-made ladies' dress shoes to the colonial market. The same vessels brought other kinds of European fancy goods, along with supplies for milliners, tailors, and other craftsmen, who, like Dagyr, produced custom goods for the local market. This was the usual course of trade. But, about the time Dagyr set up his shop, a new thing happened. Someone loaded a case of Lynn-made, ladies' dress slippers onto a ship and sent them to one of the southern colonies or sugar islands—where they sold.

We do not know what brought the Welsh cordwainer to Lynn, whether he looked the region over and selected Lynn, or was blown across the Atlantic and set down beside the Boston-Salem road entirely by chance. Perhaps Dagyr was induced to settle in Lynn by enterprising residents; by 1750, three Lynn shoemakers were making "sale" shoes in sufficient volume to employ journeymen. It was the merest seedling of an industry, but Dagyr may have been shrewd enough to see potential in what to others must have looked like a backwater. However the idea began, with that first crate of ladies' fancy shoes shipped to a southern port, Lynn found the way to earn a living.[7]

A few miles west of Bullough's Pond, just outside Natick Center, stands an unprepossessing wooden building that nobody visits despite the historic marker in the front yard. It is the workshop where Henry Wilson, "The Natick Cobbler," abolitionist, and eighteenth vice-president of the United States, learned to make shoes. It is a ten-footer, the kind of building memorialized in the Yankee habit of calling immense factories where shoes are produced "shops" (we Yankees puzzle outlanders further by calling vast, modern factories where textiles are produced, "mills"). For almost two centuries, shoemaking would be the leading industry in the most industrialized state in the union. It was an economic titan. But until the time of the Civil War, the actual shoes were made in one-story wooden buildings like Henry Wilson's forgotten shop. Some may have measured twelve feet by twelve feet, or ten by fourteen, instead of the traditional ten by ten, but their modesty of scale was undeniable.

Shoes by the tens of thousands poured from little shops where shoemakers labored without engines or mechanical power. Cutting was done by experts who did nothing but cut until they could carve a cured hide into correctly sized pieces with the least possible waste. Uppers were sent out to be bound at home by women who spent long hours perfecting the skill of stitching quickly and accurately. Finished uppers were made fast to soles with a speed and dexterity that comes only with practice. Nothing these shoemakers actually did was different in process than work performed by the country cobbler or "bespoke" cordwainer, every piece was cut by hand and stitched by hand-held needle and awl. But they wasted less leather, watched the London fashions more closely, eliminated the slack time expended by custom cobblers talking to customers and waiting for orders, and produced a good shoe at a low price. It was a proto-industrial manufactory particularly appealing in a hard-pressed farming economy because long after shoemakers in Lynn itself had become full-time craftsmen, capacity could be expanded by putting work out to farm families as far away as Maine and Vermont, where shoemaking was a welcome supplement to farm income.

The eighty thousand pair of shoes Lynn shipped in 1768 probably went as part of the mixed and speculative cargo of the era. Barrels of codfish supplemented by barrels of apples, butter, and salt pork, perhaps some fine cabinet work (a chest of drawers or set of dining chairs), and a barrel or two of shoes; on deck, there was a load of lumber, crates of fowl, and a few horses. If the price of horses was down at Savannah or Kingston, perhaps butter or dining chairs or shoes would fetch a good price at Charleston or St. John's. A captain clearing Salem harbor bound for the southern colonies never knew what would sell where; he expected to call at two or three ports before disposing of his entire cargo. Mixed lading was a hedge against uncertain markets; the system worked until the Revolutionary War cut off the West Indies market. Fortunately, the same war stopped English imports to the mainland colonies, opening an opportunity for Lynn to supply four hundred thousand pair of shoes annually by 1783. Fifty shops were operating in Lynn that year; all of them facing ruin when peace reopened American markets to a flood of English goods.

Lynn responded by dispatching commission agents to drum the countryside from Pennsylvania to Georgia, spreading sample shoes on the counter of every crossroads store. Lynn agents were willing to take untanned hides in exchange for shoes, or tobacco, or flour—whatever the countryside offered in trade. England wanted commercial paper in exchange for its shoes. Lynn was willing to barter, and willing to make exactly what the customer wanted. Sturdy boots for Pennsylvania farmers, fashionable slippers for Maryland belles, cheap brogans for enslaved Carolina field hands—Lynn supplied them all.

According to Emerson, if a man builds a better mousetrap the world will beat a path to his door. If Emerson had been in the shoe business, he would have known that it is rarely sufficient to build an improved mousetrap; the great thing is to sell it. The cordwainers of Lynn could be only as prosperous as those early commercial travelers were successful. The entire industry depended on men leaning over the wooden store counters of Georgia and Tennessee, persuading southern communities that it was in their interest to send produce north in exchange for Yankee shoes.

The success of Lynn's enterprising shoemakers was too great to be ignored; by the 1790s, cobblers in half a dozen eastern Massachusetts towns were manufacturing in bulk. Brockton had become the center of men's heavy boot- and shoemaking, while Lynn dominated ladies' and fancy goods.[8] Commission merchant houses in Boston assembled large batches of shoes for shipment to southern markets. Profits were good, though everyone knew they would be even better if the cost of manufacturing could somehow be reduced.

The first steps in the direction of cost reduction were taken early with the division of labor: replacing the skilled cobbler or cordwainer, who did everything from measuring the foot and making the last to polishing the finished shoe, with a shoeworker, who only cut, stitched, lasted, or bottomed the shoe before passing it to the next worker. Passing the shoe to the next worker often meant not passing it to the next workbench, but loading dozens of half-finished pairs for delivery to a farmhouse, where men spent the winter stitching shoes in a ten-footer. Only cutting and finishing were done in the central shop of the entrepreneur. Another key to cost reduction was the employment of thousands of women who sat at home tediously stitching pieces of leather to form "uppers," at wages far below those paid to male workers. More revolutionary was the invention, about 1810, of the pegged shoe.[9]

Shoemaking was and remains a process of many stages. Even if we skip over the processing of raw hides into leather, there remains the carving of a last in the shape and size of the foot to be shod, and the job of cutting thin leather for the upper and thick leather for the sole. Pieces of upper had to be stitched together, then stitched to the insole and to the welt, the narrow leather strip running around the insole. This welt was inserted into a slit or channel in the outsole, and sewn tight. Then the channel was sealed with glue to protect the stitching. Heels added several extra steps. And the possible flourishes, from straps to beadwork to insets of variety leathers, were limited by only imagination and taste.

About 1810, someone took an upper, inserted it between sole and insole, and united the three with a series of short, pointed, wooden pegs, inserting six or eight pegs to the inch. We can be certain of neither who he was nor where he came from, only that the obvious cost advantages made the process so popular that a Byfield mechanic soon found it worth his while to invent a mill to mass-produce wooden shoe pegs.[10]

Paul "Peg" Pillsbury was in many ways typical of the men who industrialized New England. Born one of seven sons on a Newburyport farm, he had two brothers who stayed in farming, one who became a blacksmith, one a mechanic, and two who entered the ministry. Paul settled in Byfield, where he farmed, worked as the mechanic in a small cotton mill, and invented first a corn sheller and then a bark mill for the tanning industry, before he turned his attention to shoe pegs. Oral tradition in Byfield held that Pillsbury observed the wooden pegs cobblers used to secure heels to shoes and conceived the idea of using similar, smaller pegs to replace the stitching uniting upper with sole.[11]

If "Peg" Pillsbury did not invent the pegged shoe, then someone very like him did, some Yankee with a gift for invention who lived in a shoe town in 1810. The genius of invention requires a very particular kind of inspiration: it is the knowledge that a product or process will be profitable that sets inventors to work. Cobblers had been working with wood and leather for thousands of years, but only after entrepreneurs had set up workshops to produce and ship shoes by the thousand were the potential profits from reducing labor in one step of the long process large enough to induce someone to invent the pegged shoe. And a mill to make the pegs. Pillsbury worked for three years to invent and adapt machinery, and set up a peg mill that by 1815 sent wholesale lots of shoe pegs to ten-footers all over eastern Massachusetts. It was one small step toward industrial revolution.

Surveying the evidence of two centuries ago, we are astonished that the great change should have surprised anyone, it seems so clear to us that economic conditions were so much dry tinder awaiting the igniting spark. In 1810, the year of the shoe peg, every town in southern new England was extensively engaged in manufacturing for distant markets.[12] Across the region, artisans plaited straw bonnets, felted fur and wool for hats, poured brass into molds to make buttons, filed cow horn into combs, and tempered wrought iron to shape augers. With so many hands performing repetitive tasks for so many hours, it seems obvious that someone would think of a way to do a job more quickly, more cheaply, or more easily. We must remember, though, that manufacturing districts where countless hands perform repetitive tasks for endless hours had existed nearly since the construction of the first, ancient civilizations. Lightning of the kind that ignites industrial revolutions did not strike until the 1700s, and when the thunderbolts fell, they fell not randomly but on England. And, a few years later, on southern New England, where the lightning flashes struck not in blazes of

Olympian glory, but in scarce-noticed flickers that illuminated the figure of a Yankee farmboy in a leather apron bending over a workbench.[13]

Pegged shoes replaced hours of sewing with a simple operation: drill a hole and hammer a peg. It took 298 hours to sole 100 pairs of men's medium-grade welt shoes by stitching; only 42 hours to peg the same number. True, pegged shoes with sole and insole rigidly fixed were somewhat less comfortable than shoes with the two soles sewn to a welt. But in 1845 a dozen pair of pegged boots were priced at $39 wholesale, compared with $25.50 for pegged boots of the same quality. Pegged boots and shoes soon dominated the market.[14]

More remarkable than pegged shoes was Thomas Blanchard's 1817 invention of a lathe capable of faithfully turning an irregular shape in wood. Until this point, lasts had been hand carved. In a custom shop, a last was carved to match the foot of an individual customer. Shops producing for the market used generic lasts of whatever size and shape the Yankee cobblers guessed would fit the feet of unseen customers in Virginia or Kentucky. Shopkeepers ordered shoes by the barrel and hoped that the dimensions of unshod local feet would roughly match the dimensions of recently arrived Massachusetts shoes. A customer might sift through several barrels of shoes without finding any that fit. Nor was there any way of insuring that the next shipment would have anything in the right size, standardized sizes being the very thing that had yet to be invented.

Blanchard's lathe opened a whole new world. The fact that it could turn a block of wood into a last in ninety seconds insured that by 1840 virtually all lasts were lathe-made. More important was the fact that the machine could turn out last after last of precisely the same size. Suddenly, it was practical for there to be such a thing as a size 7. A shopkeeper in Mississippi could order a dozen pair of size 7 boots and know that he would receive the size his customers needed. Modification of the Blanchard lathe soon made it possible to turn out identically sized, mirror image lasts—one for the right foot and one for the left. A public accustomed to shoes that fit the right or left foot equally well—and equally ill—responded to this latest Yankee innovation with real enthusiasm. Assured of a good fit, wholesale producers could move into the market for higher quality goods previously held by bespoke cobblers. Ladies and gentlemen of means continued to have fine footwear custom-made in eastern cities, but in new, western towns, retail establishments offering well-sewn, properly-sized Massachusetts boots and shoes served the carriage trade so effectively that custom shops were never established.

Burgeoning shoe production called a tanning industry into existence. Small, part-time tanneries had long been operated by farmers in every village. The dung and urine in which hides were "bated" came from the barn, and if the tannin-rich oak or hemlock bark required for tanning did not come from a farmer's own woodlot, he could at least employ his horses in idle seasons at turning the mill that ground tan bark to the requisite fineness. Progressive farmers used spent tan bark and liquors to manure fields. What they could not do was produce enough leather to supply an industry.

William Edwards is said to have been the first tanner to replace horse-powered mills with water power for grinding bark. His Northampton tannery shipped substantial quantities of leather to Boston in 1794. Fifteen years later, he was tanning 16,000 hides a year, soaking them in 672 vats filled with bark ground by three water-powered mills. He also replaced the immemorial and laborious process of tempering leather by hand pounding and beating with three water-powered rolling mills. Unable to buy sufficient hides in the Connecticut Valley, Edwards imported a third of his stock from South America.[15]

Voracious consumers of oak and hemlock bark, tanneries followed the forests to Maine, New York, and Pennsylvania, which all developed into major tanning centers in the early nineteenth century. Pennsylvania and New York specialized in the production of heavy, oak-tanned sole leather, and in the heavy leather belting without which the industrial revolution would have ground to a halt. The wooden cogs that had served so faithfully since Europe first harnessed water power could not withstand the speed of machinery in the new textile factories. Leather belts turned the wheels of rising industries.[16]

Oak bark was stripped from boles on their way to the mill; hemlock bark was just stripped. Hemlock lumber was worthless in a country blessed with vast stands of old-growth pine and spruce, but crews of bark strippers could make a living felling and stripping hemlock in the summer woods. Maine hemlock bark was carted to local tanneries or sent by coasting schooner to tanneries nearer Boston, which also imported Mediterranean sumac and South American quebracho bark. About 1880, commercially viable methods were developed for extracting tannin from bark, reducing bulk so far as to make the cost of shipping almost negligible. Tanners now located close to sources of hides, or close to the shoe industry to keep an eye on the changing demands of fashion, limited only by the need for a source of fresh water to wash the hides.

New York, nineteenth-century America's great port of entry, was its greatest tanning center, but eastern Massachusetts, the center of the shoe and boot industry, had a substantial tanning industry, especially the fashion-sensitive production of fine leathers for the uppers of expensive shoes, often made from imported sheep and goat skins.[17] It would be hard to name a river in eastern Massachusetts that did not host a fair-sized tanning industry in the nineteenth century, but it is easy to name the river that was the tanner's chief sewer: the Mystic, which meandered through seventeen miles of urban hills, ponds, and marshes before dumping some of the dirtiest water in the country into Boston harbor.[18]

Power machinery for the mechanical processes of grinding bark and pounding leather spread through the industry in the early 1800s, followed by a machine for splitting hides into two sheets of leather. This was a real profit center because no leather worker could split a sheet of leather with a hand-held knife. The hand process of making leather thin and even enough for the uppers of fine shoes was called shaving and involved removing—wasting—layers of leather until the desired thinness was achieved. Splitting machines doubled the supply of leather at very little cost. Steam power replaced water mills powering the grinding, pounding, and splitting machines in the 1850s (spent tan bark provided cheap fuel for steam engines), but none of these mechanical innovations altered the nature of leather making.

Hides were still soaked for months in vats of lime and water to loosen hair, which had to be scraped off with hand tools. Then the hides were soaked or "bated" in vats of urine or dung. After washing, they were tanned by soaking in ground bark and water. The tanned leather was oiled if it was to be used for harness, soles, or industrial belting; it was stretched and beaten, then kneaded with tallow if it was intended for uppers. The only nineteenth-century changes in this ancient craft were the addition of sulfuric acid to the lime bath—it speeded up the process and produced a stiffer, heavier piece of leather—and the introduction of aniline dyes derived from coal tars, forerunners of a host of petrochemical products that would soon alter the future of life on earth.

Further innovations, like innovations in most other chemical-processing industries, awaited the attention of German industrial chemists goaded by a desire to replace expensive and potentially unreliable imports of raw materials. Not until the early 1890s were commercially viable methods found to replace bark-derived tannin with a chromium-based solution.[19] The next major innovation came in 1913, when the active element in the bating process was discovered to be a pancreatic enzyme, and German chemists successfully replaced urine with enzyme extracts.[20] The fact that leather emerged from chromium tanning vats in unattractive shades of blue was a minor disadvantage compared with the fact that it emerged in hours instead of weeks. Color could be corrected. The complex, organo-metallic composition of dyestuffs was of no concern to tanners, who asked only that dyes be priced right and turn out a good-looking piece of finished leather.

Even before chromium baths and organo-metallic dyestuffs, the outflow of a tannery was foul. In 1885, the Winslow brothers of Norwood, Massachusetts, turned one million sheepskins into leather at their tannery on Hawes Brook, which flows into the Neponset River and Boston harbor. Sulfuric acid, lime, salt, aniline dyes, and a suspended and dissolved soup of tannin, excrement, vegetable-based dye, oil, grease, and bits of sheep tissue spewed from the plant, causing workers at the George Morrill printing ink factory, downstream, to complain of the "fearful stench" rising from waters fouled by tannery waste.[21]

Nothing lived in those waters. The volume of salt washed from preserved skins would alone have killed many freshwater organisms. Most that survived would have been stressed beyond endurance by fluctuating pH levels as lime alternated with tannic acid in the waste pouring from tanning vats. Oil and grease can suffocate fish by gumming up their gills even in water that is otherwise clean, just as it can kill bottom-dwelling organisms when it settles into the sediments. Great quantities of grease were washed from skins in the tanning process. Tiny pieces of tan bark, animal hair, and other organic matter kill simply by floating in the water, if they are present in sufficient volume to screen out the light needed for photosynthesis—and they were. But tannery waste was a ruthless killer mostly because it was biodegradable.

Organic waste, whether it leaves a tannery as suspended particles or in dissolved form as nitrogen or ammonia, demands oxygen to decompose. Bodies of water are not only able to decompose waste products, they actually thrive on a certain amount of decaying organic matter: it is the stuff that feeds the bacteria and plants at the bottom of the food chain. The volume of organic waste pouring from an industrial tannery was much too much of a good thing. The stench the ink plant workers complained of was the smell of hydrogen sulfide and methane, the aroma of tan bark and leather offal biodegrading, a process that rapidly used up all the available oxygen in Hawes Brook, killing anything that lived there, and produced a water column choked with organic matter racing

The leather Belting Manufactory of H. L. Fairbrother, Pawtucket, Rhode Island, c. 1880. It was situated on the Blackstone River, from which it drew water for tanning and into which it discharged waste. Courtesy The Rhode Island Historical Society. Rhi(x3)1819.

downstream to find new oxygen supplies to deplete, new reaches of water to render lifeless.

It would be grossly unfair to blame the Winslow brothers' tannery for choking aquatic life in Hawes Brook. The muddy yellow brook water was already so dirty when it reached the tannery that the Winslow brothers themselves complained of being unable to manufacture white leather. This was the fault of Isaac Ellis, owner of a mill producing Manila wrapping paper from old bagging, used rope, and scrap paper in a mill upstream from the Winslows. Ellis's effluent yellowed the brook water with ferrous sulfate, quantities of lime, and suspended bits of fiber. Only mills at the head of streams of clear water could produce white paper, white leather, or white cloth.

Across the decades of the nineteenth century, rivers died as the effluent of tanneries, paper mills, cotton mills, and other industries poured waste into the streams. An earlier New England, a New England of farmers who depended on spring fish runs for food, would have acted to save the rivers, but by the nineteenth century, New England was much richer than that. Food could be bought for money. And the shoe industry made money, enough money that the town of Lynn, where two thousand residents had scratched a living from the land in 1760, could support nineteen thousand a century later. Nearby Salem, which had twelve thousand inhabitants at the height of its Federal era maritime prosperity, had twenty-two thousand in 1860. They earned their living manufacturing furniture, candles, rope, metalware, chemicals, liquors, and—the town's largest industry by far—shoes.

The Yankee knack for making and selling shoes allowed the growth of population far beyond the numbers the land could support, generating wealth that enabled New England to purchase food and industrial feedstocks from less industrialized parts of the world. Tan bark and hides came from faraway places, but so did the flour for the shoeworker's bread, the beef he ate, the coal that warmed his house, and the wool or cotton from which his clothing was made. If the growing demand for cattle, cotton, wheat, timber, and coal meant that fields were overgrazed, topsoil exposed to erosion, hills torn open to yield coal, and forests stripped to make shoes and profits, these things happened in distant places. Massachusetts remained a green and pleasant land. Industrialization enables successful entrepreneurs to live in warm, comfortable homes in nice neighborhoods while somewhere else forests are clear-cut and hillsides gouged out for coal.

Chapter 8

Why Lightning Strikes

❧

What distinguished the British economy was an exceptional sensitivity and re-
sponsiveness to pecuinary opportunity. This was a people fascinated by
wealth and commerce, collectively and individually.[1]

—David Landes

T HE PRODUCTION OF SHOES BY THE HUNDREDS
of thousands in Yankee factories was curious from the start. In 1849,
shoe towns in eastern Massachusetts, New Hampshire, and Maine produced over half of the nation's shoes, despite the fact that the region was devoid of any resource to qualify it as shoe capital of the world. Hides came
from the Midwest, the Mediterranean, and Latin America. Local supplies of
hemlock and oak bark were supplemented by sumac, quebracho, mangrove,
eucalyptus, and other imported barks, chosen for price and availability as
well as for the properties and color they imparted to the finished leather. By
the 1860s, even the shoemakers were coming from Ireland. But by that date,
machinery had been invented that did give Massachusetts shoemakers a technological edge over the rest of the world. The interesting question is how
Massachusetts gained its huge market share before it developed a technical
advantage.

New Englanders of the 1830s routinely sailed around Cape Horn, purchased
raw cattle hides from Mexican ranchers, salted and dried them in the California
sun, sailed back around the horn, and delivered the hides to Salem tanneries
and Lynn shoemakers—who tanned the leather and stitched the shoes using
technology familiar to Spaniards since Roman times. Sailors then loaded cases
of shoes into wooden ships and sailed around the Horn again to sell Lynn boots
and shoes to those same Mexican ranchers. Richard Henry Dana, who immor-
talized the California hide drogher in his great sea story, *Two Years Before the
Mast*, scorned California prodigality.

The Spaniards are an idle, thriftless people and can make nothing for themselves . . . Their hides, which they value at two dollars in money, they barter for
something which costs seventy-five cents in Boston, and buy shoes (as like as not
made of their own hides, which have been carried twice around Cape Horn) at
three and four dollars.

Mexican California in 1834 was very different from Cambridge, Massachusetts, where Dana grew up, and where, in the course of a short walk, he could
pass a busy shipyard; observe water-powered mills weaving cloth, sawing wood,
and making paper; or see leather tanned while soap, candles, fertilizer, and glue
were made from tannery waste. He could even, if it was cold enough, watch
men saw the frozen surface of Fresh Pond into blocks of ice. Come summer,
they packed the ice in ships, insulated it with sawdust, and sold it to slake tropical thirst as far away as Calcutta.[2]

Perhaps no enterprise embodies the commercial spirit that possessed New
England so perfectly as the business of carving up pieces of winter to sell on the
wharves of Havana and New Orleans. It was not a simple business, not so obvious then as it may seem in retrospect. The insulating properties of sawdust
were hit upon only after trial-and-error experimentation with straw, sheep
skins, and other materials. Early shipments of irregularly shaped chunks of ice
melted unevenly and shifted in the hold, threatening the delicate balance of
sailing vessels and necessitating the invention of equipment capable of cutting
the surface of a frozen pond into square blocks. Worse than any technical problem was the fact that the first ice ships reaching southern ports carried a cargo
that no one wanted to buy.

Ice has a long history of luxury use in parts of the world where hot summers
alternate with cold winters, or where wealthy cities nestle against snow-capped
mountains. But ice was not regularly available in the tropics before a young
Bostonian named Frederick Tudor carried a shipload to Martinique in 1806.
The island had no icehouse and no customers interested in buying ice. In six
weeks, Tudor's entire investment was liquid.

Giving up does not seem to have been among the options Tudor entertained.
His father had lost his fortune in a real estate speculation, leaving the family with
few resources aside from Frederick's ambition and a Saugus country house with
a pond. That pond Tudor proposed to slice, ship to the West Indies, and sell, in a
determined effort to make his fortune. He had to make a fortune. In his own
view, the view of a young gentleman reduced at the age of twenty-six from
wealth to pennilessness, "a man without money is like a body without a soul—a
walking dead man."[3] Tudor succeeded—after two difficult decades, during
which he was frequently bankrupt, several times had to leave town by night to
evade a sheriff, and more than once served time in debtor's prison. There was always one more wrinkle to work out before a fortune could be built on ice.

Harvesting ice on the Kennebec River, Maine, in the late 1880s. Before the invention of a commercially viable freezing process, ice harvesting was a major industry. Ships carried Yankee ice to southern cities and as far as Bombay. The Independent Ice Company was a Washington, D. C., firm whose icehouses, visible in the background, could hold 70,000 tons of ice. Transportation was extrememly convenient—ice schooners came upriver directly to the icehouse docks after the spring thaw. Forty-nine icehouses of comparable size lined the Kennebec alone. Collections of the Maine Historical Society.

Kitchen iceboxes had to be made, insulated with sheepskin, and sold to potential ice consumers in southern ports. Tropical customers who had never seen ice had to be taught how to preserve it in the specially constructed boxes, and how to use it to preserve food. Plans for the building of efficient icehouses had to be contrived, and the icehouses themselves built, shipped, and assembled on southern wharves. Supplies of ice had to be secured in the North, even in winters when ponds near Boston failed to freeze. Competitors had to be kept from cashing in on the demand Tudor created in tropical ports; in such situations, Tudor sold ice below cost until the competitor was driven out of business. Above all, a market had to be created, even if it meant giving away shiploads of ice to create demand among skeptical, tropical populations. At the peak of the trade in the 1870s, cargoes of New England ice worth hundreds of thousands of dollars went annually to cities from Charleston to Calcutta, cities that had never known they wanted ice until Frederick Tudor sold it to them, and ice was cut in winter on every pond and river in the region—even our little pond.

For a brief period in the late 1800s, Bullough's Pond was renamed Silver Lake by a savvy local ice dealer who understood that attractive names sell goods. Half the ponds in New England were similarly renamed. Some got their names back after ice-making machines replaced pond and river ice at the turn of the century, but New England is still dotted with Crystal and Silver lakes, namesakes of an enterprising age.

What made men on one edge of a continent think of cutting and carrying ice to the four corners of the world, while on the other edge of the same continent, men were unwilling to scrape, salt, and dry their own cattle hides to fetch a better price? How was it that Salem could import Mediterranean sumac and Portuguese sheepskins to make shoes that sold in Savannah at a profit? Why, in short, was there an industrial revolution in Massachusetts before there had been one in Monterey, Tokyo, or Berlin? That these places have industrialized in our wake does not diminish the fact that the rural countryside of an insignificant province, remote, and unendowed with wealth or resources, industrialized before any nation on earth—save only England.[4]

In part, the answer is that many men thought like Frederick Tudor. Few had Tudor's luck in being born to wealth, but a great many children of respectable farmers found their prospects stunted by land shortage or population surplus. In an agrarian society, these are but two ways of describing the same problem, a problem that left young adults without prospect of enjoying the level of economic success their parents knew. Few men in any generation are willing to undertake the levels of risk and effort necessary to raise themselves to a station above that into which they were born. But threaten men and women with the prospect of falling in status, and they will make heroic efforts to save themselves from degradation.[5] Tens of thousands of New Englanders had to do something drastic, or cease to be numbered among the respectable middle class. Their response was to create new industries. Some were industries that could have been created only on foundations of recently developed technology. Others, like producing shoes for export, ice cutting, and most of the mechanical innovations in textile production, could have been attempted any time from the Middle Ages on. Why the eighteenth century? For that matter, why had so many entirely new kinds of technology chosen the eighteenth century to make great leaps forward?

Overpopulation is an old problem in the world; the traditional solutions are old, too: penury, population control, migration, and conquest. Penury has nowhere been the option of choice. Conquest of Indian lands and westward migration would come after American independence made them possible. Population control is a more interesting question. It may be that rationally planning family size according to economic opportunity is a good indicator of cultural readiness to launch an industrial revolution; family planning, that is, reveals a proclivity for rational approaches to problems.[6] Japan, which industrialized overnight by an act of will, is remarkable for having self-consciously held population and living

Cutting ice on Bullough's Pond. The ice shown being harvested on Bullough's Pond in the 1870s was stored in an icehouse on the bank for summer delivery to Newton households. Courtesy of The Jackson Homestead, Newton, Massachusetts.

standards at a constant level in the early modern period. England responded to economic limitations by keeping its birthrate low long before it industrialized. Upon crossing the Atlantic, seventeenth-century New Englanders responded rationally to the change in economic prospects by lowering the average marriage age and increasing the number of births per marriage. Individuals in these nations acted to improve their economic status and the prospects of their descendants in many ways; family planning was one of those ways. But birth control was not the primary solution to the resource crisis of the eighteenth century in Britain or America. Industrial revolution was.

That old and New England came up with a genuinely new answer indicates that there was indeed something new under the sun, something in the air of the 1750s that was yet unheard of when the Iroquois tribes began their brutal wars of expansion and English Puritans responded to an overcrowded homeland by setting forth on their migrations to new lands. In the century between the Puritan migration and the Lynn shoemaker, Englishmen noticed that the sun had ceased to revolve around the earth.

For many centuries it had been growing increasingly difficult for astronomers to make the sun, planets, and stars continue in their prescribed rotations.

The paths they took were convoluted, requiring intricate calculations to predict where a given star would be on a certain date, calculations that had to be made because the position of the earth at the center of the system of sun and stars was not to be doubted. Then, in 1543, a Polish astronomer published an accurate and mathematically parsimonious method of making astronomical calculations. The first difficulty was that Nicolaus Copernicus's method assumed that the earth revolved around the sun. The second was that according to every observable fact, Copernicus was correct.

This kind of thinking, a searching for truth logically derived from observed facts, would soon open everything to question: the existence of God, the divine right of kings, even the economic lot of the farmer in his village. Until the Enlightenment, men had been as wholly embedded in the village, the tribe, or the social group as a single blade of salt grass is embedded in its marsh. The forces that buffeted the social units in which men lived were as far beyond their comprehension as a northeast wind is beyond the understanding of a blade of grass. Certainly, such forces were beyond human control. The end of this immemorial view of self is associated with the Protestant Reformation and, more to the point, with the long struggle to secure the property rights of Englishmen, not as members of estates, but as individuals.

Before this new attitude could bring about an industrial revolution, society had first to acknowledge that if every empirical fact indicates that the earth revolves around the sun, then the earth revolves around the sun. It is a question of fact, and the pope could no more influence a question of fact than King Canute could command the tide to stop. Before we dismiss King Canute out of hand, however, we should remember that the pope succeeded for many centuries in making the sun revolve around the earth. That as many Americans today believe in astrology as in evolution. And that wealthy Chinese men continue to pay fancy prices for rhinoceros horn and sea cucumbers in the belief that consuming phallus-shaped foods will impart virility. The industrial revolution was not fomented by men who thought they could achieve virility by eating rhinoceros horn. It certainly did not begin among people living in a world in which every mountain and every tree was inhabited by a living spirit. It began among people who drew a firm line between magic and reality. European society had its mystics, and vestiges of animism lingered, but the boundary between the spiritual and the material was more sharply drawn in northwestern Europe than anywhere else in the seventeenth-century world. The apple tree Newton sat under was inanimate, and when he described the pull of gravity on the apple, he assumed that any observer sitting under any tree could observe the pull of gravity on any apple. The phenomenon did not depend upon the spirit of that particular tree. Nature, before it could be manipulated with impunity, had to become inanimate. It had to respond in predictable ways to definable laws.[7]

The same austerely rational approach to reality that produced modern science was imposed by our Calvinist forbearers on all experience. Wealth, if one possessed it, ought to be put to work producing more wealth. It was not thought out of order for an Oriental potentate simply to own gold. But hoarders of gold, are, in European terms, irrational. A rational owner invests. Experience, travel, acquaintance ought, like gold, to be turned to account. Each experience, every voyage, all new acquaintances are opportunities from which useful things can be learned. Opportunities are squandered if they result not in the increase of useful knowledge, but in mere pleasure. Time, a resource that aristocratic and primitive societies both regard as a good in its own right, becomes a raw material. The supreme raw material. Time is given by God to man. It is our responsibility to turn it to account, to see that it is used profitably on weekdays and dedicated to the glory of God on His Sabbath.[8]

The fixed cosmology of monarch, noble, and peasant began to change even before Copernicus rearranged the solar system, a crucial change, because the near universality of premodern property arrangements is one of the more astonishing instances of human consistency. In Polynesia, in Japan, in India, Persia, Mexico, and England, wherever states existed, the peasant held his land of the noble who held it of the king who might at any time levy a tribute of goods or labor. What Western Europe did was to sever the king from the land and settle it on the farmer in fee simple, which allowed land to become part of a rationally organized production process, like leather, wood, iron . . . or a workman's time.[9]

Methods of filling the royal treasury were as internationally consistent as systems of land tenure. The most popular method was to conquer some weak but wealthy nation, as when the royal treasure of ancient Spain was transferred to Rome, or when, centuries later, the royal treasuries of Mexico and Peru were transferred to Madrid. Failing that, kings controlled disfavored social groups or overly ambitious nobles with fines and confiscation. Occasional levies raised general revenue as needed. Both methods encouraged hoarding of riches and concealment of wealth, in addition to making planning impossible and many types of investment unattractive. It was unwise to put gold to work by building mills or wharves when there was no way of knowing when taxes would next be levied or in what amount. And who would start an enterprise knowing that, if it succeeded, the king might simply expropriate it?

It is difficult to imagine an industrial revolution starting in a place where the sultan, learning that a subject had invented a spinning machine and built a profitable cotton mill, was free simply to take it. Under such conditions, the most rational use of gold often was simply to hoard it.[10]

When the barons of England confronted King John at Runnymede in 1215, the key right they demanded and won was the security of private property from arbitrary confiscation. It was the first step in a long, arduous, and complex struggle to secure property rights in law, and although our revolution was part of this process, the important battles were fought and won in England. Americans were beneficiaries and heirs of a legal system that could support an industrial revolution, including mechanisms for taking private property for public economic advantage.

Market orientation, a tendency among farmers to plant not simply to satisfy local needs or to pay taxes, but with an eye on prices in distant markets, is discernable among Yankee farmers at least as early as the 1750s.[11] In that same period, Lynn cobblers moved from producing for a local market to seeking and creating demand for their output in distant markets. Success in those markets enabled the increase in volume that made specialization and division of labor possible. Division of labor produced economies of scale that resulted in economic growth as each worker produced more shoes. Increased volume also supplied the incentive for the invention of machinery and techniques that generated further economic growth. But Massachusetts boot and shoe manufacturing became a highly sophisticated, international business producing fifty million dollars worth of goods annually before power machinery was introduced.[12]

Economic growth generated by large-scale, putting-out systems of handicraft production was not a new story in the world. Medieval Flanders grew wealthy by large-scale putting-out cloth production. It was the explosion of new machines and techniques generated by the cloth industry, the metal and woodworking trades, and, albeit to much smaller extent, the New England shoe manufactory, that was new.[13] That explosion of invention, the Industrial Revolution, took place in an economy that had already experienced a commercial revolution. Which is to say that "Peg" Pillsbury invented his shoe pegging machinery in a world where farmers and craftsmen produced not for individuals with whom they had ongoing and complex relationships, but for sale in an anonymous marketplace.

New England was speeded along the path of transition to a market economy and industrial revolution by the Puritan insistence on schooling, which meant that the general population was literate and had enough arithmetic for proficiency in double-entry bookkeeping. Also, successful agricultural and maritime enterprise, particularly the profits of the neutral trade, had left a small store of capital at the disposal of many families at a time when traditional paths ceased to offer opportunity; that capital was put into workshops, mills, and agricultural improvement. And it is significant that New England had no staple crop profitable enough to make the importation of slave labor on a large scale pay. The drudgery of grinding tan bark, stitching shoes, pulping rags to make paper, carding wool, and pounding iron into shape was performed by free men, each of whom had an incentive to invent a labor-saving way to hatchel flax or shell corn. English law had long secured rights in property that allowed a man to enjoy the profits of his enterprise; American law soon moved to secure patent rights for inventors.

Not only were abundant natural resources unnecessary to start industrial revolution, they would have been a positive hindrance. China and Turkey, not to mention Barbados and South Carolina, were far too rich to give young men from respectable families an incentive to dirty their hands with cams and gears. Resource paucity is an important goad to industrial initiative; an enterprising people can actually create their own natural resources.[14] The goad to industrialization in England was not abundance of coal; it was lack of wood. France, the wealthiest and most scientifically advanced nation of the eighteenth century, was well endowed with forests, and smelted iron with charcoal. Everyone smelted iron with charcoal. It was only when England ran out of forests that Abraham Darby came up with a method of using coke to smelt iron. And it was only because the shortage of cordwood was forcing England to heat with coal that Thomas Newcomen was induced to invent the steam engine as a way to get more coal out of the ground. Coal is a commonplace stuff. It was the industrial genius of the English people that turned it into the feedstock of a revolution. England did not industrialize because it had coal; England had coal because it industrialized. That resource paucity pushed New England to industrialize is painfully obvious.

It was also important that New England was self-governing. Independent governments were able to respond to the needs of developing industry by allowing private land to be flooded for water storage behind mill dams, or taken for use by turnpike and railroad companies. Self-government was, of course, not coincidental. The same men who took up arms to defend their right to life, liberty, and property went on to start an industrial revolution, then reshaped the common law to allow the new revolution to proceed. Often, the very same men. Major Loammi Baldwin mustered the Woburn militia when the Middlesex Alarm reached that town two hours after midnight on the nineteenth of April in 1775, and marched them fast enough to play an important role in decimating the British army as it retreated from the Battle of Lexington and Concord. After the war, the major developed the Baldwin, an important variety of market apple, then taught himself engineering and designed the Middlesex Canal. Paul Revere made handcrafted silver tableware before the war; after the war he established the first American foundry capable of casting bells, and the first American rolling mill to produce sheet copper. It is fitting that Revere copper covered the dome of the new Massachusetts State House and sheathed the hull of "Old Ironsides," the USS *Constitution*.

Self-government came to a well-educated people at a moment when population growth threatened impoverishment, but had not yet caused a generation to grow up in debilitating poverty. Juncture was crucial, because while people faced with poverty may be spurred to innovative enterprise, people who have been long impoverished will lack the physical and mental capacity for such ex- ertion. New England faced the prospect of economic decline, but standards of nutrition, health, and education were high enough to enable men to search for new ways to earn a living. Shoes were only the most successful of many prein- dustrial approaches New England tried in an attempt to find something the world would buy, a problem not really solved until Yankees began to invent new kinds of machines.

Chapter 9

Peddling the Future

I have seen [Yankee peddlers] on the peninsula of Cape Cod, and in the neighborhood of Lake Erie, distant from each other more than six hundred miles. They make their way to Detroit, four hundred miles farther, to Canada, to Kentucky, and, if I mistake not, to New Orleans and St. Louis.[1]

—Timothy Dwight, 1821

IF LYNN, MASSACHUSETTS, WAS A PROVINCIAL backwater when it sent the first commercial travelers out to drum up shoe sales, Berlin, Connecticut, was the veriest boondocks. Salem harbor was, after all, within a morning's walk of even the most remote farm in Lynn; when the land ran out, Lynn loaded shoes onto ships and sent them to distant ports. Lynn might be a backwater, but it was a backwater at the edge of the Atlantic economy. When Berlin ran out of land, its sons loaded tin pans in saddlebags and plodded over the Litchfield hills.

Tin pans were a new thing in the world. The technique of coating a thin sheet of iron with a layer of rust-proof tin was invented in Germany in the sixteenth century, but only introduced to England around 1720. About thirty years later, a Scotch-Irish immigrant named Edward Pattison settled in Berlin, Connecticut, and began to make kitchenware from imported British tin-plate. Inexpensive, lightweight, rust-proof, and easy to clean, tinware found a ready market and, after a pause when importing sheet tin-plate stopped during the Revolutionary War, business boomed.[2]

Customers came to tinsmiths to order coffeepots and candle molds, just as they ordered boots from the cobbler and spoons from the silversmith, but most Berlin tinware was sold in ways new to New England workshop production. Unlike silver and iron, tin was not worked by an established network of local smiths. And tin did not compete with imported English goods; it was not profitable to ship such a high-bulk, low-value item as a tin coffeepot across the Atlantic. So Britain shipped sheet tin, Berlin men learned to fashion it into useful objects, and peddlers strapped a pair of baskets to a horse and jogged over bad roads selling canisters and saucepans, funnels and graters. Berlin became a peddling center not because the town had more underemployed men than other overpopulated farming villages, but because the Pattison's tinsmithy gave Berlin peddlers a profitable line of goods. Fairhaven, Connecticut, the eastern neighborhood of modern New Haven, had one too.

Oysters thrive on a clean, hard bottom where a regular flow of fresh water mixes with the ocean. The Quinnipiac River had disappointed New Haven's first settlers by failing to drain a vast territory of beaver ponds; its waters recompensed their great, great-grandchildren by producing oysters. Farm wagons streamed out of New Haven in early winter, heading north. Behind each driver sat barrels of oysters packed in brine, bound for the dinner tables of northern New York, Vermont, and Quebec. Far from tidewater, Fairhaven peddlers traded oysters for butter, cheese, brooms, salt pork, and homespun cloth, which found a strong enough market in the small seaport to make the long, cold, jolting drive on the wooden plank seat of a farm wagon pay.[3]

New England roads were local affairs maintained by citizens obliged to spend a few reluctant hours every year filling mudholes with desultory shovelsful of gravel. Shoveling gravel was no man's favorite occupation, but it beat paying taxes. Town meeting could have insisted on better roads, but it was hard to get a majority vote for higher taxes or more hours of conscript road work. Even if the citizens of Berlin had built a good road, they would still have had to travel on bad roads through Newington and Wethersfield to reach the Hartford market, while farmers from Meriden would have had the advantages of traveling through Berlin on the new road, gratis. For want of good roads, as much heavy hauling as possible was done in the winter months, when farmers had time on their hands and snow made bad roads into decent sled tracks. Snow is free.

Very few commodities will bear the cost of freighting over bad, indirect roads by oxcart, yet with remarkable enterprise Yankee farmers, under pressure to generate more income from less land, found crops that would. Milk, for example, was turned into butter and cheese, fruit was made into brandy, potatoes and rye into whiskey, all of which could bear the freight to a seaport. Farmers, lured by the desire to purchase goods in the cash economy and pressed by the need for cash to establish children in the world, were unrelenting in the search for cash crops.

Levi Dickinson, a Hadley, Massachusetts, farmer, began to plant broom corn from English seed in 1797. Within a decade, the farm fields of Hampshire and Franklin counties glowed with golden acres of maturing broom, and farmers spent the cold months binding the straw into flat brooms far superior to the bundles of birch twigs then in common use. Farmers in the Berkshire hills found that they could distill the essences of peppermint, spearmint, and wintergreen for profitable sale. Tewksbury and other towns in northern Middlesex County produced hops; cured over charcoal fires, it was

Road. Fred Quimby, c. 1890s. Country roads were winding, rutted, pitted and often muddy—even when the traveler did not have to deal with windfalls and washouts. This view of a southern Maine road in the 1890s gives some idea of the way things were.

Courtesy of the Society for the Preservation of New England Antiquities (neg.# 4347-B).

a crop that would profitably bear the cost of freight not only to Boston, but also to breweries in wood-poor Europe. Silk was grown in eastern Connecticut, and substantial amounts woven into cloth, although profits from raising silk were nothing compared to the profits that could be made selling mulberry trees. In a sort of horticultural Ponzi scheme, farmers bought mulberry whips at wildly inflated prices from farmers who had bought whips from a man on Long Island who had imported a superior strain of mulberry from China. Silk, the sales pitch went, sold for big money. Mulberry and silk worms could be raised in Connecticut. Everyone was going to be rich. The hitch appeared when it became clear that, even with the cost of freight from the other side of the globe factored in, New Englanders would not perform the delicate work of unwinding cocoons for rates that could compete with Chinese wages. Just as they would not undertake the painstaking process of preparing hemp for rope or flax for sailcloth at wages that could undercut the Russian peasantry. Soberer towns grew flax for household clothing production and flaxseed for export. Irish farmers, growing flax to produce fine linens, harvested when the fiber was at its peak—before the seed had a chance to mature—and found it profitable to import their seed from America. Flaxseed was also sold to a growing number of local mills, which pressed out linseed oil for the manufacture of paint. For the first time, America was growing wealthy enough to paint its houses.[4]

Profits depended on cheap transportation and, in the age of the oxcart, the only cheap transportation was by water, which made it profitable to sell Lynn-made shoes in Savannah, Georgia, but not in Worcester, Massachusetts. Worcester, like hill towns throughout New England, could hardly make a profit by farming or by manufacturing while transportation was so expensive. Everyone knew that good transportation would allow inland towns to make money from farm produce and manufactures; everyone wanted the cheap and easy access to imported goods that harbor towns enjoyed, nobody opposed improving the roads—they balked only at paying the taxes to build them. When a system was introduced that would provide the roads without the taxes, enthusiasm knew no bounds.

The Monhegan Turnpike opened in 1792, connecting Norwich, Connecticut, to New London. The new road straightened an old route, leveled the roadbed, provided better drainage with dug gutters, and smoothed the way so effectively that the twelve-mile journey, which had taken the better part of a day, could now be made in only two hours. Beyond mere speed, the new road was energy efficient. A team that had strained under a one-ton load, could, now that the road was more nearly level, move two tons easily. Best of all, the turnpike was built by proprietors who expected to recoup their investment by charging tolls—all without costing taxpayers a penny.[5]

A fever of turnpike building swept the countryside as investors hustled to get in on a good thing and boosters angled to have private companies route turnpikes through town. The new roads were far from perfect. Only a handful were macadamized. Most were simple, dirt tracks, a little straighter and a little smoother than the old roads, with fill shoveled on low spots and the tops of some hills cut down to level. At best, they were crowned—that is, built slightly higher in the middle with sloping sides shedding rainwater into dug gutters—and covered with a layer of gravel. Turnpikes were dusty and rutted in summer, muddy and rutted in spring, but they ran in lines straight to tidewater. Freight charges for a ton of goods hauled a mile by wagon over the old roads ran from thirty to seventy cents; when turnpikes opened they fell to between seven and twenty cents a mile. Suddenly, whole categories of goods that had hardly been worth producing could be profitably hauled to market.[6]

Far from quenching the demand for better transportation, turnpikes whet the appetite for something even better: canals. Nothing beat water for cheap freight rates. The South Hadley Canal opened a way around the falls of the Connecticut in 1794, making the river navigable almost to the Vermont—New

Blackstone Canal. Anonymous, undated (1840s?) oil on canvas. Although manufacturing began in Worcester County even before the Boston and Worcester Turnpike opened for business, and grew with the improved transportation that the turnpike offered, this painting of factories clustered along the canal banks at Worcester gives some idea of the boom in industrial production generated by the cheap transportation on the Blackstone Canal. Courtesy The Rhode Island Historical Society. RHi(X3)3307.

Hampshire border, a goal achieved within a few years by the opening of canals at Miller's and Turner's Falls. By 1810, the river was navigable for two hundred and fifty miles, far into New Hampshire and Vermont.

The Middlesex Canal—twenty locks and twenty-eight miles linking New Hampshire's Merrimack Valley with Boston harbor—spelled the end of commercial prosperity for the Merrimack's natural outlet at Newburyport when it opened in 1803, which was exactly what the Boston proprietors had in mind. Serving a hinterland meant prosperity for seaport towns. The easiest way to enlarge a hinterland is to steal someone else's. Boston commercial interests were accordingly perturbed by a proposed canalization of the Blackstone River, linking the isolated hill farms and fledgling industries of Worcester County with tidewater at Providence, and successfully blocked the plan for a time. Providence merchants finally succeeded in opening the Blackstone Canal in 1828. Boston fought back with iron.[7]

During the great era of American canal building it was widely understood that railroads were so expensive to build that they could never turn a profit; that they might work in England but could never run through our snowy winters or over mountain ranges as high as the Berkshires; and that Boston absolutely had to have a railroad to Albany and the Erie Canal or abandon all hope of competing with New York as a major transatlantic port.

Late on summer nights when the windows are open and the bullfrogs not too raucous, I sometimes hear a freight train on the old Boston and Worcester line. New England's first railroad, it opened for service on April 16, 1834. The train left Boston for West Newton at 6 and 10 A.M. and at 3:30 P.M. It departed West Newton for Boston at 7 and 11:45 A.M.and at 4:45 P.M. One engine, and one track, on which the engine ran back and forth as far as West Newton—which is a long way short of Worcester. It was a beginning.

The way had not been smooth. Citizens who had opposed spending tax money on turnpikes were just as firmly set against spending tax money on railroads. Salem voters opposed a railroad that would benefit Boston. Northampton voters disliked being taxed to build a line that would run through Springfield. Argument over who would be taxed and who would benefit continued until 1830; by then, Baltimore had the Baltimore and Ohio Railroad up and running.

When the Massachusetts legislature finally acted, it was only to decide not to fund any of the proposed schemes, throwing railroads into the laps of dubious private investors. Turnpikes, for all their benefits, had frequently lost money for investors. Canals had lost even more. Shareholders might make money if the farms, stores, or factories they owned profited from lower freight rates, but the shares themselves were likely money losers. Investors had to be browbeaten into buying shares in the Boston and Worcester on grounds that it was their civic duty to support a project of general public worth, even though it would probably never return a profit. Civic duty proved inadequate to the task: all the private money that boosterism and browbeating could raise ran out with the road just halfway to Albany. Only the strenuous efforts of industrial interests in Springfield and Pittsfield managed to push bond issues through a reluctant legislature to fund the completion. But it was completed. The Western, as the Boston and Worcester was renamed when it mustered ambition to reach for the Erie Canal, laid track as far as Worcester in 1835 and reached Albany in 1841, surprising skeptics who had been certain that enough money would never be raised, even if the engineering of a rail bed over the Berkshires proved feasible, which they doubted. What surprised everyone was that the trains began to turn a profit almost as soon as they began to run.[8]

The Western Railroad was supposed to divert the bounty of midwestern grain flowing east through the Erie Canal and New York harbor, to the port of Boston for transshipment to Europe. It never happened. Instead, the railroad created markets for its services that no one had dreamed of—let alone planned for. There was, of course, substantial demand for transportation of manufactured goods from rural workshops and mills; that was expected. But no one had

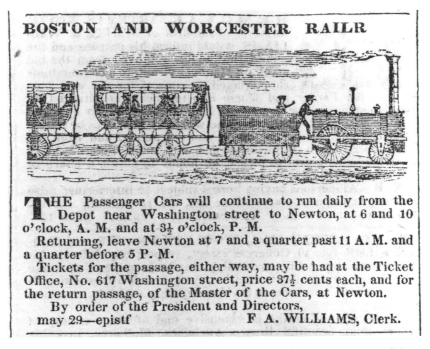

BOSTON AND WORCESTER RAILR

THE Passenger Cars will continue to run daily from the Depot near Washington street to Newton, at 6 and 10 o'clock, A. M. and at 3½ o'clock, P. M.

Returning, leave Newton at 7 and a quarter past 11 A. M. and a quarter before 5 P. M.

Tickets for the passage, either way, may be had at the Ticket Office, No. 617 Washington street, price 37½ cents each, and for the return passage, of the Master of the Cars, at Newton.

By order of the President and Directors,

may 29—epistf   F A. WILLIAMS, Clerk.

Advertisement, *Boston Morning Post,* June 23, 1834. The Boston and Worcester did not intend to offer passenger service when the first train made its first run from Boston to West Newton. Hoping that the locomotive newly imported from George Stephenson's works in England would generate some modest freight revenue, the management was surprised to discover a demand for passenger service. Their ad hoc efforts to comply with public demand were so well remunerated that they were soon delighted to run advertisements in the Boston papers announcing that the new service would continue. The ad began running in the *Boston Daily Advertiser* on May 12; it ran in several newspapers.

known that Americans had a pent-up appetite for passenger travel, no one had expected commuters, and no one had thought of milk.

Every farmer kept a cow or two; some kept as many as a dozen and made dairying a specialty, turning the cream into butter or cheese and fattening hogs on the skim. Cheese, salted butter, and salt pork made money even when shipped by oxcart; only farmers with property very near town could follow the more profitable route of selling fresh milk directly to city customers—until the railroad came. A bare two years after the first cars chugged from Worcester to Boston, farmers were loading so many cans of milk on the morning train that the line had to add special cars to accommodate them. By 1838, the job of carrying milk to Boston required an entire daily train, and a second train to return the empty milk cans.

Settlement of new villages in the seventeenth and eighteenth centuries was closely followed by the desire for roads, ferries, bridges, and wharves, but as long as commerce consisted of the occasional drove of swine or barrel of potash, extensive road improvement would not pay.[9] It was only when farmers increased their output of such market crops as broom and hops, and local workshops began to produce for distant markets, that better roads were worth building. Once increased market production generated sufficient traffic to justify road improvement, better roads made new categories of goods worth producing, which led to even more demand for transportation improvements, which made more goods worth producing. Looking at this specific chicken and this particular egg, we know which came first.

Before the incorporation of its first turnpike, Connecticut workshops were producing nails, hats, candles, shoes, leather goods, boots, wooden dishes, wooden kitchenware, wool cards, cast iron, buttons, and tin kitchenware for sale "in almost every part of the eastern states."[10] Before the first canal was dug, Yankee farmers were deciding which crops to plant and what livestock to raise not only on the basis of local needs, but according to commodity prices in distant cities.[11] No insatiable world market demanded the produce of Yankee fields and workshops. No efficient transportation system lured producers with low freight rates. The productive energy of a generation of New Englanders in need of new ways to make a living grew the crops and manufactured the goods that created the demand for transportation that called roads and bridges into being.

Berlin tinsmiths responded to the widening market made possible by the new turnpikes with increased production, with the invention of machines to roll the raw edge of a vessel over a piece of wire, forming a neat lip, and machines to flute the metal, and form concentric grooves to decorate and strengthen a piece of tinware. As roads improved, peddlers switched to carts and then to wagons, setting up distribution systems that enabled them to resupply their wagons at warehouses and Connecticut-managed workshops from Ohio to Georgia. Tinsmiths supplied this marketing system with new styles and kinds of tinware, lacquered, and painted with flowers and patriotic eagles. Peddlers increased their profits by adding an extensive line of Yankee notions to their load of tin housewares.[12]

Yankee peddlers cannily chose their lines of notions. A peddler, whether on foot, horseback, in a cart, or even in a comparatively commodious wagon, is forced to balance bulk and weight against profit. Andirons and Windsor chairs were not carried; pins, thread, scissors and buttons were. Peddlers leaving Bristol or Waterbury with such an assortment could afford to travel a long distance, stopping at isolated farms to trade for such country pay as linen rags, butter, sheepskins, homespun cloth, brooms, and ginseng. The peddler knew where to find paper mills that would buy rags collected from dozens of scattered

John Robbins, Yankee peddler, posed for this unique daguerreotype in Waltham, Massachusetts, in 1843. The making of a daguerreotype required the subject to stay perfectly still while a long exposure was made; the horse appears to have moved its head. The brooms that Robbins peddled show up clearly; we cannot know what was in the sacks piled atop the wagon. Courtesy of the Society for Preservation of New England Antiquities (neg #15520-B).

farmhouses. Butter, eggs, even a cow tied behind the tin wagon would be sold at the next market town. Something as valuable as ginseng was worth bringing home to sell at the port in Middletown. The system was useful to farmers, peddlers, merchants, and to the Connecticut artisans who made the notions.

The peddling system functioned like a protected market. Storekeepers and store customers alike shunned American products in favor of English goods with a reputation for quality, but the smooth-talking peddler came right to the kitchen door, sharpened old knives, shared tidbits of neighborhood news, and patched leaky kettles. The tinker, or tinsmith, applied a daub of inexpensive lead solder to dam the leak, a low-cost repair on a low-value pot, which would probably develop a new leak soon enough, and which cost the peddler so little that he probably did it without charge, as a good-will gesture. A "tinker's dam" came to mean for a thing whose value is below price, worth, that is, as much as a temporary patch on an old pot. With convenience and service thrown in, farm women gladly traded cheese and beeswax for knives and buttons. At a time when early textile mills were having a hard time competing with English imports, peddlers provided artisans turning out Yankee notions with a reliable, growing market, a market strong enough to lure men to set up manufacturing shops.[13]

New England at the end of the eighteenth century had both a labor surplus and a labor shortage. There was a surplus of men looking for ways to make a good living, the kind of living that that generation called a competence, work that offered a respectable position in the community, something comparable to owning a farm. That kind of respectability, in the view of the times, could only be achieved by owning one's shop or farm. It was a kind of independence inextricable from the political ideas of an era when owning a freehold, however small, meant sturdy independence, while the wage laborer, dependent on his employer, was regarded as occupying a lower station in life. The Yankee wanted his own farm, or, at least, to buy his own materials and work them up in his own shop, beholden to no man.[14]

Peddling was hardly a desirable occupation. A peddler was on the road far from home and family for weeks or months at a time. When it rained, the horses kicked mud in his face. When the sun shone, he sweated. If it snowed, icicles hung from the collar pulled high about his cheeks. Lodging might mean sleeping under the wagon, and the quality of his dinner depended on the hospitality of the farmers with whom he traded. But a man did not go into peddling for the amenities it offered. Peddling offered the opportunity to become a settled shopkeeper, wholesale merchant, manufacturer supplying other peddlers, or to save enough to buy a farm. Going to sea was a rougher life than going on the road, but it offered the opportunity to work one's way up to captain or even merchant. When this stopped being a realistic hope, Yankee boys stopped going to sea. Starting a workshop to manufacture almost anything offered a fair chance, and parents apprenticed likely boys to learn mechanical trades. Leasing farmland also held out the chance to accumulate the capital necessary for eventual ownership of western land, and was preferred to working as a farmhand.[15]

New England villages teemed with clerks aiming to become storekeepers, young mechanics intending to own their own shops, and tenant farmers saving to buy land, but men of the class who spent their lives at the workbenches of Sheffield were hard to find. Capable, energetic young men could do better than that, even young men without capital, connections, or education. To discover the difference between the penury that threatened the landless young of the 1760s, and the opportunities that beckoned young men no better endowed with education or wealth in the 1790s, look no further than Ohio.

A few years of diligent work and conscientious saving was enough to enable a young man to buy a frontier farm and stock it with animals, tools, and seed. Many a young artisan, peddler, or tenant farmer was saving to do just that. More pertinent to the industrialization of the region were the numerous young men who saw the West not as a destination, but as a fall-back position, some-where to head if all else failed; they preferred to stay home. Staying home wasn't easy. It couldn't be done at all if a man were determined to own a farm, even though farming was the only business most boys learned. It couldn't be done by salaried employment: salaried, middle-class jobs did not exist in that economy of farms and small workshops. If a man were determined to stay in New En-gland and not drop to the status of laborer, he had to start a business of some kind. If a man failed in business—if the workshop, the mill, the farm, the store went belly-up—it was always possible to go west. Knowing that Ohio was there gave men the courage to risk everything they had on new enterprise. And it eliminated wage labor as an option for all but the young and the less able.

Ohio and the vast continent stretching south and west were important in two other ways. For one thing, they established a sort of floor beneath which Americans were unlikely to sink. Wages in a country with opportunity just over the mountains could fall only so low. An underclass of hired hands living at a true subsistence level, which had seemed on the verge of developing in the 1760s, could not develop in the early national period with so much western acreage wanting labor. Lack of a laboring class made European-style large-scale production by hand difficult to establish except in trades such as shoe-making, nail heading, or the braiding of straw hats, where tasks could be par-celed out to homeworkers during slack time in the farming year. If Yankee industries were to increase production, it could only be done by inventing labor-saving devices. Secondly, Ohio, producing corn and pork on virgin land, bought all the manufactured goods that could be carried west at a rea-sonable price. When Ohio, Kentucky, Georgia, and Tennessee joined the grow-ing demand created by eastern artisans and farmers enjoying unprecedented prosperity during the Napoleonic wars, a market large enough to support a manufacturing sector came into existence.

New settlements were likely to have a blacksmith, a tanner, a gristmill, and sawmill. But until a village was large enough to support a store, the Yankee ped-dler provided everything else. Where there were settlers, there was sure to be a peddler.

Yankee peddlers filled their carts with tin kitchenware made in Berlin, horn combs from Bethel, buttons made in Naugatuck Valley workshops, scythes from Winchester, axes from Canton, Meriden pewter, stoves made in Middle-town, shoes from New Caanan, Danbury hats, Norwalk pottery, brass kettles from Torrington, screws from Wallingford. Levi and Edward Porter of Water-bury—button manufacturers, purchasers of handcrafted clockworks and cases for assembly and resale, and dealers in Yankee notions, wholesale—noticed that the peddlers whose wagons they filled with these goods could sell as many wooden clocks as they could supply.

Chapter 10

Machines That Make Machines

I was born and reared in Hartford, in the state of Connecticut—anyway, just over the river, in the country. So I am a Yankee of the Yankees—and practical; yes, and nearly barren of sentiment, I suppose—or poetry, in other words. My father was a blacksmith, my uncle was a horse-doctor, and I was both, along at first. Then I went over to the great arms factory and learned my real trade; learned all there was to it; learned to make everything: guns, revolvers, cannon, boilers, engines, all sorts of labor-saving machinery. Why, I could make anything a body wanted—anything in the world, it didn't make any difference what; and if there wasn't any quick, new-fangled way to make a thing, I could invent one—and do it as easy as falling off a log.

—Mark Twain, *A Connecticut Yankee in King Arthur's Court*

A RESIDENT OF BOSTON, SALEM, OR EVEN LYNN prosperous enough to buy a clock could choose a timepiece imported from London, or have one made by a skilled artisan who, if he did not come from England, certainly imported his tools and kept up with the latest European styles and technology. Eastern Massachusetts was part of the Atlantic economy. But when Connecticut wanted timepieces, it not only made its own, it made them with homemade tools. A New Haven clockmaker advertised: "Time pieces of various descriptions and warranted, Clock and Watch Makers' Lathes and Engines as good perhaps as can be procured in the United States."[1]

The lathes and engines referred to in this 1801 advertisement were hand- or foot-powered tools, and the advertiser's modesty about their quality may have been warranted, but procuring clocks, tools, or even clockmakers from England was more than rural Connecticut could afford. Connecticut made its own clocks and its own tools. When the peddling system developed the capacity to sell more clocks, Connecticut produced the Yankee inventor.[2]

When I was a child, Walt Disney made movies about charmingly eccentric inventors who spent their days fiddling with improbable contraptions. Neighbors, in these movies, laughed and shook their heads. But the inventor didn't care. He knew he could make the thing work. And then, to the astonishment of the town—he did! The tinkerer produced a machine that could manufacture not mere vindication, but riches, fame, and glory. However—and this was the deliciously improbable part—it always turned out that the inventor didn't care. Not about wealth. Certainly not about fame. All he wanted was to go back to his workshop and fiddle with new machines.

Eli Terry really was that kind of inventor. In 1806, when he signed a contract to make four thousand clocks in three years, the townsfolk of Plymouth, Connecticut, laughed and shook their heads. A clockmaker might, with skill and good health, make four hundred clocks in a lifetime. To make four thousand clocks in three years was plainly impossible. But suppose that by harnessing water power to cut parts in quantity, Terry really could make four thousand clocks—who would buy them? "So limited was the demand for clocks at that time, and so inadequate his means for making them, that after finishing three or four [Terry] was obliged to go out with them on horseback, and put them up [literally hang the 'tall-case' movement on a wall and set it in beat] in households where they had been previously ordered. His usual way was to put one forward of the saddle on which he rode, one behind, and one on each side in his portmanteau."[3] Eli Terry was proposing to mass-produce a complicated mechanical device, and sell thousands in a region that could afford to purchase two or three dozen clocks in a prosperous year. No wonder the townsfolk laughed.[4]

Clocks were made in Plymouth the way they were made in Europe—one at a time, usually on a "bespoke" basis. In European capitals, clocks were made of brass and steel, embellished with porcelain, jewels, and gold. Connecticut craftsmen made clocks out of brass, and out of wood for customers who could not afford brass.

Either way, in brass or wood, not even the most skillful craftsman could make more than six or ten clocks a year. A man who thought he could profitably sell more clocks might bring apprentices into his workshop, though the wages of a journeyman skillful enough to be useful were too high to make such an arrangement profitable. New apprentices, however, boys too green to put a clock together, might turn a lathe and cut wheels that a skilled craftsman could finish and use to build clocks. In the early years of the century, it occurred to a small number of Connecticut clockmakers that waterpower could be harnessed to produce clock wheels and other parts even more cheaply than it could be done by boys working foot-pedaled lathes. In 1802 or 1803, Eli Terry acquired a mill and began to produce wooden wheels for clockworks using water-powered machinery.

Wooden clockworks sold for twenty dollars in 1807, forty dollars if the buyer wanted his clockwork enclosed in a case. By 1816, Eli Terry would offer shelf clocks handsomely cased for twelve dollars wholesale, fifteen dollars to eighteen dollars retail.[5] But first he had to invent machinery that could make clock parts. It took three years and a substantial amount of Levi and Edward Porter's money. The first year Terry designed and built machinery, but produced no clocks; the second year he made one thousand clocks and improved the machinery; and in 1809, Eli Terry produced 3,000 clocks from parts turned by water-powered machinery. Then he sold the factory to two assistants, Seth Thomas and Silas Hoadley, and retreated to his workshop to design a better clock.

The clock Terry invented was a remarkable machine. In 1807, he had undertaken to construct machinery to produce, in bulk, the wheels and pinions of an ordinary, tall-case or hang-up wooden clock. By 1814, he had designed a new kind of clock, a clock calculated for mass production. The machine-made parts of Terry's first four thousand clocks made them dramatically less expensive than handmade clocks, but the wheels and pinions still had to be individually fitted by skilled craftsmen. The interchangeable parts of Terry's new, four-arbor, thirty-hour shelf clock were designed for quick assembly in identical, dust-proof cases by unskilled hands. Skilled workmen were needed only to adjust the escapement and depth the verge, cunningly placed outside the boxed works in order to make this, the one step in Terry's assembly procedure requiring the attention of skilled artisans, an efficient process.[6] Eli Terry had designed a machine to be mass-produced from interchangeable, machine-made parts. It was an idea that would change the world.

Terry's thirty-hour shelf clock, also known as the pillar-and-scroll clock for the fashionably ornamented case he sold it in, ran like clockwork and sold like hotcakes. The one on my mother's mantel still keeps fairly good time, when someone takes the trouble of winding it daily. It was sold to my great-grandmother at the turn of the century by an antiques dealer who explained that it had been handmade of wood because brass was scarce during the War of 1812, which is precisely not the point. Wood strikes us as an incongruous material for a mass-produced machine; it probably struck turn-of-the-century antiques dealers that way too. But wood was cheap and easy to work.

Within a few years of Eli Terry's invention, several hundred men in some two dozen small factories were producing Terry-style clocks, and the craftsmen who had made clocks one at a time had to become factory owners or leave the trade. From 1816, when the first of the new clocks came from the factory, until wooden clocks were supplanted by mass-produced brass clocks in the 1830s, Naugatuck Valley shops turned out tens of thousands of wooden shelf-clocks. To sell a luxury good in such volume, peddlers introduced installment-plan purchasing and the manufacturers invented model changes, in which the style of the case (not the internal clockworks), was changed to induce consumers who already owned a functioning clock to buy a more stylish model—

marketing concepts that continue to sell consumer durables today. The brass clock industry began to grow when clockmaker Joseph Ives took advantage of rolled sheet brass, first produced in this country with reliably uniform thickness and quality by Waterbury button manufacturers in the 1830s, to manufacture clockworks from wheels stamped out of brass sheets.[7] Eli Terry's wooden clocks became obsolete; his idea of designing complex machines for the ease of manufacture from interchangeable, mass-produced components would launch a thousand factories making products he never dreamed of.

Redesigning clockworks to tailor the product to an inexpensive method of production was an idea of genius, the sort of epoch-making idea that has made the inventor an American folk hero. Terry's earlier idea of harnessing waterpower to produce ordinary clock wheels was as common as baked beans. The years from the late 1780s on found Yankee artisans harnessing waterpower to myriad tasks that had always been done by hand. New England's waterfalls were put to work kneading clay for pottery, sawing marble, pulping rags for papermaking, grinding bark for tanning, rigging trip-hammers to hasten the blacksmith's task.[8] Where waterpower wasn't practical, either because a business required an urban location or because the demand for a mechanized process was too slight to justify the cost of purchasing a mill (cider mills, for example, only pressed apples for a few weeks in autumn), a horse was rigged to the power train, and mechanization proceeded apace.

Simeon North was born in Berlin, Connecticut, in 1765, not far from Eli Terry's birthplace in East Windsor, but while Terry's parents had apprenticed their son to learn clockmaking, North's prosperous parents were able to provide their six sons with farms. Simeon and his brother Levi had farms in Berlin; the family helped Asa and Noah buy farms in Vermont, while David and Stephen bought farms in New York. Simeon married Lucy Savage when he was only twenty-one, young by the standards of the era, but with sixty-six acres to farm, they could afford to marry young. What Simeon and Lucy North could not afford on sixty-six acres was to provide farms for each of their five sons and portions for three daughters. In 1795, a saw mill came onto the market on the brook that ran beside their land. North bought it, hired a man to help run it, expanded the building to include a forge and trip-hammer, and began making scythes of imported steel, which he sold, one at a time, in nearby towns.[9]

A traditional blacksmith lifts a red-hot piece of iron with tongs, places it on an anvil, and hammers it into the shape he desires, turning and shifting the work piece with tongs between blows. A trip-hammer replaces the blacksmith's strong arm with waterpower harnessed to drive the hammerblows steadily on the anvil, freeing the blacksmith to manipulate the iron piece with his tongs and greatly increasing productivity. Trip-hammer shops like Simeon North's sprang up on small streams across New England, producing quantities of tools. North was more adroit and more ambitious than most. On March 9, 1799, he signed a government contract to manufacture five hundred horse pistols.

Where Simeon North learned metalworking is not clear, although many farmers of that era did a little blacksmithing. Nor do we know whether he was trained in the gunsmith's trade, although there was a gunsmith in Berlin in those years.[10] His brother-in-law and business partner, Elisha Cheney, did, however, have metalworking skills, which he developed as a trained artisan clockmaker in an era when clockmaking involved precision work in brass and steel. Not many people in Connecticut could afford a clock made of brass and steel, metals that had to be imported, but a well-trained apprentice learned how to make them; Cheney's father, Benjamin, and his uncle Timothy Cheney were two of the finest. One of them trained Eli Terry, who also worked under Daniel Burnap, a specialist in brass clocks. We don't know which Cheney brother trained Terry, but both brothers helped train an apprentice clockmaker named John Fitch, who was among the inventors of steam engines and who built the first American steamboat that worked. It was common for men trained in one craft to switch to another where opportunity offered; for a clockmaker to become a gunsmith, locksmith, silversmith, brassfounder, machine-builder, or all of the above was nothing out of the ordinary—so long as it promised to pay.[11]

There were only a handful of skilled clockmakers in Connecticut when Eli Terry's invention spawned a boom industry, but men trained as joiners and cabinetmakers quickly became clock manufacturers; they had only to cut the parts from wood exactly the way Terry cut his. It would not have been out of the ordinary for Elisha Cheney, artisan clockmaker attempting to increase production by the use of waterpower, and Simeon North, farmer, blacksmith, and proprietor of a trip-hammer shop, to attempt to manufacture pistols, if pistol making looked like the way to make money.[12]

In 1801 Elisha Cheney moved his clock shop to the waterpower site next upstream from Simeon North's trip-hammer mill on Spruce Brook. There he used waterpower to turn wheels for traditional, tall-case clocks, and, after Terry's invention, for the works of pillar-and-scroll clocks—a product so standardized that jobbers could obtain wheels from any manufacturer and assemble them into identical clockworks. Cheney also produced screws and small metal parts for North's pistols. In 1826, Cheney sold the business to his son Olcott, who manufactured wooden clocks under his own label for several years. Unsuccessful as manufacturers, the entire Cheney family moved west in the 1830s, with the exception of the daughter who had married a North.

Simeon North could hardly have failed to draw several conclusions from Cheney's career and from the wooden-clock factories that sprang up in the wake of Terry's invention like toadstools after rain: First, that the manufacture of complex mechanisms from interchangeable, machine-made parts was not only possible, it could be highly profitable. Second, that the invention of mass-production machinery in the pistol field would put artisan gunsmiths out of business as fast as mass-produced clocks had destroyed the businesses of artisan clockmakers like the Cheney family. Even artisan gunsmiths operating sizable trip-hammer workshops would be supplanted by machinery that could mass-produce parts. Third, that attempting machine manufacturing techniques might well fail. Failure and bankruptcy were considerably more common among early manufacturers than success.

Simeon North learned these lessons well. He invented and was the first arms maker to implement a number of machine production techniques, yet he cautiously halted his pursuit of mass-produced, interchangeable parts whenever it became apparent that the single-minded pursuit of technological advance would be a poor business decision. North had five sons to launch, and in this he succeeded: four entered the gun business with their father, eventually transferring their skills and capital into hardware manufacturing; the youngest son went to Yale, taught classics, and became president of Hamilton College.

During the years when interchangeable parts were being routinely assembled into Connecticut wooden and brass clockworks, French and English armorers continued to view the concept as a kind of holy grail: interchangeable parts in complex machines were a dreamer's quest, not a goal that practical men expected to achieve in this life. Beginning in 1765, General Jean-Baptiste de Gribeauval had urged French engineers to produce small arms with perfectly interchangeable parts; this was an expensive quest at a time when fine, individually-crafted arms were available at reasonable prices, but a quest that made sense to battlefield commanders. An army engaged in the field soon found itself with heaps of disabled weapons that would require a legion of skilled gunsmiths to put back to working order, one gun at a time. By the time the muskets damaged in any single battle were in repair, the war was likely to be over. If, however, the damaged weapons had all been manufactured with perfectly identical parts, semiskilled men could take the functioning lock from one musket, the intact barrel from another, and produce working guns from a heap of useless, disabled arms. To an army in the field, weapons made from perfectly interchangeable parts would be invaluable.

Thomas Jefferson was serving as United States minister to France in 1785 when he witnessed a demonstration of interchangeability by Honoré Blanc. Under Blanc's supervision, skilled workmen had tooled the locks of fifty muskets to dimensions so nearly identical that the parts of any one lock could be taken apart and randomly exchanged with the parts of any other. Jefferson reported the wonder in letters home.

Fifteen years later, as vice-president, Jefferson watched Eli Whitney replicate Blanc's demonstration in front of an audience that included President Adams and a prestigious assembly of Congressmen and government officials. Whitney explained to Jefferson and the others that he had "invented moulds and machines for making all the pieces of his locks so exactly equal, that take 100 locks to pieces and mingle their parts and the hundred locks may be put together as well by taking the first piece which comes to hand."[13] In fact, Whitney had replicated Blanc's accomplishment precisely. He had hired skilled workmen to file perfectly identical parts by hand. As did Honoré Blanc, Eli Whitney performed his demonstration as a way of inspiring the government to fund him while he developed machinery capable of producing interchangeable parts. The similarity ends there. Blanc was a capable mechanic and inventor dedicated to the idea he promoted, although revolution robbed him of the patronage necessary to put his ideas into practice. Eli Whitney was driven by a desire to win a share of the vast profits cotton planters and textile manufacturers derived from his earlier invention of the cotton gin. He promoted mass production and interchangeable parts in order to win government subsidies and generous government arms contracts, then applied the proceeds of his arms contracts to fighting cotton gin patent suits, while in his Connecticut arms factory gunsmiths made muskets the old-fashioned way, one at a time, with hand tools. Other men would unlock the secrets of mass production and interchangeable parts.

Eli Terry's clockmaking machinery was of little direct use to arms production. First, shaping wood is a very different mechanical task from shaping hardened steel. Second, clockworks are made from round wheels, and circles are far easier to form by machine than the irregularly shaped parts of a gun lock. Third, Terry's design calculated that very slight inaccuracies could exist in the clockwork without compromising the clock's performance, once the escapement wheel and verge were properly adjusted. Clock parts, that is, could be *functionally* interchangeable and work *perfectly*. Gun parts had to be perfectly interchangeable to work at all.

In the twentieth century, machinery mass-produced from perfectly interchangeable parts has become so commonplace that we take it for granted. Not only does it make everything we buy far less expensive, it produces machines that work. The smoothly functioning machinery we use daily is made possible by the development of machine tools capable of producing large numbers of metal parts identical to within very small tolerances. Machine tools were what men like Simeon North needed to invent; they had two incentives to do so. First, whenever a machine tool or process could be devised to turn out standardized parts, products could be offered at a lower price and profits made. Second, the imperatives of war were such that the ordinance department sometimes paid to develop tools and processes whose development would not have been cost-effective in the production of market goods; but once a machine tool or process was developed for military production, it rapidly found other uses. That these machine tools were developed in the Connecticut River valley, and in nearby parts of Connecticut, Rhode Island, Massachusetts, and Vermont, was not a matter of chance.

New England had waterpower. Nothing on the scale of Niagara, but in the early years it was the many small streams the size of Spruce Brook where it ran past Simeon and Lucy North's farm that mattered. Mill seats of a few horsepowers each, available at modest prices, gave great numbers of men the opening to try their hand at doing a job a little better and a little cheaper.

New England also had the Salisbury Iron Works. Tucked in the hills of northwestern Connecticut, these iron mines are scarcely big enough to notice, but in 1800 they produced wrought iron as fine as could be purchased anywhere. In an age of primitive metallurgy, undetectable impurities in ore meant that most iron was riddled with invisible faults that caused products manufactured from it to fail. Swedish iron, naturally low in sulphur and phosphorous, was the world standard. So it is particularly interesting that Salisbury iron was better than most not because of the purity of the ore, but because of the diligence of the workmen.

Salisbury was so remote from affordable transportation on navigable water that, except by producing in limited quantity for the immediate neighborhood, an ironmaster could turn a profit only by producing iron of unusually high value. Gun-barrel iron fetched the highest price, so Salisbury ironmasters set themselves the task of reprocessing their pig iron into high-quality wrought iron, making a local source of gun-barrel quality iron available to the Connecticut arms industry in its infant years.[14]

The third special factor in favor of Connecticut as the cradle of interchangeable parts manufacture was the designation of Springfield, Massachusetts, as the site of one of the two national armories. President Washington chose Springfield not because it was located in a hotbed of artisan creativity, but because it was located on a navigable river protected from naval attack by its location just above the falls, and because the government already owned land and buildings there. The second arsenal was placed at Harper's Ferry, Virginia, because Washington, a major landowner, stood to make money if the Potomac Valley became a flourishing industrial region. The contrast between the region where one of the world's earliest industrial revolutions occurred, and the region where it did not, is starkly clear in the story of those two armories.

Harper's Ferry stood alone. No nearby industry existed and none developed. To recruit mechanics and new technology, the armory looked to New England. Virginia boys grew tobacco or went west; they did not set up trip-hammers and lathes on the fall line. Inside the armory, highly skilled artisans, often recruited from the famous gunsmith shops of Pennsylvania, crafted finely made weapons one at a time. When the ordinance department sent machine tool builders and designers of interchangeable parts technology south, Harper's Ferry gunsmiths sullenly resisted.[15]

Springfield was located in a region of farmers and farmer's sons who built machines that made things, and the difference is not completely explained even

"View from the green woods towards Canaan and Salisbury in Connecticut." The Salisbury Iron Works were an extraordinary enterprise in an agrarian countryside, sufficiently notable to draw the attention of the editors of the *Columbian Magazine* in 1789. The published view does not show the foundry buildings or the extensive forest clearance that supported the voracious furnaces, but it does convey something of the wonder an eighteenth-century traveler felt in coming upon great, billowing plumes of black smoke so unfamiliar in a nation of farmers. Courtesy, American Antiquarian Society.

by the sum of all the factors already mentioned. There are, after all, many parts of the world with waterfalls but without industrial revolutions. Many nations have mined iron without developing the technique of die forging, or imported steam engines without developing interchangeable parts manufacturing. Societies have even developed legal systems to enable land to be appropriated for canals and power dams, without finding innovative uses for the power thus generated. Certainly there are peoples who have met the challenge of overpopulation by becoming poor.

A culture is more than the sum of its parts, and a break with the past as radical as the Industrial Revolution requires something more by way of explanation than enumeration of a set of tangible resources. The Yankee was the child of Puritanism. The strong work ethic, respect for manual labor, tradition of assuming responsibility, willingness to accept risks, rational approach to life, and a certain independence of mind inculated by the Puritan heritage combined to produce the culture that produced a revolution.

Virginia, on the other hand, was a commodity-producing economy in which the upper classes self-consciously mimicked the English aristocracy.

Status accrued to ancestry, ownership of land, and ownership of slaves. Working with one's hands entailed loss of status for a white man, but even the poorest white man was superior in status to a black slave. Virginia had other characteristics that made it unlikely to foment industrial revolution: Illiteracy was high. The land grew tobacco, a high-value commodity that made the production of unprocessed raw materials profitable. And while Virginia was self-governing, government by local grandees is very different from government by officials chosen by electors of equal status, just as a ministry appointed by bishops differs from a ministry selected by the congregation in the shaping of an entrepreneurial culture. While Virginia grew tobacco, New England grew entrepreneurs.

Thomas Blanchard was born to a large family in Sutton, Massachusetts, in 1788. By the time he was a teenager, one older brother had started a trip-hammer shop to manufacture scythes while another had a horse-powered mill for making tacks. Thomas went to work for the tack-making brother, and soon devised a mechanism to count the finished tacks. When he was eighteen, he set about inventing a tack-making machine, selling the patent when he was twenty-nine for five thousand dollars—enough money to set up his own shop on a water privilege. Streams falling to join the Blackstone from the hills of Sutton and Millbury turned the wheels of many small mills, among them the gun factory of Asa Waters, who held a patent for a lathe that turned gun barrels, and had contracts to make barrels for the armory at Springfield. Water's patent lathe could machine the round barrels to taper at the firing end, but it could not machine them at the breech end where a barrel must change shape from a perfect circle to an oval with flattened sides. The breech end had to be filed by hand—until Thomas Blanchard invented a lathe that could turn ovals by machine.[16]

In 1818, Blanchard installed his new lathe in the armories at Springfield and Harper's Ferry, then returned to his Millbury shop to work out a new problem: how to make a lathe that could turn complex irregular shapes in wood. He received the patent in September, only to have it challenged by a rival inventor, Azariah Woolworth, who had invented an irregular-turning lathe while working in a Waterbury, Connecticut, wooden clock factory. Blanchard's first thought had been the market for rifle butts, while Woolworth was aiming at the large market for shoe lasts. But wood is wood: a machine that could turn one could turn the other and was likely to be profitable. Blanchard went to the clock factory to have a look at Woolworth's lathe, which turned out to be built on a different principle than his own. The two patents would contend for priority in court battles lasting several decades. Blanchard won because he had invented a better machine, worked successfully at improvements to his original idea, and was a more skillful businessman. Blanchard's patent lathe was soon turning gunstocks, ax handles, wheel spokes, scythe snaths, shoe lasts, and hat blocks—

anything a woodworking factory wanted to make, so long as they paid a royalty. Meanwhile, other men tackled the difficult problem of shaping iron by machine.

The superintendents of the Springfield and Harper's Ferry armories, on a visit to Simeon North's Middletown arms factory in 1816 (North had expanded from Berlin to a creek in nearby Middletown, where a larger flow generated more power), observed the operation of a machine to mill or shape iron, and were so impressed that they had North build and install a second machine at Harper's Ferry. There John Hall, an ingenious inventor and machine builder from Portland, Maine, was working under government contract to construct machinery that could produce his patented, breech-loading rifle with interchangeable parts. Hall made improvements on North's milling machine, which were readily copied in new versions built at North's Middletown works. We cannot be certain who in the North factory first had the idea to build a milling machine, but North's sons may have had a hand in the project. In 1808 or 1810, North's oldest son, Reuben, built a washing machine, described in family memory as "a cumbersome affair, with heavy pounders in a round bottomed box. A pulley tackle passed outside to which, on Monday mornings, a horse was attached and made to do the great washings."[17] North, his sons, and the mechanics working for and with them made further improvements until by 1832 the Norths, Hall, and the armories had the world's first machine able to "mill," or cut, flat and curved surfaces in iron with a powered, rotary cutter to a high degree of precision. Although early milling machines were built in the shops where they were used, by the 1840s anyone could buy a milling machine from the Ames Manufacturing Company of Chicopee, Massachusetts, or the Robbins and Lawrence Company of Windsor, Vermont.[18]

By 1828, John Hall and Simeon North were producing M1819 rifles with truly interchangeable parts, though the parts were not entirely machine-made. Even their wonderful, new milling machine could take iron only so far. As far, that is, as pretty close to the specified size. At that point, skilled gunsmiths set to work with files and precision gauges until the parts matched to within 0.006 inches.[19] A new century would begin before machines could do that well.

While armorers like North and Hall strove to satisfy military lust for interchangeable parts, Samuel W. Collins tried to make money by making axes. In 1826, in partnership with his brother and his cousin, Collins set up a triphammer shop on the Farmington River in Canton, Connecticut. There, blacksmiths worked, cutting a length from a bar of wrought iron, flattening it, folding it around a steel pin to keep open a hole for inserting the handle, and welding the two halves together. Next, a steel "bit" was welded onto one side to become the cutting edge; steel holds an edge better than iron, but was too expensive to use for the entire ax. The welded axhead was then tempered, sharpened on a grindstone, polished or painted, and shipped in lots to the West or to Latin America.

Thomas Blanchard's shop. The small, Sutton, Massachusetts, workshop where Blanchard invented the irregular turning lathe survived until the end of the century without exterior alteration, although there may have been interior changes between Blanchard's day and the moment when this photograph of the abandoned workshop was taken. The plain, one-room wood-frame building drawing power from a very small brook was far from unique in its era. That the undistinguished building where so important an invention was made survived to be photographed for a coffee-table book in the 1890s is extraordinary. An exterior photograph of the shop is also featured. Elbridge Kingsley and Fredrick Knab, *Picturesque Worcester* (Springfield: W. F. Adams Co., 1895). Courtesy of Concord Free Public Library.

Yankee streams were studded with trip-hammer shops. Samuel Collins stands out because he had a knack for selecting mechanics of genius and the vision to fund their work, sometimes for unprofitable years at a stretch, while they devised machines that could make axes, and because he possessed the business acumen to buy metal and sell axes at a profit in up markets and down. The most outstanding mechanic to work with Collins was Elisha Root, the man who perfected die forging.[20]

Root was born on a Massachusetts farm in 1808, a generation younger than North, Hall, and Terry, which meant that he grew up in a world where mills and machine shops dotted the countryside. At the age of fifteen, after several years of work as a bobbin boy in a cotton mill, Root began work in a Ware,

Massachusetts, machine shop. By the time he arrived at Samuel Collins's ax factory at age twenty-four, Root had worked and learned what he could in the machine shops attached to a series of Massachusetts and Connecticut mills.

Elisha Root reconceptualized the making of axes. He eliminated the labor of flattening wrought iron, folding it around a steel pin, and forging the two sides together under a trip-hammer, by arranging a series of dies and rollers that could "die forge"—or apply pressure to a mold, forming a solid piece of yellow-hot wrought iron into the shape of an ax, with an eye already punched to receive the handle. Root also automated the process of tempering axes with a machine that regulated oven heat and moved axheads through the oven on a rotating wheel. Another machine reduced the amount of hand labor required to give axes a sharp edge by "shaving" the hardened steel until it need only receive its final finish by hand on a grindstone. Root appears to have been working on further automation of axmaking when he was hired away by Samuel Colt in 1849, to design and oversee the mechanization of Colt's ambitious, new, Hartford arms factory. There, Root perfected die-forging machines to mass-produce gun parts that, while not perfectly interchangeable, required only modest amounts of hand-filing to gauge before they were ready to be fitted interchangeably into well-made, inexpensive guns.

Between die-forging and milling, Yankee mechanics could mass-produce at a competitive price any metal object that human ingenuity could contrive. Pins, guns, knives, locks, clocks, watches, buttons—familiar things made elsewhere by artisans were machine-made in New England at prices that astonished the world. Clock magnate Chauncey Jerome dined for years on a favorite story from the early days of the brass clock industry. In the early 1840s he sent a shipment of mass-produced brass clocks to England hoping to open a new market. British customs officials took one look at the clocks and the unheard-of low price on the invoice, decided that Americans were dumping goods on the English market, and confiscated the lot at the invoice price. Jerome, delighted to receive prompt payment in full—and even more delighted at the chance to tweak the lion's tail—immediately dispatched a second shipment, invoicing them again at the regular wholesale price. British customs agents, wondering, perhaps, what the American was up to, but certain that his price was dishonestly low, confiscated the new shipment and again sent Jerome the invoice price. When a third shipment arrived, customs shrugged and let Jerome's agent have the clocks.[21] England was even more astonished when Yankee precision manufacturing shops began to produce things the world had never seen before: sewing machines and typewriters.

Most inventions are not eureka moments of the kind Eli Terry perhaps experienced when it occurred to him that the clock itself could be reengineered for ease of production by machine. They are incremental improvements to existing machines of the sort that Hall, North, and other mechanics made as improved models of the milling machine passed between Middletown and Harper's Ferry, or they are innovations that affect a single step in a lengthy process. Inventions, therefore, are most likely to be made by people already working in an industry. Once Yankees started making new things, they were well positioned to make more, and newer things. Better machine tools, for example, precision measuring instruments needed in manufacturing processes, more accurate watches.

But it is also true that expertise attracts business. The sewing machine was invented not by a lone genius, but by a series of men, each of whom addressed the task of fixing stitches in cloth from a different angle, each approach only a partial success, so that patents held by sundry inventors and investors had to be pooled to produce a practical machine. The inventors came from many places. They brought their ideas to New England to be turned into working machines.

The Wheeler and Wilson sewing machine company combined the inventive genius of Allen Wilson with the business and manufacturing know-how of Nathaniel Wheeler. A Waterbury manufacturer of Yankee notions, Wheeler saw the potential of Wilson's invention and began sewing machine production with the metalworking tools he used to produce brass buttons and buckles. In 1857, Wheeler took over the Bridgeport building that had once housed Chauncey Jerome's brass clock factory (Jerome had gone bankrupt) and hired William Perry, a production superintendent, who, like Mark Twain's Connecticut Yankee, had learned to make machines that made things at Samuel Colt's Hartford armory. Perry made sewing machines the way Colt made guns: die-forging the parts, then machining them in a series of special-purpose machine tools to match the dimensions of standardized jigs, and assembling the nearly interchangeable parts into sewing machines.[22]

The Wilcox and Gibbs Sewing Machine Company merged the talents of inventor James Gibbs of Virginia and a Philadelphia hardware merchant, James Wilcox, who saw the machine's potential. In 1858, Wilcox contracted with Brown & Sharpe of Providence for the machine's manufacture. It was an odd choice. The small Rhode Island firm specialized in the manufacture of gauges, rules, and drawing instruments, in the production of tools for watchmakers, clockmakers, and jewelers, and in making fine-quality, custom clocks and watches. Brown & Sharpe possessed three small engine lathes, two hand lathes, an upright drill, and a hand planer; it mass-produced no machines. The skilled mechanics at Brown & Sharpe could easily have produced Gibbs sewing machines by hand, one at a time, at a competitive price. Instead, they designed and built a series of machines to do the job—a difficult and expensive process. The high cost of developing machinery could be defrayed only if the Wilcox and Gibbs machine became popular enough to sell in large numbers. If the machine achieved volume sales, profits from machine manufacture with interchangeable parts would ultimately be greater than for a machine produced by craft technique. But that was only half of the reason for selecting machine production. Lucien Sharpe and J. R. Brown believed that precision manufacture of interchangeable parts would produce a better machine, and that a superior machine would be its own best advertisement. Mastering the techniques of machine production, Brown & Sharpe improved production technology and ultimately became a leading manufacturer of precision gauges, calipers, and machine tools. But in 1857, it was not clear that precision manufacturing with interchangeable parts, which entailed large investments in special-purpose machinery, was the most profitable way to build machines, or even that it was the way to build the best machines.

Isaac Merrit Singer, a young actor stranded in Ohio when the traveling theater troupe in which he was playing disbanded, had an idea for a machine to manufacture printer's type. He went to Boston to try to have his idea manufactured and sold, leasing space in the shop of scientific instrument maker Orson Phelps, where he worked on a model machine. While tinkering with his type-maker in Phelps's shop, Singer decided that inventing a sewing machine might pay even better. When he came up with one, Phelps agreed to manufacture it. Orson Phelps's scientific instrument business was fairly similar to the Brown & Sharpe tool- and clock-making shop; their approaches to making sewing machines could hardly have been more different. Buying bolts and nuts from hardware merchants, and contracting for cast head, gears, and base with local job shops, Phelps's craftsmen filed and ground pieces to a fine fit as they put each machine together. In 1851 the company moved to New York, a strategic location for the man who would teach the world to sew by machine. Isaac Singer was interested in manufacturing machines only insofar as making the machines was a necessary prelude to selling them. Marketing was the great thing. He insisted that his machines be the best, but never believed that superior workmanship would necessarily translate into superior sales. Singer's marketing network taught customers how to sew by machine, advertised aggressively, offered machines on time payment plans, and designed fashionable tables and cases to hold the machines.

By the 1880s Singer's sales force could move thousands of machines every week; his factories, employing armies of highly skilled artisans, still could not make machines as fast as Singer could sell them. The company turned, somewhat reluctantly, to machine production, convinced that machine tools could never produce the fine fit they strove for. In point of fact, they were correct.

Die-forging and milling by the finest machine tools available continued to require finishing by hand filing.[23] A factory manager could have each piece filed precisely to gauge and achieve true interchangeability, which had the advantage of insuring that repair parts would fit even without the attention of a highly skilled fitter equipped with a set of hand files. Or he could have machine-made, nearly uniform parts filed, fitted, and assembled into a finished machine

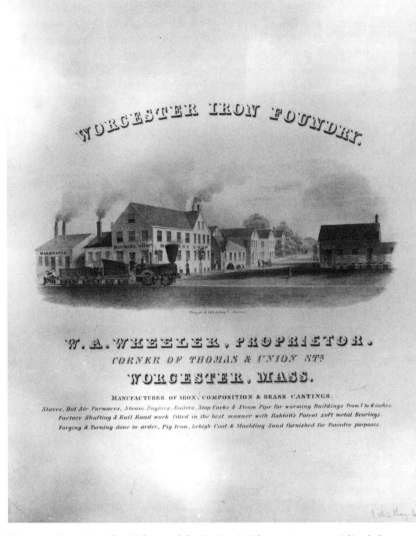

Worcester Iron Foundry. Lithograph by Benjamin Thayer. An unspecialized shop typical of the early industrial era, the Worcester Iron Foundry, operating from a collection of small buildings alongside the Boston and Albany main line, offered everything from retail pig iron and coal to domestic stoves, brass fittings, and complete steam engines.

Courtesy, American Antiquarian Society.

virtually, though not interchangeably, identical to every other machine. A third alternative was to take the nearly identical machine-made parts and assemble them into a machine equipped with an final adjustment mechanism that would compensate for any slight variance in part size, like Eli Terry's clocks. Manufacturers of typewriters chose this alternative. What a manufacturer could not do was make perfectly interchangeable parts entirely by machine. Machine tools continued to improve by steady increment until, around 1915, Ford Motor Company could turn out engines with perfectly interchangeable, wholly machine-made parts.[24] Ford's achievement, which came exactly a century after Eli Terry first exploited the potential of mass-production by machine-made interchangeable parts, came in a nation where machine production in immense factories was normal, and workshops like the one where Thomas Blanchard invented the irregular-turning lathe had become venerable antiques, displayed to tourists driving through country villages in search of quaintness and charm.[25] Nowhere was this change more dramatic than in New England, where a countryside of field and pasture had been transformed into a landscape of mill towns and cities, a transformation crafted by machine tool and arms industries that led the world in precision manufacturing.

Chapter 11

Acres Cleared and Drained

✣

When a man is obliged to maintain a family on a small farm, his invention is exercised to find out every improvement that may render it more productive. This appears to be the great reason why the lands on the Delaware and the Connecticut rivers produce to any farmer twice as much clear profit as lands in equal quantity and of the same quality upon the Hudson.[1]
—Jedediah Morse, 1784

THERE WAS NOTHING IN THE APPEARANCE OF Samuel Slater's mill to arrest the attention of passersby. The modest clapboard building looked like one of many small mills grinding corn and sawing logs beside streams draining a countryside where most people worked on farms. Ours had been a world where most people worked on farms since the Neolithic revolution and, in 1793, it was only reasonable to expect that it always would be. But in the brief half-century between the building of Slater's mill and the day in 1841 when the Western Railroad reached Albany, the immemorial round of seedtime and harvest that had dominated human life since grain and livestock were first domesticated, ceased to rule the lives of men and women in New England. Henceforth, work schedules would be regulated by a factory whistle and food would come from distant fields that those who ate it never plowed.[2]

The year New England was linked to western cornfields by rail, 1841, was the year that saw more Massachusetts workers employed in manufacturing than in farming. Less than a third of the working population of the commonwealth labored on farms that year, somewhere between a third and a half worked in manufacturing, with the remainder distributed among fishing, paid domestic work, the professions, transportation, and commerce.[3] So it is a wonderful paradox that this period of unprecedented industrialization was the heyday of Yankee agriculture, as farmers who once spread labor thinly on acres stretching toward an endless horizon, found that it paid to pour labor into smaller farms growing potatoes, eggs, and wool for the mill towns. Especially wool.

Slater Mill. This view of Slater Mill shows how easily the pioneering factory fit in among the other small, wood-frame buildings of Pawtucket Village. The original building, topped by a cupola, was even smaller; the ell was an additon. Courtesy of Slater Mill Historic Site.

Sheep have two great virtues. Their fleece is a high-value, nonperishable, low-weight product; a rare boon for remote farms. And they eat almost anything, which means that they can be raised on land too poor to grow crops or pasture cows. Remote, rocky, steep, unfertile farms could produce and sell wool at a profit.

For early settlers, the trick was not to find fancy breeds with a silky, high-priced fleece, it was to keep the sheep from being eaten by wolves. For this reason, seventeenth-century sheep farming was concentrated on islands and peninsulas protected from the threat of wolves, mountain lions, and bear. As settlement spread, these predators were eliminated by determined hunting and by habitat destruction so successful that eighteenth-century farmers in every part of New England could keep a few sheep, eat the mutton, and spin the wool for family use, without worrying about wolves. The desirable sheep of the pre-industrial era was a sturdy model that gave a fair clip of medium-grade wool, and produced a fair volume of good-enough mutton.

The sheep boom of the 1830s and 1840s was farming of a different order. It began after David Humphreys, United States Minister to Spain, brought seventy-five Merino ewes and twenty-five rams home to Connecticut in 1802, and William Jarvis, consul at Lisbon, shipped two hundred Merino rams and

three hundred ewes to his Weathersfield, Vermont farm in 1811.[4] Merinos produce fine, long-staple wool and stringy mutton, but mutton was of little interest to market-oriented farmers making good money on fleece. Wool mills rapidly became a major industry, paying well for all the high-quality, long-staple
wool farmers could supply. Sheep grazed high-quality flatlands remote from
transportation and markets, but it was in the thin-soiled hill country that sheep
farming changed the face of the land.

The Appalachian Mountains run through western Connecticut and Massachusetts, up the spine of Vermont, across the center of New Hampshire, and
into the heart of Maine; and Appalachian slopes were cleared by land-hungry
Yankees long before Merino sheep came to Connecticut. Those pioneer hill
farmers scratched a living from steep, thin-soiled fields by producing virtually
everything they ate, wore, or used—and by not eating well, dressing richly, or
using much. It was the Merino that made mountain farms profitable.

At the height of the Merino boom, well-financed farmers bought out their
hand-to-mouth neighbors. The hardscrabble hill farms, many only a generation old with a few acres of field and pasture scattered over steeply wooded hillsides, were cleared of trees to open land for pasture up the slopes and over the
tops of the Berkshires and the Green Mountains. Sheep were pastured on steep
slopes with little regard for the quantity of topsoil that washed down moun-
tainsides where grazing Merinos were turning meager soil into golden fleece. [5]

But sheep were not the only culprits. Farms of all kinds lost topsoil that had
taken thousands of years to create. Forest clearance, plowing, and grazing on
slopes as gentle as 10 per cent can cause substantial quantities of topsoil to slide
downhill, and few Yankee hill pastures sloped as little as 10 per cent. Hikers in
wooded regions can still see evidence of soil erosion where stone walls mark the
boundaries of hillside fields and eroded topsoil is banked many inches deep on
the uphill side of the wall.[6] Agricultural reformers urged contour plowing, but
reformers urge many things. When farmers tuned in to a single strain amid the
cacophony of proffered advice, it was to a voice that offered immediate profit.
In the 1830s, they heard voices sing the praises of Merino fleece, and cleared
forests to graze sheep.

Topsoil washing off the land in spring freshets flowed seaward, with predictable consequences. The tiny Saugus River flowing through the section of Lynn,
Massachusetts, that is now the town of Saugus, was just deep enough at high
tide to float a small, fully loaded ship when the first ironworks in America was
built in 1647, near the bridge carrying the main road between Boston and
Salem. A seventeenth-century ironworks consumed vast quantities of charcoal,
and among the chief attractions of the Saugus site were the acres of nearby virgin forest held as commons by the town of Lynn. The site's other attractions
were bog-iron-producing wetlands, proximity to Boston, and the small but
navigable Saugus River for power and transportation.[7]

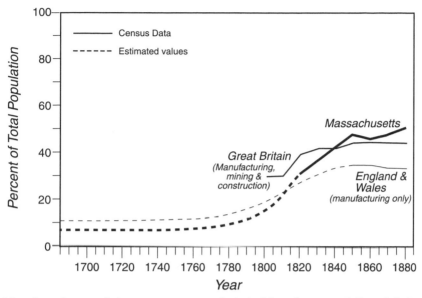

Manufacturing population as a percentage of whole, Massachusetts and Great Britain, 1685–1885. Graph from Carl Siracusa, "Manufacturing Population as Percentage of Whole, Great Britain and Massachusetts, 1685–1885," *A Mechanical People: Perceptions of the Industrial Order in Massachusetts, 1815–1880* (Middletown, Conn.: Wesleyan University Press, 1979). Numbers are derived from census data carefully discussed in Siracusa's appendix A. By permission of University Press of New England.

Charcoal was made by stacking cut hardwood around a central post in mounds ten to fourteen feet high and thirty to forty feet across, packed so precisely that no chinks or gaps were left between the logs. The entire mound was then covered with sod or damp leaves, then covered again with a layer of charcoal dust. Finally, the central post, or chimney, was removed, the hole filled with wood chips, the chips ignited, and the hole stopped with a plug. For about twelve hours the heap smoldered safely and the collier slept. Then the real work began.

Burning a heap of wood to ashes is simple; charring one was a tricky business entailing five or six days of smoldering, followed by two or three days cooling. Fire, which could destroy a season's hard labor in an hour, was only one of many threats. Gas explosions or severe windstorms might cause uneven charring, or blow off the covering, igniting the pile. Wind damage was a danger no matter how carefully a collier worked. No site could be sheltered well enough to protect it completely from sudden storms. "Soft" spots where the wood was burning rather than charring could develop rapidly, threatening the whole. The only way to test for these was to jump up and down on the smoldering pile.

When a soft spot was discovered, the covering was pulled off, the burning wood repacked or replaced with fresh logs, and the covering replaced. At any point in this operation, the wood might ignite, burning the collier.

A pile not charring properly needed to have draft holes opened, either by re-stacking sections of wood or by prodding with a long stake. Too much draft, and the whole pile might burst into flame. When an experienced eye, the set-tling of the pile, and the color of the smoke told the collier that charring was complete, cooling began, a process as delicate as charring, since strong drafts could ignite the finished charcoal even as it was being loaded into wagons. Dur-ing the long days of charring, cooling, and loading, colliers slept only at the risk of having all their labor destroyed by a sudden conflagration they were not awake to stop.

Skilled colliers demanded high wages for the grueling, life-threatening work; even local farmers willing to cut and haul cord wood in the winter demanded payment in cash. About 1650, ironworks managers seeking an alternative to paying high wages in a labor-short economy focused on Scotland, where clans-men had flocked to fight under the banners of Charles I—and lost. Sixty Scots prisoners from the battle of Dunbar were purchased as indentured servants by the ironworks, which realized substantial savings as the Scots took over the wood cutting. Some eventually became colliers. We cannot know how the Scots prisoners felt about their destiny; we do know that many of them lived to work off their indentures and become respectable members of the community, and we know that a labor-short industry will find means to supply its want—even if the laborers must arrive in chains.

An acre of virgin forest produced about forty cords of firewood. One cord made forty bushels of coal. Two hundred and sixty-five bushels of charcoal were required to make a ton of iron in Saugus' great blast furnace. In 1655, the blast furnace seems to have produced about three hundred tons of iron, but the enterprise was headed for failure. Poor management, insufficient capital, high labor costs, and a clouded title that frightened off prospective investors doomed the ambitious enterprise. Arguably, the Saugus blast furnace and slit-ting mills—cutting-edge technology in the mid-1600s—were conceived on too grand a scale for the infant colonial economy to support. Certainly, several of the skilled workmen who left Saugus were able to start small, comparatively primitive, but successful bloomery ironworks. Equally certain is the fact that extensive land clearance for charcoal production combined with nearby land clearance for farming to pour silt into the Saugus River until it was no longer navigable, not even by the diminutive commercial vessels of the era. Cheap transportation was one of the criteria the ironworks founders had specified when they chose Saugus. Now, a forced choice between high-priced land cart-age or expensive channel dredging added to the financial calculus that closed the ironworks.

Charcoal burners at the foot of Mount Agamenticus, Maine. Photograph by Emma Coleman, 1884. The finest charcoal was made in kilns, but kilns require capital to build. Making charcoal in old-fashioned pits was a poor man's employment. The superior fire produced by charcoal insured a continued demand for use in smelting and forges even after large-scale iron production had switched to fossil coal. Maine and New Hampshire had large charcoal industries into the early twentieth century. Courtesy of the Society for the Preservation of New England Antiquities (neg. # 7876-A).

A similar fate befell the Mill River in Freeport, Maine, a town that once shipped towering pine logs to England from its aptly named Mast Landing. Forest clearance washed silt downhill, extending the salt marshes at the river's mouth. Today, the old Mast Landing is a mile from saltwater. It is a story that can be told of many small landings, and, possibly, even of a harbor as important as Salem, which once had a commercial fleet so large and enterprising that traders in Sumatra and Zanzibar assumed that Salem was the name of an important and independent nation.

Salem declined as a major, international seaport because old-style merchant shipping disappeared in a modernizing economy, and because railroads shifted commercial dominance to Boston and New York, not because silt made the harbor too shallow for ocean-going ships. But if the world had not changed, Salem would still have been forced from the list of major seaports, because its harbor silted up. Salem's harbor was never deep; the "rivers" that flow into it are mere tide-marsh creeks. But the always shallow harbor was made shallower by accumulating silt, although the pattern of siltation is not as linear as it is at Mast Landing or on the Saugus River. In Salem, silt not only accumulated, it moved. Where Derby Wharf reaches seaward from the nineteenth-century customs house in which Nathaniel Hawthorne served as clerk, a low-lying section of land called Foote's Point disappeared during a storm in 1690, and did not reaccumulate in subsequent years, indicating that patterns of sediment deposition may have been altered by settlement. It may be that water currents changed after the South River was dammed to power a mill, or changed again when the river was filled to create land. Further changes in flow came as a causeway was constructed to Winter Island, and as salt marshes fringing the town were filled for building lots and wharves, altering tidal flow. Whatever the precise sequence of shifting mudflats was, the silt that washed off fields to fill Salem's harbor was available because the land had been cleared.[8]

Topsoil was washing off fields everywhere, and where conditions were right, a few years of farming could eliminate the topsoil completely. In the areas now known as the "desert" of Maine and the "sand barrens" of North Haven, Connecticut, glaciation left vast acres of sand that millennia of plant life had barely managed to spread with a thin frosting of topsoil. Pine thrives on these well-drained soils and the land may have looked fertile enough to early farmers. Once the pine forest was cleared and the land plowed, however, a single heavy rain or wind storm was able to strip the scant topsoil rapidly from a small area. Farmers termed these bare patches "blowouts." The problem was that they tended to spread. Exposed to wind, the loose sand piled up in dunes that "walked" across the landscape, burying fields and woodlots in their path. One family turned their southern Maine "desert" into a tourist attraction; the land was ruined for farming.

The problem was most dramatic on Cape Cod and along the shore of Massachusetts Bay, where much of the sandy soil of the glacial outwash plain was covered by a scrub forest of pitch pine and bear oak. English settlers had no intention of farming sand, but they cut firewood, and they turned cattle out to graze the grassy dunes near their farms, then watched in horror as the denuded sands "walked" over richer lands, burying cultivated fields and fences. Town statutes forbidding the grazing of cattle on sand dunes were powerless to stop the march, once the stabilizing grasses had been destroyed.[9]

Dennis, Massachusetts, on Cape Cod, created desert out of forest more deliberately than most towns in the furnaces of its thriving lampblack industry, where resinous knots of pitch pine were burned for the copious smoke they produced. Soot scraped from the specially constructed chimneys, or "funns" as they were known locally, was shipped to Boston and made into paint and printer's ink.[10] Denuded of pine by this profitable industry, dunes "walked" over the town; but the people of Dennis had turned to pine-burning only in desperation.

Although most of New England reached an agricultural maximum in the early nineteenth century, generations of farming with too much wind, too much sand, and too little ground cover to stay erosion had combined with overgrazed

New Hampshire Iron Factory Company, stock certificate, 1805. A small
river curls down a New Hampshire mountainside to turn the water wheel
that powers the iron foundry depicted on this stock certificate. The picture
may or may not depict an actual foundry: the same drawing appeared on a
stock certificate for a Salem, Massachusetts foundry, a few years later, with
the mountains gone and a harbor in their place. Although the great iron
ore deposits are located elsewhere on this continent, numerous small Yankee mines and foundries supplied the demand for iron at the dawn of the
industrial age. Courtesy, American Antiquarian Society.

dunes and overcut forests to reduce to sterility the once-productive land on
Cape Cod and the mainland shore of Massachusetts Bay. Eastham, for example,
was so fertile at settlement that the Plymouth Colony gave serious consideration to moving its seat of government there, to be where the best land was. By
the time of the census of 1791, walking dunes had covered Eastham's once-
renowned wheatfields and a mere 1.8 per cent of the land was cultivated.[11]

Patches of "desert" were rare, however. Most of New England was covered
with topsoil, not sand dunes; but every year there was less topsoil than there
had been the year before. Soils that required millennia to create were dimin-
ished as precious inches washed away from land less able with every rainstorm
to sustain life. But there was money in sheep. There was money in hay, apples,
firewood, and everything else a farm could produce, so land was cleared for
production.

Profits grew and land use intensified as railroads shrank the distance from
farm to market. Before rails were laid, fresh milk for the Boston market could
come from towns about as far from the city as Lexington: milk wagons on their
way to Boston market before dawn met the British troops on the road to Concord. Fresh fruit and vegetables could travel about the same distance as fresh
milk, and hay only slightly farther. Hay does not spoil, but it is of such low value

relative to its bulk that the cost of carting quickly becomes prohibitive, except where it can be freighted by water (hay for the Boston market came from islands far down the coast of Maine, where farmers turned to it as a cash crop as soon as they had clear-cut and sold the woods). But just as not every farmer can live near a market town, not every farm can be on an island. Inland farmers voted for railroad bonds. Cheap, fast rail transportation raised the value of farm produce, intensifying land use across the region and creating a direct market for one crop.

Cordwood, like hay, rose in value with the advent of cheap transportation to city markets. But the cordwood market also came right to the farmers' door, as huge volumes of wood were converted to energy in locomotive fireboxes. The Boston and Worcester operated nine locomotives in 1836 and burned 2,687 cords of firewood.[12] Nor did railroad consumption of wood stop at the woodbox; the locomotive, the cars, the bridges, stations, and watertanks—even the tracks were made of wood. Not just the ties, but even the rails themselves in early lines were made of wooden beams capped with iron. Even the bed on which the rails were laid was sometimes built of wooden blocks.

A hiker at the top of Mount Monadnock in the southwestern corner of New Hampshire today climbs through woods to a view of forest-covered hills. On the way to the summit, the curious may wonder that farmers troubled to build stone walls on slopes so high, so steep, and so heavily forested. But a century and a half ago, hikers on the same trails climbed through fenced pastures to a pinnacle from which they could look in every direction and see cleared fields and pasture, punctuated with but an occasional woodlot or orchard. The heights of the White Mountains were still forested and the woods of northern Maine were untouched, almost unvisited; the rest of New England was farmland.

It was possible to find a deer or a moose in New England of the 1850s, but only by traveling to remote and mountainous areas. Nineteenth-century Yankees were about as likely to see a deer as residents of modern Hartford are to happen upon a draft horse.

Prime game animals were hunted to the vanishing point within a few years of settlement, then prevented by lack of habitat from repopulating. In a land of fields and fences, where even the diminishing acreage devoted to woodlots was widely scattered, there was no place for large wild animals. Even small wild creatures were scarce. Wild turkeys, which require forests of mature, nut-bearing trees and reach their northern limit in the middle of Vermont, vanished completely. Populations of groundhogs and raccoons were kept in check by hunting, trapping, and, most tellingly, by farm dogs prized for their skill at ridding the fields of vermin. Mink, river otter, and muskrats were assiduously trapped for the value of their pelts. Animals that threatened livestock were hunted even more aggressively.

I was quite young when I learned that General Israel Putnam killed the last wolf in Connecticut. This bit of trivia is the only fact I remember being taught about General Putnam, and it was a puzzling thing to teach children in suburban Connecticut in the 1960s, since wolves were not a significant threat. The fact that we learned about them shows how real a threat they were in the 1740s, when Israel Putnam was young. Killing a wolf certified Putnam as the hero who made Connecticut safe for the milch cow.

Bounties certified wolves, rattlesnakes, and mountain lions as threats to the farm economy deserving of the death penalty. The last rattlesnake in Norwich, Connecticut, was killed in 1786, ending a bounty era that peaked in 1738 when the Norwich selectmen paid the ten-shilling bounty on seventy-eight rattlesnakes.[13] The last mountain lion in Vermont was killed by Alexander Crowell near the town of Barnard in 1881. The 182-pound animal (seven feet long, nose to tail) stands alongside the gun that killed it at the state historical museum in Montpelier.

Wolves, bears, rattlesnakes, and mountain lions were the target of effective eradication campaigns. Governments paid bounties, towns organized hunts of up to a hundred men to comb barrens where predators might hide, organized parties of citizens burned cedar swamps and mountain ravines to flush wolves and deny them refuge. It is thought that the alpine flora that charms hikers at the top of Mount Monadnock is the result of the burning of the original forest by farmers eager to eliminate wolf habitat, followed by erosion of topsoil from the burned-over area that has prevented the forest from growing back. Monadnock is too low and too far south to have alpine vegetation without the assistance of wolf hunters.

Those efforts succeeded. By the 1850s, large predators were a fading memory in settled farming areas. By the century's end, logging and hunting would insure that not even the mountain fastnesses harbored wolves, mountain lions, or wolverines. Lynx, fisher, and bobcat were harried almost to the vanishing point. A remnant population of black bear hung on in remote woodlands.

Overall, the amount of wildlife in New England declined as farming spread, although the change from woodland to field and pasture sometimes led not simply to decline, but to shifts in animal population. Wood warblers became less common as land was cleared, but numbers of meadow-dwelling bluebirds, bobolinks, and meadow larks reached new heights. Most forest-dwelling birds survived the tide of forest clearance, retreating to forest remnants in reduced numbers; the passenger pigeon was not so fortunate.

Passenger pigeons fed, roosted, traveled, and nested in flocks so large that an observer could stand beneath a flight "seeing neither beginning nor ending, length or breadth of these millions and millions,"[14] of birds so dense that they truly darkened the sky. The largest recorded nesting colony covered 850 square miles. From time immemorial they had flown over a forested continent, de-

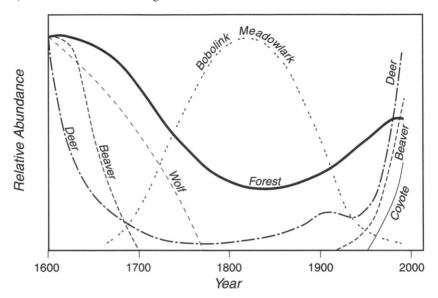

Species abundance in Massachusetts. Species abundance has varied with forest cover: Hunting and the clearing of land for farms virtually eliminated deer, but also gave rise to large populations of bobolink and meadowlarks that nest in hayfields. The return of prey species that thrive in our regrown forests has also brought back predator species, but in place of the wolves that were eating winter-weakened deer when the first settlers landed, New England forests now harbor large coyote populations. John F. O'Keefe and David R. Foster, "An Ecological History of Massachusetts Forests," in *Stepping Back to Look Forward: A History of the Massachusetts Forest*, ed. Charles H. W. Foster (Cambridge: Harvard University Press for Harvard Forest, 1998). By permission.

scending to strip the trees of nuts, seeds, and berries, their savory flesh and immense numbers a boon to market hunters, who trapped them by the thousand for sale at three pence the dozen in 1725. By 1800, the price had risen to a shilling six pence. By 1850, prices were expressed in American currency and scarcity had raised the price of a dozen pigeons to one dollar. The last game market pigeons, rare delicacies that last appeared at market in 1885, fetched six dollars the dozen. The last recorded breeding of passenger pigeons in New England was at Plymouth in 1889. A few birds eluded the commercial carnage, surviving into the twentieth century protected from hunting, but in numbers so reduced that mere handsful gathered to roost in scattered remnants of mature beech forest.

Passenger pigeons were easy targets for predators and hunters who pursued them with guns, and, more profitably, with traps. A popular technique was to sew the eyelids of a live pigeon shut, tie it to a stick, and scatter corn on the ground. Hidden nearby, the pigeoner watched for a flock to come near, then pulled a string to lower the stick, causing the captive bird to flutter like a wild bird coming to ground. When the flock alighted, lured by the stool pigeon, a tug on another string lowered a net that might trap hundreds of pigeons at a time.

Etymologists describe *stool* as an archaic term for both the decoy itself and the stick or frame to which it was tied. By whatever etymology, pigeons were easy prey—as easy for foxes and hawks as for humans. Their natural defense lay in numbers. Raccoons might steal the eggs and owls feast on the young, but no forest harbored enough predators to decimate a flock numbering in the millions. Once the magnificent flocks were reduced to a few dozen individuals, a lone skunk with a fancy for pigeon eggs could easily eat every egg in the woods. Then there were none.

Settlement had spread from the richest river valleys to thin-soiled mountain slopes as land hunger drove the young to seek a living; new pressures cleared the swamps and the woodlots. Mill towns and the growing industrial cities were insatiable. All the fruits and all the vegetables, all the milk, butter, and cheese, all the firewood, all the hay, all the meat, and all the potatoes Yankee farms could produce, Yankee cities bought at good prices. Prices good enough to make it profitable to pour fertilizer onto the land and bring marginal land into production.

Better markets made it profitable for farmers to separate the common flocks that once grazed on town lands and pen animals in individual pastures. This allowed the husbandman to fertilize a field with a herd's valuable dung, but it also guarded increasingly valuable cows and ewes from random encounters with stud of unknown antecedents. Deliberate breeding by prize rams and bulls was the imperative of the hour in the decades following independence; stone fences were the method. While many fences were built simply to clear a plowing field of stones, others were designed to allow the farmer to manage cattle. The irony was that when the profit center in Yankee farming shifted from sheep to hay in the second half of the nineteenth century, massive stone walls that had the fenced in small fields to make livestock farming profitable became obstacles to the efficient use of the mechanical mower. Some Yankee farmers buried miles of stone walls as they converted small fields into large fields that mechanical mowers could cut in long, broad swaths, but not all farmers were able to make the transition from hand mowing to mechanical harvesting.

New England's hilly landscape, laced with streams and sprinkled with swamps, lent itself well to small-field agriculture. Farmers working on foot and by hand could work their land efficiently: that ribbon-shaped field on a gentle slope planted to corn; this small, wedge-shaped patch a rich mowing field. Men mowing by hand could cut a small, irregularly shaped patch as efficiently as a large, rectangular one. Mechanization changed the equation. Even after mechanical reapers appeared that could handle rolling ground, they could be operated profitably only in large fields. Many Yankee farms, bisected by streams,

"Netting wild pigeons in New England." Hunters waiting in the blind have scattered corn on the ground under the trees where passenger pigeons roost. When enough pigeons have settled to feed on the corn, the hunters will pull the trigger rope, releasing a net that will trap hundreds of pigeons to supply big city game markets. *Frank Leslie's Illustrated Weekly,* Sept. 21, 1867, page 8. Courtesy, American Antiquarian Society.

hills, and swamps, could not consolidate scattered patches of arable land into large, regularly shaped fields. Farms with good soil, good markets, and long growing seasons foundered over the inability of mechanical equipment to harvest the patchwork of small, irregularly shaped, Yankee fields. When this republic was young, however, small fields were profit centers, and Yankee farmers eagerly walled their pastures, orchards, and cornfields.

The memorials to that era of farm profit stand in the woods of New England: miles of stone walls fencing ghost sheep in pastures that returned to forest decades ago; overgrown tangles of lilac that once bloomed in dooryards of houses long vanished; cellar holes with hundred-year-old oak trees growing through the stones. But the era of profitable farming also left memorials in landscapes it erased. The wet meadows, maple swamps, and bogs that dotted many farms had always been considered waste. Even the land hunger of the late 1700s left marshes and swamps untouched, except for wood cutting. High produce prices of the factory era made drainage pay for the first time.

Cutting down trees to make farmland was a simple process: clear a forest, create a field. From time to time, however, the land surprised the farmer. Trees would be cut on a perfectly ordinary tract of dry woodland and, instead of a dry field, the farmer would be left with a wet meadow. The uncleared land had looked little different from nearby woodland, but underground, unseen and unsuspected, impermeable bedrock lay closer to the surface, or a seemingly insignificant dip in elevation lowered the new field almost to the level of the groundwater table. In either case, trees drew moisture from the soil, creating dry ground as long as the forest cover remained. Cleared of trees, water stood on the land. When woodland cleared for the plow turned into wet meadow, the colonial farmer shrugged—perhaps cursed—relegated the soggy acreage to pasture, and cleared a new field. Wet meadows also occurred naturally, especially at the margins of rivers that flood.

As the price of hay went up, farmers surveyed their wet meadows with a new eye. Unimproved wet meadow yielded about three-quarters of a ton per acre of inferior hay. Drained, the same acre could yield a ton of timothy, alfalfa, or clover. Drained and fertilized, the same acre might yield a ton and a half. Farmers like Thomas Ward of Shrewsbury, Massachusetts, responded to the economic logic of the situation. In 1831, Ward had forty-eight acres of fresh meadow and forty-two of upland mowing. By 1865 he had drained his wet meadows until the forty-eight acres were reduced to seven, presumably situated in such a way that drainage was not feasible. This remnant he fertilized and cultivated to increase output to one ton per acre. He was also getting a ton and a half per acre on sixty-two acres of fertilized and seeded upland hay.[15] The economic logic of draining wet meadows was reinforced by the fact that muck dug from drainage channels was valuable fertilizer, and the digging could be done at times of the year when labor was cheap and demands on the farmer's time light.[16]

Wooded swamps had long been more profitably left as woodlots than cleared for farming, but the economics of woodlots changed as completely as the economics of wet meadows. New England heated and cooked with wood, and the mill villages springing up in every town made cordwood a lucrative cash crop even for farmers remote from city markets. A farmer's limited acreage produced better returns as pasture, mowing, or tillage than as woodlot—even if the woodlot was swampy enough to require drainage in addition to clearing. In Concord, Massachusetts, an old-settled town, 80 percent of the land was cleared for farming by 1771, when population pressure on the land was at its peak. In 1840, when rail transportation made cordwood, hay, and fresh milk so profitable that economic demand for agricultural land reached its zenith, 90 percent of the land was cleared.[17]

Waste is an economic judgment. Land overgrown with buttonbush and covered by standing water half the year is waste. It would not be waste if buttonbushs grew buttons. They don't. Only worthless, button-shaped flowers. The scraggly bushes are messy looking, too. Untidy beards of fountain moss hang

VIEW OF MEADOWS ON NEPONSET RIVER LOOKING SOUTHWEST FROM NEPONSET STREET IN NORWOOD.   (Before improvement.)

View of meadows on Neponset River, before and after "improvement." (Looking south-west from Neponset Street in Norwood.) Draining marshes and wet meadows, whether for agriculture or building lots, eliminated a richly productive aquatic habitat and increased the probablility of destructive floods. Commonwealth of Massachusetts State Department of Health, *Report upon the Protection of the Public Health in the Valley of the Neponset River* (Boston: State Printer, 1916), between pages 16 and 18.

VIEW OF MEADOWS ON NEPONSET RIVER LOOKING SOUTHWEST FROM NEPONSET STREET IN NORWOOD.   (After improvement.)
Approximately the same quantity of water flowing as in previous view

from the branches. In spring floods, tadpoles, fish fry, and salamander larvae dart between the dangling wisps of moss to hunt water fleas and copepods, and to escape the jaws of a hungry spotted turtle. As the land dries with changing seasons, fountain moss hangs in ugly, blackened masses, good only for stuffing the chinks in a log house, not even good for that if the householder is prosperous enough to build a proper house. Such a piece of sodden wasteland can be improved by ditching and draining, turned into an income-generating resource. Of course, the improved land will no longer produce wood frogs, spotted salamanders, and bog turtles. This was one of the hallmarks of improvement. "In draining a marsh, we add to the available surface of the world. Much of the soil of New England is undrained, cold, unproductive, wet, insoluble. But these marshes are magazines of humus; rich mines which the rivulets have carried there from the decaying leaves of centuries of vegetation, rich as the most fertile soil of the West, but now the abode of reptiles."[18] Economic calculus favored alfalfa over reptiles. And it favored timothy over salt marshes.

Spartina patens, salt marsh hay, was among the earliest resources harvested by English settlers, and it continued to be harvested from natural marshes into the twentieth century. Planted by nature and fertilized by the tide, hay could be had for only the labor of mowing. But as growing cities bid up the price of hay, farmers looked for ways of making a good thing better. That could be done by draining saltwater from the upper marsh to convert the land to higher-priced fresh hay. The process required ditching for even drainage and erecting tidegates—hinged doors that allow rainwater and seepage to drain with an out-flowing tide, but swing shut against inrushing saltwater. Ditching paid for itself in cartloads of fertile muck. Even on marshes kept in salt hay, farmers found it profitable to ditch for even tidal flow and to improve yields by shoveling the muck to fill low places where water pooled.[19]

Converting salt marsh to fresh mowing reduced habitat for shore-bird populations, a matter of little import. The birds that were good to eat had long ago been hunted to the vanishing point, while the fate of sharp-tailed sparrows and long-billed marsh wrens affected nobody's bottom line.

A third wetland type, bogs, form in cool, rainy places where the drainage is poor. If drainage were good, if streams flowed in and rivers flowed out, the pool of water in question would be a marsh or a lake. It is a bog when rainwater collects with no outlet. The still waters of bogs are oxygen-poor, and since rainwater flows through no mineral soil en route to the bog, the mineral content approaches zero. Bogs are so oxygen-poor that plant material hardly decomposes; leaf, stem, and branch fallen in a bog are preserved almost as they fall, accumulating in thick layers of highly acidic material known as peat. After eons pass, the peat becomes coal.

Most plants and animals find the acidic, nutrient-poor, oxygen-deprived conditions of a peat bog forbidding, but empty niches in the ecological web

View of the Plum Island salt marshes. Hay was stacked on wooden pilings called "staddles," built high enough to keep it above water even during a spring tide. It was moved to the barn in large, flat-bottom wooden boats called gundalows poled across the marsh at high tide. Courtesy of Historical Society of Old Newbury.

always attract occupants, and a remarkable array of living things have adapted to the unique conditions of bog life. Carnivorous plants are the most notorious—pitcher plants, sundews, and bladderworts, which compensate for the nutritional deficiencies of bog life by attracting, trapping, and digesting passing insects—but there are others. The bog is a beautiful place of rare orchids and glossy-leafed evergreens fringed with feathery spires of tamarack and spruce.

As plants begin to grow around the edge of a bog, they form a mat of roots, sphagnum mosses, and partially decomposed leaves that actually floats over silent water stained dark by humic acid. Stepping onto such a mat, the visitor stands on ground that quakes underfoot as the impact of a step makes waves in the water below.

Sphagnum moss and peat are harvested from a few boglands in Maine, but it is the cranberry that has drawn the greatest human attention to New England's bogs. Massachusetts farmers had long been aware of cranberries growing wild on local bogs; in the early-nineteenth-century drive to make the land produce more, Cape Cod farmers began to experiment with ways to reap these profitless lands by encouraging the growth of cranberries. It was not a simple process. Farmers had to discover the secrets of propagating, transplanting, and cultivating a wild plant. They learned to improve bog conditions with the right increment of sand, to supply the correct amounts of water, and to protect the ripening fruit from early autumn frosts by flooding the bogs. By the 1850s, hundreds of acres in southeastern Massachusetts were devoted to cranberries. It was an unusual farming enterprise, because cranberries paid so well that it was profitable to convert suitably located dry land into wetland.[20]

Cranberry growing is among the kinds of farming most congenial with the need to allow space for wild things to flourish in unhampered diversity. Not that wild things flourish on the mats of growing fruit in carefully controlled bogs—these are strict, profit-ruled monocultures—but bogs need reservoirs of fresh water, and in the margins of reservoirs, channels, and cultivated bogs, wetland plants and animals flourish. But biodiversity was not a goal Yankee farmers recognized; productivity was.

Last winter, after a northeaster hit the coast, my sister and I took our children for a walk on the beach at Scituate. Beaches are interesting after a storm. We were looking for pelagic birds blown onto the land, and for sea creatures stranded in the mass of tangled rockweed that storm tides had strewn many inches deep on the beach. A century ago, storms were more than a boon to amateur naturalists: they were money disguised as uprooted seaweed.

Rockweed and kelp are potent soil amendments, free to any farmer willing to load them into a cart. Contemporary property owners view the debris-covered beach as neither profit center nor natural history treasure trove; for them it is an eyesore, and an expensive one at that. The direction of our walk that afternoon was determined by the presence of a bulldozer, noisily pushing the rich jumble of rockweed, starfish, and dying crabs into heaps a front-end loader could scoop into waiting dump trucks. Seaweed rots. Town maintenance crews knew they had better move the stuff before it started to smell. Front-end loaders are expensive, but it was worth it to the taxpayers to hire them. Ocean views over a clean, fresh-smelling beach are worth money. The losers in the process don't vote.

Rotting beach wrack is a noisome thing and not even the absence of a sense of smell can make it lovely. Step close to a mass of decomposing marine life and you will find the damp, half-rotted ocean weeds alive with maggots, a sight to warm the hearts only of those beach-cottage owners that dwell in depressions in the sand: curlews, plovers, pipers. Springtime rank with putrid kelp deposited in winter storms enables nesting pairs to raise healthy broods, but few homeowners of the taxpaying species will stand for the stench. We clean beaches to shield our sensibilities from nature. Two centuries ago, farmers raked seaweed after a storm to manure the fields.

Seaweed was free. Manure from a farmer's own animals and such waste as stalks from his own fields were also free, but no farm produced as much manure as its fields needed. Fertilizing was a financial decision, requiring the farmer to calculate the price of increasingly expensive manures against the probability of improved yields. Once the original fertility of virgin soil was gone, abandoning

Loading Kelp. Photograph by Emma Coleman, c.1885. The farmer loading kelp to fertilize his fields was a common sight on nineteenth-century New England beaches. Courtesy
of the Society for the Preservation of New England Antiquities (neg. #15520-B).

the soil or renewing its fertility with manure were the only choices. Importing
nitrates from guano islands in the South Pacific and mining the fertilizing
properties of industrial by-products ranging from banana peels and cotton
seed hulls to wool washings and manure collected from urban stables, New England farmers made the land pay.[21]

Until railroads crossed the Alleghenies, western land offered competition of
only a limited sort: grain grown in the deep, virgin soils of the Midwest could
be shipped east on the Erie Canal cheaper than it could be grown at home. But
fruit, vegetables, milk, sweet butter, and meat remained necessarily local products in the days before refrigeration. As did hay, which was too bulky to pay the
freight. Yankee farmers continued to be able to sell as much hay as they could
cut until Henry Ford and his horseless carriages spoiled the market. Other farm
products lost their market with the coming of the railroad.

Responding to market demand for meat in the rapidly growing cities, Yankee farmers imported Ohio corn by canal boat to feed increased herds through
the winter. When the railroad crossed the Alleghenies, they imported young
stock by railcar to fatten and send to market. Eventually, a pipeline of ready-
for-market western stock stepped into cattle cars in Ohio and Illinois for non-
stop rides to the Brighton and Cambridge slaughterhouses, and to be loaded,
live, on ships bound for England. New England farms could no longer compete
in meat production, but demand for fresh produce was high enough to keep
good land fully cultivated and profitable. Cities were growing; the amount of

land close enough to supply fresh eggs, milk, and strawberries was not. Yankee farmers prospered until refrigerated railcars changed the equation. The first carload of refrigerated meat left Chicago in 1881; shipments of vegetables followed within the decade, beginning the long decline of New England poultry, dairy, fruit, and vegetable farming. The abandonment of Yankee farms began with the collapse of the wool boom of the late 1840s, and reached a crescendo when the automobile ended the market for hay.

Plowing stopped first. Hayfields that would once have been planted to timothy or clover were allowed to grow what nature chose, with a few cows turned in to glean what they might. The cows ate the tender leaves of birch and aspen as they sprouted in the half-abandoned pastures; they did not fancy the taste of pine needles. Year by year the aging pasture grew more brambles and less clover until it was no longer worth the trouble of opening the barway to let cows in. At that moment, the old field ceased to be a pasture and began to be a forest—a very young forest, where pine rejected by finicky cows had a head start on other trees. On these worthless, abandoned hillsides, great forests of white pine began to grow, but there was no one to watch it happen. Fields, farms, entire villages stood empty as Yankees followed opportunity to the cities.

Chapter 12

Spinning Cotton into Gold

≥≤

Aqua currit et debet currere, ut currere solebat (Water flows and ought to flow as it has customarily flowed).

—British Common law principle

COTTON WAS NOT A NEW FABRIC WHEN TECH-niques for manufacturing it spun the Iindustrial Revolution into mo-tion. It was not exotic. It was not even rare. The bushy plant, each seed clinging to myriad delicate filaments, is designed for dispersal: the fibers built to catch the wind and loft embryonic cotton plants on voyages to new homes. Nor was the art of converting filament to fabric new. People the world around have known the use of cotton since ancient times. It was spun and woven into fine cloth by the Maya, Inca, Aztec, Chinese, Indians, and Arabs.

Indian cottons were among the riches Prince Henry the Navigator sent ships around Africa to obtain. Three centuries later, they were high on the list of east-ern goods that drew Salem ships to the far side of the globe. But cotton was a luxury. Mayan nobility wore it; the Mayans who laboriously planted, picked, and spun cotton, dressed in cloth made from coarse maguey fiber. European princesses had cotton gowns; common girls had wool. The problem was seeds.

Cotton is easy to grow, prolific, productive—far cheaper to raise than an equivalent volume of wool, linen, silk, or other natural fiber. But cotton seeds cling to their fibrous parachutes for dear life. Using the primitive roller gin called a churka in India, and a manganello in Italy and Spain, a worker could clean the seeds from ten pounds of cotton in a day, but the fibers produced would not make the finest-quality cloth. For that, the seeds had to be plucked free by hand. It is thought that a highly motivated worker could pluck the seeds from about two pounds of cotton in a working day; it is known that chattel slaves commonly separated the seeds from about a pound a day. In that day, cotton went from being the cheapest natural fiber to being one of the most expensive. But separat-ing seeds was only the most labor-consuming of several expensive processes.

Cotton bolls had to be picked from the plant one by one; a good man could pick fifty pounds a day; wherever their labor could be compelled, women and children picked too. After the cotton was picked and the seeds separated, it was baled and shipped to a spinner, who had to clean it of stray bits of leaf and debris, card the fiber, and laboriously spin it into thread. Spinning cotton, in addition to being more painstaking than spinning flax or wool, produced thread that varied in strength and fineness. The fifty pounds of bolls it had taken an entire day's labor to pick, and a prohibitive thirty to fifty working days to separate from the seeds, finally produced about four pounds of hand-spun cotton thread. In the mid-1700s, a pound of spun wool took less than two days of labor from sheep to thread. A pound of linen took from two to five, while a pound of silk required six. A single pound of cotton thread required up to fourteen days' labor.[1]

Plucking seeds was far and away the most expensive step in turning cotton into fabric, so it is odd that spinning, not separating seeds, was the first process to be mechanized. But seeds were separated from cotton in the Levant and the West Indies, before raw cotton was baled and shipped to England to be spun. Five or six spinners were kept steadily at their wheels to supply a single weaver at his loom; it would never have paid to spin cotton in a high-wage nation like England if there had not been a stiff tariff on the beautifully varied fabrics of India and the fine, luxury textiles and thread of the Middle East. The British cotton tariff is a wonderful illustration of irony in economic policy.

It is not by coincidence that the Lord Chancellor sits on a wool sack: wool made England rich. Wool was both England's leading industry and England's leading export from the twelfth century on. By the time of the Restoration, England was so rich that the upper classes had begun to purchase significant quantities of luxurious imported cotton. Wool interests responded by persuading Parliament, in 1700, to enact a tariff on cotton thread and cloth stiff enough to discourage ladies and gentlemen of means from wearing cotton. Instead of ending cotton imports as intended, the tariff created a new industry as merchants imported raw cotton, which was not subject to the tariff, and had it spun and woven in England. Members of Parliament rose to defend British woolens. They increased the tariff. But, unlike wool, cotton is soft, light, and washable. It was expensive, but England was rich. And cotton was the height of fashion. Not all the patriotic rhetoric in Westminster could stop fashion; certainly no tariff could. The tariff did, however, succeed in reducing the price of cotton.

In 1733 John Kay, woolen manufacturer, invented a device to throw the shuttle across a loom at the pull of a cord, freeing the weaver's hand to press home the weft. Kay's flying shuttle doubled a weaver's productivity. Wool weavers objected to a device capable of halving the numbers employed in their traditional trade; they rioted to thwart attempts to introduce the innovation.

COTTON CLEANING BEFORE THE INVENTION OF THE COTTON GIN.

COTTON GIN FROM THE WAREHOUSE OF C. V. MAPES.

Cleaning cotton before and after the invention of the cotton gin. The generation that witnessed the replacement of laborious methods of hand manufacture by the wonder machines of the Industrial Revolution experienced no nostalgia for the grinding stoop-labor of the olden days. Industrial progress was a palpable blessing. *Eighty Years of Progress of the United States: A Family Record of American Industry, Energy and Enterprise* (Hartford, Conn.: L. Stebbins Co., 1867), 113.

But cotton was a new industry, growing so fast that available labor could scarcely supply the demand for skilled spinners and weavers. Although John Kay died a penniless exile, his flying shuttle was widely adopted by cotton weavers in the 1750s.

Kay's flying shuttle doubled the productivity of each weaver; twelve spinners now labored to supply a single loom. Into this industry in 1764, James Hargreaves introduced his spinning jenny, a machine that enabled a single spinner simultaneously to produce eight cotton threads strong enough to be used for warp. Then Richard Arkwright invented a waterframe or water-powered spinning machine and, in 1770, built a mill at Nottingham where fifty unskilled operatives tended twenty-five hundred water-powered spindles producing thread too weak for use as warp, but excellent as weft. In 1779 Samuel Crompton's "mule" combined aspects of the first two inventions in a new, water-powered machine able to spin thread at once strong enough to serve as warp and fine enough to produce the finest grades of cloth. Kay doubled productivity; Hargreaves multiplied it by eight; Arkwright, by fifty.

It still took all day to separate the seeds from a pound of cotton. A little was grown in Georgia. Not much. Planters had more profitable uses for land and labor than a fiber that multiplied costs by clinging stubbornly to its seed. Georgians talked about cotton, but they didn't intend to plant much of it until someone found a profitable way to way to separate the seeds.

Eli Whitney was far from being the first man to tackle the problem of ginning cotton. The desirability of such an invention was well-known to planters who readily calculated the potential of a fiber that was easy to grow and in high demand. Southern planters, however, directed labor; they did not handle tools. Eli Whitney was not a southerner. He was a Massachusetts farmboy with a knack for mechanical tinkering. Young men of his station and inclinations built the trip-hammer shops and mills that spawned an industrial revolution. Whitney was different. Instead of starting a workshop, he entered Yale. Perhaps it was because his inclinations were intellectual as well as mechanical, but Whitney's career path may also have been a result of his age. Born on a Westborough, Massachusetts, farm in 1765, Whitney approached adulthood in the early 1780s, a period of economic doldrums throughout New England. In the hills of Worcester County, there was not yet even the first stirring of handicraft production for distant markets. It might as well have been 1680, as far as the range of opportunities Whitney could see in rural Westborough were concerned. His family was not wealthy enough to think of sending a son to college, but Whitney was a boy of extraordinary talents. He used them to prepare under a local minister, and in 1784 at the age of nineteen, quite old for the era, entered Yale.

Yale was filled then as it is today with children of privilege, and Whitney, with only intelligence to recommend him, is said to have been reserved and ill at ease among classmates blessed with the savoir faire of social position. He used his mechanical talents to pay for his education and is remembered for having repaired the mechanism of an astrolabe that the college had expected to ship to London for repair at a cost equal to a year's tuition. At graduation, in 1792, Whitney accepted a teaching job near Savannah, traveling south with the family of the widow of General Nathaniel Greene, and staying with the family while making arrangements to begin teaching. The teaching job fell through, but Whitney had put the idle weeks to good use.

Nathaniel Greene was not born a southern planter. He grew up in Rhode Island, helped manage the family iron foundry, and married the daughter of another prosperous Rhode Island family, Catherine Littlefield. Their plantation, Mulberry Grove, was a gift from the people of South Carolina in token of Greene's brilliant strategic command of the southern Continental Army, particularly at the Battle of Cowpens. The general's early death left his widow with five young children and a plantation as deeply in debt as southern plantations in the pre-cotton era commonly were. Mrs. Greene managed with the help of a

Yale-educated Yankee, Phineas Miller, hired by General Greene as a children's tutor, who stayed to serve as estate manager. Catherine Greene and Phineas Miller would marry in 1796.

Fortune had brought the Greenes to Savannah and established them in southern society, but a decade as chatelaine of a plantation could not make Catherine Greene southern enough to believe that a college graduate degraded himself by working with his hands. She encouraged Whitney to try to solve the ginning problem, supported him with hospitality and the use of a workshop, and when several weeks of labor produced a working model in the early spring of 1793, proudly invited the plantation owners who were both her friends and Whitney's prospective customers to view the machine. One or more of these gentlemen broke into the workshop at night and stole the model. Or, being gentlemen, they may have directed hired or enslaved hands to perform the physical labor of stealing the valuable machine.

It is an injustice and an irony that an invention may be too valuable for protection by patent law. Whitney and Miller obtained patents, formed a corporation, set up a Connecticut factory to manufacture gins, and spent most of their lives in patent infringement litigation that consumed Miller's modest fortune along with Catherine Greene's larger fortune, forced the sale of her plantation, and absorbed most of the proceeds from Whitney's arms contracts. The legislatures of South Carolina, North Carolina, and Tennessee eventually voted modest cash gifts to Whitney, but his lifetime income from the invention that made Dixie rich seems to have amounted to somewhat less than his legal fees.

Whitney's gin featured a crank that moved the cotton onto rotating, saw-toothed wheels, which pulled fiber through narrow wire slots, separating it from the seeds, which fell to the bottom. It was so elegant in its simplicity that any good mechanic could copy the model. Every mechanic in the South seems to have done so. American planters produced 3 million pounds of raw cotton, all separated from its seeds by hand, in 1792, the year Eli Whitney graduated from Yale. They planted and harvested 5 million pounds in 1793, when pirated copies of Whitney's gin were available to savvy planters near Savannah, and 8 million the year after that. Sixty million pounds were harvested in 1803, when Whitney's gin was ten years old, 1,650 million pounds in 1860.[2] Finding a Southern jury willing to convict in a cotton gin patent infringement suit was as easy as finding a southern plantation owner who picked his own cotton.

British cotton production soared as ginned cotton turned what had been a modestly profitable business into a spectacularly successful one, and Francis Cabot Lowell of Boston wanted a piece of it.

To be fair to Lowell, he was not merely greedy. In the decade and a half following graduation from Harvard, Lowell made a substantial fortune as a merchant shipper. Times were hard for merchant shipping during the embargo, would continue to be hard through Mr. Madison's War, and get really bad when

Britain reentered international trade after defeating France. But times are usually hard and Boston merchants would continue to make fortunes during Mr. Lowell's lifetime and after. What Francis Lowell wanted was not money but security of fortune.[3]

Merchant shipping was a knowledge-based enterprise in an era when information moved slowly and unreliably. Profit and loss depended on the price of pepper in Sumatra, the stocks of coffee in the port at Mocha, or the arrival of enough tea to glut the New York market. Every voyage was a bet that a certain cargo would sell at an acceptable profit in a particular port at a particular time—a bet that the merchant might win or might lose. Once the ship left Long Wharf, a Boston merchant could not even place his own bets. He had to rely on the ability of his captain or supercargo to purchase cargoes and choose ports of call where profits would be found. Four, five, or twenty successive voyages might end in profit. The next twenty might lose more money than the first twenty had earned. Ships might be lost at sea, captured by pirates, or confiscated by unfriendly governments. Fortunes were made on a single voyage. Fortunes were wiped out in a single season.

Lowell had been searching for more dependable investment opportunities for some time. In 1808, with a partner, he built India Wharf on the Boston waterfront, counting on dockage fees and the rental of warehouse space to provide a steady return on the investment. India Wharf was profitable, but there was a limit to the number of wharves needed even in a flourishing seaport. Like other Americans with cash to invest, Lowell put some money into frontier land. Then, in 1810, accompanied by his wife and young sons, Lowell boarded a ship bound for England.

At what point Francis Lowell decided to become a textile manufacturer is not certain. Britain was jealous of its machines and forbade the export of textile machinery as well as the emigration of anyone with the skills to build such machines. If Lowell sailed with the intention of observing and replicating the methods of British success, he was too sly to tell anyone. In Boston, in London, in the British textile districts, and to the owners of British textile mills he visited, Lowell presented himself as a gentleman of means in need of a rest from business for reasons of health, traveling for pleasure with his family. Perhaps it was even true, at least at first. But another Boston merchant, Nathan Appleton, joined the Lowells in Scotland, and when they returned to Boston they built a cotton mill.

Power spinning was already widespread in England and in small Yankee yarn mills, but England at the time of Lowell's visit was only beginning the process of developing power looms. Upon his return to Boston, Lowell hired Paul Moody, a brilliant mechanic who had trained as a weaver and worked as a machine and mill builder. Together they designed and built a working power loom. They then designed the necessary winding, warping, and dressing machines to complement the loom. Finally, in 1813, at the site of a dam across the Charles River between Waltham and Newton that had previously powered the wheels of a paper mill, Francis Lowell built his manufactory. It was the first mill in the world to accept deliveries of raw cotton, card it, spin it, weave it, and send out bolts of finished cloth. English mills would not abandon hand weaving in favor of power looms for another generation.

Lowell's mill was capitalized with four hundred thousand dollars raised from a small circle of Boston merchants. Dividends averaged a spectacular 17 percent in the early years, a period when inflation was nil and government bonds paid 5 percent. Even these impressive profits would soon be dwarfed by the profits Lowell's associates made by selling inflated shares of existing mill corporations to new investors, while quietly transferring personnel, capital, and equipment to new corporations. Lowell's mill turned cotton into gold as fast as his new power shuttles could fly.

Owners of several Rhode Island spinning mills were working to develop power weaving even before Francis Lowell went to England, and had looms of their own design at work not long after the Waltham mill opened. By the late 1820s, power looms were even appearing in wool mills, although wool is more difficult to spin and weave by machine than cotton.[4] Wool manufacturing expanded steadily in absolute terms, but claimed a constantly shrinking market share as consumers opted for lightweight, easy-to-wash cotton.

There seemed to be no limit to the quantity of cotton the market could absorb. Lowell's Boston Associates expanded the mill at Waltham to produce inexpensive, durable cotton sheeting, while smaller manufacturers found profitable niches making higher quality dress goods. Before Lowell's mill was ten years old, the power of the Charles River was judged inadequate to supply the potential of cotton manufacturing and the associates moved to create an entire city dedicated to the spinning, weaving, and coloring of cotton goods at a waterfall on the Merrimack. Lowell, Massachusetts, was a memorial to Francis Cabot Lowell, who died in 1817, still a young man. But not even the immense waterpower at Lowell could satisfy the demand for cotton; soon the Boston associates were damming the Merrimack for new mills at Lawrence, Nashua, and Manchester.

Along the Blackstone, the Merrimack, the Thames, cities were conjured out of cornfields by the market for yard goods. Water turned the wheels of industry because it was cheaper and more reliable than steam power—provided a would-be manufacturer had the requisite capital. A steam engine could be had for a modest price compared to the large investment required to build the dams, spillways, power canals, and headwater reservoirs needed to power a large mill; but steam engines entailed unending expense for wood or coal, while waterpower, after a system was built, was virtually free. It was free, that is, according to standard accounting methods. The great dam across the Merrimack at Lawrence, the largest dam in the world when it was built in 1848, ended fish runs on the river, but no account was rendered for depletion of the fishery.

New England's hunger for profit collided with legal doctrines protecting the free passage of fish. The issue was joined at the Lawrence Dam. English common-law rights, reiterated in a series of colonial Fish Acts, explicitly forbade any miller from obstructing the free passage of fish; either a fishway must be constructed or a breach made in the dam in springtime. Yet the same legislature that passed the fish laws had, in 1848, passed a statute allowing the proprietors of the Lawrence Dam to pay upstream fishermen for usurpation of their rights in the manner of dam owners who paid farmers when fields were flooded by power reservoirs. Justice Lemuel Shaw of the Supreme Court of Massachusetts considered the shad, considered the cotton mills, and ruled that the legislature had the power to decide "whether the public good expected from the fishery . . . or the public advantage . . . from building up a large manufacturing town . . . should preponderate."[5]

A choice had to be made, and it was. Anadromous fish runs were a valuable resource, but if doing without shad, salmon, eels, and alewives was the price of progress, it was a price New England was eager to pay.[6]

Fish runs were only the most obvious of the productive cycles ended by dams. Guiding a canoe down even so remote a river as the West Branch of the Penobscot, through alternating stretches of white and flat water, the contemporary voyager notices that the river has turned lazy. At the moment of realization the Penobscot is narrow, there may be moose in the shallows and a bald eagle overhead, but the water is not wild anymore—it is scarcely moving. Miles upstream from the dam at Ripogenes Gorge that creates Chesuncook Lake, the demand for hydropower has stilled the wild river.

A lake is not a bad thing; it is only a different thing than a river. A fast river harbors brook trout; a lake, whitefish and bass. A rational society might swap brook trout for whitefish as the price of cheap power. But in spite of its name, Chesunkook is not a lake. Like the myriad other bodies of water created by damming Yankee rivers, it is a reservoir. And the differences, although they were not apparent to Chief Justice Lemuel Shaw when he ruled on the Lawrence Dam, are significant. The surface of a natural lake is stable, shrinking only gradually in the driest of seasons, whereas it is the duty of a reservoir to rise rapidly after rain and shrink as fast as the economics of power generation dictate.

There is no reason to believe that Chief Justice Shaw took the loon into consideration in rendering his decision. There is certainly no reason to believe that he was anti-loon—no one who has seen a loon or heard its maniacal yodel echo through the night could be. Someone who has watched these masterful swimmers attempt to walk, however, may be forgiven a chuckle. As a pedestrian, the loon is a pathetic failure, and knows it. Loon chicks are no sooner

A View of the Lawrence Dam. Ink and watercolor by Marshall Tidd. The building of the great dam across the Merrimack at Lawrence in 1847 was a triumph of financial and industrial know-how. When a choice had to be made between fish and waterpower, the choice was easy to make. Courtesy of American Textile History Museum, Lowell, Mass.

hatched than their parents take them for a cruise. They spend their infancy waterbound, safely carried on their parent's back. Because they walk with only slightly more skill than the average fish, loons must nest at the water's edge. Reservoirs lack the most productive part of a lake: a stable edge. If power demand suddenly draws the reservoir down, the loon nest is left stranded many rods from water. If spring rain held back by a dam submerges the small island where cautious parents chose to build, there will be no young. Largemouth bass and bluegill sunfish suffer when eggs laid in nests carefully scooped on the bottom of the reservoir's shallow edge are abruptly left high and dry. Eggs laid in warm, shallow water at a reservoir's edge rapidly chill and die when power management decisions suddenly submerge them in many feet of water.

A reservoir shore is a sterile thing; fluctuating waters prevent a dependable waterline and the development of a lakeshore community. The buttonbush, cattail, and pickerelweed of a natural shore harbor the young, anchor the egg sacks, and feed the larvae that feed the minnows that feed the great fish of the deep waters. Reservoirs—lakes without shores—contain different and fewer fish than natural lakes. Below the dam, the river contains no fish at all.

Once there were rivers. Now there are reservoirs alternating with dry river-beds. Below the dams lie dry, rocky bottoms that sprout only empty beer cans. Downstream, past the dry rocks robbed of life by the dam, water gushes fitfully from a pipe to make something that looks like a river, except that it lacks a river's natural edges and a river's natural rhythm of spring flood and summer shallow. It lacks northern pike that spawn in spring-flooded meadows, and brook trout that swim in cold, constant waters. Intermittent spurts of power-company largesse struggle to make a river with increasing success as distance from the power dam and the contributions of small tributaries unite to even the flow, until, far from sight of the dam and out of earshot of whirling turbines, the river slows in the backwater of yet another lake without a shore.

Unquenchable demand for power led the great cotton mills to reach north and grasp the sources of the Merrimack. Dams were built across the outlets of Squam (Golden Pond) Lake, Newfound Lake, and Lake Winnipesaukee in the 1840s and 1850s, raising the lake surface by several feet after rain, stockpiling water for use when power demands at Lowell dictated. Across New England, lakes, swamps, rivers, and brooks were turned into power reservoirs, and although the industries whose wheels they turned have largely vanished, the dams remain. Many generate hydroelectric power, but dozens of old dams with heads too small to interest a power company lie abandoned, stolidly holding back the waters of small ponds and, sometimes, marking the upstream limit of spawning runs for no reason except that no one will pay to remove them.

The old mill on Bullough's Pond last ground corn in 1876. The dam and its shallow, marshy pond attracted the attention of a real estate development company that replaced the seventeenth-century dam with concrete in 1897–1898, landscaping the banks of a new, smaller pond intended as the centerpiece of a residential neighborhood. The new dam lacked a fishway, but there was little hope of smelt making their way up the filthy sewer that the Charles River had become. After 1908, there was no hope at all. In that year the last free-flowing stretch of the river, from the Watertown Dam to the harbor, became another in the series of reservoirs that check the Charles in its halting progress from Hopkinton to the sea.

Tides once rose and fell on the Charles as far upstream as Watertown. The river's long mouth was a life-birthing estuary of such broad proportions that early explorers were deceived into thinking that the Charles was an important river. It is, of course, a river of no significant length, but the headlands and peninsulas that make Boston a sheltered harbor foiled fresh water in its rush to the sea and resulted in a highly productive estuary. Here were acres of fertile salt marsh, oysters that had to be cut in half before they would fit in a man's mouth, flounder as big as a dinner plate, sturgeon the size of a canoe, and flocks of migrating ducks that darkened the sky. Deterioration began almost immediately: hunting, fishing, the damming of small streams like Smelt Brook that cut off fish runs, and the dumping of offal that fouled the waters. By the nineteenth century, tides rose and fell not in salt marshes, but on mud flats filthy with the effluent of sewers and slaughterhouses. Boston wearied of the stench, and in 1908, a dam was built across the mouth of the Charles that stopped the tide from falling and liberated Brahmin nostrils from the twice-daily stench of be-fouled mud flats.

The new dam's sole imperfection was that sluice gates letting the river waters flow out to sea shut twice daily to keep out the inrushing tide. Even this was not so much an imperfection as an inability to see the future. The system func-tioned well for decades, furnishing Boston with a boat basin and waterfront promenades never fouled by the noxious odors of low tide in a dirty harbor. Meanwhile the city and its suburbs grew, constructing new housing and miles of asphalt roads, greatly increasing the amount of runoff in the wake of a heavy rain. In 1954 and 1955 Hurricanes Carol and Diane, respectively, visited Boston. Diane poured twelve inches of rain into the Charles River basin in just two days, rain that rushed off rooftops and paved roads with astounding speed, piling up behind a dam unable to drain the Charles River basin at high tide. Boston became a reservoir; some neighborhoods filled with two and a half feet of water; storm sewers backed up and streets became canals. When the flood ended, Boston built a new dam, equipped with six 2,700-horsepower diesel en-gines, able to pump 8,400 cubic feet of water a second into the harbor even against the combined forces of high tide and a major storm surge.

Today, the Charles River basin is an urban reservoir; it is sterile, compared with the bountiful estuary nature provided, but as beautiful and well loved as any river in America. The fish ladders don't work very well, but boat locks at the Charles River Dam are opened to allow passage of anadromous fish, and the alewife run on the Charles is flourishing, although smelt and shad run in disappointingly small numbers.

A smelt considering a run up our little brook would first confront a freshwa-ter reservoir where every instinct leads her to expect the rush of freshwater mixing with salt in a springtime estuary. Should she overlook this monstrous substitute for an estuary, manage to locate the mouth of her ancestral brook where it enters the Charles just below the Watertown Dam, and swim up the few yards of water flowing freely over a gravel bed, she would have to negotiate more than a mile of concrete pipe before emerging into a narrow, concrete canal flowing through suburban backyards. Then there would be a second cul-vert under the playing fields of Newton North High School and, finally, a few rods of rocky, fast-flowing, oxygen-rich, natural bottom perfect for spawn-ing—before the dam at Bullough's Pond blocks further upstream passage. The ubiquity of dams and culverts goes a long way toward explaining the paucity of smelt. Oysters and sturgeon don't exist in the modern Charles at all. But dams have their uses.

Samuel Slater, Samuel Collins, Francis Lowell, and their peers built cities on land where family farms once stood. Fields that had produced a few tons of hay were made to yield yard goods, farm tools, Yankee notions, and jobs.

In the decades following independence, men and women were the leading Yankee export crop as, year after year, the young assessed their prospects in overcrowded farming communities and headed west. Around the year 1820, circumstances changed. Steady employment in one of the new mills not too far from home became an alternative to leaving forever, and part of the westward stream was diverted to Slaterville, Collinsville, Lowell, and a hundred other mill towns.[7]

Lowell's famous mill girls, hired to work the new looms for a few years between childhood and marriage, were the exception, a category called into being by well-capitalized industrialists who had seen England's dark satanic mills and recoiled from the dangers of creating a permanent class of factory workers. Even this isolated exception lasted a scant two decades. Most mills were staffed by families. Father and children took production jobs, while mother increased household income by taking in boarders. Many families found such situations beat the alternative of piecing a living together by farming a few rented fields, hiring out as day labor, and taking in outwork stitching shoes or plaiting straw bonnets. Not everyone wanted to go west and, because setting up and stocking a frontier farm cost money, not everyone could afford to. For those who could not or would not go, mill towns beckoned.

Small semiattached cottages built for early-nineteenth-century mill families still stand in many towns, often near an abandoned dam at the outlet of a body of water with a name like Knife Shop Pond, although the knife factory has long disappeared and even the old mill ponds are disappearing, filling with sediment and turning into woods. One series of such dams I know well begins at the outlet of Lake Massapoag in Sharon, Massachusetts, a Boston suburb that has virtually no industry today. But in 1820, Sharon, like all Yankee farm towns, was also a factory town.

Massapoag Brook exits Lake Massapoag near a site that was made available to become a town beach after the immense icehouse that once occupied the site burned to the ground. There is no visible sign that the beach was once the site of a large, commercial ice-cutting operation. Indeed, few sunbathers guess that the beach itself is artificial, built of sand trucked in to satisfy the twentieth-century craze for swimming and melanoma. It is impossible to know precisely what the original brook looked like, since, as early as the 1760s the channel was deepened to draw down water in the lake and make it easier to recover bog ore for the nearby iron industry. At some later point, a dam was built so that the lake could become a power reservoir; in the nineteenth century no fewer than six industrial plants drew power from dams on this creek—a rivulet that is at no point too wide to jump across.

Hammershop Pond, behind the first of the series of dams below the reservoir, powered a gristmill, then, from 1825 to 1835, a cotton mill, before becoming a shop where up to a hundred men worked producing leather-cutting knives for the shoe industry. In the last decade, from the vantage point of a friend's kitchen window, I have watched Hammershop Pond lose about a third of its surface to rapid siltation. The next reservoir in line, Knife Shop Pond, has entirely disappeared. It is a damp meadow turning rapidly into woods with a brook running through, and a ruined dam. Downstream, the brook feeds Mann's Pond. Not many years ago, when this pond was drawn down so that the dam could be repaired, a stone wall could be seen running down the pond bottom to the original brook and back up toward the woods—survivor of a time before farm fields were drowned to power millwheels. A small mill was erected here in 1831 to weave mattress ticking. In the late nineteenth century, a handsome, two-and-a-half-story brick mill on this site wove cotton duck. Nothing is left but foundations, a row of millworkers' housing, a pond rapidly silting in, and the old dam. Next downstream a dam was built in 1809 creating Trowel Works Pond to power a mill spinning thread for fine cotton shirting. When that mill went out of business, a new owner wove bedding and upholstery fabric, before selling out in 1852 to the owner of the knife works upstream, who used his new mill to make trowels. This intensity of industry on a single, small brook in a farming village was typical, not unique. Other little brooks in the same small town powered other mills. Industrial New England in the first half of the nineteenth century was built on innumerable millstreams, large and small. Nearly every fall of water in New England powered a mill producing tools, machines, paper, leather, teapots, and an endless web of yard goods.

Chapter 13

Cities of Steam

❧

Coal, in truth, stands not beside but entirely above other commodities. It is the material energy of the country—the universal aid—the factor in everything we do. With coal almost any feat is possible or easy; without it we are thrown back into the laborious poverty of early times.[1]

—W. S. Jevons, 1865

THE WORLD CHANGED FOREVER IN A CLOUD OF water vapor escaping from a primitive engine in an English coal mine. Looking back, we can perceive harbingers of change in the mists of the Middle Ages, and argue that the Industrial Revolution had its tentative beginnings when men first used overshot wheels to harness the power of falling water, invented a working clock, or replaced drop spindles with spinning wheels.[2] We would not be wrong in asserting the importance of these and other medieval inventions, only disingenuous in implying that cams, gears, cranks, or flywheels changed the terms of life on this planet. They did not. Steam did.

Cranks and flywheels were spinning fast when that first, clumsy steam engine began to drain water from a Wolverhampton coal mine in 1712, and a revolution would have taken place even if the steam engine had never been invented. Even if no means had ever been found to run machinery by burning coal, the commercial revolution already underway would have insured that factories, machine tools, and manufacturing cities would have sprung into being. Their growth, however, would have been checked by human inability to convert stored sunlight to mechanical power—except by feeding it to an ox. Oxen are fussy eaters. They consume only the solar energy that can be temporarily stored in hay, rather than the infinitely greater quantity locked in fossil fuels.

The limitations on growth in a world without engines powered by fossil fuel are severe, though not quite as severe as our petroleum-fueled generation may imagine. New England's great textile mills, its machine shops, the mills that produced clocks, guns, bicycles, and sewing machines from interchangeable

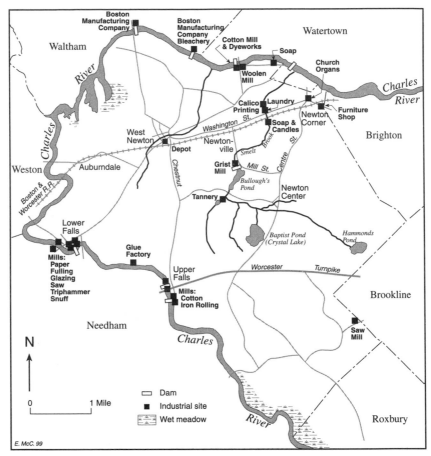

Newton, Massachusetts, 1834. When the Industrial Revolution came to New England, it happened everywhere at once. Workshops sprang up on every waterfall and every crossroads in the region. This map of Newton in 1834 shows the density and diversity of manufacturing that existed in one agricultural town the year that the first railroad in the region began to operate. Although Newton is only a few miles from Boston and therefore had somewhat more and larger enterprises than most, an array of mills and workshops manufacturing in bulk lots for shipment over the town line was found in every Yankee village. Eliza McClennan, Mapworks, work by Peter Stott for the Massachusetts Historical Commission in the collection of the Newton Historical Society, Jackson Homestead.

parts, even the sewing machines, guns, clocks, and bicycles that they produced, all operated without power from fossil fuel. Before steam locomotives, goods were shipped considerable distances with some degree of efficiency on mule-towed canal barges and square-rigged sailing ships. When a sailing ship needed repair, it was maneuvered into position over a wooden cradle set on a marine railway. A horse attached to a capstan turned a massive reduction gear, heaving cradle and ship out of the water.

Horses are still capable of turning capstans, but a contemporary marina owner would doubt your sanity if you suggested using one. Horses are expensive; they have to be fed and hay is expensive. Gasoline is cheap. And unlike horses, engines don't consume fuel on days when no boats are winched out of the water. Hay is the key. In a world without engines, a vast acreage of hayfields was needed to fuel the horses. And while wind may be free, the large crews that spread canvas on masted ships ate three meals a day. There is, as Malthus knew, an absolute limit to the amount of hay and wheat that can be grown on a finite amount of land. What Malthus did not understand was the potential of engines that could perform work without inputs of hay, wheat, or even potatoes.

Fossil fuel was the key that unlocked the door to riches beyond King Midas's dreams—all the gold in the royal countinghouse could not switch on an electric lamp or buy an airline ticket. So it is ironic that bad little boys and girls discover lumps of coal in their stockings on Christmas morning: it was coal that saved us from a lifetime spent behind a plow pulled by a plodding ox.

Thomas Newcomen did not set out to change the world when he branched out from making and selling iron coal-mining tools to build the world's first working steam engine. His immediate motive was profit, and in this the invention of the steam engine was not different from Simeon North's invention of the milling machine or Elisha Root's refinement of die forging. From one perspective, however, Newcomen's approach was a step into a world as new as that seen by Copernicus.[3]

North and Root, like the men who invented the waterwheel, the printing press, and the lathe, were craftsmen. They were, to be sure, craftsmen of brilliance and vision, but they were nevertheless, craftsmen, whose hands manipulated tools and materials and sometimes, by genius and diligence, made a new thing in the world. Newcomen was a craftsmen too, an ironmonger, owner of a firm in the business of making and supplying tools.

Several social removes from the forges where Newcomen's workmen hammered mining tools out of iron, a world existed in which gentlemen boiled water on laboratory stoves to make pistons move, and created vacuums in copper cylinders. These gentlemen aimed to learn what air and water were, an activity then just coming to be known as science. Newcomen's genius was to familiarize himself with the theoretical and experimental work on vacuums and steam, then apply this knowledge to building an engine that could pump water

Two-horsepower engine powering a threshing machine, Lincoln County, Maine, early 1900s. Photograph by Joseph Leighton. Horses powered a wide variety of machinery before the advent of portable gasoline engines. Dogs and goats were also made to power small engines. Human treadmills, familiar in many parts of the world, were never common in this country, although foot-treadles were routinely used to operate small machines such as lathes. Courtesy of Maine State Museum, Augusta.

from coal mines. The notion of applying scientific principles to industrial processes is so familiar that it requires an effort to remind ourselves that the Industrial Revolution was almost completely innocent of science. Except for Newcomen and his "fire engine," the Industrial Revolution clanged into noisy existence without the help of scientists or scientific principles, and flourished virtually without scientific input until the middle of the nineteenth century.[4]

The second way in which Newcomen's fire engine was different from all that had gone before and much of what would come afterward, was that the by-product of steam generation possessed the power to change the terms of life on this planet. But that was not imaginable in 1712. All that could be known then was that a clever new way had been found to power the pumps in deep coal mines.

Newcomen's clumsy, expensive, five-horsepower contraption did not inspire a generation to search for ways to apply scientific principles to practical problems; it did not even inspire much interest in steam engines. They were useful for pumping water and that was about all, at first. Early steam engines burned prodigious quantities of fuel to generate small amounts of power; coal mine owners could afford that. Improvements came slowly; a century after Newcomen's invention steam was competitive only when there were compelling reasons why the work could not moved to a site with waterpower. England, with little waterpower, turned early to steam. Early American engines drained mines in New Jersey, moved boats on waterways, and crushed sugar cane on Louisiana plantations too flat to generate waterpower; they would not replace water as the prime movers in Yankee factories until several crucial improvements had been made.[5]

The Industrial Revolution is sometimes defined as an explosive burst of innovative activity applying mechanical power to manufacturing. By this definition the overture ended and the first movement of the symphony of industrialization began in 1769. That was the annus mirabilis.[6] In 1769, James Watt successfully separated the steam engine condenser from the cylinder, and Richard Arkwright introduced cotton spun by waterpower.

In a Newcomen engine, steam entering a cylinder pushed a piston up. Cold water then squirted into the cylinder, causing the steam to condense and creating a vacuum that allowed atmospheric pressure to push the piston back down. In Watt's new design, steam moved from the piston cylinder to a condensing chamber, obviating the need for the cylinder to cool down after each stroke, an innovation that reduced fuel costs by over two-thirds. Unfortunately, James Watt's wonderful new engine could not actually be manufactured in 1769. To operate efficiently, a Watt engine required each piston to fit tightly within its cylinder. Although a skilled craftsman was able to drill a smooth, concentric cylinder for the working model, technology did not exist that would enable Watt to manufacture full-size engines at a reasonable price.

Watt's idea was made functional by John Wilkinson's 1774 invention of a boring machine capable of hollowing cylinders with a fairly smooth, concentric cavity. (Wilkinson was trying to build a machine that could bore the holes in cannon.) Cylinders, that is, in which a piston could work without excessive loss of power from steam escaping around the irregularly bored tube. Watt's dependence on Wilkinson's work was part of the normal process of invention: advances in technology make other, unanticipated improvements possible. Only after Wilkinson succeeded in boring cannon, could Watt turn his nifty idea for an improved steam engine into an actual, working engine. The steam engine that conquered the world in the 1850s would be the product of a century and a half of incremental improvements.

The most important American contributions to the process were made by Oliver Evans, the brilliant inventor from Delaware and Philadelphia who moved high-pressure steam power from theoretical possibility to working reality, and George Corliss, creator of the automatic variable cutoff, or "Corliss," engine. Before Corliss, steam was what regions and industries resorted to when unable to use waterpower, compared with which steam was expensive and delivered an irregular stroke damaging to machinery and to the materials being processed. Corliss's automatic variable cutoff engine regulated engine speed and power, varying the period of steam admission during each stroke by use of a variable cutoff device in the valve gear, and by using a governor to determine the point and degree of expansion on each stroke.[7] These improvements increased engine efficiency—which is to say they reduced fuel consumption—but the more important effect may have been that they made the engines run smoothly. Before Corliss, a manufacturer of fine fabrics concerned about power surges breaking threads and spoiling machinery would have chosen waterpower. After Corliss, he would choose steam.

The son of a country doctor in Washington County, New York, George Corliss opened a general store in his hometown of Greenwich in 1838 when he was twenty-one. The young storekeeper developed a stitching machine, received a patent, and, in 1844, took his patent to Providence, Rhode Island, in quest of a machine shop where he could develop a working model. Corliss's sewing machine did not work out; when he was offered a job as draftsman and designer in the machine shop of Fairbanks, Bancroft, and Co., he sold the store and moved his family to Providence.[8]

Providence was dense with machine shops and surrounded by cotton mills; but the region was running out of unharnessed waterfalls. It did not take a genius to see that improving the steam engine could be worth a fortune; it did require genius to make the improvements. Successful inventors of any era can be divided into two groups; those who had the business acumen to manufacture and sell their inventions, along with the resources and will to win patent suits, and those who died poor. It is a pleasure to record that George Corliss died a wealthy man, having lived to see a Corliss engine—specially built and the largest engine in the world to date—displayed at the center of the 1876 Centennial Exhibition. President Grant and Emperor Dom Pedro of Brazil threw the switch that turned the engine on and powered all of the equipment on display in Machinery Hall. Only the mechanically inquisitive noted the presence in the hall of a small German engine, a technical curiosity in which the pistons were powered by small explosions of gas mixed with air.[9]

But in 1849, George Corliss was neither rich nor famous. He was a young machine shop owner who had bought out his original partners and claimed that his steam engine was able to supply steady power no matter how many or how few machines a factory owner wished to run at a given moment, while saving so much fuel that it would pay for itself. Mill owners were skeptical. Corliss made them the kind of offer James Watt made to skeptical English industrialists a century earlier: he would install the engine free and take as payment the savings industrialists realized on fuel bills. One of his early clients, the James Steam Mill of Newburyport, Massachusetts, was offered the choice of outright

Newport, Rhode Island. Engraving by Samuel King, 1795. Colonial cities were situated where Yankee farm produce could be shipped to the sugar islands and the profits used to pay for imports. This picture of Newport shows the commercial fleet at anchor. Windmills behind the town indicate Newport's lack of falling streams and adequate sites for tide mills. Courtesy The Rhode Island Historical Society. RHi(x3)213.

purchase at $10,500, or paying Corliss five times the first year's savings on the mill's fuel bill. The company elected to pay Corliss what it saved in fuel; it ended up owing the inventor $19,734. The details are well documented because Corliss had to take them to court to collect.[10] At the end of a century and a half of incremental improvement, the condensing (Watt), high-pressure (Evans), automatic variable cutoff (Corliss) steam engine (Newcomen) had emerged with the power to build cities.

Cities in eighteenth-century America were understood to be places where the products of the countryside were traded for the products of countries on the other side of the sea; the ideal location was a protected deep-water harbor where rivers brought country produce to tidewater. A glance at a map of New England will confirm that New London, Portsmouth, and the other colonial cities offer just such sites. Even such apparently inland towns as Norwich and Hartford were located at the head of river navigation; if they had not been ports they would not have become sizeable towns. Early-nineteenth-century industrialization built cities in new kinds of places, locations where falls of water offered power, which explains the location of such Rhode Island factory towns as Woonsocket, Pawtucket, and the aptly-named cotton mill village of Arkwright. But even as these towns were being built, steam was about to make them obsolete.

The broad sweep of Narragansett Bay is out of all proportion to the size of the rivers that flow into it. Above Providence, the Blackstone River descends from the hills of central Massachusetts, and although the Blackstone was the hardest-working river of the nineteenth-century America, it was and remains insignificant in every other way. The Blackstone is a very small river. It is, however, larger than the Taunton, the river that flows into the eastern reaches of Narragansett Bay. East of Bristol, where the bay changes its name to Mount Hope, past Somerset, where the bay starts to be known as the Taunton River (despite the fact that it is still a salty tidal estuary deep enough for oceangoing vessels), lies the little town of Dighton.

Every town on Narragansett Bay was home port to seagoing ships when the republic was young, even towns as small and as far inland as Dighton. While Dighton never rivaled Newport or Providence, in 1800 the village at the head of the estuary was an international port of entry with a customs house and a not inconsiderable commercial fleet. Fall River, a town slightly closer to the open ocean, was a much less significant place. Its anchorage was too poor to attract mariners; it would have remained a farming hamlet if not for an unusual asset:

COLLINS & CO.'S WORKS. COLLINSVILLE, CONN.

Collins and Company's Works, Collinsville, Connecticut. Factory towns like Collinsville were creatures of the Industrial Revolution. Neither city nor village, Collinsville was defined by a single industry: Collins and Company, which made axes and plows. Power came from a reservoir built in the hills above the town. In contrast with the colonial seaports, several of which went on to become manufacturing cities with the advent of steam, the water-powered mill towns died with the industries that built them. Horace Greeley, et al. *The Great Industries of the United States* (Hartford, Conn.: J. B. Burr & Hyde, 1872), 124.

the Fall River (the brook shares its name with the town), which flows a total distance of 2,300 feet and drops, in that brief space, 132 feet, providing nine mill seats. Not many waterpowers lie within whistling distance of saltwater anchorage. In 1811, local investors built a cotton mill.[11]

That first mill was built in a farming village of 1,296 people. Thirty-five years later Fall River was a bustling mill town with over 10,000 inhabitants, who earned their living in cotton mills strung like beads along the stream. But not until the steam engine arrived did the factory town become a large city. It is a minor irony that in America's premier city of spindles, iron was the first local industry to turn to steam.

New England iron production had long been an essential support of farming, housekeeping, and shipbuilding. Both forests to make charcoal and local bog iron ore were running short when a group of Providence businessmen, which included Samuel Slater's brothers-in-law Abraham and Isaac Wilkinson, bought land on the Fall River. They built the Fall River Iron Works in 1821 on waterpower almost at sea level: it was designed to use iron mined in Egg Harbor, New Jersey, and bituminous coal from Nova Scotia to supply iron fittings to the Rhode Island shipbuilding industry. The entrepreneurial spirit soon branched out into hoops for whale oil casks, castings for machinery, and nails. By 1831 the strongest line was nails. Kegs of them were sent up the Hudson and west on the new Erie Canal.[12] A Massachusetts foundry could smelt New Jersey ore with Nova Scotia coal to supply Ohio farmers with nails only until the furnaces of Pittsburgh came on line, but even after its western nail trade collapsed, the Iron Works flourished by supplying iron machines to the burgeoning cotton industry.

The first New England cotton mill to shun water in favor of coal was built in Providence by Samuel Slater in 1827. Steam-powered cotton mills followed at a slowly increasing pace through the 1830s and 1840s, their numbers always dwarfed by the many new water-powered mills.[13] Some early steam mill owners were inspired by a desire to add on to an existing mill at a location where water power had been exhausted. Some were motivated, as Slater seems to have been, by a desire to locate a mill near bleacheries and print works and—this was crucial—in a seaport where the newest English and French designs could be copied quickly. Some may have been inspired by an owner's desire to possess the newest in technology, even though it was less efficient than the old technology. Most of the increase in steam mills, however, was driven by a new factor: labor shortage.

Labor supply was near the bottom of the list of problems confronting the first Yankee cotton mill owners. Mechanical difficulties, markets, financing, debt service, overdue accounts, drought, and spring freshets were problems for cotton industry pioneers. Labor was not. Landless Yankee families flocked to mill jobs, as did the daughters of Yankee farm families—for a decade or two. But by the 1840s, the supply had dried up even as the labor demands of the

cotton industry expanded. Cities were flourishing, the West was opening, opportunity abounded: it was not easy to attract labor to remote mill towns. One
solution was to build mills in seaboard cities where labor might be found. As
solutions go, this one was only as good as contemporary steam engines, and
they were less than perfect.

The Fall River Iron Works had a more compelling reason for turning to
steam. Cotton, a high-value commodity, could bear the cost of freight to remote waterpower sites. An iron foundry, however, had to be located where coal
and ore could arrive by water and, equally important, had to be near the mills
and machine shops it served. Mill machines were not a standardized commodity. Machinery was constantly evolving, being altered, needing repair and spare
parts—the ironworks had to be near the customer; the Fall River works was.
Business for the ironworks serving the thriving industrial region surrounding
Providence was so strong that the waterpower on the Fall River could not supply the needs of the growing plant. In 1840 the Fall River Iron Works broke
ground for a steam-powered mill. Trip-hammers and bellows did not need the
protection from power surges that delicate muslins required; the new power
source was an immediate success.

The first Fall River steam cotton mill came on line in 1843, but the advantages
were not enough to inspire many imitators. Fall River's second steam mill did
not open until 1852, but the third, which opened in 1859, was powered by a Corliss engine. After that, investors rushed to build in coastal locations where high
humidity gives elasticity to cotton fibers, leading to less breakage and reducing
the frequency of adjustments to the machinery. Humidity also reduces friction,
allowing the cotton fiber to run through the machinery more smoothly, Cotton
worked in humid conditions produces less airborne dust, which must be cleaned
from the delicate machinery. Employers knew the effect of dust on workers'
lungs, where it caused interstitial lung disease, but this was not a consideration
of interest, since they were not obliged to compensate disabled former employ-
ees. Transportation, however, was a significant cost, one that made location in a
seaport attractive once steam power became competitive with waterpower.

The number of spindles in Fall River doubled between 1859, when the town's
first Corliss engine was installed and 1865. By 1875 it had quadrupled, making
Fall River a city of forty-five thousand people and the largest producer of cotton textiles in the nation.[14] To reach this pinnacle, Fall River had pulled one
more ace to go with its already strong hand of deep water anchorage, humid
climate, and location near the machine shops and merchant entrepreneurs of
Providence. Fall River had clean water.

Water from Watuppa Pond, source of the Fall River, and from the smaller
Stafford Pond was clean enough to support bleacheries and calico printing
works. No river water could compete with the purity of these pristine, spring-
fed ponds, certainly not the Merrimack at Lowell, downstream from the mills

of Nashua and Manchester. The mordants, dyes, acids, and bleaches that went into producing Fall River's fashionable printed goods were flushed into Narragansett Bay. That was another advantage of location: the waste disappeared without any expense or inconvenience to the Bordens, Durfees, and Chaces in their elegant Victorian mansions. If we are to take the Fall River magnates to task, however, it is not fair to do so over effluent. The ocean was so vast and the works of man so puny that no one in the world had yet suggested that harm could be done by pouring chemical waste into the ocean. People who see beyond the understanding of their generation are rare in the world; we call them saints, prophets, or cranks—their vision is not a fair standard by which to judge others. The best thinking of a person's own generation is a fair yardstick, and it is by this reckoning that the magnates of Fall River fail to measure up.

Their failing, if men who built a great industrial city can be accused of failing, is that they failed to see beyond cotton. Fall River took the wonderful engine Thomas Newcomen gave the world and used it to spin cotton; to weave, print, dye, and bleach cotton; even to power an ironworks that produced machinery to manufacture cotton. They failed to find new things to make. When cotton left, Fall River died, and the mill towns of New England died with it: Lowell, Lawrence, New Bedford, Taftsville, Woonsocket, Chicopee, Slatersville, Norwich, Manchester, Pawtucket, Nashua, Lewiston. When low labor costs made it cheaper to process cotton in southern states, the cotton cities of New England became empty shells, places of abandoned mills and vacant housing.

The decline was slow. It started as the South recovered from the Civil War and began to industrialize, and continued for eighty years—three generations during which the young, the educated, and the able left the Yankee mill towns. There was a final burst of activity as the industrial muscle of the nation strained to produce the material needed to defeat the Axis powers. Then everything stopped. Wheels that had spun for a century, mills that had woven a revolution, were outmoded, unwanted. By the 1960s, the old industrial cities, with no jobs and no hope, offered only the opportunity for immigrants to find housing cheap enough to live on the income a welfare check afforded.

The immigrants of the 1960s and 1970s, predominately Puerto Rican, did not have fewer skills than Irish immigrants of the 1840s. Those descendants of French-Canadian and Irish mill workers who still inhabited the old textile cities did not have less ambition than their ancestors. It was the world, not the workers, that had changed. From the day Samuel Slater set his spinning mill in train there had been jobs for able-bodied, willing men and women, regardless of their lack of formal education. Now there were not.

The 1950s and 1960s were a dismal period in the economic history of New England. Only the artificial prosperity of World War II masked the fact that decline had begun to set in much earlier, certainly as far back as the mill closings of the Depression.

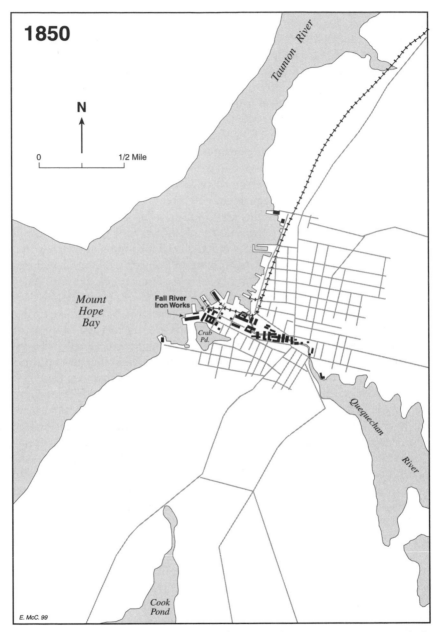

1850

N

0　　　　　　1/2 Mile

Taunton River

Mount Hope Bay

Fall River
Iron Works

Crab Pd.

Quequechan River

Cook Pond

E. McC. 99

Fall River, Massachusetts, in 1850 and 1877. The power of steam to create an economy is demonstrated by these two maps. Until 1850 the growth of the town was limited by the amount of waterpower available; cotton mills are strung like beads along the river, each only as large as the available waterpower permitted. After the introduction of the Corliss

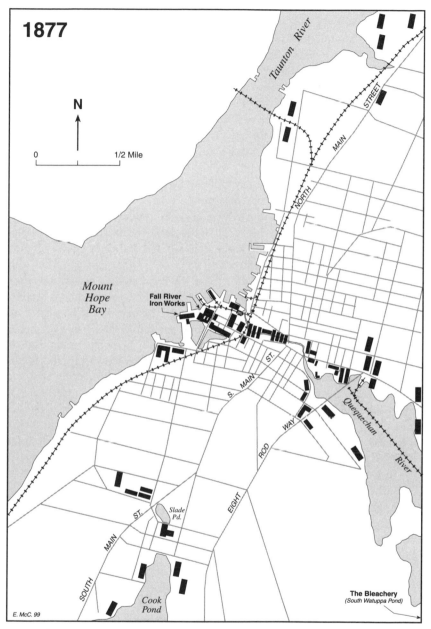

1877

N

0   1/2 Mile

Taunton River

STREET

MAIN

NORTH

*Mount
Hope
Bay*

**Fall River
Iron Works**

S. MAIN ST.

ST.

Quequechan

ROD WAY

EIGHT

River

ST.

*Slade
Pd.*

MAIN

SOUTH

*Cook
Pond*

The Bleachery
(South Watuppa Pond)

E. McC. 99

engine, the existing mills expanded and new ones sprang up in every direction. It was as though all limits on growth had gone up in steam. Map by Eliza McClennan, Mapworks, based on 1850 map by H. F. Walling in the collection of the Fall River Historical Society, and on 1877 map of Fall River, O. H. Bailey and J. C. Hazen, Boston.

The problem was not that cotton mills were moving to the Carolinas, that automobile companies founded at Waltham had moved to Detroit, that the sewing machines patented from Providence machine shops were manufactured in New Jersey, or that the territories and nations to which we once exported shoes now manufactured their own. Since 1640, the region's success has depended entirely upon thinking of new products first, marketing them aggressively, and coming up with the next new thing as old industries moved away to be closer to markets or raw materials. The New England economy declined not because cotton moved south, but because the inventive and entrepreneurial spirit failed.

The silence that would one day fall over New England's spindle cities was far in the future when Yankee entrepreneurs built the cotton mills of Fall River. The problem of the hour was not industrial decline, but where to find enough labor to man the machines. Then the potato crop failed in Ireland and, for the first time since the Long Parliament sat in defiance of Charles I, there was immigration to New England.

Millions of Irish left Erin because there was no industrial revolution taking place in their homeland and without one there were no jobs and no revenue to pay for imported food when the potatoes rotted. The question of why there was no Irish industrial revolution has no simple answer. Ireland had a coast, but, unlike Brittany, no commercial fishery; good natural harbors, but, unlike Norway, no vessels in the carrying trade; cattle, but, unlike Massachusetts, no tanning or shoemaking beyond domestic requirements; kelp, but, unlike Scotland, no burgeoning early-nineteenth-century industry converting seaweed into chemicals. Whatever it is that creates a spirit of enterprise in a culture, nineteenth-century Ireland lacked it. And if such a spirit is contagious, then it is not easy to catch; moving to New England was certainly not enough to infect the Irish. But if crossing an ocean did not make the Irish into entrepreneurs, it did convert them into valuable raw material.

Pushed from their impoverished, overpopulated homeland, Irish laborers of the 1820s and 1830s found work in English mills. Among the fleets of ships bringing the resources of the world to England's burgeoning cities were freighters carrying lumber from New Brunswick. The lumber carriers filled their holds with coal and salt at west of England ports, and carried these cargoes to Ireland, where, since there was no westbound cargo to take on, they were willing to carry emigrants to Halifax for fifteen shillings. The wages of a season in a New Brunswick lumber camp bought a ticket to Boston, which was the metropolis of the Canadian maritime provinces.[15]

Boston may have been the commercial capital of the maritimes, but Canada was British, and England had a strong interest in maintaining communication with its colonies. In 1841 a Post Office Commission of Inquiry on behalf of Her Majesty's Government determined that the best route for sending the mail from England to Canada was by steamship to Boston, then north by rail.

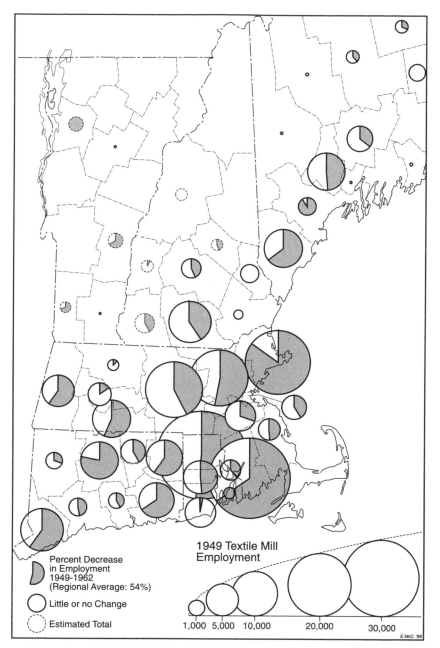

Percent Decrease in Employment 1949-1962 (Regional Average: 54%)

Little or no Change

Estimated Total

1949 Textile Mill Employment

1,000 5,000 10,000   20,000   30,000

E.McC. '99

Industrial employment in New England declined in the post–World War II era as textile manufacturing moved south and shoe manufacturing moved offshore. The machine tool, armaments, and paper industries remained strong, while the electronics industry was being invented in Cambridge and its suburbs. R. C. Estall, *New England: a Study in Industrial Adjustment* (New York: Praeger, 1966), 58. By permission.

Cunard Line steam packets, subsidized by the British government to carry the mail, began regular service in 1842, giving Boston swift, dependable transatlantic service, and forcing competing carriers to lower their rates. By the 1840s when the Irish potato crop failed, Boston was a familiar destination to which even the poor could afford a ticket; the near-destitute could even travel in the hold of a lumber freighter returning to Halifax empty. Few Irish famine victims, however, would have the luxury of planning their route of emigration.[16]

Immigrants from other nations, even those forced from home by poverty or persecution, selected a destination. When the potato famine hit Erin, the Irish simply fled. Escaping death, they took what passage they could and got off the boat where it docked. Fate carried many to New York, a booming metropolis and one of the great immigrant magnets of the age. For others, the landfall was Boston.

A city of ninety-three thousand in 1840, Boston earned a living as it had always done, by merchant shipping and by supplying the hinterland with goods and services. As Massachusetts industrialized, the city warehoused, marketed, and shipped manufactured goods, predominantly shoes and cloth, from the state's burgeoning mill towns. There was manufacturing in Boston, but it was craft industry carried on in the myriad small workshops of the mercantile city. Demand for unskilled labor was slight. Then, in less then a decade, two hundred and thirty thousand Irish immigrants arrived.

Boston did not welcome the Irish, but neither did it panic or take up collections to send them elsewhere; for several years the city ignored them. When Boston did notice the Irish, it saw that they were destitute, and therefore willing to work at rates far below standard wages. This drew the attention of mill owners, who hired Irish workers and lowered wages. Railroad contractors hired Irish laborers on contract, housed them in primitive camps, charged them for board and supplies, and sent them back to Boston no better off than when they signed on. Profits in these industries were so high that railroads would have been built and cotton woven even at the high wages native workers demanded. But other industries were called into existence by the poverty and abundance of Irish labor.

Ready-to-wear clothing started at the low end of the market. Just as the mass production of shoes began with slaps and brogans for enslaved farmhands, the first shirts, jackets, and breeches available off the rack were made for sailors. At a time when all clothing was made within the family or by custom tailors, seamen often found themselves in sudden need of inexpensive clothing in a strange town. It was a small market, easily supplied by waterfront storekeepers who contracted with journeymen tailors in slack seasons. Potential existed for the market to expand, but only if labor were cheap enough.

Cheap Irish labor arrived almost simultaneously with the invention of the sewing machine. The apparently endless supply of destitute immigrants willing to work for half the pay native labor commanded inspired entrepreneurs to break the complex task of tailoring a suit of clothes into individual steps, give each immigrant a sewing machine and a single, rapidly performed task, and create an efficient new industry almost overnight. Cheap clothing poured from Boston shops to supply the needs not only of mariners, but of enslaved southerners, forty-niners in the gold camps of California and, a few years later, the Union Army.

Other industries took advantage of the availability of steam power and cheap labor to transform New England's old mercantile cities into important manufacturing centers. Within a decade of their arrival, famine refugees were laboring in ironworks, sugar refineries, brass foundries, shipyards, oil refineries, glass factories, and dozens of other enterprises that to succeed had to locate near the good transportation, ready markets, and skilled entrepreneurial and engineering talent of a major city, but that would have been stymied by labor shortage had the Irish not arrived. Additional jobs were created as steam transformed the city's workshops into small industries.

Efforts to create an efficient steam engine scaled to the power needs of a small workshop failed; steam power could be produced economically only on a large scale. Small shops could, however, locate beside a large factory and power machinery by linking a belt to their neighbor's power train. Another solution was the power building, a manufacturing plant with a large, central engine built by a real estate entrepreneur who leased both manufacturing space and a power source to small firms. Both solutions to the power needs of small-scale manufacturing drew industry from farming villages into the cities, where Irish immigrants met the demand for labor. Little mills on small streams were abandoned as manufacturing concentrated in large cities with railroads and harbors.

The great good fortune of Irish famine refugees was timing. Good fortune is, of course, a cruel label to apply to a people driven from their homeland by devastating famine. But, for the refugees, it could have been worse. They could have been driven from home into a world that didn't need them. Had tens of thousands of unskilled, destitute refugees landed on the wharves of Boston in 1755, 1810, or 1935, the welcome they would have gotten would have been less than tolerant. Not because they were Catholic, although that fact did not help New England accept the Irish, but because they were not needed. Labor in a market where it is already surplus is a threat to the civil order. The Irish had the good luck to arrive in a commercialized economy poised to exploit the potential of steam and wanting only labor to enjoy dynamic growth. Irish refugees supplied labor in large and profitable volume. Yankees did not like them very much; the economic value of the Irish explains why they were not driven back into the sea as the Acadians had been in 1755.

Second- and third-generation Irish began to move into the ranks of skilled labor and the professions, albeit at a slower rate than other immigrant groups. What the Irish did not do was start businesses or create new products, and the list of great Irish engineers and scientists for the entire century after the famine migration would be even shorter than the list of Irish entrepreneurs. In Oscar Handlin's stark assessment, "Fecundity was the only contribution of the Irish towards a solution of the community's social problems." Generation after generation, the Irish supplied New England with labor. And, although Handlin was considering Boston when he wrote those words, the same could have been said of the French Canadians who left their impoverished farming province to work in Yankee cotton mills and shoe shops.[17]

Irish and French Canadian immigrants and the first several generations of their American-born descendants were notably resistant to the American drive for upward mobility. This resistance is particularly evident when the Irish are contrasted with upwardly mobile Scandinavian immigrants, who arrived in New England equally destitute and from similarly impoverished, peasant backgrounds, although Scandinavians were far less literate than the Irish, and, of course, unable to speak English. Anti-Irish discrimination fails as an explanation because the racism the Irish faced was no worse than the racism faced by Jewish immigrants. It is true that Irish and Canadian immigrants resisted the dominant, Protestant culture in order to preserve their Catholic faith. And it is true that members of a large immigrant group succeed better in preserving cultural traditions than do members of a small or fragmented group, if only because they need less often to associate with members of other groups. The very success of Irish cultural integrity is the core of the question: there were strands in Irish culture that were different from the ethos of the society into which they had come, differences that were antithetical to the capitalist, entrepreneurial spirit that made New England rich.

In some ways the Irish were as exotic as the Pacific islanders Yankee sea captains met on whaling voyages, whose homelands Yankee missionaries and merchants colonized in the same decades that saw Irish immigration to New England. The islands of Polynesia produced breadfruit and taro and fish in such abundance that by working two or three hours a day the lower classes easily produced a bounty of food. Polynesians were as clear as any people on earth in their view that work was a thing required to achieve an end, not an end in itself. No Polynesian with the leisure to spend his days surfing ever berated himself for not having gotten more work done. The world envied them. From Paris to Chicago it was understood that paradise was to be found on the Island of Tahiti, where men were not required to earn their bread by the sweat of their brow.

Boston was no bountiful Polynesian island, but neither was an Irish immigrant who was willing to work very likely to starve. Not that anyone accuses the Irish of being unwilling to work, only of being unwilling to continue working once the needs of the day had been provided for. No one accuses the Irish, as a group, of being stupid; even derogatory stereotypes of Irishmen portray the very opposite of dullness.[18] The Irish as a group lacked not the ability but the ethos that drove other immigrants to improve their economic status. The social inertia of the Irish immigrant community from the famine generation until World War II was not a matter of incapacity or of thwarted opportunity but of choice. The Irish chose to enjoy the day. Why defer until tomorrow the good things of life when they can be enjoyed now?

This pre-modern attitude toward work and leisure is common to almost every known society from the hunting-and-gathering tribes studied by anthropologists to the great empires of Europe and Asia. It is the modern attitude, sometimes called the protestant ethic, with its demand for productive labor, even from those who already have plenty, that is the aberration in human attitudes.

Choosing leisure once the needs of the season were provided for was no improvident choice in the Loire Valley, where verdant pastures and fertile fields provide ample sustenance, nor are the residents of the Chengdu Basin in Sichuan likely to starve as long as they maintain the canal system that has kept their region free from drought and flood for the last twenty-two hundred years. The supervisors of the Chengdu irrigation canals do not need to invent innovative water-control mechanisms. They need simply to maintain the canals and plant the rice exactly as it has always been done. Pre-modern attitudes toward work and leisure are viable in regions where resources are ample to meet the needs of the population. But in a region such as New England, where the population had outgrown the ability to feed itself by the end of the eighteenth century, prosperity depended on continuous entrepreneurial and technical innovation. Proximity to Ireland and Quebec was a short-term economic boon and a long-term economic blow. Neither of the two dominant nineteenth-century immigrant groups in the region gave birth to inventors or entrepreneurs. This failure, serious as its consequences were for the New England economy, may not have been as disastrous for the region as the failure of old Yankee stock to produce new generations of entrepreneurs.

Francis Lowell got what he wished for. The industry he created not only paid steady dividends for the lifetime of his widow and children, it set his grandchildren up in life very nicely. In fact, in a nation where popular wisdom holds that families go from shirtsleeves to shirtsleeves in three generations, it is interesting to note that many fortunes made in the neutral trade of the Napoleonic wars and used to build cotton mills, still support the descendants of the founders. The Ames family, whose ancestor turned an 1790s Easton blacksmithy into an ironworks that produced the shovels that turned the soil in the California gold fields and dug the trenches on Civil War battlefields, invested those profits in the Union Pacific Railroad, and still lives in an Easton mansion set in a stately park designed by Frederick Law Olmstead. William Weld, the recent governor of Massachusetts, enjoys the returns on a shipping fortune made in the neutral trade. As do his children.

Wealth maintained so long grows conservative, which may explain why New England industry aged with the Victorian century and why few new industries were born in the region in the first part of the twentieth century. But it is also true that after the middle of the nineteenth century, ambitious New England youth followed opportunity west. Just as Yankee boys after the Federal period ceased going to sea and turned to manufacturing, Yankee boys after the Civil War ceased to found industries in New England. They continued to found industries, but they did so in New York, Chicago, and California.

My own family left the farm in the 1830s and 1840s. Some came to the cities from farms in western Connecticut; others, whose own ancestors had migrated to Nova Scotia in the 1760s, returned to New England and settled in Boston. They did not become factory hands but, starting in a small way, manufacturers and importers of hardware who eventually left Boston and Waterbury for greater opportunity in New York. The leap from a farm, even a Yankee farm, would have been harder had they waited until the 1870s or 1880s. Whereas in the first half of the century, industrial capitalism was a new frontier with opportunity open for any energetic young man to seize, after the Civil War, the industrial economy of New England was mature and not only immigrant groups but factory hands of native ancestry found upward mobility in the ossifying Yankee economy a slow and difficult climb. Few factory hands, Yankee or immigrant, created new industries in the New England of the late nineteenth century.

By 1900, shoes, textiles, and precision engineering were mature industries, the major streams of immigration had already arrived, and the economy of industrial New England was settling into a comfortable old age. Factory hands lived in crowded cities giving birth to new generations of factory hands. Around the cities, mile after mile of abandoned farmland reverted to forest just as the steam engine was rearranging the population. New England Indians were a people of the littoral; they lived along the water's edge, leaving upland district remote from fishing opportunties lightly settled, if at all. Colonial New England was arranged in precisely the opposite fashion, with people almost evenly spread across a landscape of farms and rural villages.[19] Even the coming of industrialization rearranged the population only slightly at first, concentrating growth in mill villages scattered along streams. Steam power brought people back to the littoral, to Bridgeport, New Haven, Providence, and Portland; to large cities on the estuaries.[20]

Population grew even as it shifted toward the coast. At the time of the colony's first census, in 1764, 245,698 people lived in Massachusetts; 398,787 in 1790; and 523,287 in 1820, when the Industrial Revolution was getting underway. The total passed one million just after 1850 and two million in the 1890s. Most of those people lived in cities and almost all of the region's cities were built on rivers at tidewater. The consequences of urban growth for the waters of New England were about to become apparent.

Chapter 14

The Maine Woods

✤

The reckless disregard of forest property which characterized the early lumbering operations of the state has been replaced by sensible methods for preserving and perpetuating the forest.[1]

—Census report, 1884

BEFORE THE ADVENT OF INEXPENSIVE COTTON cloth, body linens were made from—linen. And when linen chemises were so worn out that even the thriftiest housewife could find no way to turn, patch, cut down, or even use a square of worn fabric as a wash rag, the scraps were sold to a paper mill. Linen rags make good paper. Cotton rags do not. Cotton fiber fresh from the gin makes excellent paper, but new cotton has almost always been too expensive to be put to such use. Cotton fibers that have been woven into summer dresses, washed a thousand times, cut down to serve as baby clothes or polishing rags, washed, and reused until they are of no use in a household are too fragile to make paper. This is an important point in a world where fiber is in short supply—not that a paperless world is inconceivable.

Written documents do not absolutely require paper, they can be created on any number of substances, ranging from the bamboo slats employed by ancient Chinese scribes to the black basalt of the Rosetta Stone. Parchment, papyrus mats, clay tablets, rolls of fine silk are all more or less serviceable and more or less awkward to manipulate, transport, and store—not to mention expensive to manufacture. It was a tremendous advance when paper of the modern kind, flat sheets manufactured from macerated vegetable fiber, was first presented to Emperor Ho-Ti of China by the courtier Ts'ai Lun in the year 105 C.E. Although Ts'ai Lun's introduction took centuries to work its way around the globe, it was Chinese-style paper that would make Gutenberg's printing press possible.

Paper is made by breaking vegetable matter down to a pulp of cellulose fiber suspended in slurry. The pulp is formed into sheets, traditionally, by dipping a

Paper Maker

"Paper Maker" and hand-dipping paper in China. The process of making
paper did not change materially from the time of its invention in second-

century China until the invention of the Fourdrinier machine in eighteenth-century England. Until that machine was perfected, paper was made in exactly the same way the world over, as shown in these early-nineteenth-century images of British and Chinese papermakers. Note the freshly dipped, still-moist sheets of paper hung to dry on lines behind the British journeyman. "Paper Maker," *The Book of Trades* (White Hall, Pa., 1805), 55. Courtesy, American Antiquarian Society. Hand-dipping paper in China. John Scarth, watercolor and pencil. Courtesy, Peabody Essex Museum, Salem, Mass. (M-9758-59).

screen mounted in a frame into a vat of pulp of just the right consistency while vibrating the mold to spread the slurry evenly and cause the fibers to inter-twine. Excess water drains off through the screen. These damp sheets are lifted from the mold and air-dried before use. Dipping paper was a skilled and tedi-ous craft, mastered after a lengthy apprenticeship and fairly well paid. It was also unpleasant. The constant bending strained men's backs, while immersion inflamed and irritated the skin, eroding the vatman's fingernails until they dis-appeared. Production was limited by the slowness of the process, but paper was in limited demand before Gutenberg, and even after the introduction of printed books, it remained an expensive, hand-produced, luxury good.

Fiber was reduced to pulp by a pounding process, either with a hand-held mortar and pestle, or with trip-hammers driven by foot pedal or waterwheel. The first important mechanical advance in papermaking since Ts'ai Lun's time came because the Dutch lacked waterpower. Windmills, the ingenious Dutch substitute, could not deliver enough power to enable Dutch papermakers to compete with the large, water-powered trip-hammers macerating rags in Ger-man paper mills. A seventeenth-century Dutch workman whose name has been lost to history designed a wooden roller fitted with iron blades that re-volved against a plate made of stone or iron. The Hollander, as modern ver-sions are still called, efficiently lacerated rags in a large, wooden tub, produc-ing excellent pulp.[2] As useful an invention as the Hollander was, it paled before the invention of a machine designed to turn pulp into continuous rolls of paper, eliminating the time-consuming and highly skilled labor of hand dip-ping each sheet.

The Fourdrinier papermaking machine was invented in France by Nicholas Louis Bobert in 1798, but it was perfected and brought to commercial success by two British stationery merchants, Henry and Sealy Fourdrinier. Larger, more complex, and requiring both more power and more skilled labor than the spin-ning and weaving machines in contemporary cotton mills, a Fourdrinier oozed a continuous web of liquid pulp onto screens that vibrated to entwine the fi-bers, then passed the web through rollers and onto felted conveyors, all the while draining, squeezing, and applying suction to vacuum water away from the web until a roll of paper emerged.

Before the invention of mechanical papermaking, American production was limited by the number of skilled papermakers a mill owner could hire, train, and retain to hand-dip paper sheet by sheet. But paying the kind of wages that would have attracted enough sober, steady, skilled men to meet the rising demand for paper would have put any mill owner foolish enough to attempt it out of busi-ness. They made do by constantly training apprentices, paying the highest wages they could afford, importing papermakers from countries where wages were low, employing a labor force notorious for rowdy drunkenness, and hiring away other mills' papermakers with bonuses and other inducements. Expansion on a scale that could meet the burgeoning demand for paper was made possible only by the invention of the Fourdrinier.

It was an age of invention, and other machines followed the Fourdrinier. New mechanical cutters to prepare rags for the Hollander; washing machines and bleach that allowed mills to make even the dirtiest rags into white paper; machines that applied size to writing paper, trimmed edges, and ruled lines onto ledger paper. The cumulative effect was increased output and a series of small reductions in the price of finished paper.

The hand mills that produced paper before the invention of the Fourdrinier collected rags from and supplied paper to small regions using modest water-wheels to power a Hollander, but water's role in the papermaking process was far more crucial than its use as a power source in those preindustrial mills. Pure water was the most crucial ingredient in papermaking—and the rarest. Naturally occurring taints, such as high iron content, could mar the finished product; effluent from upstream users was anathema. Which is why a young man named Zenas Crane rode through the Berkshires in 1799 examining springs.

Crane was born in Milton, Massachusetts. His family was prosperous and his father was part owner of a paper mill on the Neponset. The father died while Zenas was an infant, leaving the young man no fortune except for the skills he would acquire working in his older brother's paper mill at Newton Lower Falls. At twenty, Crane wanted to start a mill of his own and calculated, correctly, that opportunity would be brighter in a late-settled region like the Berkshires, where the entire county boasted not a single paper mill, than in the economically developed areas along the coast.

The mill Zenas Crane built with financing from local investors was designed to turn Berkshire rags into paper for Berkshire use, which it did. As the years passed, a handful of similar mills were started in other Berkshire towns. There were four paper mills in Berkshire County by 1809, unremarkable except as indicators that the world was changing. Two or three mills and some importation from England had met the needs of even the most economically developed colonies. Connecticut had no paper mill at all until one was started in Norwich in 1776; New York got its first mill, at Hempstead, only in 1768. Yet by 1810 nearly every town had a local mill; the ones that didn't had local promoters interested in luring a papermaker to town. As the pace of commercial life quickened, the demand for newspapers, account books, writing paper, wrapping paper, almanacs, and books of all kinds burgeoned. A local mill was the best way for local printers and merchants to insure their supply of paper, and an important indication that a town had moved beyond its agricultural origins and was on the road to commercial prosperity.

New York was the largest and fastest-growing city on the continent, but one glance at the Hudson confirmed that, produce as many rags as it might, the city could not make its own paper. The Berkshires, on the other hand, had plentiful

PLATNER & SMITH. LEE, MAS⁵

The virtuous republican mother teaches industry to her children in this lithograph by Nathaniel Currier before he teamed up with Ives. We are intended to see republican virtue in the Roman dress and to understand that industry is being taught from the beehive. The slatted windows of the drying lofts identify the building as a paper mill.

Lithograph by N. Currier of Platner and Smith paper mill, Lee, Massachusetts. Courtesy, American Antiquarian Society.

clear water. Between 1819 and 1829 Berkshire County erected ten new paper mills, a threefold increase; since the new mills were larger than early mills built to serve local needs, the productive capacity of the local industry actually increased fivefold.[3]

Berkshire County was America's leading center of paper production; its market was New York, the young nation's leading city. A steady flow of rags traveled up the Hudson, and fresh supplies of paper moved down, slowed only by the tedium of overland transportation from mill to riverboat, and by winter, when ice closed the Hudson. Business correspondence between the two centers was unchanging: New York merchants wrote to Berkshire manufacturers enjoining them to increase their production of paper; Berkshire mill owners wrote to New York merchants beseeching them to send more rags.

Not that papermaking required linen rags. Paper can be made from the fiber of myriad plants, and the list of plants that make good paper is a long one. The list of vegetable fibers available in sufficient volume and at a low enough price to be of practical interest to paper mill owners was, however, distressingly brief. Almost all paper in Europe and America was made of linen rags. Linen rags were inexpensive, they made excellent paper, the technique of working them had become familiar, and until the advent of cheap cotton clothing, they were widely available. As cotton garments began to replace linen, a partial solution was found by blending available cotton rags with stronger linen rags, but by early nineteenth century, not all the cotton and all the linen rags added together could meet the growing demand.

Mechanization made the supply problem only worse. Every innovation enabling mill owners to produce more paper at cheaper rates created fresh demand for their product. Linen rags were imported from Europe by the shipload to meet the paper demands of Americans, who shifted from linen to cotton clothing more rapidly than Europeans, and, industrializing faster, purchased more paper even as they generated fewer linen rags. Worn-out jute and hempen rope purchased from shipyards was used to make Manila paper, although scrap rope could not be made into white paper. Worn-out sails could, and were much sought-after by the voracious mills. The most bizarre episode in the quest for new sources of rags was surely the use of cloth wrappings taken from Egyptian mummies. Shiploads of bodies were stripped of their fine linen wrappings and of the papyrus filling used by ancient embalmers, but even in mummy procurement mill owners encountered competition. The Egyptian government, regarding the relics with Islamic disdain for pagan relics, permitted the use of pre-Islamic bodies as locomotive fuel on the new Suez railroad.[4]

Grave robbing was a mere stopgap. The pressing need was to find a new source of fiber. Cattails, bark, cabbage stocks, hop vines, thistle, wasps' nests, peat, corn husks, and asbestos were all made into paper by entrepreneurial experimenters, but the only alternative fiber used on a large commercial scale in this country was straw. Straw had the advantage of being readily available, even if mill owners had to be prepared to purchase and store a year's supply during the grain harvest. There was some expense in cleaning the dirt and foreign matter that inevitably clung to the straw. But the greatest shortcoming was that the cellulose fibers of straw are short, forcing papermakers to mix linen pulp with the straw; even so the straw paper proved more brittle and less durable than rag.[5]

The potential of wood fiber from America's vast forests escaped no one in the industry, but there were obstacles. Paper was a small-scale, undercapitalized industry, even in Berkshire County, where forty-one paper mills in 1855 represented by far the largest concentration in the nation.[6] Mills were owned and managed by papermaking families who financed expansion by reinvesting profits in plant and equipment. They knew that any new raw material would entail the underwriting of lengthy experimentation and expensive retooling. As a group, Berkshire mill owners hung back from innovation as long as there was money to be made from familiar materials. They had begun manufacturing straw paper only after a Pennsylvanian worked out a profitable process. Now they were waiting for someone to invent a process for making paper from wood. Friedrich Gottlob Keller obliged.

Keller, a weaver from Hainichen, Saxony, invented an efficient process for reducing blocks of wood to fiber with a grindstone. He built a working model, but such an invention faced a limited future unless someone undertook to finance its commercial development. Heinrich Voelter, director of a paper mill in Bautzen, Saxony, was the man for the job. Keller patented his invention in 1840. In 1846, Voelter bought the patent and hired a Wurttemberg machinist, I. M. Voith, to make the machine practical for commercial-scale production. Even with adequate financing, the job took time, but by 1852 Voelter had two plants turning out linen-and-wood paper in volume.[7]

Alberto Pagenstecher had nothing to do with the paper business. An engineer from Wiesbaden, he made a fortune building railroads in South America. An early venture capitalist, Pagenstrecher was looking for ways to invest his fortune and mentioned his quest to a young relative, Albrecht Pagenstecher, who was living in New York. Albrecht had happened recently to hear his friend, piano maker Theodore Steinway, mention that a German manufacturer had mastered the technique of producing paper from wood. Albrecht and Alberto wrote to Albrecht's brother, Rudolph, still in Germany, who went to see Voelter.

America's first wood pulp mill opened in Curtisville, Massachusetts in 1867, with ownership divided among the three Pagenstechers, Steinway, Voelter, and one Ferdinand Hoffman. The owners imported a skillful and experienced mechanic named Frederick Wuertzbach and five German operatives to run the mill, using second-growth poplar cut from abandoned Berkshire County pastures as feedstock. With a decade and a half of German industrial research and development behind it, the Curtisville mill was an instant success.[8] The first

American newspaper to be regularly printed on wood pulp paper was the *New Yorker Staats-Zeitung.*[9]

Wood paper was far from perfect. What a papermaker wants from a plant is cellulose fiber, the longer the better, but separated in any event from noncellulose plant matter. Grinding wood produced fibers that were so short and weak they had to be mixed with linen to make paper. Worse, the grinding process did nothing to separate the desirable cellulose fibers from the lignin and resins that, however useful to a growing tree, are contaminants in a paper slurry. Because the fibers were short, paper made from ground-wood fiber tore easily. Because the slurry was impure, it yellowed quickly.

In its favor, ground-wood paper took ink well and it was cheap. Cheapness can be a paramount virtue. Ground-wood paper was so cheap it created its own market, lowering the price of newsprint so far that a penny-press sprang into existence with a voracious appetite for more newsprint.

Ground-wood pulp mills multiplied rapidly. Still, it was apparent that a fortune would be made from a process that could produce higher-quality paper by removing the lignin and resin from wood while preserving the long cellulose fibers. Men were working on the problem even before the first ground-wood mills came on line. The first practical method was developed by two Englishmen, Hugh Burgess and Charles Watt, who received a patent in 1851 only to discover that no English financier would back them while they developed a commercial process. The English financiers may have been correct. Not because industrial development is a lengthy, costly process with no guaranteed payoff, although it is, but because wood in England was scarce and dear. The two English inventors received an American patent in 1854 and began making paper at Gray's Ferry on the Schuylkill near Philadelphia. Their technique entailed boiling wood chips in a caustic alkali solution under pressure and at high temperatures to dissolve the lignin and separate it from the cellulose, followed by washing the fibers with water. Though Watt and Burgess went bankrupt, the process they developed worked.[10]

An alternative process, in which wood chips were cooked in sulfurous acid, was also developed near Philadelphia by chemist Benjamin Tilghman, who had the misfortune of solving the chemical problems while failing to work out a practicable manufacturing process. That was done by Carl Ekman in Sweden and George Fry in England, whose patents were purchased by the Sayles brothers of Providence, Rhode Island, where the first American sulphite process mill was built in 1884.[11] With three commercially viable processes available for turning paper into trees, the new problem was finding enough trees.

Maine was not supposed to be a woodlot. It was surveyed and laid out in neat townships by men who had every expectation that Maine would be settled in the same orderly fashion as Massachusetts and Vermont. As the nineteenth century began, they confidently assumed that Maine would soon be cleared for tillage and pasture.

Township lines still run across the map of Maine, marking portions of acreage calculated to support a village, a school, and a church. But Maine's empty townships are not like Tinmouth, Vermont, where empty cellar holes testify that, in its day, Tinmouth was a prosperous village and the shiretown of Rutland County. More than half of the state of Maine was never settled at all. The township lines on the map are the only indication that anyone ever expected that it would be. Although immigration to Maine from the settled parts of New England boomed in the 1790s, by the turn of the century, American farmers took note of the short growing seasons on Maine's thin, rocky, glacier-scoured soil, and moved to Ohio. Efforts to attract settlers continued long after a dispassionate observer would have called a halt, but the truth was that in a nation that could grow corn in Indiana and wheat in Nebraska, the only crop that it paid to grow in Maine—Aroostoock and its potato farms excepted—was wood.

When settlers failed to come, lumbermen did, entering the Maine woods like children searching a bowl of M&Ms for the red ones. The lumbermen wanted white pine, and in their search for the finest lumber from the most profitable species, they ignored everything else. Settlers near tidewater cleared land and cut cordwood, but the deep woods of Maine were only culled for pine until, in the late 1840s, pine began to run short. With the pine gone and the cities of a growing nation hungry for timber, the lumbermen came back, like children who have eaten all the red M&Ms and now want the yellow ones. This time they wanted spruce. Great logs of red spruce were cut, headed, limbed, and stacked along winter rivers to be carried to mills on the spring freshet. Wooden lumber camps sprang up like mushrooms after rain, stood for a season where there were stands of pine or spruce near a river, then rotted back to the soil.[12] Two and a half centuries after the first English ax felled a tree in Maine, great forests still stood. There were almost no large-diameter pine or spruce left standing near a river in 1870, but a vast forest of balsam fir, maple, birch, hemlock, beech, and half-grown spruce spread over half the state while, in southern Maine, farms abandoned soon after statehood supported young forests of poplar and white pine.

Paper mills came for the same reasons that made Bangor the nation's leading lumber port: forests, water, and proximity to market. There were more trees in Oregon, but they were all the way out in Oregon. There were no more trees in Berkshire County: within twenty years of the building of the first ground-wood pulp mill, Berkshire County's woodlots and second-growth forests were depleted and papermakers had begun to look elsewhere for uncut forests, pristine streams and new sources of power. They found them Down East.

The first Maine pulp mills were small affairs, locally financed and often unsuccessful, but the potential of the industry was so apparent that Boston and New York money moved to take advantage of the Maine woods on a grand

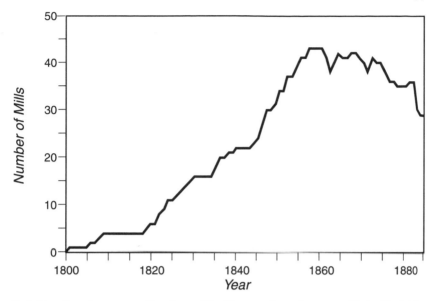

Berkshire County paper mills, 1800 –1885. The number of paper mills in Berkshire County increased as the Industrial Revolution created demand, then fell in the 1880s, when Berkshire County ran out of second-growth timber to feed the wood-pulp mills.

Judith McGaw: *Most Wonderful Machine: Mechanization and social change in Berkshire papermaking, 1801–1885.*

Copyright ©1987 by Princeton University Press. Reprinted by permission of Princeton University Press.

scale, building large, highly-capitalized papermills, constructing immense dams to power them, and moving to insure the wood supply.[13]

When Maine's first wood pulp mills were built in the 1870s, the vast forests of Michigan were being carried to market. By the 1890s, when the Maine paper industry expanded aggressively, logging was in its heyday in the upper midwest and forested acreage in Maine, long since stripped of pine and large spruce, was exceedingly cheap. It would stay cheap while the old-growth forests of Wisconsin and Minnesota were stripped of virgin timber and loggers moved on toward Oregon and California. Papermills were the only buyers of Maine land, and they were buying reliable supplies of feedstock, not forests.

A forest is the ultimate sustainable ecosystem: capable of producing valuable wood, while maintaining populations of wildlife, plants, and microorganisms. A well-managed forest can do all this, forever, while absorbing carbon dioxide and generating the oxygen that sustains life on earth. It is also a place of great beauty.

A walk in an old-growth forest is nothing like a walk in the woods. It is, perhaps, the quality of light in old growth that makes it so different from the second growth woods of contemporary experience. Light filters and sifts through a canopy far overhead, reaching the ground in green translucence like light seen from the bottom of a clear sea, or it slants between giant boles in bright fingered shafts, piercing the half-light to spotlight a few square inches of forest floor. That floor is not the carpet of oak leaves in a suburban woods. It is damp and soft, tufted with fern and upholstered with mosses that cover the ground and grow seventy and eighty feet up the trunks of trees. The trunks are of such immense girth that where they lie fallen, the way is impassible. Air in the old growth is moist even in a dry season. Beech and hemlock sprout in the deep, rich soil, and on the tops of rotting stumps and boles that strew the ground interspersed with thickets of viburnum, laurel, and yew. The old growth is also gone. The last intact northern hardwood forest in New England, three hundred acres in Colebrook, Connecticut, was logged in 1913. Only fragments remain, scattered on steep, inaccessible hillslopes.

Less majestic than old growth, a mature, second-growth northern hardwood forest is nonetheless a magnificent thing. Maple, birch, beech, spruce, hemlock, and white pine create a forest that blazes with autumn glory and carpets the spring with flowers. Northern hardwood is the forest that nature plants in two-thirds of New Hampshire and almost the whole state of Vermont. It was the forest of Berkshire County before the farmers started clearing land, and the forest of northwestern Connecticut before the ironworks started cutting cordwood. It is the forest nature plants in Maine.[14]

The northern hardwood forest is not merely beautiful; it is an efficient machine for combining mineral earth with sunlight and water to create topsoil. Trees do not perform this masterwork of creation; forests do. A forest is more than trees. A forest is the trees, the warblers, the trailing arbutus, the caterpillars, the chipmunks, the millipedes, the arthropods, the fungi, and the soil bacteria. Especially the arthropods, the fungi, and the soil bacteria, of which there may be more than ten million in a single gram of topsoil. Before there can be a forest there must be topsoil.

Half the volume of healthy topsoil is made up of mineral elements—sand, silt, and clay—but almost nothing grows in pure mineral soil. To produce a forest requires the mixing of water and air into the mineral soil until each constitutes 20 to 25 percent of the total mix, and it requires the addition of humus, the dark, organic element that is the breakdown product of decaying plants and animals. Humus comprises 5 to 15 percent of the material in productive topsoil and it is arthropods, fungi, and bacteria that turn maple leaves into humus. Without their deconstructive labors, fallen maple leaves lie on the forest floor, and the calcium they contain stays locked in dead cell walls.

Calcium, phosphorous, nitrogen, potassium, and magnesium are the crucial and usually scarce elements of plant life. Hydrogen, carbon, oxygen, sulfur, and iron, no less essential, are omnipresent on the face of the earth, but the first five are hard to come by, largely because they are useful to plants only in soluble form. Nitrogen, for example, must be wrested from the atmosphere by one of a small number of plants with associated root bacteria capable of converting the airy element into growing tissue. Calcium is found in any number of common sedimentary and igneous rocks, but only a few plants and microorganisms have the knack of using mineral calcium. When a forest gets hold of a bit of calcium or nitrogen in the tissue of a plant, it latches on, breaking a dead bit of nitrogen-fixing alder root down to humus, drawing it up through the roots and into the needles of a white pine, and, when the pine sheds its needles, breaking them down to humus for use by another plant.

As long as the needles fall into the litter to be broken down and used again, the forest holds its own in the immemorial cycle of growth and death, even gaining a little as it accumulates reserves of the five scarce elements and the layer of fertile topsoil deepens with each passing century. If the total amount of phosphorous, nitrogen, potassium, magnesium, and calcium locked into the fiber and resin of wood removed from a forest is equal to the quantities of those elements the forest community can wrest from air and from mineral soil, then the harvest is sustainable. Selective, limited harvest can continue forever without diminishing the forest. Unless the timber is removed with heavy equipment in a warm season.

There are many ways to kill a forest. One of the simplest is by tamping it down. Loggers of the ox and axe era worked in winter not because they were environmentalists aware that hard-frozen ground protects topsoil from compaction, although it does, but because it was easier to move logs over snow- and ice-covered ground. No such constraints hamper modern logging. Mammoth feller-bunchers capable of mechanically cutting and limbing a tree as easily as a gardener clips a branch, move into the woods in all seasons, packing down the earth beneath their treads. Mechanical harvesters are expensive machines, but even with price tags of half a million dollars, they are cheaper than paying the wages of a crew with chain saws. It is an economy of the short term, because mechanical harvesters kill soil insects and microorganisms when their vast weight compacts the soil, and the hard-packed soil they leave behind makes it impossible for seedlings to put down roots and exceedingly difficult for even planted seedlings to grow.[15]

The harvested site, bare of vegetation, bakes in the sun, becoming far too hot and dry to sustain the life of whatever soil organisms survived the logging in uncompacted patches and might have renewed the forest. The soil, with no growing plants to hold it in place, washes away easily, a disaster most logging companies try to mitigate by diverting runoff into uncut areas, where undisturbed topsoil readily absorbs the muddy water and its burden of nutrients. While this technique keeps soil nutrients from being lost downstream, the cutover acreage has lost much of its productive capacity.[16]

Nature is forgiving. When a tree is limbed and the trunk skidded out of the woods, insects and fungi immediately set to work reducing its branches and leaves to humus that will support a new generation of trees. Because most of the nutrients in a living tree are found in the leaves and growing branches, a forest from which only boles are removed retains nutrients that enable it to sustain growth.[17] But loggers do not always leave the nutrient-rich branches in the woods. In a process called whole-tree harvesting, everything down to the leafy twigs is chipped and pulped for papermaking or turned into electricity in biomass energy plants, leaving the land less productive with every harvest.[18]

The forest that the paper companies came north to harvest in the 1890s was a mixed ecosystem with a dozen species of trees dominated by birch, beech, and maple; spruce, hemlock, and white pine played important roles; while oak, ash, and others had bit parts. One of the few firm axioms in ecology is that diverse ecosystems are more productive than monocultures, and a mixed hardwood forest produces far more wood than a single-species stand. It is also more resistant to disease.

There were in Maine whole forests where spruce and balsam fir dominated, but these were the cold, wet places where nothing else would grow—along parts of the western border with Quebec, on foggy Atlantic headlands, in high mountains and low peat bogs. Where the land was good, a mixed forest grew, and the mixed forest made the land good. Spruce creates a biological near-desert wherever it grows.

Spruce needles decay slowly, leaching a dilute acid solution into the soil as rain flows over thick carpets of fallen needles. Earthworms, millipedes, slugs, and bacteria are loath to live in the acid soil under a spruce tree. When the neighborhood changes from mixed hardwoods to spruce, only the fungi stay to continue their slow labor of decomposition. Bacteria, arthropods, and other denizens of the topsoil die. Rainwaters leach away the crucial nutrients stored in their decomposing bodies, nutrients that made the growth of the topsoil-producing, mixed-species forest possible. Dilute acid seeping from spruce needles dissolves the components of the mineral subsoil, washing away everything except the quartz. Dig a hole in the spruce forest and, just below the forest mold of slowly decomposing twigs and needles, you will find a layer of fine, ash-colored sand. It is quartz, the only mineral the acid bath washing down from spruce needles fails to dissolve; it offers no sustenance to plant or animal. Russians call this nutrient-poor soil *podzol* (ash-soil) for its pale grey color. Few Americans dig holes in the spruce forest. Pioneer farmers knew better than to settle on spruce lands. Once soil is reduced to this level, it will not support a mixed hardwood forest. It will not support agriculture. It will grow only spruce.[19]

Spruce, fast-growing with strong fibers and light color, had become the pulpwood of choice by the 1880s. Lumberjacks cut thousands of cords of red spruce too young to make saw timber to feed the pulp mills, then they cut beech, maple, hemlock, birch, and fir, but it was apparent that not even Maine's vast forests would last forever. As each tract was cleared, paper companies managed their cutover land for spruce. Young black and white spruce, species of the tundra, will grow in the impoverished soil, dry conditions, exposed winters, and hot summers of a clearcut, where red spruce, a child of the shady, moist forest, is loath to put down roots. As the paper companies cut the mixed hardwood forest and replaced it with spruce, parts of the Maine forest became paper plantations, as ecologically diverse and sustainable as cotton fields.[20] Cotton fields require regular fertilization. It is not profitable to fertilize something as vast as a spruce plantation when the payoff lies at the end of a forty-year cutting cycle.

Aspen trees stubbornly sprouted where the paper companies wanted a profitable spruce monoculture in Maine, but the companies sprayed herbicides to reduce would-be mixed aspen-spruce forests to spruce monocultures. Generations of heavy cutting and suppression of mixed-species regrowth in favor of spruce often resulted only in degraded stands of brush dominated by the low-value pioneer species, birch and aspen.[21] Given time, a degraded landscape of aspen, birch, and bramble turns itself back into a forest, but it takes decades or centuries, not the few years an intelligently cut stand requires for regeneration.

For much of the present century, however, the Maine forest was not intelligently cut. It was thoroughly neglected. Paper companies may have wanted the land to grow spruce, but pulpwood was so cheap and lumber came in such plenty from the vast, virgin forests of the West that it hardly seemed worthwhile to manage a Maine forest. Some lands near mills were managed and even planted for spruce monoculture, but vast acreages were carelessly high-graded by loggers who cut only the most profitable individual trees of every species, leaving a ravaged stock of less desirable trees growing on intact soil. Lumberjacks with their band saws took only the valuable trunks, leaving the branches to rot. When the loggers left, the woods recovered. Some forms of neglect can be benign.

World War II changed the way men went into the woods. The direct effects of the war were an increased lumber harvest as America geared up for war production, and the fleeting novelty of camps of German prisoners of war working as lumberjacks. The effects of the technological spinoffs would be far greater. Aware that the war would be fought on wheels, in 1941 the war department sponsored development of the jeep. It was not elegant, but it could go places no motorized vehicle had gone before.[22] By the time the war ended, army contractors had developed motorized chain saws as well as cargo trucks capable of driving off-road and tractors able to tackle rugged terrain. The nature of man's assault on the woods changed. The change accelerated about 1960 with the introduction of new, fat-tired trucks designed for lumbering, but the Maine woods were buffered from the full impact of the changes by the existence of the western forests. As long as the virgin forests of the West still stood, Maine was only lightly cut. Cutting declined from its turn-of-the-century rate in the middle decades of the century, when more wood grew each year in Maine than was harvested. In about 1970, demand caught up with dwindling supply, and the loggers came back to Maine.[23]

Demand came from paper companies expanding mill capacity to keep up with growing markets, from lumber mills filling demand the now cutover forests of the American West could no longer meet at prices that had long made Maine timber unprofitable, and from renewed demand for cordwood created by the oil crisis. For the first time since the turn of the century, in the 1970s more wood left the Maine woods every year than was being grown. For the first time ever, wood was being harvested by huge machines in clearcut swaths that left the topsoil bruised and impoverished. The hot, dry, compacted soil of some clearcuts were growing nothing but bramble thickets ten years after heavy-wheeled feller-bunchers stripped them of trees, a situation that would not look unusual in much of the rain-scarce West, but that is shocking in New England's humid, forgiving climate.[24]

Frighteningly little is known about how the topsoil functions. Recent examination of the soil of an old-growth forest in the Pacific Northwest reveals that there are about eight thousand arthropods on the site. Not eight thousand individual, minute invertebrate creatures. Eight thousand different species of microscopic insects at work shredding the detritus of a forest.[25] Study of microscopic soil process is too recent for all of the creatures even to have been identified, let alone studied, but we do know that soil communities vary by site, that different insects, bacteria, and fungi are found under different species of tree and in different kinds of soil, that the leaves in a mountain birch forest are decomposed by a very different community than are the needles of a hemlock grove. And we know that the soil community remnant in a large clearcut is uniquely impoverished. We do not know how or whether soil communities recover from clearcutting.

We know, however, how to manage forests to increase yield and improve forest health.[26] It can be accomplished by following five simple principles. The first of which—never remove lumber faster than the forest can grow new wood—sounds so obvious, we forget that doing precisely the opposite is one of the things that made America rich. The forests that Europeans found on settlement were a huge bonanza. We didn't plant them, we didn't manage them, we didn't thin undesirable trees or do a release cut to improve the stand. We simply walked in and took the harvest. When the first colonists landed, a squirrel could have traveled from Cape Cod to the Mississippi without ever leaving the treetops. The squirrel had to stop at the Mississippi only because the river is too wide to jump across; a squirrel provided with a boat could have continued its journey some considerable while before reaching the grasslands. The eastern half of this continent was a vast forest. The mix of species varied, but the forest was continuous. That forest provided an immense, unearned timber dividend that accrued to the first comers in 1607 and continues to accrue today, when old-growth timber is felled in California, Oregon, Washington, and Alaska. It has been hard to realize that the free lunch is over, that the topsoil accumulated over presettlement millennia can be depleted in mere decades, and that any large sawtimber future generations will need must be planned and husbanded.

The second principle of sustainable forestry is that yields are maximized by growing timber on long rotations. Forty-year-old trees yield low-grade fiber and narrow planks of weak, knotty wood. Only wood that grows for one hundred, two hundred years, or longer, depending on the species, yields the clear, wide boards needed for fine cabinetry and the strong timber useful in building construction. More to the point is the fact that mature trees add more wood annually than young growth. Waiting until each tree reaches the peak of its growth curve, at an age of one hundred or one hundred and fifty years, maximizes the amount of wood that can be produced on a given tract of land.

The third forest management principle is known as uneven-aged management; it entails cutting the forest in small patches and harvesting selected, individual trees within a stand. This is the way Indians cleared the land. Except in areas where they clear-cut the coastal plains, Indian cutting of small fields in the forest protected the integrity of the topsoil community by insuring that when the field was abandoned, neighboring species would move into the opening and allow the forest to recover. The method works. A small cut is quickly reseeded with native species and decimated topsoil microorganisms can be replenished from the intact soil adjacent to the cutover area. Woodlands where individual trees at the peak of their productive life are selected by thoughtful foresters can retain remarkable stability of species and high yields over a very long time.

Ecological balance, the fourth principle, is based on an assumption of profound ignorance. We do not know everything about how a forest functions, but we are quite certain that it does function. By managing our harvest in ways that preserve the viability of every species known to live in a forest, we can insure the future health and productive capacity of the land as efficiently as if we fully understood how the system worked.

The final principle, that extreme care must be taken not to damage the topsoil, is not conceptually difficult, but it is widely disregarded. In fact, all five principles of sustainable forestry are ignored by corporate forest owners because in an investment environment where five years is regarded as long-term, they are economically absurd.

A corporation that decides to invest money in timber is deciding not to invest the money elsewhere. Part of the cost of growing trees must be calculated as the opportunity price of not investing the money in ways that would have paid a dividend during the decades it takes a tree to grow to harvestable size. If a tree will take eighty years to reach harvestable size, and interest rates during that time are at 4 percent, the tree will have to return $23 in year eighty for every dollar invested in year one (in constant dollars allowing nothing for inflation). If interest rates are 7 percent, every dollar invested in trees will have to return

$224, and if interest rates are 10 percent every dollar will have to return $2,048.[27]

Maine pulp mills, understanding the implications of these figures, put very little money into active forest management. Release cuts, culling, and other management techniques improve the yield of a stand, but almost never by enough of a margin to justify paying a forester now for work that won't pay off for forty or eighty years. The numbers are bad enough to make an observer wonder why pulp mills invest in land at all.

The key reason is that the mills own only a fraction of Maine's industrial forest, but it is a large enough fraction to supply the mills at times when prices charged by other landowners are too high. Large enough, that is, to keep prices permanently low by giving mill managers the ability to force prices down by cutting on company land in periods of short supply. Company lands, moreover, were purchased over many decades, but always at times when prices were low. There is little debt service involved, only the opportunity cost of owning land that might be sold for profits that could be invested elsewhere. In recent years, many northwoods owners have done exactly that.[28]

Buying timberlands can be profitable if the value of standing wood is high and if the wood is immediately cut and sold. Buying land at timberland prices and selling it at house lot prices is very profitable. The unprofitable thing is to tie money up in land that will not produce a harvest for decades.

Owners are aware that clear-cutting will degrade the soil, but degraded soil is about as relevant to a paper corporation's annual statement as Ts'ai Lun's expense accounting for the effort he put into inventing paper. These companies are not in the topsoil business. They are not in the business of growing forests. They are in the business of taking a profit out of the woods. Because all business costs are analyzed in terms of the opportunity costs of the investment, soil depletion that will reduce the productivity of the land by 100 percent at the harvest of the first generation of trees, reduces the current value of forest land by less than 1 percent. Depletion of forest soils that will leave land incapable of producing a crop of trees in one hundred or two hundred years are irrelevant to corporate profit calculations.[29] Managing a forest to maximize the sustainable yield of wood or to insure the future productivity of the topsoil would be fiscal irresponsibility on the part of corporate officers who owe a fiduciary duty to the shareholders.

Altering forest policy in a way that would maximize wood production and insure healthy lumber harvests for future generations is probably beyond the political capacity of a poor state dominated by a single industry. It may be beyond the capacity of any single nation-state: managing forests for sustainable yield would simply drive paper and lumber jobs offshore, unless nations cooperated to protect a shared future. This lack of control is distressing to the residents of Maine who are able to envision the many ways sustainable forestry policies would improve the state economy. But there is more distressing news in the wind.

Chapter 15

Pure Waters

❧

One of the most remarkable qualities of running water is that of self-purification . . . when the most noxious matter has been thrown into a running stream, all traces of it have disappeared in the course of a few miles.[1]

—Frederick Rice, 1872

W HEN I WAS A GIRL, MY FAMILY WENT EVERY
summer to the Thimble Islands off the Connecticut coast. There
are hundreds of islands in the Thimbles, but only a few large
enough to be inhabited. Of these, some have dozens of houses, and some, like
the island of my girlhood summers, have only a single home. That house fascinated me.

Nothing about it had been changed since it was built as a summer residence
in the 1890s. Light in the grand rooms and the immense, polished-walnut
butler's pantry on the first floor came from gas jets, which was unusual in the
1960s; light upstairs in the bedrooms was provided by kerosene lamps that had
to have their chimneys cleaned, wicks trimmed, and reservoirs filled daily. The
bedrooms all had sinks, echoes of the washstands that preceded indoor
plumbing, while the bathrooms boasted cast-iron tubs enthroned on ball-and-
claw feet with separate taps labeled for salt and fresh water, sinks that stood on
pedestals, and toilets operated by pull chains pendant from varnished wooden
tanks perched near the high ceiling. Water arrived from the mainland via pipes
on the seabed and the entire, elaborate plumbing system ended in an outfall
behind the kitchen that poured raw sewage into Long Island Sound.

Those pipes, the long, expensive-to-maintain system bringing fresh water to
Lewis Island and the short, rusty pipe dumping sewage into the sound, epito-
mize American attitudes toward plumbing: spare no effort to obtain clean
water and don't worry about what comes out the other end of the pipe. The
irony is that the grand Victorian summer mansion on Lewis Island was built
with a fortune made in oysters.

Before tacos, before pizza, even before hot dogs, Americans ate oysters. The ultimate fast food, oysters waited in harborside restaurants until a customer walked in. They were ready to eat as fast as they could be shucked, and they were so cheap, a hungry man could eat his fill for pennies. If oysters were the simplest, cheapest food, they were also the most elegant. When Victorian gentlemen in white tie and tails sat down to a seven-course dinner of dishes with pretentious French names, oysters certified the elegance of the evening. Packed with ice, oysters were shipped far inland. When canning developed, tinned oysters were sold in outposts too remote even to receive iced shipments. Americans ate oysters, raw, fried, stewed, on the half-shell or in a Meissen china dish. Immense demand and inexhaustible supply conjured a great industry into being.

Oysters grow as far north as Nova Scotia, but it's hard for them. Spawning takes place in water that has reached temperatures of sixty-eight to seventy degrees Fahrenheit, a situation that, as vacationers who have attempted to swim at Old Orchard Beach, Maine, know, does not often occur along the Maine coast. North of Cape Cod, perfectly healthy oysters with a normal interest in sex may wait several years for a season with favorable spawning conditions, but when their season comes, they are fecund beyond imagination: each mollusk releases tens of millions of eggs or sperm. If temperature and current are right, the eggs and sperm get together to make free-swimming larvae called spawn. To live, the spawn must set, that is, attach to a hard, clean surface on the bottom of an estuary where the water is neither fresh nor as salty as deep-sea water.[2]

Oysters are sedentary creatures and, since they live in shallow water, easy to catch. Fishing efficiently eliminated the population in northern waters where spawning was infrequent. Oysters were scarce near Boston by the late seventeenth century and unknown in commercial quantity north of Cape Cod by the late eighteenth. Even the famous commercial oyster fishery at Wellfleet harbor disappeared, every last mollusk eaten before it could spawn. After 1775, the 'Wellfleet' oysters served in Boston oyster houses were transplants, Long Island Sound or Chesapeake oysters carried to Wellfleet for a few months' growth before being sold in Boston.[3]

Long Island Sound is a far more hospitable home for oysters than the cold waters north of Cape Cod. It is shallow; rivers constantly replenish the food supply and keep the water slightly fresher than the ocean; and temperatures are warm enough for spawning every year. In the early years of British settlement, oysters were harvested for local use just as they had long been harvested by Indians. The survival of the oyster population was not in doubt: the number of people living near tidewater was small, while the supply of oysters was huge. Commercialization of the Yankee economy changed that. Shipment of barreled oysters by the wagonload began about 1800 and created a market for every oyster in the estuaries. A law intended to conserve the oyster population closed the fishery during the spring and summer to allow the oysters to spawn and set, but

Tonging oysters, Seekonk River, 1904. Courtesy The Rhode Island Historical Society. Rhi (x3)2273.

when the legal season began on November 1, Fairhaven Harbor was rimmed with boats that began their race to the grounds while the town clock was still pealing midnight. Within days, the floor of the estuary had been scoured clean of oysters, most of which, too small to eat, were resold to men living near shallow bays where they would grow to market size. By the 1830s natural production of young oysters could no longer keep up with demand.[4]

The obvious recourse was to Chesapeake Bay. Fleets of coasting schooners brought southern oysters to northern markets, and it was not long before someone noticed the efficiency of carrying small oysters north, replanting them in Long Island Sound, and harvesting them after they had grown to market size. Transportation costs were lower and the perishable inventory was then near market to be harvested on demand. Since importing southern oysters was necessarily less profitable than harvesting local stock, the economics were ripe for oyster farming to develop.

Mediterranean oystermen have been farming since Roman times, catching the set on shells or clay tiles suspended from floats and laying these out on proprietary grounds. By the 1840s, Connecticut oystermen were experimenting with ways to catch the "set" of the free-swimming oyster larvae.[5] The process was not smooth. American oysters differ from Mediterranean in preferring to set on the sea floor, and while clean shells could be strewn on a firm bottom for their convenience, if the shells lay in the water more than a few days they became coated with algae and the spawn would not set. Modern oystermen monitor water temperatures and lay down shells when conditions are ripe for spawning, but the careful studies of molluscan sexual practice that make accurate prediction possible were not available to nineteenth-century oystermen. Old-time oystermen watched the weather, opened brood oysters to look for "spawn in the neck," strained the waters of the sound with sieves of fine cloth to look for larvae, and lay shells on the sea floor when they calculated that the spawn were ready to set. If spat failed to set, they dredged the shells back up and spread them in the sun to dry for next year. Almost always, the spat set.

Very few larvae are lucky enough to find a clean bit of shell or rock to attach to under natural conditions; under the management of oyster farmers spreading shells, millions of spat successfully set. State and local governments, with Connecticut in the lead, made oyster farming pay by selling and leasing plots of the sea floor. With their growing grounds protected from interlopers, farmers could afford to set out brood oysters and spread shells to collect spat in shallow estuarine waters. They dredged the shells and replanted them in deeper waters where oysters grow but don't set, freeing the valuable nursery grounds for next year's set. Two- and three-year-old oysters were sold to farmers in shallow bays on Long Island itself, where the meat acquired a finer flavor and lost the greenish tinge imparted by the high iron and copper content of Connecticut waters. Cotton nets were dragged across proprietary sea bottoms to remove predatory starfish. In 1898, the Long Island Sound oyster catch reached 15,218,614 bushels, worth $1,249,071.[6] This, in 1898 dollars (which bought a gallon of cleaned oyster meat for ninety cents), was a major industry, profitable enough to build for its owners mansions like the one on Lewis Island.

Waterbury, Connecticut, never was a fishing village. It was a farming town where water flowing down the hillslopes was put to work manufacturing buttons, clocks, tools, and, especially, brass hardware. The largest mill in town was the Scoville Manufacturing Company, which, by 1850, had used all of the water-power potential on its site and was installing a 125-horsepower steam engine. To supply clean water to run the engine, it was necessary to construct a private aqueduct from a spring on a nearby hillside.

Steam mills were not the only consumers demanding new water supplies. Households wanted increasing supplies of water as they became more affluent. Towns wanted ready supplies to fight fires. And, as cities grew crowded, there was a demand for water purity that could no longer be guaranteed by backyard wells and natural springs. Waterbury mill owners and groups of private citizens piped water in from springs in the hills, but it quickly became apparent that even if there had been enough springs to go around, which there weren't, it would be far cheaper to build a reservoir and a municipal water system.[7]

Public works projects of this scale are not agreed upon and built overnight, but by 1868 Waterbury had built a reservoir and water pipes ran to every household that paid for the privilege. The system proved so popular that in 1880 a second reservoir came on line. In that year one-eighth of the houses in Waterbury used their new, piped-in water to operate modern water closets, which emptied into backyard cesspools or were conducted by private sewers to streams flowing into the Naugatuck. Cesspools are designed to allow liquids to flow into the surrounding soil while solids are held in a tank for later removal. Everyone without cesspool or private sewer used what was called a privy vault, an arrangement whereby privy wastes collect in a below-ground tank usually constructed of brick. Town ordinances in Waterbury as elsewhere specified that these vaults be watertight, but neither the ordinances nor the vaults actually were. Once a year the vaults were emptied. Wastes from vaults then joined wastes from cesspools, and were carted out of town to a pit where they were composted, before being spread on farm fields as fertilizer.

Privy vaults for the disposal of human wastes had been part of the urban waste disposal system for centuries. Other parts of that system included a dry well in the back garden into which bath, laundry, and dishwater were poured to be absorbed by the surrounding soil, the pouring of wash basins into street gutters in neighborhoods too crowded to have backyards, and the underlying truth that where water must be drawn from a well or carried from a public spring, there is a limit to how much of it will be used. It is an axiom of political science that every initiative has its unintended consequence. With the arrival of piped water, the waste disposal system broke down.

Households connected to the new water mains increased their use of water exponentially. Some of the new flush toilets and sink and bathtub drains let into sewers constructed to carry off rain water, which festered in dry weather and sometimes overflowed on rainy days. Some new water closets let into privy vaults, which overflowed even when it was not raining. In crowded neighborhoods there was no space to build cesspools, and when the volume of newly available water poured into privy vaults designed to hold only nightsoil, the ground became saturated with human waste and the aroma of an untended latrine permeated the air. Worse, waste-saturated soils contaminated wells serving households not hooked up to city water, causing epidemics of dysentery, typhus, and cholera. All of which might have failed to trouble residents of Waterbury's finer neighborhoods, where houses were set in spacious gardens with ample room for cesspools and many homes had private sewers that carried wastewater to the Naugatuck River, if not for the fact that typhus and cholera epidemics that started in tenement districts sometimes carried off members of prosperous families. To secure itself from this threat, uptown Waterbury decided to install sewers.[8] In 1877, just a decade after the arrival of piped water, Waterbury voted to construct sewers. When

they were built, effluent from the city's water closets would flow in the Naugatuck and the people of Waterbury would be safer from disease.

The Waterbury town fathers did not act in isolation.[9] Ten years was a fairly
standard gap between the first flush of municipal water through the tank of a
water closet, and the decision to construct an expensive municipal sewer system.
By the end of the century, every city in the region was building a sewer system or
expanding an antiquated one. These town fathers were not building sewage
treatment plants. They were building sewers: pipes to carry wastewater away in
simple faith that, diluted by the natural flow of rainwater, rivers would purify
themselves. They did not worry about the ocean at all. It was far too vast for the
sewage of Waterbury, Connecticut, to have an impact, even if the town's sewage
had gotten that far, which it would not. It would be purified by natural processes
as it flowed down the Naugatuck, or, at the very latest, after that river reached the
Housatonic on its journey to the sea.

The town fathers were not wrong. At least, not entirely wrong. At least, not at
first.

The Housatonic with its average annual flow of 23,300 gallons per second is
a fair-sized river. The one thousand Waterbury residents flushing their new
water closets into private sewers in 1880 were correct in assuming that the river
could take care of it. Rivers do that. Aerobic bacteria can break down almost
any organic substance into benign chemical components—so long as there is
sufficient oxygen present. The problem, of course, is volume. Any household
may pour its waste into the Housatonic in full confidence that the river will
break it down and no harm done; when every household and factory in a river
basin does so, available supplies of oxygen are quickly depleted. Organisms deprived of oxygen die. Year by year the volume of effluent pouring into Long Island Sound increased, although even in the 1890s, most of the nightsoil produced by urban Connecticut households was collected in privy vaults or
cesspools and spread on Connecticut fields. The number of households with
sewage connections increased gradually in the wake of the introduction of
piped water, until, about 1900, the number of sewer systems pouring factory
and human waste into the waterways suddenly doubled and the oysters failed to
set. The set was light in 1901, failed in 1902, failed again in 1903, and would continue to fail.[10] Oystermen were puzzled: the brood oysters looked healthy; temperatures were warm enough; they had spread clean shells on the seabed as they
had done for decades. Yet the set failed. The oystermen may not have known
whom to blame, but in 1922, the conservation commission of New York knew
in what direction to look.

> The parents of seed oysters are to be found in the natural growth beds well up
> these estuaries. The requirements of commerce have caused these streams to be
> lined with bulkheads, dredged to considerable depths and the towns and industries

which have grown up around them have polluted the waters of the harbors. All of these causes, together with over-fishing of the grounds, have resulted in complete or partial extermination of parent oysters, and it seems that the present failure to obtain seed is due to a combination of these causes.[11]

Actually, it was only one of the above.

River and sewer waters laden with dissolved nutrients entered a sound alive with microorganisms almost as infinite in their variety as in their numbers. Plankton exist in such extreme diversity because each minute member of the Kingdom Protista has evolved to exploit a unique niche, thriving in a particular mix of salinity, light, and temperature, consuming a particular selection or blend of the available nutrients, and, not incidentally, nourishing certain of the organisms on the next step up the food chain. Alter the nutrient supply and the mix of microorganisms changes. Nutrient mixes in an estuary change

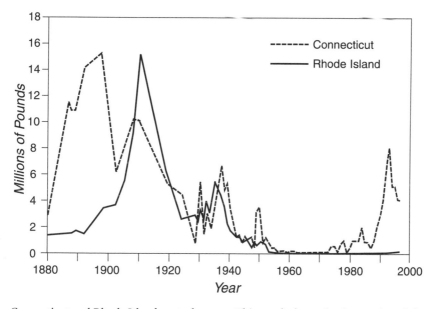

Connecticut and Rhode Island oyster harvests. This graph shows the devastation of the Connecticut beds around 1900, the industry's shift to Narragansett Bay, and the parallel decline of the Rhode Island beds. In 1987, the Connecticut Department of Agriculture working through its Bureau of Aquaculture and Laboratory Services at New Milford began a concerted effort to research the conditions of oyster culture and restore the Connecticut industry. The graph reveals both the success of the effort and the difficult conditions that continue to plague shellfish in the polluted waters of Long Island Sound.

Statistics on the oyster harvest have been compiled since 1880 by the National Marine Fisheries Service, http://www.nmfs.gov.

by season, in the wake of storms, and with variations in the weather. The nature
of the plankton community changes with the fluctuations. Alter nutrient inputs in a way both drastic and consistent, and strange things occur.

Great South Bay, the long, brackish lagoon on the south shore of Long Island, was once one of the nation's premier oyster grounds, home of the famous
Blue Point oysters beloved of gourmets. Natural beds between Smith's Point
and Nicholl's Point near Fire Island provided seed oysters for growing beds
from Moriches to Jamaica Bay. The fishing villages edging Great South Bay
made a good living from oysters, with fifty thousand acres under cultivation in
1916. Prosperity came also from catering to the needs of wealthy hunters who
came out from the city for the migratory duck season, and from the growing
number of wealthy families building seaside summer houses.

It was the ducks that finished the oysters in Great South Bay. Not wild ducks
migrating through; ducks raised for market on large, specialized farms. When
duck farming started, oystering began its decline, about 1940. By the mid-1950s,
there were forty duck farms and six million ducks pouring effluent into the bay,
or into streams that run into the bay. The nutrient load altered the phytoplankton community: a vast bloom of *Chlorophyta*, *Nannochloris atomus*, and *Stich-
ococcus* sp. dominated the waters to the exclusion of all others. Although oysters
can eat these small, green algae, when they eat nothing but, they starve and
die—just as sailors fed on a diet of hard tack will die of scurvy even though
hard tack provides ample calories. During the duckling decades, thousands of
acres of Great South Bay oyster bottom that once produced prized Blue Points,
produced only a bumper crop of serpulid worms.[12]

Nutrient enrichment causes algae blooms, events in which a single species
or a small number of species dominates the water column. If the blooming
algae happen to lack the nutritional components vital to growth, the oysters
die. The complex of algae blooming in Great South Bay were one such group.
There are others. At bloom density, *Prorocentrum minimum*, a red tide dino-
flagellate, will kill 100 percent of oyster spat within 14 days. At 33 percent of
bloom density, it will kill 43 percent of the spat within 22 days.[13] Although 33
percent of bloom density might not be high enough to elicit cries of "red tide,"
it would cause what oystermen would call a poor set. *Prorocentrum minimum*
bloom where sewage flows.[14]

There is no way of knowing exactly which microorganisms might have
bloomed along the Connecticut coast in 1902, but the evidence points to a
bloom of a protist of a type that fails to provide adequate nourishment to oyster
spat, blooming in sufficient volume to exclude other organisms from the water
column. The blooms were induced by a sudden and dramatic increase in the
sewage loadings of Connecticut waters.[15]

With set failing along the entire Connecticut oyster belt, oystermen looked
to Narragansett Bay for financial salvation. Connecticut firms moved swiftly to

colonize Rhode Island waters, buying rights to the seabed and replicating proven techniques of mariculture. It worked for a few years. Then, in 1914, the set failed in Narragansett Bay, and it continued to fail,[16] just as it had failed in Long Island Sound. The house where I spent my childhood summers was available for us to rent because the family fortune that built it was made in the oyster industry, and the oyster industry died.

The death of the Connecticut oyster industry was of concern only to oystermen. Deaths from epidemics of typhoid fever caused a concern far more widespread.

Typhoid was plainly linked to crowded, filthy conditions; but nineteenth-century medical science was unable to determine the nature of the link. Some thought that the problem lay not in the conditions but in the people who endured them. According to this theory, immigrant mill workers were a slovenly lot and there was little the city fathers could do to help people whose personal habits were so filthy that they would die of typhoid fever under the best of conditions.

A second theory, that typhoid was transmitted by waterborne organisms, would have been more persuasive if scientists had not looked at the water. But they did look, with microscopes and chemical tests. And there was nothing in the water. Typhoid bacillus had been isolated in the feces of fever patients and the organism examined under microscopes. Medical opinion was divided: some thought typhoid bacilli caused the disease, others that it merely indicated the fever's presence. When investigators turned their microscopes on sewage-polluted water, however, the bacillus wasn't there. Advocates of the waterborne germ theory of disease were in the position of believers in UFOs; rational people demanded to see a Martian.[17]

The third and most popular theory blamed thick air—miasmas, fumes rising from ground saturated with privy waste, which rose in disease-bearing clouds and infected those who inhaled them. The tight correlation between neighborhoods with filthy, sewage-saturated soils and high death rates from typhoid fever supported the theory. By the 1870s, the obvious linkage led the city fathers of Lowell and Lawrence, Massachusetts, to plan to install sewers to pipe waste away from the privies of crowded neighborhoods and into rivers where the action of flowing water would purify it.

Concord, Manchester, and Nashua, New Hampshire; Lowell and Lawrence, Massachusetts, are cotton mill towns strung like beads along the Merrimack. As population burgeoned, every Merrimack mill town except Nashua faced the need to replace wells with new water sources, for the same reasons of foul-smelling water and fear of fires that had forced Waterbury to act.[18] Nashua was spared the expense of building a reservoir only because it was blessed with a large stream of clean water, Pennichuck Brook, that had been tapped to create a municipal water system when the mills were built in the 1850s. The other

Merrimack towns depended on wells until the 1870s, when Concord built an aqueduct from a natural lake, Long Pond, and Manchester built a reservoir.[19] Lowell and Lawrence would have liked to build reservoirs too. Unfortunately, they had no access to suitable reservoir sites.[20] Tapping the Merrimack seemed to be the only option.

Industrial effluents, which poured into the river from every mill, were not perceived as pollutants, since they were understood to have important purifying properties that improved water quality.[21] The dirtiness of river water was merely visual, and could be remedied by gravel filtration beds in the waterworks. With commendable efficiency, Lowell and Lawrence addressed their sewage and water problems simultaneously, digging up the streets to lay the pipes for both a city sewage system and a city water supply.

It was true that the intake for the Lawrence water supply would lie a mere nine miles below the Lowell sewage outfall; this was not perceived as a problem. The Merrimack, with an average daily flow of six thousand cubic feet per second where it passes Lawrence, is such a large river that dilution alone was believed capable of eliminating any nuisance from sewage. The engineers who designed the Lowell and Lawrence water systems had faith in the power of the Merrimack to purify itself. "The sewage of Lowell is diluted with from 600 to 1,000 times its volume of water, and then flows a dozen miles to Lawrence, much of the refuse from the mills acting as a precipitant to disinfect it."

According to Massachusetts law, an unlimited volume of sewage or industrial effluent could be poured into a stream provided only that the outfall was located twenty miles above the drinking water intake. The law did not apply to the Merrimack, which was exempted from clean water laws because of the economic importance of the cotton manufactory.

In 1873, Lowell installed gravel filtration beds and began drinking Merrimack River water. In 1876, Lawrence did the same. Death rates from typhoid fever, which had been very high when the cities drank well water and sewage sat in privy vaults, fell.[22]

Upstream, Manchester and Concord, New Hampshire, encountered the usual problems of cities that install water systems without installing sewers. They decided to build sewer systems. Nashua sent its sewage down Pennichuck Brook. The sewage of Fitchburg and Leominster flowed down the Nashua River to join the Merrimack above Lowell. The sewage of Framingham, Maynard, and Concord, Massachusetts, flowed down the Concord River to join the Merrimack above Lawrence. The rivers of New England were being turned into open sewers, but it could not be helped: "Until we have better means of disposal of our refuse than at present, some of our rivers must be used, more or less, to scavenge the countryside."[23]

While by no means convinced that disease could be transmitted by water, the people of Massachusetts were worried enough by 1886 to spend some money

Cotton printing works, Pawtucket, Rhode Island, 1951. At the bottom of the photograph, outfall pipes can be seen disgorging effluent from the Paramount Printing and Finishing Mill directly into the Blackstone River. Before the Clean Water Act, most industrial waste was discharged directly into rivers or into municipal sewage systems with no provision for treating chemicals. Courtesy The Rhode Island Historical Society. RHi (x3)2507.

finding out. They were also thrifty enough to decide that money could be used more effectively by a state agency than by individual towns. In 1887, the Lawrence Experiment Station of the board of health was charged with studying the purification of water in conjunction with state-funded microscopy, bacteriology, and chemistry laboratories at the Massachusetts Institute of Technology. The university had no funds for building laboratories or supporting research, but with state funding, William Sedgwick, professor of biology, was able to buy equipment and begin the scientific work of identifying the microorganisms in contaminated water, while at the Lawrence Experiment Station, Sedgwick's colleagues and students devised methods for removing bacteria from water.

A deadly typhoid epidemic struck Massachusetts in the winter of 1890 – 1891. It killed everywhere, but in Lowell the death rates were so shockingly high that the board of health brought Professor Sedgwick in to investigate. Sedgwick's microscopy laboratory had not actually found any typhoid bacilli in the Merrimack by November of 1890. Sixty-four residents of Lowell died of typhoid fever that month.

Sedgwick interviewed the families of each of the deceased, following the trail of death up the Merrimack to the North Chelmsford home of the earliest identified victim of the epidemic, where he found a privy emptying into Stoney (Stony) Brook. From Chelmsford, he traced the contagion down Stony Brook to the Merrimack and to sequential epidemics in Lowell and then in Lawrence. Two years later, Sedgewick traced a new epidemic through Lowell, Lawrence, and on down the Merrimack to Newburyport. There were still no typhoid bacilli visible under Sedgwick's microscope, but the sequencing of death from privy to river to water tap was so dramatic that the world saw and believed. In Massachusetts, they began to filter the water.[24]

It was not possible yet to see every waterborne pathogen, but engineers at the state-funded Lawrence Experiment Station developed a sand and gravel filter bed capable of removing invisible pathogenic bacteria from polluted water. After publication of Sedgewick's 1891 report on waterborne typhoid contagion, scientific and popular opinion swung firmly behind the need to purify drinking water. The new filter beds began purifying drinking water for the city of Lawrence in 1893; the technology soon spread throughout Europe and America.

The story of the Lowell water supply resonates because the people drinking the contaminated water were neither wealthy nor powerful; most of them were impoverished Irish immigrant factory hands. Lowell, Lawrence, and Holyoke were all built by the same circle of Boston families. Those families, the owners of the mills, drank reservoir water. The quality of the water we drink and the air we breathe is linked to social status; this would be a commonplace tragedy if it were merely the story of people named Cabot and Lowell letting poor immigrants die of typhoid. It is, instead, a tale of virtue. Once the nature of the threat was clear, the body politic moved swiftly and decisively to end it. Scientists and engineers were funded to find a solution, and when a method of water purification was devised, it was rapidly implemented, even though it cost money and even though the people threatened were mere immigrant mill hands.

Yankees were good at solving problems, and the problem of waterborne disease had been solved. The rivers of New England continued to be sewers—low-cost viaducts carrying off domestic and industrial effluent. Effluent killed the rivers, of course, the smelt, the salmon, the oysters in the estuaries. But death was not, in this case, permanent. The indigo dye and dust washing from a cotton mill, the sizing and fiber from a paper mill, even the salt and acid pouring from tanning vaults killed only on a temporary basis. Tan bark, sawdust, or mill washings might accumulate in the stream bed in such quantity that they could kill long after a mill was abandoned, just by filling the water column with debris, blocking light, and absorbing oxygen. But if the mill were abandoned, if the tannery stopped spewing untreated effluent, if sewage ceased to be poured

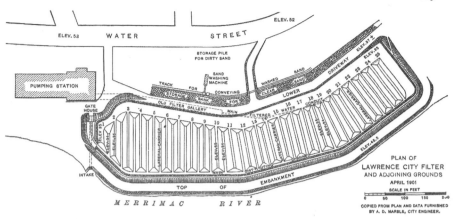

PLAN OF
LAWRENCE CITY FILTER
AND ADJOINING GROUNDS
APRIL 1901
SCALE IN FEET

COPIED FROM PLAN AND DATA FURNISHED
BY A. D. MARBLE, CITY ENGINEER.

Lawrence filterbed. Water drawn from the Merrimack was filtered through a series of sand beds, ending the typhoid epidemics that had repeatedly devastated the city. Lawrence poured its own sewage directly into the Merrimack to flow downstream to Newburyport. Allen Hazen, "Lawrence, Massachusetts City Filter: A History of Its Installation and Maintenance," American Society of Civil Engineers Transactions, paper #906 (vol. 46, December 1901). Courtesy American Textile History Museum, Lowell, Mass.

into the river, the river would recover. It might take years or decades, but as long as the pollutants were materials in their natural forms, a time would come when shad would again swim upstream to spawn and eel again make their autumn passage to the Sargasso Sea.

Then nineteenth-century industrial engineers began to alter the chemical nature of the materials they processed, and it ceased to be true that time could heal all wounds.

Baltimore had been the first American city to build a railroad and it was the first to declare the advent of a new age by lighting up the night with gas jets. Boston followed Baltimore in illumination as it had in rails, piping gas to affluent homeowners in 1822. It was a wonder. At the turn of a key, city folks made night into day without the inconvenience of trimming wicks, refilling oil reservoirs, or scraping up candle drippings.

The gas in question was not the natural gas we use today. It was coal gas, produced by baking coal over low heat and capturing the escaping fumes. It was produced in massive quantities in nearly every American and European city, and the hundreds of cooking ovens quickly became coated with a residue of coal tar that had to be scraped off and disposed of. Coal tar, or creosote, was useful in coating railroad ties, but even with railroads being laid across entire continents, there was more of the smelly, black ooze than anyone knew what to do with.

Born and trained in Germany, August Wilhelm von Hoffman, England's leading chemist, suspected that the black goo might prove useful as a chemical feed stock. Von Hoffman, hoping to derive or synthesize the antimalarial drug quinine from coal tar, sent one of his students home on Easter vacation in 1856 with a packing case full of chemicals and instructions to work on the problem. The student, William Henry Perkin, failed to synthesize quinine (a goal American chemists would finally achieve in 1944 under the pressure of a world war in the tropics), but he did produce a colorfast, purple dye.[25] It was the first commercial, synthetic chemical. Perkin, whose father was a success in the construction business, dropped out of the Royal College of Chemistry in London to go into the dye business. Von Hoffman is said to have been disappointed to see a student with great potential as a research chemist leave to go into business. Perkin made a fortune. His new dye, Aniline Purple, or Mauvine, was such a success that the color became the fashionable shade of an era: the mid-Victorian years are also known as the Mauve Decades. Below cotton mills, the rivers ran purple.

Von Hoffman lost patience with the British penchant for favoring business over research and returned to Germany, where government backing created the first great departments of chemical research. By the end of the century, Germany had far outdistanced England both in researching and in manufacturing chemicals of all kinds. America, imitating British and German technique, was self-sufficient in the production of bulk, inorganic chemical products such as chlorine, phosphates, and sulfuric acid, but dyestuffs and other fine chemicals derived from coal tar had to be imported from Germany. Bright young Americans went to Germany to study chemistry, and in 1903 one of the returnees, Arthur A. Noyes, who had earned his doctorate at the University of Liepzig, established the Research Laboratory of Physical Chemistry at the Massachusetts Institute of Technology. There chemists could study and work in the style of the great German universities, aloof from the business of manufacturing.

Noyes's colleague, William Walker, could not have disagreed more with this goal. In 1908, Walker established the MIT Research Laboratory of Applied Chemistry. Here the brightest young men could master both the best techniques of chemical manufacturing and the most advanced ideas of research chemistry, a combination known as chemical engineering. In 1916, Walker founded the School of Chemical Engineering Practice, the first chemical engineering department in the world. This was the school that trained the men who established the petrochemical industry.

Petroleum derivatives can do almost everything. (Coal tar derivatives can too, of course, but they cost more.) Petroleum is the stuff of twentieth-century life. We fertilize our fields with it, wrap our food in it, propel our vehicles with it and build them out of it. We wear it, clean our clothes with it, and substitute it for nearly every material we once used: ivory, silk, clay, wood, linen, wax, and leather are mere affectations of the wealthy in a world where plastic is everything. Unlike these obsolete materials, petrochemicals are not inert.

The number and diversity of persistent toxic chemicals already in circulation is sobering. The trichloroethylene (TCE) that workers at Grace Chemical Corporation in Woburn, Massachusetts, used to clean grease from machinery, and poured onto the ground when it was no longer useful, did not evaporate and it did not biodegrade.[26] It worked its way through the ground and into the town well; children who drank from the well died of leukemia.[27] The dioxin produced when paper is bleached with chlorine does not break down after it leaves the paper mill. It moves in unaltered state through air, soil, and water, insinuating itself into the food chain and accumulating in the fatty tissues of animals that give birth to malformed young. The polychlorinated biphenyls (PCBs) used to insulate the transformers produced in General Electric's Pittsfield, Massachusetts, plant, are intrepid travelers, moving through the food chain with aplomb, showing up on remote Pacific islands where albatrosses give birth to chicks with crossed bills and club feet, and in remote Arctic ice shields where some polar bears are failing to give birth at all.[28]

Synthetic chemicals—TCE, PCBs, dioxin, and others—are thought to wreak reproductive havoc in animal populations by imitating the action of naturally occurring hormones, which they are capable of doing even when present in vanishingly minute quantities. They are capable also of reducing intelligence and disrupting mental function in human children in the quantities in which they are already present in our food supply.

Americans aware of these findings have reacted by drinking bottled water and avoiding fish from waters known to be contaminated, much as the citizens of Lawrence reacted to the presence of typhoid in the water supply by installing filter beds. Filter beds effectively removed typhoid bacillus from the water supply. Dealing with persistent chemicals is not that simple. Not only is it impossible to filter all traces of PCBs and other persistent synthetic chemicals from the air we breathe and the foods we consume, it is not practical to supply nursing polar bears with bottled water. We can, however, stop producing persistent synthetic chemicals. There are no industrial applications in which these chemicals are the sole viable manufacturing process, although there are many instances in which they are the least expensive known process. There are no instances in which continued production of persistent, hormone-mimicking chemicals is less expensive than the risk of giving birth to malformed, deficient human beings.

Raw sewage no longer flows from outfall pipes. Not on Lewis Island, not in Waterbury, not in Lowell.[29] Since the passage of the Clean Water Act of 1972 our waterways have been getting cleaner. Not clean enough for oysters to spawn in New Haven Harbor or for fish caught in the Concord River to be safe to eat (Concord River fish contain mercury in toxic levels, a legacy of the dye industry). Not yet. Although it is in our power to make them so. The technology exists. All that is lacking is the kind of political will that led the people of Massachusetts to remove invisible typhus bacillus from the water supply.

Chapter 16

Fishing for Profits

꙳

Why are the cattle on a common so puny and stunted? Why is the common itself so bare-worn, and cropped so differently from the adjoining enclosures?[1]
—William Foster Lloyd, 1833

COD IS NOT AN ELEGANT FISH. POETS DO NOT write epics celebrating the prowess of cod fishermen. It is never featured at royal banquets. Anglers do not invest in expensive rods and creels or book flights to exotic destinations in the hope of hooking cod. Yet a large, wooden codfish occupies a place of honor behind the speaker's chair in the Massachusetts State House. The state house cod is at least as appropriate as the sack of wool that rests under the chair of the Lord Chancellor of Great Britain, and for the same reason. Codfish are money.

England is a nation of shopkeepers, as is Massachusetts. Napoleon intended to mock the British entrepreneurial spirit with that quip, which is why the British have been repeating it with pride ever since. British enterprise defeated Napoleon just as American enterprise saved the French from the consequences of their own shortcomings in two World Wars. Frenchmen look down their noses on nations whose leaders sit upon a woolsack, or convene beneath a wooden fish—French deputies have more style. I am Yankee enough to be proud of our wooden cod; it represents something important even if we were stupid enough to kill the fishery it commemorates. I lament the fate of our cod fishery, but I am proud of the fact that the Massachusetts economy has not withered with the demise of our oldest and most enduring enterprise. Cod fishing, plebeian as it may be, was the enterprise that launched the New England economy. In a region virtually devoid of locational or natural resource advantages, codfish were the grand exception. There, the people of a thin-soiled, winter-beset province found nature's bounty.

Oceans in general are as sterile as a granite outcrop. Nutrients, the bodies of dead plants and animals, settle to the ocean floor. Sunlight, without which no photosynthesis can take place and almost no food chain can start, is available only in a shallow zone near the surface. In the deep ocean, the sunlit surface and the nutrient-rich bottom are separated by a wide band of lifeless water, which is why the ocean is generally empty of fish. Only near land, where surface and bottom meet, do waters teem with life. Because the deep sea is so sterile, sailors in the position of Captain William Bligh, forced by mutineers to sail from Tahiti to the Dutch East Indies in an open boat, are more likely to starve than to survive by eating fish. Bligh and his men did not die, but only because of the captain's iron will and the fact that he was one of the greatest navigators the British Navy ever produced. They did not survive by catching fish. There are almost no fish in the deep ocean. (There are islands between Tahiti and the Dutch colony Bligh was sailing toward, but although their inshore waters offered fish, the people living on the islands were cannibals. Bligh preferred the risk of starvation to voluntarily becoming part of the Melanesian food chain.)

George's Bank, far enough into the Atlantic to be as sterile as the deep ocean Bligh crossed, teems with fish. This is because the floor of the sea rises here, coming within twenty feet of the surface at points and staying within 100 meters of the surface over an area 150 kilometers wide by 280 kilometers long. Twice daily a tidal surge rises from the bottom to course over the shoals, bringing nutrients from the ocean's floor up to fertilize the sunlit surface waters where plankton feed and multiply. The result is codfish. Also halibut, haddock, hake, and flounder.

George's Bank, which lies east of Cape Cod, was discovered much later than the Grand Banks off Newfoundland. The abundant stocks of fish on George's Bank first came to the attention of sperm whale hunters out of Nantucket in the 1720s. It was not long before the Marblehead cod fleet was working the bank regularly. Fishing ceased during the War of Independence, and the closure of West Indian and continental markets to American goods after that war meant that the industry did not recover quickly. With foreign markets closed, New England's rich, inshore fishing grounds were adequate to supply domestic demand. It was not until inshore fishing grounds began to be depleted, about 1830, that men again started fishing George's Bank, mostly for halibut.[2]

Those gargantuan fish were so plentiful that a crew dropping handlines over the rail could fill the hold completely—fifteen thousand pounds of halibut—in a single day. The halibut bonanza lasted about two decades. Halibut is a slow-growing species; it reaches sexual maturity at nine or ten years of age, which makes it difficult to recover from population collapse. Halibut stocks in George's Bank and the Gulf of Maine still have not recovered from the overfishing of the 1830s and 1840s.

Cod fishermen also returned to the bank in the 1830s, but cod, which begin to spawn at five or six years of age, withstand human predation better than halibut. It was a steady fishery, producing profitable hauls for boats from

Provincetown. By Nickerson & Smith. 1883. Cod flakes filled every spare inch of land in Provincetown, Massachusetts, in the 1870s. Dried and salt cod supported Yankee fishing towns for two and a half centuries. Courtesy of the Society for the Preservation of New England Antiquities (neg. #17132-B).

Gloucester and lesser ports, and salt fish for the nation's tables. Change came not from overfishing but from new technology: ice and railroads. Boats that headed out with holds packed with chopped ice could spend a day or two on the bank and come into port with a load of fresh, iced cod, haddock, or flounder, which sold for more than salt cod. It was, of course, more profitable to bring fresh fish into a large city full of dinner tables than into a small fishing town like Gloucester. And it was most profitable to bring a load of fresh haddock to the wharves at Boston or New Bedford where the fish were immediately transferred to refrigerated railcars bound for the New York market. Provincetown and other small ports that specialized in salt cod shriveled with the advent of refrigerated railcars. Gloucester fought back.

In 1923, New York inventor Charles Birdseye moved to Gloucester and developed a successful technique for quick-freezing fish without serious loss of quality. As Birdseye's process spread, fishing boats had the choice of selling to fresh or frozen fish processors in New Bedford, Point Judith, and Boston, or to frozen fish processors in Gloucester, Portland, or Rockport, Maine. The only other commercial port to prosper into the middle years of the twentieth century was Eastport, Maine, where sardines were packed in tins. All other Yankee fishing ports shrank into backwaters, serving, at most, a local market for fresh fish with day boats working inshore.

After World War II, even Gloucester and Boston faded, threatened by lower wages in Iceland, Norway, and Canada, where fisheries were subsidized by governments keen to maintain employment. Admitted to the United States under very favorable trade agreements, imports soon dominated the American market in frozen fish. Only the fresh-fish market continued to be served by American boats. But fishing is a very minor part of the American economy in the twentieth century, even in New England. The sacred cod still hangs behind the speaker's chair in the Massachusetts State House, but the few thousand fishermen in the state have little political clout. In Washington of the 1950s, they had none at all. The United States government had bigger fish to fry than the decline of a historic industry. The attention of national leaders was focused on Soviet expansion, and on keeping Canada, Norway and Iceland happy, prosperous, and capitalist. Allowing Canadian and Scandinavian fish to undercut and destroy an American industry was part of the price of fighting a cold war. The irony is that when the Russians finally launched a full-scale assault on American territory, the casualties were not soldiers, but fishermen.

Soviet scouts cased George's Bank in 1961. The fleet followed: gill-netters and side trawlers that took 63,000 metric tons of herring from the bank in 1961. Russian appetites were not sated. The fleet swelled. Immense, steel-hulled models of cutting-edge technological efficiency vacuumed the sea floor clean of fish. Soviet trawlers cruised in phalanxes; any fish that escaped the nets of one ship was immediately swept up by a sister ship cruising to port and slightly aft. At the peak of the feeding frenzy in 1973, ships from Russia, Britain, Poland, East Germany, West Germany, Japan, Bulgaria, Spain, Canada, Romania, Italy, and France caught 950,500 metric tons of fish on the bank. Although several foreign nations had ships on the banks, the Russians took the lion's share: 832,800 metric tons netted by Soviet factory trawlers that gutted, flash froze, and packaged the fish for market. American boats took 203,000 metric tons that year. The next year the Soviets were back. By 1976, there were so few fish in the sea that the catch fell to half what it had been in 1973. Appalled, Congress passed the Magnuson Fisheries Conservation and Management Act declaring that the territorial waters of the United States extended two hundred miles offshore.[3]

Fish market, Newburyport, Massachusetts. By H. P. Macintosh, c.1870s. The abundance of seafood that dayboats once brought to market is glimpsed in the bounty available at Newburyport in the 1870s; the indoor hall of the fish market is shown in the inset. Newburyport was neither a large city nor a transshipment point for fish. Everything in the market was locally caught for local consumption. A dayboat going out of Newburyport today would bring back far fewer and smaller fish. Courtesy of the Society for the Preservation of New England Antiquities (neg. #12142-B).

The New England Fishery Management Council immediately established quotas for cod, haddock, and yellowtail flounder, all badly depleted by foreign factory fleets. Stocks began to recover. Buoyed by the new territorial boundaries and by signs of stock recovery, fishermen pushed for the quotas to be lifted. Since fishing interests controlled the Fishery Management Council, they didn't need to push hard. In 1982, regulation was abandoned and Yankee fishermen, encouraged by federal tax incentives, plunged heavily into debt, buying new boats with sophisticated loran fish finders and other navigational gear. There was money in fish. The bonanza would be short-lived.

By 1989, the Fishery Management Council admitted that cod, haddock, and yellowtail flounder were dangerously depleted in Yankee waters. In August 1991, Federal judge David Mazzone entered a judgment in a Conservation Law Foundation lawsuit forcing the National Marine Fisheries Service to impose a plan to end overfishing. Under severe pressure from fishing communities where the imposition of quotas would mean the loss of livelihoods and economic hardship, the Fisheries Service dithered until the fish were gone. Finally, in December 1994, fishing on George's Bank and in southern New England waters was closed on an emergency basis. Fishing is still closed, as scientists study the complexities of population dynamics and wonder if stocks will ever recover.

Sustainable levels for a fishery are notoriously difficult to calculate. Year classes of infant fish fluctuate wildly in size, according to such variables as water temperatures, ocean currents, and class sizes of significant predators. The interaction of species complicates the picture. The crash of the cod population, for example, has been a boon for lobster fishermen, since cod eat young lobster. Almost all fin fish feed on their own young and on the young of all other fin fish, so a decline in halibut removes an article of diet from the codfish who prey upon young halibut, but simultaneously removes the grown halibut from the list of predators that feed upon young cod. All of which makes forecasting fish populations about as simple as predicting where the stock market will be in six months. If fished at moderate levels, however, the banks were once capable of producing cod, halibut, and haddock forever. The cod fishing was sustained for centuries and in Iceland, where they manage well, it still is.

Scientists doubt the ability of New England fisheries ever to regain their former abundance. For one thing, the fish we do not catch can be as important as the fish we do. Haddock is a coveted food species, while little skate is scorned by cooks and held in consequent contempt by fishermen. The two species share an appetite for crab and clam dinners. When haddock are overfished, the little skate population, which suddenly has all the rock crabs and clams on George's Bank to itself, explodes. A new year's class of young haddock will find it hard to compete for food with the overwhelming numbers of little skate. It is unclear when, if ever, the species will regain numerical balance. Halibut, fished out over a century and a half ago, still have not recovered.[4]

New England fishermen face the same dilemma faced by seventeenth-century Indian beaver hunters, a dilemma known as the Tragedy of the Commons, after William Forster Lloyd's famous description of cattle on a commons. A dairy farmer or cattle rancher has every incentive to pasture only the number of cattle his land will support without destroying the turf by overgrazing. By ruining his own pastures, he will, after all, reduce the income he may expect from his cattle in years to come. Farmers grazing cattle on a commons, however, have every

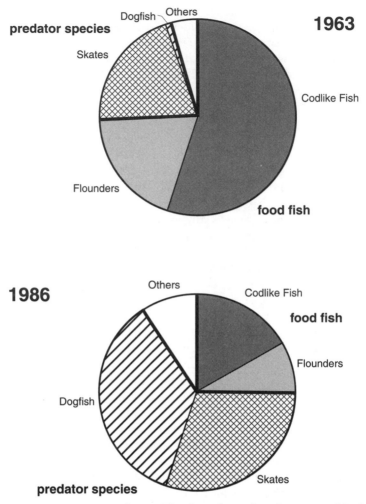

Predators versus prey, 1963 and 1986. The chart dramatizes the catastrophic shift in species in the Gulf of Maine, where increased numbers of dogfish and skate prey on the still-declining stock of cod and haddock. Philip W. Conkling, *From Cape Cod to the Bay of Fundy: An Environmental Atlas of the Gulf of Maine* (Cambridge: MIT Press, 1995), 95. By permission.

incentive to graze as many cattle as they can buy, since the cost of overgrazing will be divided among all the owners, while each individual pockets the entire profit on the cattle he owns.

Just as every Indian who located a beaver pond had either to kill all the beaver in it or know that someone else would soon take them for his own profit, fishermen have long known that any fish they refrain from catching will soon be taken up by some other boat's nets. The cost of depleting George's Bank is widely spread, but the profit of a full hold accrues to the man who caught the fish.

Haddock and cod are born and live their entire lives at the edge of the continental shelf, but many of the fish they feed upon spawn and feed in salt marshes and coastal estuaries. Many of these estuaries are too polluted to produce anything. Lost estuarine productivity affects fish populations in ways that are poorly understood.

The story of the siege of Boston is well known. After the debacle at Lexington and Concord, the British, finding themselves surrounded by an army under the command of a provincial militia colonel calling himself a general, faced the difficult problem of dispersing the rebels and putting down the rebellion. From General George Washington's perspective, the problem was how to force the British to leave Boston. He solved it by placing cannon on Dorchester Heights, cannon that pointed down into the occupied city.

The occupation of Dorchester Heights, on the night of March 4, 1776, under the direction of generals Washington, Knox, and Putnam, went like clockwork. When British sentries spotted the new fortifications, Lord Howe, the British commander, decided to evacuate Boston. It was a turning point in the War for Independence, so it is scarcely surprising that students of military history should come to Boston to stand on Dorchester Heights, admire Washington's strategy, and shake their heads over Howe's failure to fortify the heights before Washington thought of it. A handsome monument stands where Putnam and Knox emplaced the cannon that lifted the siege of Boston. It is located in a small, elegant park just behind South Boston High School; you can stand there and take in a panoramic view of Boston. What you cannot see is Dorchester Heights.

The heights of Dorchester Neck were cut down and carted to the shore to fill a wide, shallow bay, and create the extensive acreage of rail yards and warehouses that once spread between the old monument and downtown, the site where the new Boston Convention Center is now being built. It took a lot of dirt. When they had used up Dorchester Heights—the remnant hillock was saved only because it was a useful site for an early-nineteenth-century reservoir—they brought fill in by rail. The technology was well established. Every thriving port in New England was filling marshes and estuaries to create real estate. In the two centuries following American independence— two centuries of industrialization and increasing prosperity—biologically productive wetlands yielded to more economically productive land uses. Between 1780 and 1980, Connecticut filled or drained 74 percent of the wetlands that once covered 670,000 acres, while even Maine, the least developed New England state, lost 20 percent of its original 6,460,000 acres of bog, swamp, and marsh.[5] Wetlands were drained for farming, dredged to improve navigation, and filled for building lots. Whether a marsh becomes a marina, a

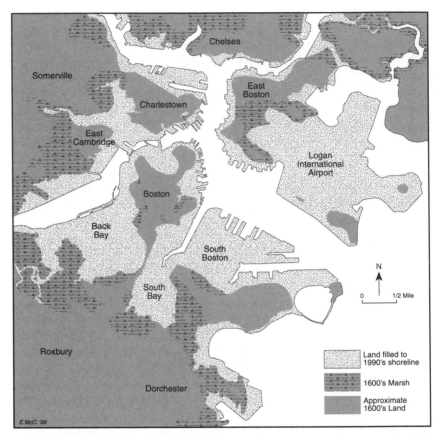

Boston in 1630 was a living estuary fringed by productive salt marshes, virtually all of which have been filled in during nearly four centuries of European habitation. Eliza McClennan, Mapworks.

housing development, or a hayfield, it ceases to produce fish and waterfowl.

Human appetite for fish did not increase noticeably between the eighteenth-century discovery of George's Bank and the twentieth-century discovery that there were almost no fish left on the bank. Human population did. A growing population demands more fish even as growing cities and industries reduce the capacity of the waters to produce them. Lowered productivity caused by water pollution is not a minor problem, but it is a solvable one. We know how to enjoy indoor plumbing and the products of modern industry without fouling our estuaries; we lack only the political will to act. The problem of a human population so large that it fills marshes and cuts down forests even while demanding more fish, wheat, and wood is more difficult.

The population of New England outgrew the ability to feed itself two centuries ago. It did not seem to matter at the time. As early as the eighteenth century, Yankee entrepreneurs were able to carry home profits sufficient to hold the wheat fields and pastures of Maryland in thrall. The specter that struck Yankee economic planners in the 1930s was the horrifying realization that with the decline of so many historic industries, we were losing our ways to pay for vital imports. Economic powers that lose this edge become backwaters. Fortunately for New England in the 1930s, there was a war just starting.

While America fought Germany and Japan, there was work for every hand and every factory. Even obsolete mills with Victorian machinery worked long shifts filling orders for the war effort. Less visible at the time were the millions of dollars poured into developing radar, radio, sonar, missiles, telemetry, and computers at the Massachusetts Institute of Technology. Unfortunately, for the New England economy, the war ended, and when it did, the old mills were abandoned, and urban industrial neighborhoods and entire industrial cities stood jobless and hopeless as old Yankee industries moved south, west, and offshore.

Economic planners asked to evaluate the economic future of New England after the war saw little to inspire optimism. Textiles, paper, shoes, and precision manufacturing were leaving New England to move closer to raw materials or closer to customers. Only financial services in Boston, insurance in Hartford, and machine tool manufacturing in the Connecticut Valley could be called healthy industries. Beyond these three centers, the forested landscape pockmarked with decaying mill towns was best suited to a future as prime moose habitat.

We had a moose in Boston last year. Young moose go walkabout in spring. This one wandered into Cleveland Circle at rush hour, made an appearance on the morning news and led wildlife officers on a day-long chase before they finally found him taking a nap along the trolley line that runs through Newton Center. He is presumed to have come to Boston looking for a girl. Adolescent males looking for girls frequently range Cleveland Circle, a neighborhood of cinemas and restaurants just off the campus of Boston College.

Perhaps the oddest thing about a young moose walking from New Hampshire to Massachusetts in a mating mood is that his quixotic quest might actually have succeeded. Massachusetts began to abandon its farmland long ago, and where corn and hayfields reverted to forest, wildlife has come back. Slowly, lagging the regrowth of pine and oak by several decades, deer have returned to our woodlands and river otters again play in the streams. Bald eagles and wood warblers nest where cows once grazed, and wood ducks swim on beaver ponds in states where beavers were unknown for centuries. Even the large predators, timberwolves and mountain lions, are moving back into Maine and northern New Hampshire.

When the beaver hat fell from fashion's favor, there were still beaver in a handful of redoubts in the Rocky Mountains and the Canadian shield. They began to spread east and south. Remnant southern populations also spread north. There were remnant southern populations because southern pelts were never worth much—only cold winters produce valuable pelts. The hard-working rodents reclaimed their historic range pond by pond, reappearing in West Stockbridge, Massachusetts, in 1920. By the 1990s there were beaver in every New England state and the Massachusetts Fisheries and Wildlife Department was forced to run an efficient trapping program to keep them out of the cranberry region. Beaver carry the deadly, waterborne disease giardia, and the potential for economic damage if beaver were allowed to live near cranberry bogs is considerable.

In other parts of Massachusetts, the beaver population flourished to the extent that fur trapping again became a viable economic pursuit. In the early nineties, thirteen hundred pelts were taken annually, worth about $140,000, a harvest as desirable as it was sustainable because beaver are expensive neighbors.[6] Staff and friends of the Broadmoor Audubon Sanctuary on the banks of the Charles River in suburban Natick were delighted when the first beaver seen in town since the early seventeenth century turned up in 1989. The new beaver dam immediately flooded large sections of the Sanctuary's boardwalk system, necessitating costly reconstruction. The Audubon Society remains staunchly probeaver despite the price of new walkways. Not everyone does.

Beaver fell trees onto buildings and power lines, cut down expensive nursery-grown saplings planted by suburban homeowners, destroy trout habitat, flood septic systems, and undermine roadbeds by rechanneling streams. Massachusetts alone spends about $100,000 a year repairing beaver damage to roads, including Route 128, which circles Boston and the computer industry. I have not yet seen a beaver on Bullough's Pond, although Newton now has a small herd of wild deer, and a wild turkey is raising a family in town this summer.

Predicting the future is always the enterprise least likely to succeed. Despite the decline of its historic industries and the increased populations of bear and coyote in our regrown forests, New England did not turn into an economic backwater. Instead, in the 1970s and 1980s, there was an economic revival known as the Massachusetts Miracle. Some miracles are made in heaven; this one was made at the Massachusetts Institute of Technology.

Boston Tech, as MIT was known for the first half-century of its existence, was founded in a world where the sons of prosperous families received a classical education while the sons of the working classes were taught to read and cipher, then sent to work in factories and shops. There were virtually no institutions that could teach a boy how to build an engine or survey a road in the 1860s.[7] Boston Tech began life with the modest goal of teaching likely sons of the laboring classes to do these things, though it rapidly expanded into other fields that colleges were neglecting, notably chemistry and physics. With the introduction of these subjects, a battle was joined for the soul of the institution: should the faculty of MIT seek to understand the nature of chemical composition—an activity known as science, or study how to apply chemistry to producing desirable goods—an activity known as chemical engineering? This battle had an outcome impossible in most wars: both sides won.[8] MIT became a leading university in both science and engineering. From the Cambridge campus have come the field of electrical engineering, the petrochemical industry, the computer industry, the vacuum tube, the Polaroid camera, and more.

The Massachusetts technology region spreads like a fan west and north from its epicenter on the MIT campus. Avionics, vacuum tubes, magnetrons, electronic switches, radar, sonar, and satellite photography were developed and manufactured by enterprises spun out of MIT, mostly with research funding provided by the United States Department of Defense.[9] It is ironic that in the region that led the nation in its opposition to the War of 1812, the Mexican War, the Spanish American War, the Vietnam War, and the Cold War, military spending has long floated the economy. The pattern was fairly straightforward. The United States government, in mortal dread first of Germany and Japan, then of Soviet Communism, poured vast sums into the development of weapons systems. MIT was the nation's finest science and engineering university. Government contracts for the development of advanced weapons systems were quite logically awarded to the university best qualified to carry them out. The money that flowed into MIT played a large role in winning World War II and sustaining the Cold War. Government contracts are not, however, always awarded on the basis of qualification.[10]

When the Kennedy administration decided to build a space center, the expectation was that it would be built near MIT, where virtually all work in that field was then being done. Vice-President Lyndon Johnson, of Texas, and Congressman Albert Thomas, who represented Houston and chaired the Independent Agencies Subcommittee of the House Appropriations Committee, wanted the National Aeronautic and Space Administration (NASA) mission control center for Texas. That there were no scientists or engineers in relevant fields working in Houston was not beside the point; it was the whole idea. Johnson was aware of the deficiencies of his state in the technology field; by snatching the space center he created a new industry for Texas. With Washington paying the bills, engineers and scientists flocked to Houston.[11]

Contracts awarded to MIT were never so baldly political as the idea of building a space center in a city so devoid of a scientific community as Houston was in 1962, but many of the decisions were political, and MIT was politically wellplaced. MIT's Vannevar Bush was science advisor to President Roosevelt; MIT's James Killian was science advisor to President Eisenhower; MIT's Jerome Wiesner was science advisor to President Kennedy; Lee DuBridge of the MIT Radiation Lab advised President Nixon; H. Guyford Stever of MIT worked for

both Nixon and Ford. Massachusetts also had a powerful Congressional delega-
tion, and, unlike many of his Cambridge constituents, Speaker Thomas P.
O'Neill harbored no antiwar sentiments that would lead him to work against a
defense contract for a Massachusetts laboratory. It may have been true that pol-
iticians brought home the bacon in the form of defense contracts, but it was a
fact that MIT boasted the finest chefs and best equipment for processing that
kind of bacon.

In 1940, Vannevar Bush, an associate professor at MIT and partner in a small
business that manufactured vacuum tubes for radios, was serving as director of
the National Research and Defense Committee, which put him in a position to
know that the government was about to fund a research team to develop radar,
a top-secret British innovation. Vannevar Bush phoned home. It took only a
few hours for MIT's James Killian to arrange laboratory and hangar space, and
clinch the deal. The MIT Radiation Laboratory—Rad Lab—working at wartime speed, produced flying radar, a gun-laying system, and the long-range
navigation system that became LORAN. Bowles arranged for his small vacuum
tube firm, operating out of an old textile mill in Waltham, to bid on some of
the magnetron contracts coming out of Rad Lab. By 1945, the firm, which was
called Raytheon, was producing 80 percent of all magnetrons and was
launched on a trajectory to become a major arms manufacturer.[12] Harvard is
the unimportant university in Cambridge.

In the mid-nineteenth century, when men were talking about founding Boston Tech, the Connecticut Valley (the region stretching from Springfield
through Hartford to New Haven, then along the shore through Bridgeport,
Norwalk, and Stamford) was already the leading center in the world for mass-
produced, precision-engineered goods. This was the place to which inventors
brought their new creations to have them manufactured. In 1925, when Frederick Rentschler decided to leave the Wright Aircraft Corporation and manufacture air-cooled aeroplane engines, he came to Hartford, where he went into
business with a successful but small firm manufacturing machine tools, typewriters, bicycles, and industrial machinery. The name of the firm was Pratt and
Whitney; it continues to build jet engines for the air force and the nation. Sikor-
sky in Stamford built the helicopters for the wars in Korea and Vietnam; the
navy built its submarines at Electric Boat on the Thames River estuary. America
pictured Connecticut as a chain of commuter suburbs strung along the New
Haven Line out of Grand Central station; the reality was that the state prospered as the precision manufacturer of aircraft and submarines, a prosperity
that would come crashing to a halt when the Cold War ended. But during the
half-century that followed Pearl Harbor, the Pentagon poured money into the
state, precision manufacturing made Connecticut rich.[13]

In 1962, my family drove from Connecticut, where my father worked for an
engineering firm, to spend Thanksgiving weekend in Boston, where we were

taken to admire the new Prudential Insurance Tower. Going to Boston to admire something new was a novel experience. For a hundred years, for the lifetimes, that is, not only of my grandparents but of my great-grandparents as well, the world came to Boston only when it wanted to admire something old. Better than any major city in America, Boston has preserved its colonial public buildings, its Federal neighborhoods and Victorian cityscape. The handful of office towers built in the 1920s did little to alter the impression that the city's streets were waiting for the arrival of a film crew to shoot a movie based on a Henry James novel. In 1960s Boston, fresh meat was sold in the market stalls under Faneuil Hall, wooden trolleys carried you out to the street-car suburbs, and the fishing fleet still tied up down at the wharves. Today, while the lion and the unicorn still decorate the facade of the Old State House, and the dome of the new state house that Bullfinch built in 1795 is still covered with the gold leaf that replaced Paul Revere's rolled copper sheathing in 1861, Boston is no museum piece. A booming economy of glitzy office towers and upscale entertainment draws talent from around the planet. Information technology and biotechnology industries have recently joined electronics, computers, and a financial services sector that has flourished since seventeenth-century merchants met at the Town House to sell shares in overseas voyages. Parts of the world struggle to cope with the environmental consequences of poverty. New England faces environmental threats that are the wages of affluence.

Chapter 17

Terrarium Earth

≈

> One of the toughest things for a population biologist to reconcile is the contrast between his or her recognition that civilization is in imminent serious jeopardy and the modest level of concern that population issues generate amount the public and even among elected officials.[1]
>
> —Paul R. and Anne H. Ehrlich

W HEN I WAS A GIRL SCOUT THERE WAS A FASH-
ion for making terraria. The idea was to take a glass container, such
as a large jar with a rubber stopper, put a layer of topsoil in the bottom, plant an artistic array of mosses and ferns, then seal the jar. If everything were done properly, the artificial ecosystem would live for many years, an enclosed garden sealed in an endlessly self-sustaining cycle of growth and decay. More frequently, some weed species would sprout and fill every cubic inch of the jar in a rampant orgy of growth before turning to slime and dying. Closed ecosystems exist in exquisitely delicate balance.

The New England landscape is about as natural as the terraria we made as children. Bullough's Pond was created by a seventeenth-century gristmiller; its present size and shape were determined by a nineteenth-century real estate developer; and a twentieth-century department of public works decision nearly turned it back into a marsh.

Americans first became conscious of environmental problems in the years leading up to the first Earth Day in 1970. Among the many ameliorative steps taken as a result of that great awakening was a decision to pour less rock salt onto icy roads in Massachusetts. There is no question that the salt strewn onto winter roads to keep them safe in bad weather wreaked environmental havoc on freshwater streams and ponds; no one regrets the decision to replace road salt with a less-damaging mixture of salted sand, but the change did have an unforeseen impact on our pond. So much sand washed off Newton roads after winter storms that, by the time we moved here in 1990, broad stretches of the pond were only a few inches deep, while yellow iris and cattails were encroaching on the edges.

Because the dam prevents silt and debris from washing downstream, Bullough's Pond, like all mill ponds, requires periodic dredging. Mill owners dependent on water power consider dredging as part of the ordinary cost of doing business. The old mill on Smelt Brook ground its last sack of corn in 1875; after that, there was no miller with an economic incentive to dredge the pond. Newton paid for a dredging in the 1920s, and the pond was due for another even before the switch from road salt to sand. In the 1970s, the accelerating transformation of Bullough's Pond into a marsh was a boon for some area residents: black-crowned night herons, little green, and great blue herons stalked the shallows, feasting on small fish and frogs. Most of the neighborhood, however, did not approve. Betsy Leitch, who moved from Brooklyn Heights into a house on the banks of the pond in 1968, disapproved most emphatically. Betsy did not disapprove silently. She decided that allowing the pond to fill with marsh weeds was quite simply wrong. She founded the Bullough's Pond Association in 1984 and spent the next decade trying to persuade Newton that the old mill pond ought to be dredged.

Money was the obstacle, of course. Backhoes and bucket loaders cost a great deal; while no one at city hall opposed dredging the old mill pond, no city official was exactly eager to pay for the work, either. Betsy Leitch and her closest ally, Peter Conde, circulated petitions, dug up old photographs of public ice skating on the pond, pointed out its value as a scenic focal point for the neighborhood, and succeeded in rallying the support of the neighborhood so effectively that, in 1992, State Senator Lois Pines inserted a budget line in a State Transportation Bill appropriating $260,000 for dredging the pond. The appropriation was made as a flood control measure.[2] Floods in the Smelt Brook drainage basin had indeed damaged roads in the neighborhood, yet there can be no doubt that it was a case of a wealthy neighborhood represented by a powerful state senator managing to obtain funding that might not have been available in more plebeian circumstances. Southern New England is full of aging mill ponds turning quietly into marshes. This particular pond was dredged because it is the picturesque darling of a well-connected neighborhood.

As the scheduled dredging approached, a valve near the dam was opened and water gushed out of the pond. It was like draining a giant bathtub. In ecological terms it was both bonanza and debacle. Hundreds of small-mouthed bass were swept through the valve and died in the creek bed below the dam after the flood had passed. Sandpipers patrolled the empty pond bottom, gleaning a feast of stranded creatures, while common mergansers, which I had never seen on this pond before, arrived to eat the fish that concentrated in the narrow creek bed that still ran across the muddy bottom of the erstwhile pond. Members of the Massachusetts Herpetological Society carried the snapping turtles away to safety.

I was getting breakfast on a February morning in 1993 when the distinctive rumble of a category three earthquake shook the house. A category three is the kind of temblor that causes the house to vibrate and makes loosely stacked dishes rattle in the cupboard without causing any real damage. Of course, big quakes start pretty much like small ones and I have a well-honed earthquake reflex. Just as I opened my mouth to shout for the children and rush for the doors, the shaking stopped; through the windows I saw the bulk of an enormous piece of earth-moving equipment rumble past the house. The thing was large enough to shake well-built houses on their foundations. It was labeled "Komatsu," the name of the Japanese manufacturer; by mid-morning it was dredging the pond.

The Komatsu worked steadily for days, scooping soil into dump trucks that carried it to cap an old landfill on the Newton-Waltham line. Eight feet down, the shovels reached bedrock, and stopped digging. Then the valve was closed and the pond filled again. It looks exactly as it did before it was dredged, except that we get very few herons nowadays. The deepened waters are better suited to buffleheads, hooded mergansers, and cormorants—birds we rarely saw when the pond was turning into a marsh. No snapping turtles with two-foot carapaces emerge to bury their eggs on spring afternoons. The neighborhood association decided that they were ill-suited to suburban life and neglected to ask the Herpetological Society to return them. Yellow iris still fringe the pond in spring. All in all, it is a very fair imitation of nature. The entire New England landscape is but an imitation of nature. Our ponds, woodlands, and meadows are a landscape sculpted, planted, and limited by human activity. From Bullough's Pond's fringe of yellow iris, a recently introduced Eurasian species, to Maine's spruce forests, an industrial monoculture that stands where a mixed forest once grew, the New England ecosystem is what we have made it.

At the apogee of Yankee farming 75 to 85 percent of the land in southern New England was cleared for field and pasture. One by one the pastures were abandoned, as freight trains carried the produce of midwestern farms to New England. By the 1970s, forests covered the hillsides, laced with ribbons of highway connecting urban islands in a sea of trees.[3] These postagricultural forests are very different from the forests New England Indians knew, and only partly because Indians no longer burn the undergrowth to favor mast-producing species.

Looking from my kitchen window up the wooded slope behind our house, I can see the remnants of a chestnut stump rotting slowly back to earth. It died in the chestnut blight of the 1930s, but chestnuts are tenacious, even now young trees sprout from old roots, pushing their way toward sunlight in a desperate effort to grow large enough to produce fertile fruit. Every shoot is doomed to failure. When they are about twice the height of my teenage sons, a bright orange fungus that arrived at the Bronx Zoo in 1904 with a shipment of exotic chestnut trees imported from the Far East will girdle the trunks, cutting off nutrients and water. All of the magnificent chestnuts, once among the dominant trees of the American forest canopy, have died. Worse, they did not die alone.

American elms once towered over the floodplain forests of New England rivers. Later, with their umbrellas of branches that split from the main trunk high above the utility poles that string electric wires along our streets, they shaded every Yankee town. Now they are gone, slain by Dutch elm disease. The hemlocks that stood sentinel on the cool, northern slopes of our hills are dying, attacked by woolly adelgids, a tiny insect whose egg sacks look like fuzzy white balls glued to the foliage of the victim. The adelgids arrived on the Pacific coast from Japan. No one knows precisely how they traveled. In Japan they infest spruce trees, which survive the assault, as do the Western hemlocks that host them in the Pacific Northwest. Since the adelgids arrived in Virginia in about 1960, however, eastern hemlock have been falling before the onslaught like infantry cut down by machine-gun fire. Dogwoods, slender trees that light the forest understory with springtime flowers, are dying of anthracnose. Not as fast as hemlock, which succumb within a year of the arrival of adelgids in a region. Anthracnose fungus first speckles the leaves, then forms cankers on the bark, then girdles the trunk, causing dogwood trees to yellow and shrivel in slow death. No one knows where the dogwood anthracnose originated, only that it is killing the trees. So, while we can choose to live in a forested land, we cannot choose to live in a forest that resembles the one that grew here before we introduced Old World diseases to American trees.

The beautiful, wooded hills of West Virginia are full of coal. It is the cheapest source of energy on the planet, as long as no bill is rendered for the loss of life and property that billows out of the smokestack. Ohio's electric utilities are not held accountable for the health of the atmosphere. They are responsible for supplying reliable, inexpensive electricity, and the most efficient way to do this is to burn coal. Coal-burning power plants belch clouds of acrid black smoke that make life unpleasant in the neighborhood and bring slow death to things living downwind: plants, forests, insects, humans. But while the blighting of neighborhood forests and lungs remains common in China and Eastern Europe, coal-fired death clouds were eliminated in this country by the passage of the Clean Air Act of 1970. Scrubbers installed in smokestacks eliminated many of the most offensive particles, while the construction of smokestacks two hundred, three hundred, and even four hundred feet tall cleared the air in midwestern cities.

Emissions still billow from smokestacks. After all the requirements of the Clean Air Act are satisfied, sulfur dioxide pours from tall new smokestacks not into the neighborhood of the power plant but into air currents far above the surface of the Buckeye State. Hundreds of miles east of the Ohio Valley, the sulfur dioxide mixes with rain and falls on New England as a dilute acid solution.

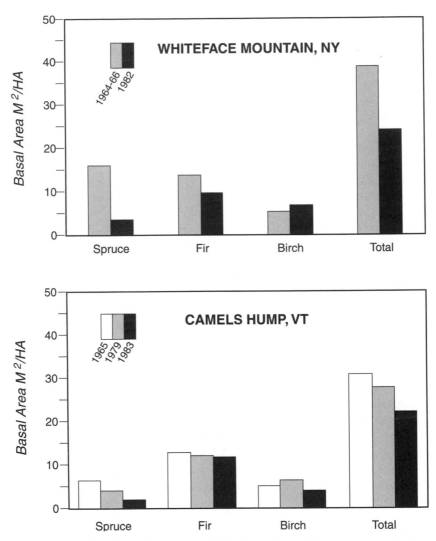

Changes in live basal area of major species in boreal forests. The trees are smaller because airborne pollutants kill them before they grow to full size, creating opportunity for a slight increase in birch, a light-loving species that springs up where other trees have died. Arthur Johnson and Thomas Siccama, "Decline of Red Spruce in the High-Elevation Forests of the Northeastern United States," in *Air Pollution's Toll on Forests and Crops*, ed. James MacKenzie and Mohamed T. El-Ashrey (New Haven: Yale University Press, 1987), 197. By permission.

On cloudless days it ends its ride on the jet stream by simply settling, as dry deposition, onto the needles and leaves of trees growing on the slopes of mountains higher than the smokestacks of Ohio are tall. When it rains, acid waters wash over the ground into the soil.[4] Like the acids that form when spruce needles decompose, acid rain kills denizens of the topsoil; fertility leaches away.[5]

The problem wouldn't be so severe if New England were made of softer stuff. Soils in regions of limestone bedrock contain elements that neutralize acids and mitigate the impact of pollution on the soil. But New England is founded on granite. Granite bedrock is powerless to neutralize the acid waters that fall on our mountains and hills, rainwater so highly acidified that numerous lakes and ponds that once supported fish are now sterile, too acidic for fish or even algae to live in. Our mountain lakes are beautifully clear. Many abandoned granite quarries are so utterly free of algae that you can see a hundred feet down to the rocky bottom. Nature is supposed to be murky.

One of the joys of mountain hiking is the sudden emergence from cloud to bright sunshine, not because the weather has cleared but because the hiker has climbed above the clouds. The cloud line is often lower than the four-thousand foot summits of the White Mountains, and it is quite common to start up a trail on an overcast morning and emerge at midday on a sunlit peak looking down on cotton-wool clouds stretching toward the blue horizon. In that constant mist, a cloud forest grows. Balsam fir and red spruce bearded with lichens, their roots spread about with Indian pipe and chanterelle mushrooms. Eerily beautiful in the hazy mist that condenses and drips water onto the moist forest floor. Beautiful and virtually sterile. Lichen. Spruce. Fir. Fungi. Little else grows in the thin, acid soil buried in snow from September to May. Even these may be doomed by the mists that once sustained them. A hiker along the Appalachian Trail can watch trees dying from Georgia to Maine, and be certain that, bathed in mist as acid as vinegar, trees are also dying in places through which the trail does not pass, in New York, Quebec, California, Norway. Acid rain is killing trees everywhere; it is killing them fastest downwind from major industrial cities and in mountains swathed in acid clouds.

Acid kills by causing cell walls to collapse, by damaging the stomatal wax plugs that enable conifer needles to exchange gases with the atmosphere while conserving water, and by leaching nutrients from needles and leaves.[6] But it is not industrial pollution alone that is killing the forest. It is cars.

Air is composed of 78 percent nitrogen in the form of N_2 (two nitrogen atoms forming a single molecule), and 21 percent oxygen in the form of O_2. Oxygen and nitrogen. Separate and stable. Turn the key in the ignition of a Chevy Suburban, however, and the heat in the engine causes nitrogen and oxygen to combine, forming oxides of nitrogen. Should one of these nitrous oxide (N_2O) or nitric oxide (NO) molecules happen to bump into an oxygen molecule in direct sunlight, the sunlight may cause the N_2O and the O_2 to break up and recombine as N_2 and O_3. O_3, three oxygen atoms formed into a single molecule, is a gas known as ozone. Ozone is rather like a swarm of bees, a marvelous, useful thing so long as it is in a remote location doing the work it is supposed to do. Bees, as every lover of honey will agree, are admirable creatures, paragons of industry, exemplars of productive excellence. Should a swarm decide to move in with you, however, your perspective on them would change radically.

The ozone we hear the most about is the ozone that is most remote from us, the layer of ozone in the upper atmosphere that forms a protective barrier shielding us from the deadly ultraviolet rays of the sun. Until recently, that was pretty much the only ozone there was. Before the Industrial Revolution, only an occasional thunderstorm generated enough heat to produce ozone in the lower atmosphere, and the output of thunderstorms was unimportant because ozone breaks down to harmless forms of oxygen in about two days in warm weather, and lasts a mere month in cold seasons. While it lasts, however, it is the leading element in the reddish-brown haze known as smog, and it causes a world of trouble.

Ozone damages the membranes of chlorophyll-containing mesophyll cells of plants, reducing photosynthesis; it "bleaches" the cells the way the oxidants in Chlorox bleach laundry. Crops in areas of high ozone exposure show small, white flecks, as though someone had sprinkled minuscule droplets of laundry bleach on the green leaves. In effect, someone did. And bleaching stunts the growth of the plant.[7]

Oxides of nitrogen in concentration as low as one part per billion generate ozone levels high enough to injure the health of plants, but only very remote regions with favorable weather patterns have concentrations of oxides that low.[8] The only ingredients needed to create ozone are automobiles and sunshine, and these are ubiquitous. Where cars are numerous, ozone levels soar, and smog drifts over the countryside in a deadly haze. The forests of Maine are being killed by every Ford on the New Jersey Turnpike, every Volvo in Connecticut, and every pickup truck in New Hampshire.

The combined effects of acid rain and ozone haze are devastating. Weakened by nutrient leaching, stunted by nutrient-depleted soil, with leaves impaired in their ability to photosynthesize, the trees succumb. The immediate cause of death may be natural, even mundane: drought, cold, pear thrips, woolly aphids. Healthy trees withstand the onslaught; forests weakened by acid and ozone die.

The spewing of harmful elements into the air as a by-product of industrial processes is not new. Lead was thrown into the atmosphere by bronze age smelting in sufficient volume that traces are detectable in core samples taken from the Arctic ice caps. The difference is scale. Ancient Greek metal furnaces did throw lead into the atmosphere, but the only people who died from lead poisoning were Greek craftsmen and the people who drank and ate from lead-contaminated vessels. When Minoan bronze smelters deforested their hillsides to make charcoal, civilized life on Crete collapsed. Civilization itself moved to new lands with uncut forests and continued. Ancient civilizations abused and exploited the environment, but the numbers involved and the technology employed dictated that the damage was only local. Not until the Industrial Revolution did human societies gain the ability to threaten the ability of the planet as a whole to sustain civilization.

The air we breath is mostly nitrogen (78.09 percent), although the smaller (20.95 percent) oxygen component is not inconsequential. Neither are the minuscule quantities of argon (0.93 percent) and carbon dioxide (0.03 percent). Not even the trace elements are insignificant. Neon, helium, methane, krypton, hydrogen, xenon, and ozone are all found in minute quantities in the first forty to fifty miles above the surface of the earth, the zone known as the lower atmosphere. Carbon dioxide, for example, constitutes a mere 0.03 percent of the lower atmosphere, calculated according to relative volume, and is virtually transparent to incoming solar radiation. When solar heat in the form of terrestrial infrared radiation attempts to pass through the atmosphere outbound, however, some of it is absorbed by atmospheric carbon dioxide and trapped in the atmosphere, just as a greenhouse lets solar heat in but not out. This greenhouse effect is a marvelous thing.

We could not have evolved on a planet as hot as Mercury, or on one as cold as Pluto. As far as we know, no life has evolved on Mercury or Pluto. It is our atmosphere that fits planet Earth for life, at least, for mammalian life, and the presence of carbon dioxide molecules trapping some but not all of the earth's infrared radiation on its way out of the atmosphere keeps the planet comfortable for us and our kind. If we weren't already calling this mechanism the greenhouse effect, we might dub it the Goldilocks effect for its ability to keep the temperature just right—not too hot and not too cold. What would happen if we increased the amount of carbon dioxide in the atmosphere just a little, say by 25 percent?

A 25 percent increase in atmospheric carbon dioxide would lead to hotter weather and a loss of soil moisture, causing significant crop losses in tropical and temperate regions. It would destabilize weather patterns, increasing the severity and frequency of major storms. There would be more floods, bigger hurricanes, and more devastating wind storms and blizzards. Weather in general would become more extreme as weather patterns were destabilized; we would have severe cold snaps, deadly heat waves, and unprecedented droughts. Arctic ice flows would freeze later in the fall and melt earlier in the spring, disrupting the marine food chain. We know that's what would happen because it is happening already. Higher temperatures, severe storms, unusual weather patterns, disrupted food chains, and significant crop losses are all well documented, as is the phenomenon causing them. This century has seen a 25 percent increase in the amount of carbon dioxide in the earth's atmosphere. In recent years, atmospheric carbon dioxide has been rising at nearly 0.5 percent per year.

Fossil fuel combustion is not the only culprit, nor is carbon dioxide the only greenhouse gas. Atmospheric water vapor traps heat radiating from the surface of the planet, which is why deserts are so cold at night, while midnight in the humid tropics can be nearly as hot as noon. Atmospheric methane, nitrous oxide, chlorofluorocarbons, and ozone are also powerful greenhouse gases, and all are being spewed into the atmosphere at unprecedented rates by agricultural and industrial processes. Leading producers of atmospheric methane, for example, include the waterlogged soils of rice paddies and the digestive tracts of cattle. Acreage devoted to both rice and cattle has been increasing rapidly worldwide. Agriculture is also a leading producer of atmospheric carbon dioxide.

The clearing of forests releases carbon dioxide not only when the trees are burned, but even when they are sold as lumber. That's because the humus-rich topsoil of the forest floor is a major carbon sink: when a forest floor becomes a farm field, organic matter in the soil decomposes, and some of the carbon enters the atmosphere. People alter the balance of the greenhouse mechanism simply by allowing population to grow to a point where demand for food causes forests to be cleared for range, flooded to grow rice, or developed into suburban housing estates. People alter the chemical balance of the atmosphere even more rapidly by burning fossil fuel.

Coal, oil, and natural gas are burned in such volume that the amount of carbon dioxide pumped into the atmosphere by their combustion is measured in gigatons, units of a billion tons. Six gigatons of carbon are added every year to an atmosphere that already has enough. Prosperity, which has the capacity to alleviate many problems, exacerbates this one.

Almost from the first whistle of a Boston and Worcester engine, there were men who saw the possibilities. Not the possibility that fossil fuel burned in locomotive engines might alter the planet's climate; that particular nightmare was far in the future. The vision that changed the face of the land was that of living in a country house like an English gentleman, while still being able to catch the 8:09 to the office.

New England's first railroad had barely made its first run when the first commuter suburb sprang into existence on West Newton Hill. Country life in the suburbs of the 1830s was a rich man's privilege. It required the wherewithal to build not just a house, but also a stable to keep the horses that pulled the carriage to and from the station, and servants' quarters, since no daily woman could walk to a remote suburban house. The middle classes, even the comfortable middle classes, lived where they could walk to the office, school, and shops. The very wealthy had always had the privilege of rural residence. What the railroad made possible was a new lifestyle for the family man whose accumulating fortune still required him to appear daily at the office. He could be at his desk until 5:00, take the 5:15 from the city, and by 5:45 be a country squire.

The rural seats of those railroad commuters of the 1830s were islands in an agricultural sea, which ought to have pleased them, since the English gentry they self-consciously emulated were farmers. Yankee farming was at its historic zenith and except for the handful of stately homes clustered around its rail stations, Newton was a market garden town, growing cucumbers and strawberries for Boston. New England's first suburbanites enjoyed a view of plowed fields.

Automobiles killed the farms. Even though railroad tracks ran through every Victorian town, horses were required to pull wagons to the depots, and hay was required to feed the horses. Land was kept in cultivation to feed the horses, and New England farmers steadily increased hay production until horseless carriages arrived. Then the fields were abandoned, the land between the cities reverted to forest, and the people in the big houses on the hills began to have a view of oaks and maples instead of heifers and turnips.

The only drawback to the automobile in the 1920s and 1930s was that not every family could afford one. Roads were paved and the prospering classes rolled into town in their new automobiles, but mill hands and clerks remained pedestrians compelled to live where they could walk either to their jobs or to a trolley. Under this constraint, cities grew in strips of two- and three-story homes nestled close to the trolley lines. Where the trolley ended, the city stopped. There was a thin suburban fringe, then the woods began. A pilot soaring over New England in one of the new flying machines would have seen a rolling landscape of dense woodlands, the thick canopy of chestnut and maple pierced intermittently by the spire of a Congregational church, marking the spot where farmers once worshipped. Very occasionally, the pilot would have flown over a city. But the cities were compact, and soon the little biplane would have been over countryside again, with nothing but trees in view. Even the narrow country roads lay hidden beneath the sheltering forest. Then the automobiles began to infiltrate the forest.

The house we live in was built in 1923. Older houses in our neighborhood have detached, two-story garages with second-floor doors that swung open to admit bales of hay in the days before carriages were horseless. Owners of homes newer than ours park their cars in garages built as attached wings of the main house, and the most modern houses of all incorporate the garage into the body of the house, because, I suppose, by the 1960s the car had become a member of the family. In the 1920s, when our house was built, Americans were not yet so comfortable with auto-mobiles. Our garage is a separate building. It has the same pitched roof, clapboard siding, and twelve-light windows as the house, but it is a thing apart, almost as though the builders were a little afraid of the new machines they owned. They should have been.

Cars brought to cities the kind of unbounded growth fossil fuels bestowed on the economy. Newton was a suburban, bedroom community with forty thousand residents the year Henry Ford introduced the Model T, a suburb so desirable that builders constructed houses on every eligible lot, yet farmers in the Oak Hill section continued to send quantities of strawberries and lettuce to market. No rail lines or trolleys ran through Oak Hill, so no one wanted to build a suburban house there. The automobile changed the equation. Henry Ford made every piece of land within a reasonable drive of downtown a desirable site for a suburban house. Demand from hordes of new, suburban drivers caused governments to build new roads and pave old ones.[9] And each new road brought more of the countryside within reasonable driving distance of downtown, which encouraged more people to own cars. In the process, trolley lines were dismantled and railroad tracks abandoned. The movement to automobile-dependent suburban lifestyles was not entirely the result of free choice. In 1926 General Motors created a subsidiary corporation that spent the next thirty years buying trolley lines and ripping up the tracks, in the face of vociferous protests from trolley patrons.[10] But General Motors understood that commuters deprived of trolleys would be forced to buy cars. The federal government also worked to pave the countryside, virtually mandating suburbanization with subsidized highways, tax deductions that went to homeowners but not apartment renters, and business tax policies that encouraged corporations to vacate aging buildings in favor of new premises far from the urban core.[11] But it was American infatuation with the idyll of life in a private home set in its own green lawn that drove the exodus to the suburbs. More Americans now live in suburbs than in cities, and few suburbanites can buy so much as a bottle of milk unless they can find the car keys.

Cars pump pollutants and carbon dioxide into the atmosphere. And every square mile paved for roads or parking lots is a square mile that is not a meadow or a forest absorbing carbon dioxide and supporting life.

I love my car. It allows me to drive across the river to the library I use in Cambridge, check out a heavy armload of books, stop at the fishmonger in Brookline, or the vegetable store in Watertown, and pick my children up after school. Yet my idea of a civilized transportation system was defined by a year we spent on the Stanford campus in Palo Alto, California, where I only backed the car out of the driveway to take a Sunday drive. I rode my bicycle to the library and my husband commuted to his office by bicycle; many of his colleagues walked. I brought my groceries home on a bike and could ride to the bookstore, the copy store, and the post office. Not only did our children ride to and from school on safe, well-marked bicycle lanes, our daughter was able to ride to the stable whenever she wanted to exchange her bicycle for a horse. And our son, the student journalist, pedaled to interviews with the school board president and our state representative. In an entire year I did not drive a single carpool.

We can redesign our neighborhoods to make automobiles superfluous in our daily routine, while keeping them around for their wonderful convenience when traveling to out-of-the-way destinations or hauling ten bags of groceries. We can design automobiles that neither pollute nor exhale carbon dioxide. What we cannot do is to go on commuting to work in Chevy Suburbans. There are too many of us.

The question of what we can and cannot do without threatening the viability of this planet's biosphere rests on a series of calculation trading numbers against impact. There were only about ten million human beings alive before the Neolithic Revolution.[12] With only ten million people on the planet, even if every housewife in the world had driven a Range Rover on her daily round of gathering wild wheat and pinenuts, the impact on the atmosphere would have been slight. If there were a mere ten million human beings on earth today, we could all eat steak and drive Chevy Suburbans with impunity. Five billion of us cannot all ride *mopeds* without destroying the stability of our climate. Five billion of us could, however, live comfortably in a billion homes powered by solar electricity and located within walking distance of school, work, and the grocery store.

Chapter 18

The Third Revolution

❧

The fact that, of all organic beings, man alone is to be regarded as essentially a destructive power, and that he wields energies to resist which nature is wholly impotent, tends to prove that though living in physical nature [man] is not of her, that he is of more exalted parentage, and belongs to a higher order of existence than those born of [nature's] womb and submissive to [nature's] dictates.[1]
—George Perkins Marsh, 1864

INDUSTRIAL REVOLUTION WAS A DEPARTURE from old patterns of energy use. It marked a transition from the use of the product of this year's sunlight to the use of the product of fossil sunlight—from the use of wood and hay to use of coal and petroleum as fuel and industrial feedstock. Industrial Revolution was also a departure from old patterns of thought. The world before Newcomen, Darby, and Watt was a world wherein wealth was understood to exist in constant volume. Wealth was a bag of gold, a field, a flock of sheep. If the rains failed in Cornwall forcing people living there to send gold or cattle into Essex to buy grain, then men in Essex were richer and men in Cornwall were poorer, but it was understood that the amount of wealth in the world had not changed. Fossil fuels meant that wealth, like the energy supply, was susceptible to unlimited growth. Economics is the most cheerful of sciences, for while physics, chemistry, and biology recognize limitations, the growth curves set in train by the harnessing of coal and petroleum have recognized no upper boundary. It is no coincidence that Adam Smith published *The Wealth of Nations* within a decade of James Watt's invention of the condensing steam engine, nor was it a coincidence that both men worked in that hotbed of Calvinism, Glasgow, Scotland.

Chemistry and physics are themselves children of the Industrial Revolution, or of the rationalism that was its intellectual counterpart. From the dawn of history, the material basis of civilization had been immutable. Wood, clay, iron, flax: there might be innovations in their use, clever craftsmanship, such new techniques as pottery glaze or the combination of linen warp and woolen woof that produces linsey-woolsey, a fabric more durable than either parent. There might even be the discovery of a new thing—like the Chinese discovery of the technique of making fabric from the cocoon of the silk worm—but no crafts-man could alter the nature of things. Alchemists and magicians might attempt to transform a base metal into gold, but no sane customer carried a barrel of mineral oil to an alchemist in the hope that it would be turned into silk or ivory. Beginning with Copernicus, our ability to decipher the laws of nature grew so rapidly that in the twentieth century we routinely carry oil to the chemist and expect him to turn it into ivory and silk or their functional equivalent. It soon became the new orthodoxy to believe that there was no material problem science could not solve, only some that it had not solved yet. Omnipotence, long an attribute of the divine, had become a attribute of humanity. There was nothing we could not achieve.

By the middle decades of the twentieth century, chemicals and materials derived from petroleum were omnipresent, as were the petroleum-derived persistent toxic chemicals generated in the manufacturing process. But Newcomen and Darby were no more responsible for PCB contamination than Bismarck was responsible for Hitler. The central problems brought on by the Industrial Revolution are that the fuels that make life comfortable and pleasant now threaten to destabilize the climate upon which our lives depend, and that the effect of the chemicals we produce seems to be disrupting the process of reproducing life itself.

We are hardly likely to choose to return to life as it was before Thomas Newcomen unlocked the power of fossilized sunlight. The prospect of living on the hot and stormy planet global warming is even now bringing into being is equally unappealing, even if it were tenable. It is more heartening to entertain the possibility that we are even now in the early stages of a Third Revolution in energy use, following up the Neolithic Revolution's harnessing of photosynthesis and the Industrial Revolution's harnessing of fossil energy with the development of efficient solar power, supplemented by wind power, thermal power, fuel cells, redesign of existing energy demand, and other even more creative alternatives. The fact that our current level of scientific knowledge and technological prowess are inadequate to the task is not beside the point—it is the point.

Revolutions become necessary when the existing system ceases to function satisfactorily. They organize society in new ways. This revolution, the Third Revolution, will entail the discovery and deployment of new kinds of energy and materials. The alternative proposition, that there must be a limit to growth, is not popular. The quality of life has been improving for Europeans and peoples of European extraction for several centuries now. The progress has been erratic, and there have been episodes of retrogression, but the direction overall has been toward steadily increasing comfort. More recently, several non-European nations have joined and even begun to lead the upward movement. Proposals that we should, as a species, switch to vegetarianism, stop riding in motor cars, or give up our television sets are greeted with horror equally by residents of Newton, Massachusetts, who live in ten-room houses and drive Jeep Cherokees, and by Pakistani farmers saving to buy their first motor bike.

Population growth has been a constant since the first modern humans walked in Africa. It accelerated with the coming of the Neolithic Revolution and exploded with the success of the Industrial Revolution. Agriculture allowed population to grow far beyond the numbers supportable by hunting and gathering. The American nexus of corn, beans, and squash, for example, allowed the population of southern New England to grow to several times the number the land could support when people earned their living by hunting and gathering. The Industrial Revolution allowed the population of twentieth-century New England to grow to many times the number that were supported by the pre-industrial agriculture of the 1700s. Yet population growth was not merely an effect, but also a cause of those two earlier revolutions.

The Neolithic Revolution began when population growth forced gatherers to take control of the process of photosynthesis by saving and planting seeds.

The Industrial Revolution began when population growth and the consequent wood famine in England pushed Thomas Newcomen to invent a way to convert fossilized sunlight to mechanical power and induced Abraham Darby to invent a way to smelt iron with fossil material. The Industrial Revolution began in New England because there were more young men than there was arable land, forcing some of those surplus men to invent new kinds of machinery. Industrialization, specifically the substitution of fossil fuel for hay and wood, was a development so liberating of economic growth from resource constraints that human population increased from the eight or nine hundred million people living when the Industrial Revolution clanged into motion, to over five billion people on the planet today.

We are being pushed into a Third Revolution by the same forces that pushed us into the first two: the pressure of population on limited resources. If it is to succeed, this revolution must result in a planned and orderly decrease in the numbers of human beings on this planet, even as it results in improved standards of living for all.

Pressure for change comes from the land, as it did when the competition of growing populations for static resources brought about the Neolithic and Industrial revolutions, but it comes in new guises. At some point, we will quite literally run out of the amount of land needed to grow food. That time is not yet here, although it will come sooner if ozone pollution, acid rain, and global warming continue to reduce crop yields. What we have already run out of is land that can be cleared for agriculture without doing severe damage to the atmosphere. Every acre of forest that we cut adds to the burden of global warming. That is true whether we are discussing an acre of Indonesian rainforest cut to supply lumber for a construction site in Tokyo, an acre of Maine spruce cut to feed a pulp mill, or an acre of Angolan woodland cut for fuel wood by subsistence farmers.

The climatic thermostat known as the greenhouse effect threatens us with a hot and stormy future unless we clean up our fossil-fuel burning habits immediately, but it is not the only natural system in jeopardy. It is certainly not the only natural system whose degradation threatens our well-being.

Upper atmosphere ozone is perhaps the best-publicized of the natural systems we have disrupted. As essential to the upper atmosphere as it is detrimental at ground level, ozone hovers in a thin, stratospheric shield protecting the biosphere from ultraviolet radiation. The ozone is depleted by chlorofluorocarbons (still widely used in refrigerants in the third world and—often illicitly—in the United States as well), which break down to release free chlorine atoms, which in turn break ozone molecules apart. When the stratospheric ozone shield is depleted, humans develop skin cancer and cataracts. Ultraviolet radiation also attacks plants, reducing crop yields and killing phytoplankton, the basis of the marine food chain.

We have been destroying the topsoil even longer than we have been depleting the ozone layer. While seams of coal and iron deep below the surface of the earth have brought wealth to individuals and civilizations, life itself depends on the first ten inches of the earth's crust, the topsoil. Sumer, Indus, Babylon, Crete, Greece, Ethiopia, Carthage: the great civilizations of the ancient world fell when they had exhausted their topsoil, just as Cape Cod ceased to support agriculture when Yankee farmers let the topsoil blow away. Topsoil can be ruined by removing the cover and exposing the land to erosion. It can be destroyed by irrigating in ways that allow salt to accumulate, by grazing-induced desertification, by clear-cutting forests to cause podsolization, or by quite simply exhausting the soil with overcropping. The complex structure of healthy topsoil is so poorly understood that is unclear whether the natural, microbial community, once destroyed, can ever be reconstructed. It is clear that large regions of once-fertile farmland have been rendered sterile by human carelessness, and that much of the world's farmland requires steadily increasing applications of soil amendments to maintain crop yields. The Iraqi deserts that lie where ancient Babylonians grew wheat stand as monuments to heedless destruction. Even greater threats to human welfare may be invisible.

Petroleum-derived industrial feedstocks have allowed us to expand our supply of everything from rayon dresses to plastic lawn chairs without devoting arable land to the fields of flax and the forests of saw timber from which dresses and chairs used to be made. Automobile dashboards, disposable picnic forks, and children's toys could all be made from metal or wood, but an automobile made entirely from steel and wood, with leather seats and glass windows, would be outrageously expensive to build and so heavy that it would burn prohibitive amounts of fuel. The difficulty is that the manufacture of plastics releases persistent toxic chemicals into the environment, and these chemicals disrupt the reproductive function of animals causing them to produce deformed young. They may be able to do so in humans, as well. The task for materials science in the Third Revolution is to find chemically inert substitutes for the petroleum derivatives we now favor as industrial feedstocks.

In addition to lacing our food, water, and soil with hormone-disrupting synthetic chemicals, we are aggressively depleting forests, estuaries, fishing shoals, marshes, aquifers, lakes, and coral reefs. It would be difficult to locate a natural system not degraded by the chemicals we pour into our air and water or by rough handling in the guise of filling, digging, plowing and mining.

Is our tenure on this planet really threatened by the filling of a salt marsh in Fairfield County for use as a garbage dump? Every salt marsh that is filled or dredged makes the waters of Long Island Sound a little less productive. Yet filling one marsh, pouring the effluent of one town into a river, or allowing carbon dioxide to billow from the stack of one electrical generating plant has an impact that is demonstrably negligible. It is, moreover, the right of the owner of a piece of land to develop the property. Or is it?

American jurisprudence derives from English common law, and while the common law never recognized the rights of naiads, it did give standing to the expectation that water would be allowed to flow "without diminution or obstruction." Mills were built under common law in colonial America as they were in England, but the miller had no common law right to hold back so much water in a dry season as would reduce the natural flow of the river and prevent users downstream from watering their cattle. Nor was the miller permitted to build a dam so high that water held back in a wet season inundated the fields of owners upstream from the mill. The miller was also required to open the dam in spring to allow the fish to run.

Two legal principals guided judges when a farmer came to court accusing a miller of building an illegal dam, the same principles that applied in all cases regarding real property. The first was always to rule in favor of the natural uses of land; and when it said "natural" the common law meant "agricultural." By the time England had kings whose names we remember, men and women had forgotten that there had ever been a time before the introduction of agriculture, or that there was anything unnatural about a plowed field. The second principle was that once a user was established astride a resource, no subsequent development would be allowed to interfere with that use. In practice, these principles prevented would-be mill owners from building mill ponds big enough to hold back large water powers, from holding onto the reserves necessary to keep their wheels turning in dry seasons, and from building new mills upstream from an existing mill. In a world itching to industrialize, the common law was holding back progress. It had to be changed, and it was.

Massachusetts took the first step in 1795, revising its seventeenth-century mill act to specify that the owner of a mill seat on any navigable stream was permitted to build a dam that flooded upstream land. Annual compensation payments were required, but the farmer whose fields were ruined was forced to accept the payments. He could not tear the dam down to remove standing water from his fields, as the common law—which called destroying a mill dam "abating a nuisance"—would have permitted him to do. He could not sue for trespass, or sue for punitive damages, or ask the court to enjoin the miller for flooding his land and creating a nuisance. All he could do was watch his fields be ruined and accept the annual compensation. In the judgment of the Massachusetts legislature, a few drowned fields were a small price to pay for the progress and profits industrial revolution brought.

The courts not only agreed with the new legislation, they went further than the assembly had gone. In a sweeping reform of centuries-old principles, judges cleared a path for industrial development. No longer would courts protect "natural and customary" uses of land. Henceforth they would act to remove legal obstacles to commercial development of land and natural resources.

The common law held people responsible for the consequences of their actions, whether those consequences were deliberate or unintended. If a farmer started a fire on a calm day for some ordinary, productive purpose such as disposing of agricultural waste, and a spark quite accidentally wafted into a neighbor's hayloft and burnt down the barn, the farmer who started the fire was liable for damages. This is called strict liability. After 1830, wood-burning locomotives charged though the countryside spewing ash and sparks, and, incidentally, setting fire to cornfields, barns, and woodlots. Irate farmers sued with every expectation of collecting damages: the law was plain enough. Railroad companies objected that if they had to pay for every little barn that happened to burn down, they would scarcely be able to run a train. The courts listened. Strict liability was jettisoned in favor of a new standard. Henceforth there would be no damages paid for fires that occurred as a consequence of business done in the ordinary way. Only if a plaintiff could demonstrate negligence would a railroad have to pay damages. The owner of a coal-burning, electricity-generating plant in Ohio, whose smokestacks send death to a sugar bush in Vermont is not obliged to pay the farmer for the dead trees or for the value of the maple syrup they would have produced. Under common law, the Vermont farmer could have sued to abate the nuisance and a judge would have shut the coal-burning plants down. Under contemporary laws, Ohio's coal-burning power plants are within their rights when they spew carbon dioxide into the air, as are the pickup trucks of Vermont farmers, and the lawnmowers of Middlesex County, despite the fact that all of these ordinary and productive activities have the direct consequence of killing trees in downwind forests. The cumulative effect of all this burning of fossil fuel is to alter the atmosphere and warm the climate. Even if the law allowed us collectively to sue the perpetrators of climate change, we could only sue . . . ourselves.

We have now reached a point where the legal priorities that made the Industrial Revolution possible are threatening to destroy the function of natural systems that make life possible. There is an emerging societal consensus that our first priority must be to defend the integrity of natural systems that provide us with a stable climate, a functioning atmosphere, healthy oceans, rivers, lakes, and soil, and that we must move to insure that the food we eat, the air we breathe, and the water we drink are free of toxic substances. Legal principles shaped in the early years of the Industrial Revolution to enable the economic exploitation of natural resources are being reshaped to defend the integrity of life-sustaining natural systems.[3]

Under the legal standards in place since the beginning of the Industrial Revolution, entrepreneurs have been encouraged to build mills and enjoy the profits, while not being held accountable for such downstream costs as crops destroyed by air pollution and estuaries rendered lifeless by industrial effluent. It is little wonder that industries accustomed to profits artificially inflated by a system that allowed them to pour harmful waste into the air and water at no charge, should object when a change of accounting methods is suggested. Yet just such a change is being implemented by legislatures and courts responding to public opinion.

Louisiana Pacific operates a paper mill in the tiny northern California town of Samoa, near one of the great surfing beaches on the Pacific coast. As a result of a lawsuit by the Surfrider Foundation, the mill was recently forced to alter its production process to meet a standard that would have been unimaginable only a few years ago: Louisiana Pacific must prove, via an ongoing program of bioassays, that mill effluents are not impairing the capacity of coastal species, including abalone, sea urchins, and giant kelp, to survive and to reproduce.[4] It is the sort of standard that we may soon expect to see applied to economic activity of all kinds, not because it is reasonable, straightforward, and wise, but because the law responds to shifts in the way individuals view the world. An emerging consensus now views our common interest in the functional integrity of natural systems as more important than the right of individuals to extract a profit from those systems.

Charles Darwin deserved his position as the most hated man of the nineteenth century. If people before Darwin knew anything of a certainty, they knew that humankind, made in the image of God, was separate from and superior to the rest of creation. The threat in Darwin's work lay in the idea that humans were a species within the animal kingdom. We who had been like the angels were rudely told that we were mere animals, like warthogs and guinea pigs.

The alternative to addressing the implications of being demoted from beings created in the image of God to members of the animal kingdom is to refuse to acknowledge our demotion. To refuse to let them strip you of your epaulettes, to go on giving orders as though you were still an officer. Behave, like Charles Stuart, as though you were actually king of England, and perhaps they really will put you on the throne. Since Newcomen, we have behaved as though our species was exempt from the laws of nature. We know that when other species experience rapid population growth, they soon experience population crashes. We observe when species deplete a vital resource, they die, as fish die that deplete all the oxygen in a pond, or ungulates die when they have eaten all of the grass. We only shrink from applying these rules to ourselves.

Charles Stuart became Charles II of England in 1660, but restoring the king could not revive the discredited idea of absolute monarchy, which is why Charles II's great-nephew was known as the Young Pretender and not as Charles III, despite the fact that he behaved all his life as though he were the rightful king of England. Pretending to be king worked for Charles II; it did not work for Bonnie Prince Charlie, because the divine right of kings was an idea whose time had passed.

The idea that the human species is exempt from the laws of nature is, like the divine right of kings, an idea whose time has passed. Human exemption from natural constraints still has defenders—especially in departments of economics. Perhaps this is not surprising in a world where we still have monarchists among us, but it is puzzling nonetheless because, like self-government, the idea that mankind is part of nature is wonderfully liberating.

Our ancestors entrusted both their immortal souls and their livelihoods to God's mercy. Rainfall, locusts, the silting of a harbor: all were in God's hands. Children were taught the prayers for rain much as our children are taught to understand the water cycle. It must have been terrifying to have to depend so completely on One so little known. Of the little we can know of God, one certainty is that the intentions of the Divine are unknowable.

About nature, on the other hand, we know a fair amount. Since Galileo developed the scientific method, we have put ourselves in the way of knowing a great deal more. Not enough to prevent every misfortune, but enough so that, if we apply what we have learned with humility and diligence, we can increase the physical security of our lives. Our immortal souls we continue to entrust to God's mercy. The fate of our fisheries, cornfields, and atmosphere would be more secure if guided by our best understanding of natural science.

It is the replacement of the arrogant assumption that humanity is above nature with the realization that we are part of nature that is bringing on the Third Revolution in technology. Ten thousand years ago we were expelled from the Garden of Eden into a world of private property and agriculture. Three hundred years ago we began the passage from a world of hayfields and woodlots to a world of steam engines and synthetic chemicals. The marvel of industrialization was that natural limitations—the laws that govern the birth

of a lamb and the growth of a leaf—no longer seemed to set a limit on the possible. The Industrial Revolution turned night into day, annihilated distance,
and enabled us to fly higher than ever Icarus dreamed. The realization that not
only are we part of nature, but that the natural world sets limits to what we can
do need not prevent us from illuminating our homes, speaking with friends
thousands of miles away, or flying across continents. It does caution us to find
ways to do these things without destroying our world.

Epilogue

᪾

And God blessed them, and God said unto them, Be fruitful, and multiply, and replenish the earth, and subdue it: and have dominion over the fish of the sea, and over the fowl of the air, and over every living thing that moveth upon the earth.

—Genesis 1:28

IT MUST HAVE SEEMED LIKE A MARVELOUS PROM-ise to those who first heard it. The whole green and blue planet with its teeming life presented as a gift by God to the people He created. True, the gift was ever so slightly absurd. What does it mean to have dominion over tigers when tigers routinely eat people?

Perhaps 'subdue and have dominion over' was not a gift at all, perhaps it was more of an injunction. It certainly described the ambitions of the bronze-age farmers and shepherds who heard it. The goal of the Neolithic revolution was to subdue and have dominion over nature, which was accomplished by domesticating animals, plants and whole landscapes. It was slow work and there is a sense in which we can view dominion as an injunction that it has taken ten thousand years to fulfill, or as a marvelous gift that it has taken us ten thousand years to unwrap. Very slowly at first, with breathtaking momentum in recent centuries, mankind has indeed multiplied and subdued the earth. Deserts, jungles and Arctic ice have lost their ability to resist human intrusion. Today tigers are an endangered species and there is no place on this planet too remote to be affected by industrial civilization. We posses a degree of mastery over our world that our ancestors only worked toward and wished for. Be very careful what you wish for.

There is a red-tailed hawk patrolling the edges of Bullough's Pond this March morning. On some passes it swoops low enough to show me the bright russet of its tail, startling against the late snowfall that still blankets the banks. A walker stops to gape as the bird comes in for a landing on a telephone pole.

He is not, I think, a bird watcher. A bird watcher would not look stunned by the grandeur of the predator that has set down on this quiet, suburban street. Awed, yes; stunned, no. Awed admiration of a hawk in flight is a natural response even from watchers who have seen many. Surprise is not. Red-tailed hawks are seen with some frequency by those who know where to look. In March in New England it is often necessary only to look up as thousands of hawks fly toward Canada, stopping, as this one has, to pick up a snack on the way.

Red-tailed hawks are beneficiaries of civilization, of farming, grazing and, most especially, of the invention of the telegraph pole. Hunters of open spaces, they patrol our interstate highway system, perching on utility poles as they watch for an unwary rabbit to show itself. There are many more red-tailed hawks in our deforested landscape now than there were when Columbus arrived.

From the perspective of a red-tailed hawk, Bullough's Pond would be an attractive hunting ground even if it had been allowed to turn into a marsh. The buffleheads and hooded mergansers fishing for their dinner this spring morning would, of course, not have come to visit a marsh. Herons visit far less frequently since the pond was dredged, but fishing ducks now pay leisurely spring and fall visits, their sleek black-and-white bodies glinting in sunlight as they dive for prey. We have decided quite deliberately that this watercourse should be a pond and not a marsh, but we have decided so much more.

Our actions determine not only which watercourses will be ponds and which will become marshes, but which species will live and which will die, which will give birth to deformed young and which will driven from their places on earth by species imported from across an ocean. Even the temperature of the planet itself is now determined by human activity. Dominion has given us both the fruits of nature for our enjoyment and the ability to determine which fruits will grow. With that ability comes responsibility for our own future. We are like the man who yearned to be king, only to discover after his coronation that governing is not so simple as wishing to govern.

Unlike all of the generations that came before us, we cannot take the functioning of nature for granted. We continue to depend on the daily miracles of photosynthesis and the water cycle as utterly as did our remotest ancestor. The difference is that nature now depends upon us as inevitably as we depend upon nature. Human actions now plot the course of life on this planet.

To watch the activity on this pond, to stand still long enough to watch a kingfisher plummet from its roost and emerge with a fingerling quivering in its bill, is to gain the impression that one is witnessing an instant of nature wild and timeless. It is nothing of the kind. From the yellow Eurasian iris that ring the pond in springtime to the loitering herring gulls, so much more numerous near human habitation than ever they were in wilder times, Bullough's Pond, like the entire New England landscape, is a mere imitation of nature in a world shaped by human hands.

NOTES

1. *From Time Immemorial (pp. 1–14)*

1. A. D. Hope, "Conversation with Calliope," *Texas Quarterly* 5(2):229 (summer 1962).
2. Caleb Vance Haynes, "When and from Where Did Man Arrive in Northeastern North America: A Discussion," in *Amerinds and Their Paleoevironments in Northeastern North America, Annals of the New York Academy of Sciences* (New York: 1980), 288 (1977): 165–166; Dean R. Snow, *The Archaeology of New England* (New York: Academic Press), Chapter 3.
3. Maurice Robbins and George A. Agogino, "The Wapanucket No. 8 Site: A Clovis-Archaic Site in Massachusetts," *American Antiquity* 29 (4):509–513 (1964).
4. Margaret B. Davis, "Phytogeography and Palynology of Northeastern United States," in *The Quaternary of the United States*, ed. Herbert E. Wright, Jr., and David Frey (Princeton: Princeton University Press, 1965) 377–401; Margaret Davis, "Late Glacial Climate in Northern United States: A Comparison of New England and the Great Lakes Region," in *Quaternary Paleoecology*, ed. Edward J. Cushing and Herbert E. Wright (New Haven: Yale University Press, 1967) 11–43; Margaret Davis, "Palynological and Environmental History during the Quaternary Period," *American Scientist* 57 (3):317–322 (1969); Ronald B. Davis, T. E. Bradstreet, R. Stuckenrath, and Harold W. Borns, "Vegetation and Associated Environments During the Past 14,000 Years Near Moulton Pond, Maine," *Quaternary Research*, 5 (3):435–466 (1975).
5. Paul Martin, *Pleistocene Extinctions: The Search for a Cause* (New Haven: Yale University Press, 1967).
6. Dr. Ross D. E. MacPhee, at the Museum of Natural History in New York, is the leading investigator of the germ theory of Pleistocene extinction.
7. Dean R. Snow and Kim M. Lanphear, "European Contact and Indian Depopulation in the Northeast: The Timing of the First Epidemics," *Ethnohistory* 35 (1):15–33 (1988). See also Daniel Gookin, *Historical Collections of the Indians in New England* (1674), reprinted in *Collections of the Massachusetts Historical Society*, Third Series, vol. 1 (Boston: Massachusetts Historical Society, 1806), 141–229.
8. I use *agriculture* and *farmer* in their common English senses. Horticulture is the term used for cultivators of crops who lack domesticated animals. Southern New England Indians certainly cultivated grain and lacked farm animals, but they also managed forests in much the way gamekeepers on the great English estates managed theirs: modifying plant communities to increase forage and meat production. To call New England Indians horticulturalists is therefore to omit a significant aspect of the system of food production. A term such as game-keeping horticulturalists would be accurate, if unwieldy. I have used agriculture although it is stretching a definition in the case of a people who neither herded nor kept domesticated animals, with the exception of the dog.

9. Roger Williams, *A Key into the Language of America* (1643; reprint, Providence: Roger Williams Press (1936), 112–116; Ann Marie Plane, "New England's Logboats: Four Centuries of Watercraft," *Bulletin of the Massachusetts Archaeological Society* 52 (1):8–17 (spring 1991).

10. B. J. Borque, "Comments on the Late Archaic Populations of Central Maine: The View from Turner Farm," *Arctic Anthropology* 12 (2):35–45 (1975); Douglas S. Byers, "The Eastern Archaic: Some Problems and Hypotheses," *American Antiquity* 24 (3):274–276 (1959); Douglas S. Byers, "The Nevin Shellheap: Burials and Observations," *Papers of the R. S. Peabody Foundation for Archaeology*, vol. 9 (Andover, Mass.: Foundation Phillips Academy, 1979).

11. James A. Tuck, "Early Archaic Horizons in Eastern North America," *Archaeology of Eastern North America* 2 (1):72–80 (1974); William A. Ritchie, "The Archaic in New York," *New York State Archeological Association Bulletin* 52 2–12 (1971); William A. Ritchie and Robert E. Funk, "Evidence for Early Archaic Occupations on Staten Island," *Pennsylvania Archaeologist* 41 (3):45–59 (September 1971); Paul L. Weinman, T. P. Weinman, and Robert E. Funk, "The Pickle Hill Site, Warren County, New York," *New York State Archaeological Association Bulletin* 39, 18–22 (1967); Snow, *Archaeology of New England*, chapter 4.

Archaeological evidence for the archaic period is scarce, in part because of sea level rise that has inundated coastal sites. Archaeologists therefore infer some patterns from nearby parts of New York, or generalize from evidence found on Maine headlands that have remained on the coast and above sea level for several millennia.

Salvage archaeology laws are an example of ordinances that function exceedingly well and precisely as intended. Developers who come upon evidence of ages past are required to put projects on temporary hold while archaeologists examine the site and preserve the artifacts. These serendipitous digs have added immensely to our understanding of prehistory.

12. The paucity of archaeological evidence on the question fuels a lively debate over the date of agricultural origins in New England. Snow, *Archaeology of New England*, argues for a pre–1000 C.E date. In Patrick Munson, "The Origins and Antiquity of Maize-Bean-Squash Agriculture in Eastern North America; Some Linguistic Evidence," in *Variations in Anthropology*, ed. D. W. Lathrap and Jody Douglas (Urbana: University of Illinois Press, 1973), Munson suggests a far earlier date based on the existence of a common word for corn in the reconstructed proto-Algonquin language; Lynn Ceci, "Radiocarbon Dating 'Village' Sites in Coastal New York: Settlement Pattern Changes in the Middle to Late Woodland," *Man in the Northeast* 39, 1–28 (spring 1990), postulates a far later date, just before contact, on the basis of the paucity of agricultural remains vis-à-vis hunting-gathering remains in excavated sites, poor soil, and cold conditions during the little ice age; Jeffrey Bendremer and Robert Dewer, "The Advent of Prehistoric Maize in New England," in *Corn and Culture in the Prehistoric New World*, ed. Sissel Johanessen and Christine Hasforf (Minneapolis: Westview Press, 1994), find widespread archaeological evidence for farming a full millennium ago; David Demeritt, "Agriculture, Climate and Cultural Adaptation in the Prehistoric Northeast, *Archaeology of Eastern North America* 19, 183–202 (1991) concurs, correlating the evidence with areas

of locally optimal conditions, as does Barbara Luedtke, "Where Are the Late Woodland Villages in Eastern Massachusetts?" *Bulletin of the Massachusetts Archaeological Society* 49 (2):58–65 (1988). Most recently, Kathleen J. Bragdon, *Native Peoples of Southern New England, 1500–1650* (Norman: University of Oklahoma Press, 1996), moves the date of widespread adaptation of agriculture closer to the present and rates the extent of dependence on corn and beans low in the total diet.

The discussion that follows is informed by the work of Mark Nathan Cohen, *The Food Crisis in Pre-History* (New Haven: Yale University Press, 1977), and Esther Boserup, *Population and Technological Change: A Study of Long-Term Trends* (Chicago: University of Chicago Press, 1981).

13. David J. Bernstein, *Prehistoric Subsistence on the Southern New England Coast: The Record from Narragansett Bay* (San Diego: Academic Press, 1992) Kevin McBride and Robert Dewar, "Prehistoric Settlement in the Lower Connecticut River Valley," *Man in the Northeast* 22, 37–66 (fall 1981).

14. Christopher Levett, *Voyage into New England* (1638), reprinted in Massachusetts Historical Society Collections, third series, vol. 3 (Boston: Massachusetts Historical Society, 1843) 178.

15. David W. Black and Ruth Holmes Whitehead, "Prehistoric Shellfish Preservation and Storage on the Northeast Coast," *North American Archaeologist* 9 (1):17–30 (1989); Russell J. Barber, *The Wheeler's Site: A Specialized Shellfish Processing Station on the Merrimac River*, Peabody Museum Monograph 7 (Cambridge: Harvard University Press, 1979); L. A. Brennan, "The Lower Hudson, A Decade of Shell Middens," *Archaeology of Eastern North America*, 2 (1):81–93 (1974); Bragdon, *Native People*, 85, cities evidence that decreasing use of shellfish on Cape Cod between 1000 and 1300 C.E. coincided with the beginnings of agriculture.

16. Snow, *Archaeology of New England*, 182.

17. The richer the environment, the longer even a large, sedentary population could wait before turning to maize, as demonstrated in Bragdon, *Native People*. Bragdon describes a Tripartite Settlement Model of river-valley dwellers who turned to agriculture well before 1300, estuarine residents who resorted to corn only after 1300, and a possible third adaptation: small bands of upland hunter-gatherers. Estuaries, according to Brandon, provided such a wealth of shellfish and other food that large, settled populations could use clams as a dietary staple, supplemented with fish, eggs, fowl, and wild rice. Eventually, of course, human population got ahead of even the fecund clam.

One puzzling aspect of Bragdon's work is her assertion that "farming (is) at best a risky proposition in most areas of coastal southern New England" (86). In northern New England, it is. But southern New England has an ample, reliable growing season and dependable rainfall. The region furnished reliable harvests even during the "Little Ice Age" of the seventeenth and eighteenth centuries. Perhaps she is misled by the fact that the region is not farmed today. This is not due to climatic conditions. It is because modern farm equipment operates so much more efficiently in the vast, flat expanses of the plains that it does not pay to plow the small fields of New England at American wage rates. Small-field agriculture is well supported by natural conditions in southern New England.

18. Lucianne Lavin, "The Morgan Site, Rocky Hill, Conn.: A Late Woodland Farming Community in the Connecticut Valley," *Bulletin of Connecticut Archaeological Society* 51 (7):7–22 (1988); Lavin demonstrates that Iroquois-style pottery was introduced to the Connecticut Valley about 1170 C.E., contemporaneously with corn farming. James B. Petersen, "Evidence of St. Lawrence Iroquoians in Northern New England: Population Movement, Trade or Stylistic Borrowing?" *Man in the Northeast* 40, 31–39 (1990); Gordon M. Day, "The Eastern Boundary of Iroquoia: Abenaki Evidence," *Man in the Northeast* 1, 7–13 (1971); Snow, *Archaeology of New England*, 307.

19. Snow, *Archaeology of New England*, 333; Bert Salwen, "Indians of Southern New England and Long Island: Early Period," in *Handbook of North American Indians*, vol. 15, ed. Bruce Trigger (Washington, D.C.: Smithsonian Institution, 1978), 165–166.

2. *Improving Nature (pp. 15–21)*

1. Francis Higginson, *New-England's Plantation* (1630), *Proceedings of the Massachusetts historical Society* 62 (Salem, Mass.: reprinted by the Essex Book and Print Club, 1908), 32.

2. The border between the agricultural South and the hunting and gathering North is not an abrupt transition. Snow, *Archaelogy of New England*, believes that inhabitants of the Merrimack basin were farmers, people living in the valleys of the Androscoggin and Kennebec were but partially committed to horticulture, and residents of the Penobscot were not agriculturalists.

3. William Cronon, *Changes in the Land: Indians, Colonists and the Ecology of New England* (New York: Hill and Wang, 1983).

4. Howard S. Russell, *Indian New England Before the Mayflower* (Hanover, N.H.: University Press of New England, 1980), 142–145.

5. Quoted in Cronon, *Changes in the Land*, 66.

6. Douglas Worth, *Once Around Bullough's Pond: A Native American Epic* (Dublin, N.H.: William Bauhan, 1987), 13.

7. Marc Lescarbot, *Nova Francia: A Description of Arcadia, 1606*, trans. P. Erondelle, London 1609 (London: reprinted by Routledge, 1928), 93.

8. Russell, *Indian New England*, 126–129.

9. Ibid., 125.

10. For descriptions of the deforested aspect of the New England coast see Captain John Smith, *Works* (1608–1631; reprint, Edward Arber, ed., Birmingham: English Scholar's Library, 1884), from *A Description of New England* (1616), 204; Charles F. Carroll, *The Timber Economy of Puritan New England* (Providence, Brown University Press, 1973), 49; Lawrence C. Wroth, *The Voyages of Giovanni de Verrazzano, 1524–1528* (New Haven: Yale University Press, 1970); John Winthrop, *Winthrop's Journal*, ed. James Kendall Hosmer (New York: C. Scribner's Sons, 1908), 258; William Wood, *New England's Prospect* (1634; reprint, Alden T. Vaughan, ed. (Amherst: University of Massachusetts Press, 1977), 38, 59.

11. Carrying clams to inland sites with plentiful wood was an option. Clams do spoil rapidly, although not too quickly to make transportation feasible if you are hungry

enough to dig them in winter. Transporting whole clams, however, is heavy work. Indians saved the labor of shucking by steaming them open for curing, and the labor of lugging clams in the shell by transporting only the cured meats. From every angle, deforestation of the coast meant more labor, or impoverished diet, or both.

12. Lynn Ceci, "Fish Fertilizer, A Native North American Practice?" *Science* 188 (4183):26–30 (1975), overset everyone's childhood Thanksgiving lesson by arguing that Europeans taught Indians to dung the corn hills with fish, not the other way round. Russell, *Indian New England;* Neal Salisbury, *Manitou and Providence: Indians, Europeans and the Making of New England, 1500–1634* (New York: Oxford University Press, 1982); Nanepashemet, "Smells Fishy to Me: An Argument Supporting the Use of Fish Fertilizer by the Native People of Southern New England," in *Algonkians of New England: Past and Present*, ed. Peter Benes (Dublin Seminar for New England Folklife, Boston: Boston University, 1993) all argue for fertilization as a precontact Indian practice.

3. The Economics of Extermination (pp. 22–34)

1. W. R. Cochrane, *History of the Town of Antrim, N.H.* (Manchester, N.H.: Mirror Stream Press, 1880. Reverend Cochrane had, of course, never seen a beaver.

2. David Beers Quinn, *England and the Discovery of America, 1481–1620* (New York: Knopf, 1974), chapter 1.

3. Sherburne F. Cook, "the Significance of Disease in the Extinction of the New England Indians," *Human Biology* 45 (3):485–508 (1973); Sherburne F. Cook, "Interracial Warfare and Population Decline Among the New England Indians," *Ethnohistory* 20 (1):1–24; Snow, *Archaeology of New England*, 31–42 (1973).

4. Dean R. Snow, "Abenaki Fur Trade in the Sixteenth Century," *Western Canadian Journal of Anthropology* 6 (1):3–11 (1976).

5. Charles Francis Adams, *Three Episodes of Massachusetts History*, 1892; Cook, "Significance of Disease"; Cronon, *Changes in the Land*: H. F. Dobyns, "Estimating Aboriginal American Population: An Appraisal of Techniques with a New Hemispheric Estimate," *Current Anthropology* 7 (4):395–416 (1966); Billee Hoornbeck, "An Investigation in the Cause or Causes of the Epidemic Which Decimated the Indian Population of New England, 1616–1619," *New Hampshire Archaeologist* 19, 35–46 (1976–77) Herbert U. Williams, "The Epidemics of the Indians of New England, 1616–1620, with Remarks on Native American Infections," *Bulletin of the Johns Hopkins Hospital* 20, 340–349 (1909).

6. Salisbury, *Manitou and Providence: Indians, Europeans, and the Making of New England, 1500–1643* (New York: Oxford University Press, 1982), 98–109.

7. Robert J. Naiman, Carol A. Johnston, and James C. Kelley, "Alteration of North American Streams by Beaver," *BioScience* 38 (11):757 (December 1988). Robert S. Rupp, "Beaver-Trout Relationship in the Headwaters of Sunkaze Stream, Maine," *American Fisheries Society Transactions* 84, 75–85 (1954). Robert J. Naimen, Jerry M. Melillo, and John E. Hobbie, "Ecosystem Alteration of Boreal Forest Streams by Beaver," *Ecology* 67:1254–1269 (October 1986).

8. William Wood, *New England's Prospect*, ed. Alden T. Vaughan (Amherst: University of Massachusetts Press, 1977), 37. On abundant springs even on offshore islands, see Captain John Smith, *Works 1606–1631*, ed. Edward Arber (Birmingham: English Scholar's Library, 1884), *A Description of New England*, 1616, 203.

9. R. Rudeman and N. J. Schoonmaker, "Beaver Dams as Geologic Agents," *Science* 88 (2292):523–525 (December 2, 1938).

10. It is, of course, possible that my hypothetical beaver were killed earlier, their pelts sold to French fur traders who frequented the coast. It is even possible that they never existed at all, outside of my imagination. I only hypothesize that native communities in the 1600 to 1615 period were still well enough organized not to kill every beaver in a colony, and even if they had, the beaver population had fifteen years to recover between the great epidemic of 1615 and the settlement of Massachusetts Bay. In all events, the essential point here is that, whenever particular beaver colonies in an area were exterminated, all were doomed by the intensification of fur trading precipitated by the great Puritan migration.

11. Bernard Bailyn, *The New England Merchants in the Seventeenth Century* (Cambridge: Harvard University Press, 1955), 622.

12. Dutch figures from Francis J. Moloney, *Fur Trade in Colonial New England, 1620–1676* (Cambridge: Harvard University Press, 1931); William Bradford, *History of Plimouth Plantation, 1620–1647*, ed. Worthington Chauncey Ford (Boston: 1912), 229.

13. Wood, *New England's Prospect*, 106.

14. Nurit Bird-David, "Beyond 'The original Affluent Society': A Culturalist Reformulation," *Current Anthropology* 33 (1):25–47 (1992).

15. Neal Salisbury, *Manitou and Providence; Indians, Europeans and the Making of New England, 1500–1643*; Oxford University Press, 1982, p. 148.

16. Lynn Ceci, "Wampum as a Peripheral Resource in the Seventeenth Century World System," in *The Pequots in Southern New England: The Fall and Rise of an American Indian Nation*, ed. Lawrence M. Hauptman and James O. Wherry (Norman: University of Oklahoma Press, 1992); Paul Robinson, "The Struggle Within: The Indian Debate in Seventeenth Century Narragansett County," Ph.D. diss., SUNY Binghamton, 1990.

17. Bradford, *History of Plimouth*, 203.

18. Moloney, *Fur Trade*; Ruth A. McIntyre and William Pynchon, *Merchant and Colonizer, 1590–1622* (Springfield, Mass.: Connecticut Valley Historical Museum and Princeton: Princeton University Press, 1961); Stephen Innes, *Labor in a New Land: Economy and Society in Seventeenth Century* (Springfield, Princeton, 1983); Sylvester Judd, "The Fur Trade in the Connecticut River in the Seventeenth Century," *New England Historical and Genealogical Register*, vol. 11 (Boston, 1957), 217–219; Bailyn, *New England Merchants*.

19. William R. Baron and David C. Smith, *Growing Season Parameter Reconstructions for New England Using Killing Frost Resords, 1697–1947*, Maine Agricultural and Forest Experiment Station, Bulletin 846 (Orono: University of Maine, November 1996), 30.

20. Snow, *Archaeology of New England*, 51–66.

4. Salt-Watered Prosperity (pp. 35–55)

1. Letter to Arthur Young, December 5, 1791, quoted in Samuel Blodgett, *Economica; A Statistical Manual for the United States of America* (1806; reprint, New York: A. M. Kelly, 1964).
2. Larzer Ziff, The Career of John Cotton (Princeton: Princeton University Press, 1962), 60.
3. The economic crisis of the 1640s is masterfully explicated in Bernard Bailyn's *The New England Merchants in the Seventeenth Century* (Cambridge: Harvard University Press), 1955; E. N. Hartley, *Ironworks on the Saugus* (Norman: University of Oklahoma Press, 1957).
4. Bailyn, *New England Merchants*, 83.
5. Letter to John Winthrop quoted in Bailyn, *New England Merchants*, 85.
6. The debate over whether colonial farming in New England was community and subsistence-oriented or market-driven continues. See Alan Kulikoff, "The Transition to Capitalism in Rural America," *William and Mary Quarterly* 46 (January 1989): 120 –144; Christopher Clark, *The Roots of Rural Capitalism: Western Massachusetts, 1780–1860* (Ithaca: Cornell University Press, 1990). My argument is not so much that colonial farming was market-oriented as that it was market-dependent. Whether the farmer directed his efforts according to conditions in distant markets (Betty Hobbs Pruitt, "Self Sufficiency and the Agricultural Economy of Eighteenth Century New England," *William and Mary Quarterly* 41 [July 1984]: 333 –364) as he certainly did by 1750 (Winnifred Barr Rothenberg, *From Market-Place to a Market Economy: The Transformation of Rural Massachusetts, 1750– 1850* [Chicago: University of Chicago Press, 1992]) or operated wholly within a traditional, cooperative, self-sufficient neighborhood (Michael Merrill, "Cash Is Good to Eat: Self-Sufficiency and Exchange in the Rural Economy of the United States," *Radical History Review* 14 [winter 1977] 42–71; James Henretta, "Families and Farms: Mentality in Pre-Industrial America," *William and Mary Quarterly* 25 [January 1978]: 3 –32) he depended utterly and absolutely on distant sources of supply for three crucial kinds of goods: land, culture, and salt and edge tools.

   Once the initial allotment of a town was used up, which took only two or three generations, new land was gotten by purchase and money was gotten by selling in the market. Land was also gotten by political allocation. Land-hungry families did band together to get land acts passed by colonial legislatures, but only until land in the colony in question had all been allocated. Land-hungry Connecticut families could not get land in New Hampshire except by purchase. Land is also gotten by war. The Connecticut farmers who settled Vermont took the land from New York, partly by force of arms. Soldiers in colonial wars with the French were also rewarded with land grants. It is, however, hard to imagine a father deciding to provide for his sons by starting a war and encouraging them to enlist. For individual families, the strategy was to get cash, and use the cash to get land.

   As for culture, New England Puritans explicitly chose not to live in cultural isolation from the mainstream of English Puritan society. The expenditure on books, on a master for the grammar school, and on a minister was miniscule. But these expenditures were as essential to life as water itself. Water was available in every town. Books entailed dependence on distant markets.

Finally, many imports to farm towns reflect a taste for some degree of comfort, but it was possible to live as English farmers without window glass or molasses. Many towns, however, had no local source of iron or salt, without which agricultural life was impossible.

Money had to be earned for these three kinds of necessities, and money was earned in the market.

7. Beaver meadows producing four tons to the acre are described in Henry Wansy, *An Excursion to the United States of America in the Summer of 1794* (Salisbury, 1798), 197, cited in Cronon, *Changes in the Land*, 107.

8. Howard Russell, *A Long, Deep Furrow* (Hanover, N.H.: University Press of New England, 1982) 14; Jeremy Belknap, *History of New Hampshire* (1792; reprint, New York: Johnson, 1970), vol. 3, 58–59, 113–119.

9. John Josselyn, *New England Rarities Discovered* (London, 1672; reprinted Boston, Massachusetts Historical Society, 1972), pilhannaw bird described on p. 8.

10. Bradford, *History of Plimouth*, 362.

11. Samuel Deane, *The New England Farmer* (Boston: Wells and Libby, 1822); Clarence Albert Day, *History of Maine Agriculture, 1604–1860* (Orono: University of Maine Press, 1954); Clarence H. Danof, *Change in Agriculture: The Northern States, 1820–1870* (Cambridge: Harvard University Press, 1969), 117–119; Benjamin Vaughan, "An Account of the Method of Preparing Woodlands for Cultivation, Used in the Vicinity of Maine, from Latitude 44 to Latitude 45 North," in Gilbert Chinard, "The American Philosophical Society and the Early History of Forestry in America," *Proceedings of the American Philosophical Society* 98 (2):444–488 (July 18, 1945).

12. Christopher Jedrey, *The World of John Cleaveland* (New York: W. W. Norton, 1979), 59; Kenneth Lockridge, *A New England Town: The First Hundred Years* (New York: W. W. Norton, 1970) 71.

13. Estimates based on Jedrey, *World of John Cleaveland*, 195, and Robert Gross, *The Minutemen and Their World* (New York: Hill and Wang, 1976), 213–214.

14. Jedrey, *World of John Cleaveland*; Laurel Thatcher Ulrich, *A Midwife's Tale* (New York: Knopf, 1990); Jane Nylander, "Provision for Daughters, The Accounts of Samuel Lane," *House and Home, The Dublin Seminar for New England Folklife Annual Proceedings* (Boston: Boston University Press, 1988), 11–27.

15. Francis Jackson, *History and Settlement of Newton* (Boston: Stacy and Richardson, 1854).

16. Day, *History of Maine Agriculture*, 66.

17. A complete review of the extensive literature on colonial New England population history is available in John J. McCusker and Russell R. Menard, *The Economy of British North America, 1607–1789*, 2d. ed. (Chapel Hill: Institute of Early American History and Culture, University of North Carolina Press, 1991).

18. Kenneth Lockridge, *A New England Town: The First Hundred Years* (New York: W. W. Norton, 1970), 147–161; Lockridge finds less of a tendency to emigrate than, for example, Robert Gross, *The Minutemen and Their World* (New York: Hill and Wang, 1976).

5. This Well-Watered Land (pp. 56–72)

1. Baron Justus von Liebig, *Letters on Modern Agriculture*, ed. J. Blythe (London: Walton and Maberly), 179.

2. Joseph Goldenberg, *Shipbuilding in Colonial America* (Charlottesville: University of Virginia Press for the Mariner's Museum, 1976), 18.

3. Phyllis Deane, *The First Industrial Revolution* (Cambridge: Cambridge University Press, 1967), 103.

4. William Carlton, "New England Masts and the King's Navy," *New England Quarterly* 12 (1) 4–18 (March 1939), Robert Albion, *Forests and Sea Power* (Cambridge: Harvard University Press, 1926); James J. Malone, *Pine Trees and Politics: The Naval Stores and Forest Policy in Colonial New England, 1691–1775* (Seattle: University of Washington Press, 1964).

5. Estimate of the value of shipping export from Jacob M. Price, "A Note on the Value of Colonial Exports of Shipping," *Journal of Economic History* 6, 721. (1976).

6. Gary Kulik, "Dams, Fish and Farmers; Defense of Public Rights in Eighteenth Century Rhode Island," in ed. Steven Hahn and Jonathan Prude, *The Countryside in the Age of Capitalist Transformation* (Chapel Hill: University of North Carolina Press, 1985), 25–50.

7. Charles F. Carroll, *The Timber Economy of Puritan New England* (Providence: Brown University Press, 1973), 70–71.

8. James Eliot Defebaugh, *History of the Lumber Industry of America*, vol. 2 (Chicago: The American Lumberman, 1907), 442.

9. Richard Lee, *Forest Hydrology* (New York: Columbia University Press, 1980).

10. Sidney Perley, *Historic Storms of New England* (Salem, Mass.: Salem Press Publishing and Printing Company, 1891).

11. United States Department of Agriculture, *The Changing Fertility of New England Soils*, Agricultural Information Bulletin no. 133 (Washington, D.C.: Government Printing Office, 1955).

12. Jared Eliot, *Essays upon Field Husbandry in New England and Other Papers, 1748–1762*, ed. Henry Carman and Raxford Tugwell (New York: Columbia University Press, reprinted 1934), 17.

13. Samuel Deane, *The New England Farmer* (Boston: Wells and Libby, 1822).

6. To the Farthest Port of the Rich East (pp. 74–86)

1. The spoil (riches) of Ind (India, the Indies, the Orient) to the uttermost gulf.

2. William B. Weeden, *Economic and Social History of New England, 1620–1789* (1890; reprint, Williamstown, Mass.: Corner House Publishers, 1978), vol. 2, 734–735; Lyman Horace Weeks, *A History of Paper Manufacturing in the United States, 1690–1916* (1916; reprint, New York: Burt Franklin, 1969); James M. Swank, "The Manufacture of Iron in New England," in *The New England States*, ed. William Davis (Boston: D. H. Hurd and Co., 1897), 359 ff; John W. D. Hall, "Ancient Iron Works in Taunton," *Old Colony Historical Society Collections*, no. 3 (1885):131–162; William

Bartlett Murdock, *Blast Furnaces of Carver, Plymouth County* (Poughkeepsie, N.Y.: privately printed, 1937); Arthur Cecil Bining, *British Regulation of the Colonial Iron Industry* (Phila.: University of Pennsylvania Press, 1933); Orra L. Stone, *History of Massachusetts Industries* (Boston: S. J. Clarke Publishing, 1930).

3. John J. McCusker and Russell R. Menard, *The Economy of British North America, 1607–1789* (Chapel Hill: University of North Carolina Press, 1985), 108.

4. Alexander Starbuck, *History of the American Whale Fishery from Its Earliest Inception to the Year 1876* (Washington, D.C., 1878); Joseph McDevitt, *The House of Rotch; Massachusetts Whaling Merchants, 1734–1828* (New York: Garland, 1986); Peter J. Coleman, *The Transformation of Rhode Island, 1790–1860* (Providence: Brown University Press, 1963), 9–10.

5. *The Writings of Thomas Jefferson* vol. 4, ed. Paul Leicester Ford (New York, 1892–1899), 88; Alexander Hamilton, "Report on Manufacturers," December 5, 1791, in *American State Papers, Finance*, vol. 1, Washington, D.C.: United States Department of the Treasury), 123.

6. Caroline F. Ware, *The Early New England Cotton Manufacture; A Study in Industrial Beginnings* (New York.: Russell & Russell, 1966), 9.

7. Kenneth M. Wilson, *Glass in New England* (Sturbridge, Mass.: Old Sturbridge Village Publications, 1969), 22–27; David Starbuck, "New Hampshire's Earliest Glass Factory: The New England Glassworks, 1780–82," *Historical New Hampshire* 39 (182) 45–63 (spring/summer 1984).

8. Samuel Batchelder, *Introduction and Early Progress of the Cotton Manufacture in the U.S.* (1863; reprint, George Rogers Taylor, ed., New York: Harper and Row, 1969); George S. White, *Memoir of Samuel Slater* (Philadelphia, 1836); Ware, *Early New England Cotton Manufacture*, 19–22; Barbara Tucker, *Samuel Slater and the Origins of the American Textile Industry, 1790–1860* (Ithaca: Cornell University Press, 1984).

9. Ware, *Early New England Cotton Manufacture*, 31.

10. Foster Rhea Dulles, *The Old China Trade* (Cambridge, Mass.: Riverside Press, 1930).

11. John Ledyard, *A Journal of Captain Cook's Last Voyage to the Pacific Ocean* (Hartford, 1783); Jared Sparks, *The Life of John Ledyard, the American Traveller* (Cambridge, Mass.: 1828).

12. John R. Jewitt, *A Narrative of the Adventures and Sufferings of John R. Jewitt* (Middletown, Conn., 1815); Foster Rhea Dulles, *The Old China Trade*; Adele Ogden, *The California Sea Otter Trade, 1784–1898* (Berkeley: University of California Press, 1941); Paul Chrisler Phillips, *The Fur Trade*, vol. 2 (Norman: University of Oklahoma Press, 1961) chapter 33.

13. Dulles, *The Old China Trade*; Phillips, *The Fur Trade*, vol. 2, chapter 33.

14. Timothy Pitkin, *A Statistical View of the Commerce of the United States of America* (Hartford: Hamlen & Newton, 1817), 176; John Reinhoel, "Post-Embargo Trade and Merchant Prosperity: Experiences of the Crowninshield Family, 1809–1812," *Mississippi Valley Historical Review* 42 (2):230 (1955).

15. Victor Clark, *History of Manufacturers in the United States* (New York: McGraw Hill 1929), 35.

16. *American State Papers: Naval Affairs*, vol. 2, 27–29.

17. Alfred W. Crosby, Jr., *America, Russia, Hemp and Napoleon: American Trade with Russia and the Baltic, 1783–1812* (Columbus: Ohio State University Press, 1965), 20 ff.; *American State Papers; Naval Affairs,* ed. Walter Lowrie and Matthew Clarke (Washington, D.C., 1832–1861), class 4, vols. 1–3, 28 ff.; James F. Hopkins, *A History of the Hemp Industry in Kentucky* (Lexington: University of Kentucky Press, 1951); John Hutchins, *The American Maritime Industries and Public Policy, 1789–1914* (Cambridge: Harvard University Press, 1941).

18. Samuel Eliott Morison, *The Maritime History of Massachusetts* (Boston: Houghton Mifflin, 1921); Crosby, *America, Russia, Hemp and Napoleon.*

7. *Cobbling a Living (pp. 87–95)*

1. Samuel Blodget, *Economica: A Statistical Manual for the United States of America* (Washington: privately published for the author, 1806).

2. Kenneth Lockridge, "Land, Population and the Evolution of New England Society." *Past and Present: A Journal of Historical Studies* 39 (April 1968): 62–80; Lockridge, *A New England Town, The First Hundred Years;* Philip Greven, *Four Generations: Population, Land and Family in Colonial Andover* (Ithaca: Cornell University Press, 1970); Daniel Smith, "The Demographic History of Colonial New England," *Journal of Economic History* 32 (1) (March 1972): 165–183; Robert A. Gross, "The Problem of Agricultural Crisis in Eighteenth Century New England: Concord, Mass., as a Test Case," unpublished paper, December 29, 1975, Concord Free Public Library; Richard Easterlin, "Population Change, and Farm Settlement in the Northern United States," *Journal of Economic history* 36 (March 1976): 45–83; Bruce Daniels, *The Connecticut Town: Growth and Development, 1635–1790* (Middletown, Conn.: Wesleyan University Press, 1979), chapter 2; Toby L. Ditz, *Property and Kinship: Inheritance in Early Connecticut, 1750–1820* (Princeton: Princeton University Press, 1986); Christopher Clark, "Household Economy, Market Exchange and the Rise of Capitalism in the Connecticut Valley, 1800–1860," *Journal of Social History* 13 (2):187, n.2 (winter 1979), which seems, contrary to Clark's own interpretation, to support Lockridge; Christopher M. Jedrey, *The World of John Cleaveland: Family and Continuity in Eighteenth Century New England* (New York: W. W. Norton, 1979), 58–94.

3. Smith, "Demographic History," 165–183.

4. David Klingman, "Food Surpluses and Deficits in the American Colonies, 1768–1772," *Journal of Economic History* 31 (3):553–569 (1971).

5. Ernest Bragg, *The Origin and Growth of the Boot and Shoe Industry in Holliston Where it Began in 1793 and in Milford, Massachusetts Where It Continued in 1795 and Remained into 1950* (privately published, 1950).

6. John C. MacLean, "The Cabinet Maker and the Maritime Community," Essex Institute Historical Collections, no. 121 (Salem, Mass.: Essex Institute, 1985), 1–20; Clark, *History of Manufactures in the United States, vol. 1, 1607–1860,* 111, cities manuscript mercantile papers of 1736 and 1748 to establish volume of furniture exports; William G. Schiller, "The Comb Industry in Newburyport and West Newbury,"

Essex Institute Historical Collections, no. 121 (Salem, Mass.: Essex Institute, 1985), 202–209; Mary Musser, "Massachusetts Horn Smiths: A Century of Combmaking, 1775–1875," *Old Time New England* 68 (Winter-Spring 1978): 59–68; Perry Walton, *Combmaking in America* (Boston: privately printed, 1925); buttonmaking in Constance Green, *History of Naugatuck, Conn.* (New Haven: Yale University Press, 1948), 59; and in Stone, *History of Massachusetts Industries,* 245, which gives myriad examples of market-oriented craft manufacture; lace in Timothy Dwight, *Travels in New England and New York,* vol. 1 (Cambridge: Harvard University Press, 1969), 320, which details numerous examples of market-oriented craft manufacture, as do many reviews of the federal economy, Jedidiah Morse's *American Geography,* 1789, for example, which lists hollow ware, wool cards, shoes, and nails among the more important exports from the port of Boston in 1788, and enumerates local manufactures including wooden dishes and kitchenware "sold in almost every part of the eastern states," along with nails made for shipment to other states, "in almost every town and village" (217).

7. Blanche Hazard, *The Organization of the Boot and Shoe Industry in Massachusetts before 1875* (Cambridge, Mass.: Harvard University Press, 1921); Paul Faler, *Mechanics and Manufacturers in the Early Industrial Revolution: Lynn, Massachusetts, 1780–1860* (Albany: SUNY Press, 1981); Alonzo Lewis and James Newhall, *History of Lynn, Essex County, Massachusetts* (Boston: John Shorey, 1865); John Phillip Hall, "The Gentle Craft; A Narrative of Yankee Shoemakers," Ph.D. diss., Columbia University, 1953.

Although I do not advocate such a theory here, there are scholars who assign a very large role to such chance factors as the settlement of a Welsh cordwainer in Lynn. In such a theory, economic growth generates sufficient feedback, once begun, as to be self-sustaining. A single craftsmen who settled in a town for no reason other than pure chance, might cause an industrial revolution to begin, much the same as the proverbial butterfly flapping its wings in chaos theory. See, for example, N. F. R. Crafts, "Industrial Revolution in England and France: Some Thoughts on the Question 'Why Was England First?'" in *The Economics of the Industrial Revolution,* ed. Joel Mokyr (Totowa, N.J.: Rowman and Allanheld, 1985).

8. Reasons for the division are difficult to discern, although once specialization began, the skills workers developed would have encouraged it to continue. Dagyr and the skills he brought may have been a factor. Certainly the many small seaports north of Boston had large populations of employable females, both widows and the wives and daughters of poorly paid seamen. Access to Salem and imported fine stuffs was undoubtedly a factor. What was not a factor was the difference in soil quality alleged by Malcolm Kier and quoted by Faler. Kier wrote that poor soil north of Boston encouraged manufacturing, while rich soil to the south kept men in farming. Massachusetts soils vary widely over very short distances, but no farmer ever envied Brockton in particular or southeastern Massachusetts in general its rich soil. It is more to the point to remark that shoemaking developed in parts of Essex, Norfolk, Worcester, and Plymouth counties with poor soils, not on the richer soils of Middlesex and the Connecticut Valley. Kier and Faler also fail to realize that Hingham, Marion, Wareham, and other sleepy south shore villages were thriving

seaports in the shoe era—to say nothing of Plymouth, New Bedford, and Providence. The point is not that the north shore had more seaports than the south shore, but that Brockton is significantly further from the coast than Lynn. Malcom Kier, *Manufacturing Industries in America: Fundamental Economic Factors* (New York: Ronald Press, 1920), 220–221; Faler, *Mechanics and Manufacturers*, 24–25.

9. Ross Thomson, *The Path to Mechanized Shoe Production in the United States* (Chapel Hill: University of North Carolina Press, 1989), 34.

10. Candidates for the home of the pegged shoe include Milford, Byfield, Hopkinton, and Spencer, Massachusetts; Homer, New York; and Norwalk, Connecticut—by 1810 shops in all six towns were producing pegged shoes. Thomson, *Path to Mechanized Shoe Production*, 34.

11. *Shoe and Leather Reporter*, July 16, 1868.

12. The first comprehensive survey of American industry was compiled in 1810 by Tench Coxe and published in 1814 under the title, *A Statement of the Arts and Manufactures of the United States of America for the Year 1810.*

An informal survey illustrates the correlation between land shortage and proto-industrialization.

I have culled from Coxe's county-by-compilation of industrial production, a list of industries producing goods in volume for distant markets by artisanal or handicraft methods. I have omitted counties listed as producing small quantities of items such as shoes and nails, because small quantities may be for local consumption. But when a single Connecticut county produced $348,791 worth of hats in 1810, we may be certain that they were shipped over the county line. Excluded from this list are seaport run distilleries (distilleries listed processed fruit and grain) and maritime industries generally, traditional household manufacturers—soap, tallow candles, cloth—in which manufacturing for sale cannot be distinguished from manufacturing for consumption, and urban luxury trades, along with iron foundries, since they were located near iron mines, not according to the necessity for communities to industrialize. Such early industries as cotton spinning and manufacture of machinery for cotton mills are included along with woolens produced in factories, which is to say, large commercial shops without power-driven looms or spindles.

The manufacturing in question was mostly by hand, but "by hand" does not mean small-scale or crudely organized. Straw hat braiding and shoe and boot making were efficiently organized, large-scale, well-capitalized businesses, even though the actual work was performed by hand in scattered farm households. Tinware was distributed by a peddling network with distribution depots nationwide.

A pattern emerges. Every county in Massachusetts, Connecticut, and Rhode Island, except Cape Cod and the islands, was manufacturing in volume for distant sale. The cape and the islands presumably turned to the sea when the land ran out. Also producing for export, although in notably lower volume than Southern New England, were the four southernmost counties in New Hampshire, and the four Connecticut River valley counties of Vermont—the old-settled, land-hungry, parts of these states. Manufacturing in Maine was negligible, except in old-settled, densely populated Cumberland and Hancock counties. The three southern states and ten counties in the three northern states that emerge from Coxe's survey as manufacturing districts were all settled before 1760. Even in Caledonia County, Vermont, and Hancock County, Maine—pretty far north—two generations born on frontier farms had already grown up and carved farms of their own from available land. Manufacturing appeared where land was not available, not in recently settled parts of Vermont, New Hampshire, or Maine.

List of counties and their protoindustrial manufactures by state:

MAINE

Cumberland

carriages	nails
hats	shoes
liquor	wool

Hancock

augers and bits	hats

MASSACHUSETTS

Dukes
salt

Norfolk

boots and shoes	nails
brushes	playing cards
cotton (spinning and weaving)	straw bonnets
hats	whips
lace	

Worcester

boots and shoes	liquors
clocks and watches	nails
cotton (spinning and weaving)	spinning wheels
guns	straw bonnets
hats	wire cards
horn combs	

Plymouth

cotton (weaving)	nails
hats	spinning wheels
lace	whips

Bristol
cotton (spinning and weaving) straw bonnets
hats   tacks
nails   wool
salt

Barnstable
salt

Middlesex
boots and shoes   nails
carriages   printer's ink
clocks and watches   straw bonnets
cotton (spinning and weaving) whips
hats   wire cards
lace

Essex
boots and shoes   horn combs
chairs   nails
cotton (spinning and weaving) steel thimbles
hats

Hampshire
brooms   liquor
cotton (spinning and weaving) straw bonnets
guns   tin plate
hats

Berkshire
essence of spruce   nails
hats   rakes
liquor   spinning wheels

NEW HAMPSHIRE

Rockingham
cotton   nails
liquor

Stafford
cotton

Hillsborough
cotton   nails

Cheshire
cotton

VERMONT

Orange
cotton   nails

Windsor
cotton   spinning wheels
horn combs   tinware

Caledonia
boots and shoes   straw bonnets
liquor

Windham
buttons   nails

RHODE ISLAND

Providence
cotton   machinery for cotton mills
factory turning screws   straw bonnets
lace

Washington
cotton   nails
machinery for cotton mills   salt

Newport
cotton

Kent
cotton   wool

Bristol
hats   shoes

CONNECTICUT

Hartford

buttons	liquor
cotton	pottery
guns	tinware
horn combs	wooden clocks

New Haven

buttons	horn combs
cotton	straw bonnets
guns	tinware
hats	wooden clocks

New London

| cotton | silk |
| hats | |

Fairfield

| cotton | horn combs |
| hats | pottery |

Windham

cotton	silk
hats	straw bonnets
horn combs	

Litchfield

carriages	liquor
cotton	straw bonnets
hats	tinware
horn combs	wooden clocks

Middlesex

cotton	horn combs
guns	liquor
hats	

Tolland

| cotton | straw bonnets |

13. Adam Smith, of course, believed that expanding markets made a division of labor possible, and that division of labor led to invention. *An Inquiry into the Nature and Causes of the Wealth of Nations* (1776; London: reprint, Oxford University Press,

1976), 96–97. I will not presume to enter the debate by declaring with T. S. Ashton, *The Industrial Revolution, 1760–1830* (Oxford, 1948), 62, that invention is the mother of necessity, or join D. E. C. Eversley, "The Home Market and Economic Growth in England, 1750–1780," in *Land, Labor and Population in the Industrial Revolution*, ed. E. L. Jones and G. E. Mingay (London: E. Arnold, 1967), in wondering where manufacturers are to be found who produce goods without some prior indication that a market exists. Shoe pegs were invented to sell to a known market in a flourishing industry.

14. Thomson, *Path to Mechanized Shoe Production*, 34–36.
15. Agnes Hannay, *A Chronicle of Industry on the Mill River* (Northampton, Mass.: Smith College Studies in History, 1936), 27–28.
16. Louis W. Arny, "Early Days of Leather Belting" (New York: National Association of Leather Belting Manufacturers, 1918).
17. Lucius Ellsworth, *Craft to National Industry in the Nineteenth Century: A Case Study, The Transformation of the New York State Tanning Industry* (New York: Arno Press, 1975), Edgar Hoover, *Location Theory and the Shoe and Leather Industries* (Cambridge: Harvard University Press, 1937).
18. Massachusetts Division of Water Pollution Control, *Summary of Water Quality, 1990.* Publication 16,501-107-25-11-90 CR.
19. John Arthur Wilson, *The Chemistry of Leather Manufacture* (New York: Chemical Catalogue Company, 1928); Fred O'Flaherty, William Roddy, and Robert Lollar, *The Chemistry and Technology of Leather*, vol. 2 (New York: Reinhold Publishing, 1958).
20. J. Wohlgemuth, "Gundriss der Fermentmethoden," (Berlin: J. Springer, 1913), cited in Wilson, *Chemistry of Leather Manufacture*, 321.
21. *Report of a Commission Appointed to Consider a General System of Drainage for the Valleys of Mystic, Blackstone and Charles Rivers, Massachusetts, U.S.A.* (Boston: State Printers, 1886), 86–87.

8. Why Lightning Strikes (pp. 98–106)

1. David Landes, *The Unbound Prometheus: Technological Change and Industrial Development in Western Europe from 1750 to the Present* (Cambridge: Cambridge University Press, 1969), 66.
2. Richard O. Cummings, *The American Ice Harvests; A Historical Study in Technology, 1800–1918*, Berkeley, University of California Press, 1949.
3. Henry Pearson, *Proceedings of the Massachusetts Historical Society* 65 (October 1933): 169–215; Richard O. Cummings, *The American Ice Harvests: A Study in Historical Technology, 1800–1918* (Berkeley: University of California Press, 1949); and Tudor's own account in the *Third Annual Report of the Boston Board of Trade January, 1857* (Boston: Boston Board of Trade, 1857), 79–82.
4. None of the factors suggested here as conditions of industrialization is sufficient to explain the phenomenon. A constellation of the factors worked together to bring forth an industrial revolution. But the study of each nation where such a revolution has taken place reveals a slightly different constellation. There is no single recipe.

5. I differ here, ever so slightly, from Joel Mokyr, *The British Industrial Revolution; An Economic Perspective* (Boulder: Westview Press, 1993), 36 ff. In New England, even more than in old England, where he establishes the importance of the mechanism, rank and status were accorded to successful entrepreneurs. I see evidence not so much of young men setting out to become magnates, as of a great many young men setting out to become modestly prosperous, and sometimes ending up magnates. I believe that a serious ambition to climb to the top of the pyramid is rare in any era, and therefore less potent as an economic motor than the ambition not to be degraded.

   In 1996–1997, I lived in Silicon Valley. It was a boom town where serious fortunes were being made in suburban office parks and yet the conversation was not so much about how to become a millionaire as whether to try. Becoming a millionaire, an option regarded as open to those with certain technical skills, was widely seen as attainable by following a specific route: (1) Find a likely-looking start-up company. (2) Take a job with the understanding that the salary will be low but the work will be demanding and there will be stock options. (3) Work sixty-to-eighty-hour weeks, subsist on cold pizza and Diet Coke, don't even think about having a life outside the office, and hope the company makes it big. (4) When the company fails, seek a new start-up and try again.

   The belief, so widespread as to be universal in the Valley, was that it would take an average of three tries and six to ten years to become a millionaire. Yet not everyone with the requisite technical skills was joining a start-up and trying to become a millionaire. Many, many people with that option decided instead to take a well-paying job offering financial security but no prospect of ever amassing more than a moderately comfortable estate.

6. David S. Landes, *The Unbound Prometheus: Technical Change and Industrial Development in Western Europe from 1750 to the Present* (London: Cambridge University Press, 1969), 22. It is also true that family limitation is widely practiced in primitive societies, although this was not so well established when Landes wrote as it is now.

7. Ibid., 21.

8. Ibid.

9. Ibid., 16.

10. Ibid.

11. Winifred Barr Rothenberg, *From Market-Places to a Market Economy: The Transformation of Rural Massachusetts, 1750–1850* (Chicago: University of Chicago Press, 1992). Stephen Innes, *Creating the Commonwealth: The Economic Culture of Puritan New England* (New York: W. W. Norton, 1995), argues that the commercialization of Puritan culture was complete at the time of settlement.

12. Boston Board of Trade, Isaac C. Bates, Secretary, "Boot and Shoe Trade," *Third Annual Report of the Government, Presented to the Board at the Annual Meeting on the 21st of January, 1857* (Boston, 1857), 98–100.

13. Dating an industrial revolution is difficult. The 1790s saw a Yankee explosion in the application of waterpower to tanning, papermaking, wool carding, and other traditional manufactories. The decade also saw proto-industries emerge in tinware,

broommaking, woodenware, buttonmaking, combmaking, and iron toolmaking, and the expansion of shoemaking. In 1793, Eli Whitney invented the cotton gin and Samuel Slater's mill began spinning cotton by waterpower using British technology. It was the decade when New England began to become a manufacturing region.

The second decade of the 1800s saw the first burst of important Yankee inventive activity: The pegged shoe in 1810, the power loom in 1813, clocks from interchangeable parts in 1814, Simeon North's first milling machine around 1816; the Blanchard lathe in 1817. It was the decade when New England first produced technologies that led the world.

1813–1814 was the Yankee annus miribilis. In 1813, the first power looms went into production at Waltham, Massachusetts, and in 1814, Eli Terry's pillar and scroll clocks—the world's first complex machine mass-produced from interchangeable parts—came off the line at Plymouth, Connecticut.

14. Paul David and Gavin Wright, "Increasing Returns and the Genesis of American Resource Abundance," Stanford University, Center for Economic Policy Research, publication 472, July 1996.

9. Peddling the Future (pp. 108–117)

1. Timothy Dwight, *Travels in New York and New England* (New York, 1821; reprint, Cambridge: Harvard University Press, 1969), Letter 1, Journey to the White Mountains.

2. Shirley Spaulding DeVoe, *The Tinsmiths of Connecticut* (Middletown, Conn.: Wesleyan University Press, 1968); Dwight, *Travels*, Letter 1.

3. Henry Rowe, *History of New Haven* (New York: Munsell & Co., 1887).

4. Howard S. Russell, *Long Deep Furrow; Three Centuries of Farming in New England* (Hanover, N.H.: University Press of New England, 1976); John H. Martin, "Broomcorn, the Frontiersman's Cash Crop," *Economic Botany* 7 (1953): 163–181; Gregory Nobles, "Continuity and Commerce; A Case Study of the Rural Broommaking Business in Antebellum Massachusetts," *Journal of the Early Republic* 4 (1984): 287–308; Arthur H. Cole, "Agricultural Crazes: Neglected Chapter in American Economic History," *American Economic Review* 16 (1926): 622–639; Nelson Close, "Sericulture in the United States," *Agricultural History* 37 (1963):225–234; L. P. Brockett, *The Silk Industry in America* (Brooklyn, N.Y.: Silk Industry Association of America, 1976); J. H. Cobb, *Manual Containing Information Respecting Growth of the Mulberry Tree, With Suitable Directions for the Culture of Silk*, 4th ed. (Boston 1839); Winifred Barr Rothenberg, *From Market-place to a Market Economy: The Transformation of Rural Massachusetts, 1750–1850* (Chicago: University of Chicago Press, 1992).

5. Dwight, *Travels*, Letter 44, Journey to Berwick.

6. George Rogers Taylor, *The Transportation Revolution* (New York: Holt, Reinhart, Winston, 1951); Frederic J. Wood, *The Turnpikes of New England* (Boston: Marshall Jones Co., 1919); P. E. Taylor, "The Turnpike Era in New England," Ph.D. diss., Yale

University, 1934; Roger Neal Parks, "The Roads of New England, 1790 –1840," Ph.D. diss., Michigan State University, 1966. R. Szostak, "Institutional Inheritance and Early American Industrialization," in *The Vital One: Essays in Honor of J. R. T. Hughes*, ed. Joel Maky, Research in Economic History, Supplement 6 (Greenwich, Conn.: Joi Press, 1971): 287–308, explicates the debt to mechanisms developed in English law enabling turnpike and canal incorporation and the taking of property by eminent domain. Without these legal mechanisms, transportation improve ments would have been blocked or delayed no matter how greatly desired.

7. Christopher Roberts, *The Middlesex Canal, 1793–1860* (Cambridge: Harvard University Press, 1938); William Lincoln, *History of Worcester* (Worcester, Mass.: Moses D. Phillips, Co., 1837).

8. Edward Chase Kirkland, *Men, Cities and Transportation: A Study in New England History, 1820–1900* (Cambridge: Harvard University Press, 1948), 2 vols.; Stephen Salsbury, *The State, The Investor and the Railroad: The Boston and Albany, 1825–1867* (Cambridge: Harvard University Press, 1967); Alvin F. Harlow, *Steelways of New England* (New York: Creative Age Press, 1946); Benjamin Thomas Hill, "The Beginnings of the Boston and Worcester Railroad," *Proceedings of the Worcester Historical Society*, September 1901; Massachusetts General Court, House of Representatives, *Report of the Select Committee of the House of Representatives of Massachusetts on the Practicability and Expediency of Constructing a Rail Way from Boston to the Hudson River, at or near Albany* (Boston: True and Greene, State Printers, 1827); Edward Chase Kirkland, "The Railroad Schemes of Massachusetts," *Journal of Economic History*, 5 (2):145 –171 (1945); Klaus Peter Harder, *Environmental Factors of Early Railroads: A Comparative Study of Massachusetts and the Pfalz Before 1870* (New York: Arno Press, 1981), chapters 2 and 5; *Report of the Board of Commissioners of Internal Improvements in Relation to the Examination of Sundry Routes for a Rail Way from Boston to Providence* (Boston, 1828); *Report of the Board of Commissioners for the Survey of One or More Routes for a Railway from Boston to Albany* (Boston, 1828); *Springfield Gazette*, December 9, 1835 (describing the purchase of shares in the Western as public service, not profit-motivated, decision); Charles Webster [pseud. Berkshire], *Brief Remarks on the Rail Road Proposed in Massachusetts* (Stockbridge; Charles Webster, 1828); George Bliss, *Historical Memoir of the Western Rail Road* (Springfield, 1863), 31. Share purchases averaged less than one thousand dollars, taken with small expectation of profit but with the understanding that rail roads meant general prosperity.

9. See, for example, discussions of early demand for transportation improvements in Charles E. Clark, *The Eastern Frontier; The Settlement of Northern New England, 1610–1763* (New York: Alfred Knopf, 1970), 339 –341; Richard Bushman, *From Puritan to Yankee; Character and the Social Order in Connecticut, 1690–1765* (Cambridge, Harvard University Press, 1967), 114.

10. Jedidiah Morse, *The American Geography* (1789; reprint, New York: Arno Press, 1970), 217; DeVoe, *Tinsmiths; History of Naugatuck*, 71 (pewter buttons); Kenneth Howell and Einar Carlson, *Men of Iron: Forbes and Adam* (Lakeville, Conn.: Pocketknife Press, 1980). Rothenberg dates the revolution in agricultural market orientation to the 1780s in the papers collected in *From Market-Places to a Market Economy*.

11. Rothenberg, *From Market-Places to a Market Economy*.

12. DeVoe, *Tinsmiths*; Dwight, *Travels*, Letter 1; John Joseph Murphy, "The Establishment of the American Clock Industry; a Study in Entrepreneurial History," Ph.D. diss., Yale University, 1961.

13. Murphy, "Establishment of the Clock Industry," 140, describes the financing of a new workshop making blotters, faucets, and combs by a man in the wholesale peddler supply trade.

14. I do not find Gordon Wood's picture ("Inventing American Capitalism," *New York Review of Books*, June 9, 1994) of "Ordinary farmers . . . working harder and increasing their productivity when they found that there were genteel goods available for them to purchase," persuasive. The evidence cited (Robert Buel, Jr., "Samson Shorn: The Impact of the Revolutionary War on Estimates of the Republic's Strength," in *Arms and Independence: The Military Character of the American Revolution*, ed. Ronald Hoffman and Peter J. Albert [Charlottesville: University Press of Virginia, 1984], 157–160) to demonstrate that the productive surpluses of Connecticut agriculture declined during the war, making it difficult for Continental quartermasters to purchase provisions, because the imports for which the farmers desired to trade their surplus were not available, seems weak in face of the active willingness of American farmers to sell to British and French quartermasters. I submit that it was inflated continental currency, not an import dearth, that caused a production decline and a pause in the development of market capitalism. (Richard Buel, Jr., *Dear Liberty: Connecticut's Mobilization for the Revolutionary War* [Middletown, Conn.: Wesleyan University Press, 1980] 257–267; and R. Arthur Bowler, *Logistics and the Failure of the British Army in America, 1775–1783* [Princeton: Princetown University Press, 1975].) If instead of being motivated by a newfound consumerism, increased market production was inspired by the traditional impulse to establish oneself and/or one's offspring, then a pause at a time when the wages of increased productivity were paid in inflating scrip, followed—as it was—by a surge when currency supply stabilized after the war, was a sensible response by the people involved. It was the good fortune of many Yankees to do so well in efforts to earn a living, that they were able to become consumers. Consumerism was not an original motivating factor, but the outcome and fuel of continuing economic growth.

15. Charles Danhof, *Change in Agriculture: The Northern United States, 1820–1870* (Cambridge, Harvard University Press, 1969), 87–94.

10. Machines That Make Machines (pp. 119–135)

1. Quoted from a New Haven advertisement of 1801 for the "Clock Manufactory" of Sibley & Marble by Penrose Hoopes, *Early Clockmaking in Connecticut* (New Haven: Tercentenary Commission of the State of Connecticut, 1934), 9.

2. On the question of where mechanized production developed and why, it is of interest that eighteenth-century Connecticut boasted one immigrant British clockmaker in the eighteenth century, Thomas Harland, who arrived at Norwich in 1773.

Tradition holds that he had intended to settle in Boston, but was diverted by political troubles there to Norwich, a town positioned at the head of navigation on the Thames, which gave it a fillip of prosperity as a transhipment point for agricultural produce, and some status as a market town. Harland set himself up in the style of a British master workman; it is said that in 1790 he employed ten or twelve apprentices to produce forty clocks and two hundred watches. He also employed a tinsmith to produce kitchenware, and he retailed jewelry, silver, and pewter. English-born, he increased production workshop-style, and by purchase of goods wholesale for retail sale. (Penrose Hoopes, *Connecticut Clockmakers of the Eighteenth Century* (New York: Dodd, Mead, 1930).

3. Quoted from an article by Henry Terry, Eli Terry's son, published in the *Waterbury American*, June 10, 1853, and reprinted in Kenneth Roberts, *Eli Terry and the Connecticut Shelf Clock* (Bristol, Conn.: Ken Roberts Publishing Co., 1973).

4. Chauncey Jerome, *History of the American Clock Business for the Past Sixty Years and Life of Jerome Chauncey Written by Himself* (New Haven, Conn.: F. C. Dayton, Jr., 1860); Henry Terry, "A Review of Dr. Alcott's History of Clock-Making: By a Clock-Maker," *Waterbury American*, June 10, 1853, reprinted in Roberts, *Eli Terry*.

5. Donald R. Hoke, *Ingenious Yankees: The Rise of the American System of Manufactures in the Private Sector* (New York, Columbia University Press, 1990), 56.

6. Ibid.

7. Kenneth Roberts, *The Contributions of Joseph Ives to Connecticut Clock Technology, 1810–1862* (Bristol, Conn.: American Clock and Watch Museum, 1970).

8. Among examples of early harnessing of water power to mechanical tasks in an array of industries: pottery in J. Ritchie Garrison, *Landscape and Material Life in Franklin County, Massachusetts, 1770–1860* (Knoxville: University of Tennessee Press, 1991), 221; Orra Stone, *History of Massachusetts Industries* (Boston: S. Clarke, 1930), cites a Lenox marble quarry sawing marble by water power in 1800 (154), seven trip-hammers in operation in Sutton in 1793 making scythes, axes, hoes, and nails—Stone cites numerous towns with trip-hammer smiths shops in the period (1963); paper maceration in 1786, and tanyard bark mill 1790 in Agnes Hannay, *A Chronicle of Industry on the Mill River* (Northampton, Mass.: Smith College Studies in History, 1936).

9. S. N. D. North and Ralph H. North, *Simeon North; First Official Pistol Maker of the United States; A Memoir* (Concord, N.H.: Rumford Press, 1913).

10. North and North, *Simeon North*; Felicia Dayrup, *Arms Making in the Connecticut Valley: A Regional Study of the Economic Development of the Small Arms Industry, 1798–1870* (Smith College Studies in History, 1948; reprint, York, Pa.: George Shumway, 1970).

11. See, for example, biographies of Ezra Dodge and David Lowrey, clockmakers and gunsmiths, in Penrose Hoopes, *Connecticut Clockmakers*. Hoopes, looking only for evidence of clockmaking, found clockmakers of Cheney's generation producing everything from church bells to stocking looms.

12. An article by Henry Terry, Eli Terry's son, published in the *Waterbury American*, June 10, 1853, and reprinted in Roberts, *Eli Terry*, refers to the clockmaker who trained his father as Mr. Cheney. The Cheney-Fitch connection and the details of

Elisha Cheney's life are found in Hoopes, *Connecticut Clockmakers*. Hoopes reprints the following advertisement from December 19, 1800: "Wanted, at the Pistol Manufactory at Berlin, five or six Journeymen Lock Filers to begin by the 15th of Feb. next. Those that can come well recommended may meet with good encouragement by applying to North and Cheney." A clear statement of partnership. In their memoir, North's sons remember that their father "never had a partner except, for a short time, about 1811, when he entered into some sort of working agreement with his brother-in-law, Elisha Cheney, the clock manufacturer, who for a time finished some of the screws and pins used in the pistols." North and North, *Simeon North*, 35. Cheney's real estate purchases and family history are covered in Catharine M. North, *History of Berlin, Connecticut* (New Haven: Tuttle, Morehouse and Company, 1906).

The Cheney-North partnership is the sort of link between clockmaking and small arms that Merrit Roe Smith demands in his review of Donald Hoke's *Ingenious Yankees* in the *Journal of Economic History* 51 (1):245 (1991) The careers of Harland's apprentices are discussed in Murphy, "Establishment of the Clock Industry," 3 1n.

13. Jefferson quoted in Constance Green, *Eli Whitney and the Birth of American Technology* (Boston: Little Brown, 1956), 133.

14. Robert Gordon, "Materials for Manufacturing: The Response of the Connecticut Iron Industry to Technological Change and Limited Resources," *Technology and Culture* 24 (4):602–634 (October 1983).

15. Merritt Roe Smith, *Harper's Ferry Armory and the New Technology: The Challenge of Change* (Ithaca: Cornell University Press, 1977).

16. Carolyn Cooper, *Shaping Invention: Thomas Blanchard's Machinery and Patent Management in Nineteenth Century America* (New York: Columbia University Press, 1991), 17–18.

17. North, *History of Berlin*.

18. Merritt Roe Smith, "John H. Hall, Simeon North, and the Milling Machine: The Nature of Innovation Among Antebellum Arms Makers," *Technology and Culture* 14 (4):573–591 (October 1973); Edwin A. Battison, "The Cover Design: A New Look at the 'Whitney' Milling Machine," *Technology and Culture* 14 (4):592–598 (October 1973); Robert B. Gordon, "Who Turned the Mechanical Ideal into Mechanical Reality?," *Technology and Culture* 29 (4):744–778 (October 1988); Robert B. Gordon, "Simeon North, John Hall, and Mechanized Manufacturing," *Technology and Culture* 30 (1):179–188 (January 1989).

19. Gordon, "Simeon North," 183; Gordon, "Who Turned the Mechanical Ideal"; Smith, "John Hall."

20. Paul Uselding, "Elisha K. Root, Forging, and the 'American System,'" *Technology and Culture* 15 (4):543–568 (October 1974); Robert B. Gordon, "Material Evidence of the Development of Metalworking Technology at the Collins Axe Factory," *Journal of the Society for Industrial Archeology* 14 (2):19–28 (November 1988); Hoke, *Ingenious Yankees*, chapter 3.

21. Jerome, *History of the American Clock Business*.

22. Frederick Bourne, 'American Sewing Machines,' in *One Hundred Years of American Commerce*, ed. Chauncey DePew (New York: D. O. Haines, 1895), 524–539; Grace

Rogers Cooper, *The Sewing Machine: Its Invention and Development* (Washington, D.C.: Smithsonian Institution Press, 1976); David Hounshell, *From the American System to Mass Production, 1800–1932: The Development of Manufacturing Technology in the United States* (Baltimore: Johns Hopkins University Press, 1984).

23. Hounshell, *From the American System to Mass Production.*
24. Hounshell, *From the American System to Mass Production, 232.*
25. See the pictures of Blanchard's mill in Elbridge Kingsley and Frederick Knab, *Picturesque Worcester* (Springfield, Mass.: W. F. Adams Co., 1895).

11. Acres Cleared and Drained (pp. 136–154)

1. Jedediah Morse, *The American Geography* (1784; reprint, New York: Arno Press (1970), 261.
2. Treating the United States as a unit masks the reality of American industrialization, and may be as anachronistic as it is unenlightening. The several states were certainly not separate and independent nations in the crucial decades (for the study of industrialization) from 1790 to 1840, but neither were the United States a single nation, although we were tending in that direction.

    It is not at all clear that residents of Connecticut (or Massachusetts or Rhode Island) in 1815 would, if put to the test, have defined themselves as Americans first and citizens of Connecticut second. We know that when Virginians were put to that test in 1861 they overwhelmingly answered "Virginian." Cultural homogeneity within New England was extreme; cultural differences among regions were very large. (The roots of regional cultural distinctiveness are best explicated in David Hackett Fischer's *Albion's Seed*.) In addition to being anachronistic, assessing the process, and especially the causes, of American industrialization through the lens of national statistics may lead us to miss important phenomena. We might, for example, fail to observe that Massachusetts in 1841 was more thoroughly industrialized than England (exclusive of Wales and Scotland) was at the census of 1851.
3. Carl Siracusa, *A Mechanical People; Perceptions of the Industrial Order in Massachusetts, 1815–1880* (Middletown: Wesleyan University Press, 1979), tables 5 and 6.
4. Harold F. Wilson, "The Rise and Decline of the Sheep Industry in Northern New England," *Agricultural History* 9 (1): 25(1935); J. E. Wing, "Merino Sheep," in Liberty Bailey, *Cyclopedia of American Agriculture* 5th ed. (New York: Macmillan, 1917), vol. 3, 619.
5. Clarence Albert Day, *History of Maine Agriculture, 1604–1860* (Orono: University of Maine, 1954); Chester Whitney Wright, *Wool Growing and the Tariff: A Study in Economic History of the U.S.* (Cambridge: Harvard University Press, 1968); L. G. Conner, "A Brief History of the Sheep Industry in the U.S.," Annual Report of the Association of the American Historical Association for the Year 1918 (Washington, D.C.: Government Printing Office, 1921) vol. 1, 89–197; Robert F. Balivet, "The Vermont Sheep Industry, 1811–1880," *Vermont History* 33, 243–249 (1965); Harold F. Wilson, "Rise and Decline of the Sheep Industry in Northern New England," *Agricultural History* 9 (1):12–40 (1935); Howard Russell, *A Long, Deep Furrow* (Hanover, N.H.:

University Press of New England, 1976; Harold Meeks, *Time and Change in Vermont: A Human Geography* (Chester, Conn.: Globe Pequot, 1986).

6. John Donald Black, *The Rural Economy of New England* (Cambridge: Harvard University Press, 1950), 224–225.

7. E. N. Hartley, *Ironworks on the Saugus* (Norman: University of Oklahoma Press, 1957).

8. William Cronon, *Changes in the Land* (New York: Hill and Wang, 1983), 149, describes similar silting up of harbors at Boston, Barnstable, Nauset, and New Haven, where between 1765 and 1821 the town wharf had to be extended 3900 feet. Salem Harbor is much smaller and more enclosed than New Haven.

9. John Stilgoe, "A New England Coastal Wilderness," *Geographical Review* 7 (1): (January 1981); Lawrence Geller, *Pilgrims in Eden: Conservation Policies at New Plymouth* (Plymouth: Pilgrim Society, 1974); Timothy Dwight, *Travels in New England and New York*, 1821 (reprint ed. Barbara Miller Solomon, Cambridge: Harvard University Press, 1969), vol. 3, Cape Cod journey.

10. Edna Cornell, "Smoky Gold," *Old Time New England*, 31 (2):41–43 (1940).

11. Peter Stott, "Economic Development," in *Historic and Archeological Resources of Cape Cod and the Islands* (Boston: Massachusetts Historical Commission, 1987.

12. John White, *A History of the American Locomotive: Its Development: 1830–1880* (Baltimore: Johns Hopkins University Press, 1968) 84.

13. Bruce Daniels, *The Connecticut Town* (Middletown, Conn.: Wesleyan University Press, 1979), 151.

14. William Wood, quoted in Dorothy Snyder, "The Passenger Pigeon in New England," *Old Time New England* 45, 61–72 (1935).

15. Andrew Baker and Holly Izard Patterson, "Farmers' Adaptations to Markets in Early-Nineteenth Century Massachusetts," In *The Farm*, The 1986 Annual Proceedings of the Dublin Seminar for New England Folklife, ed. Peter Benes (Boston: Boston University Press, 1988), 105–107.

16. The New England agricultural press began to urge the draining of wet meadows, swamps and peat bogs as early as there was a New England agricultural press. To judge by reports published in these periodicals, the *New England Farmer* in particular, farmers were actively draining wetlands by the 1820s. (See, for example, the report of the profitable draining of an "ash pocosin," peat bog, in the May 13, 1825 issue, p. 330.) Farmers wrote to inquire about methods, responded to the editor's questionnaires on the subject, and submitted drained meadows for agricultural prizes.

17. Robert Gross, "Culture and Cultivation, Agriculture and Society in Thoreau's Concord," *Journal of American History* 69 (June 1982): 42–61.

18. George Works, "The Soil of New England," an address to the Worcester North Agricultural Society, from *Abstract of Returns of the Agricultural Societies of Massachusetts* (Boston: State Printer, 1865), 31.

19. David Smith, Victor Konrad, et al. "Salt Marshes as a Factor in the Agriculture of Northeastern North America," *Agricultural History* 63 (2):270–294 (1989); David Smith and Anne Bridges, "Salt Marsh Dykes as a Factor in Eastern Maine Agriculture," *Maine Historical Society Quarterly* 21 (4):219–226 (1982); Betsy Woodman, "Salt Haying, Farming and Fishing: The Life of Sherb Eaton, 1900–1982," *Essex*

Institute Historical Collections (119):165–168 (1983); Twenty-Second Annual Report of the Massachusetts Board of Agriculture (Boston, 1874), 328–342, on the controversy surrounding the draining of the 1,412-acre Green Harbor River marsh in Marshfield; and *New England Farmer,* particularly January 26, 1827, 210; February 2, 1827, 217; May 5, 1826, 324; and June 23, 1826, 381, for farmers' opinions on the economics of cutting naturally fertilized salt hay, versus draining and converting to upland mowing requiring seeding and manuring.

20. References on cranberry growing are gathered in Joseph Thomas, *Cranberry Harvest* (New Bedford, Mass.: Spinner Publications, 1990).

21. For example, see the chemical analysis of industrial by-products for use as fertilizers in the Twelfth Annual Report of the State Agricultural Experiment Station at Amherst, Mass., for 1894, published in Boston in 1895. Richard Wines, *Fertilizer in America:From Waste Recycling to Resource Exploitation* (Philadelphia: Temple University Press, 1985).

12. Spinning Cotton into Gold (pp. 157–167)

1. Labor calculations from Henry Hobhouse, *Seeds of Change* (New York: Harper and Row, 1984), 144.

2. Cotton statistics are conveniently gathered in Stuart Bruchey, *Cotton and the Growth of the American Economy, 1790–1860* (New York: Harcourt Brace, 1967).

3. Robert Dalzell, *Enterprising Elite: The Boston Associates and the World They Made,* (Cambridge: Harvard University Press, 1987).

4. David Jeremy, *Transatlantic Industrial Revolution: The Diffusion of Textile Technology between Britain and America, 1790–1830's* (Cambridge: Harvard University Press, 1981); Caroline Ware, *The Early New England Cotton Manufacture: A Study in Industrial Beginnings* (1931; New York: Russell & Russell, 1966); John William Lozier, *Taunton and Mason: Cotton Machinery and Locomotive Manufacture in Taunton, Mass. 1811–1861* (New York: Garland, 1986); Barbara Tucker, *Samuel Slater and the Origins of the American Textile Industry, 1790–1860* (Ithaca: Cornell University Press, 1984); Jonathan Prude, *The Coming Industrial Order: Town and Factory Life in Rural Massachusetts, 1810–1860* (Cambridge: Cambridge University Press, 1983); Gary Kulik, Roger Parks, and Theodore Penn, *The New England Mill Village, 1790–1860* (Cambridge, Mass.: MIT Press 1982); Robert Brooke Zevin, "The Growth of Cotton Textile Production after 1815," in *The Reinterpretation of American Economic History,* ed. Robert Fogel and Stanley Engerman (New York: Harper and Row, 1971), 122–147. Wool is discussed in Elizabeth Hitz, *A Technical and Business Revolution: American Woolens to 1832* (New York: Garland, 1986); introduction of power weaving on page 261.

5. Commonwealth vs. Essex Company, quoted in Theodore Steinberg, *Nature Incorporated: Industrialization and the Waters of New England* (Cambridge: Cambridge University Press, 1991).

6. Fish ladders were tried and found wanting, both because they wasted water that was wanted for power generation, and because they worked so poorly. Gary Kulik,

"Dams, Fish and Farmers: Defense of Public Rights in Eighteenth Century Rhode Island," in *The Countryside in an Age of Capitalist Transformation*, ed. Steven Hahn and Jonathan Prude (Chapel Hill: University of North Carolina Press, 1985).

7. See statistical tables in Peter McClelland and Richard Zeckhauser, *Demographic Dimensions of the New Republic: American Interregional Migration, Vital Statistics, and Manumissions, 1800–1860* (Cambridge: Cambridge University Press, 1982), table C-1. Domestic migration flows from New England until 1820, records a slight in-migration in the 1820s, out-migration again in the 1830s, and substantial in-migration in the 1840s, when industrialization was in full swing. By the 1850s, New Englanders were leaving again.

There was a simultaneous movement of population within the region, from countryside to towns, and, therefore, from north to south, that continued through the century.

13. Cities of Steam (pp. 169–188)

1. W. S. Jevons, *The Coal Question: An Enquiry Concerning the Progress of the Nation, and the Probable Exhaustion of Our Coal Mines* (London, 1865).
2. John Clapham and Herbert Heaton, economic historians of the 1930s and 1940s, rejected the idea that there was an industrial revolution, pointing out the absurdity of referring to a process that unfolded over the course of generations as though it were a sudden event. A more recent summary of the assault on the concept of industrial revolution is found in David Landes, "The Fable of the Dead Horse; or, the Industrial Revolution Revisited," in *The British Industrial Revolution; An Economic Perspective*, ed. Joel Mokyr (Boulder, Colo.: Westview, 1993).
3. L. T. C. Rolt, *Thomas Newcomen: The Prehistory of the Steam Engine* (David and Charles Dawlish, 1963; Richard Hills, *Power from Steam: A History of the Stationary Steam Engine* (Cambridge: Cambridge University Press, 1989.
4. Rupert A. Hall, "What Did the Industrial Revolution in Britain Owe to Science?" in *Historical Perspectives: Studies in English Thought and Society*, ed. Neil McKendrick (London: Europa Publications, 1974).
5. Louis C. Hunter, *A History of Industrial Power in the United States, 1780–1930*, vol. 2: *Steam Power* (Charlottesville: University Press of Virginia, 1985).
6. A term first applied by Donald Cardwell, *Turning Points in Western Technology* (New York: Neale Watson Science History Publication, 1972).
7. Hunter, *A History of Industrial Power*, 2:257.
8. Mary Corliss, *The Life and Work of George Corliss* (New York: American Historical Society of New York, 1930). In a reflection of John Adams's well-known observation that his generation had to study war that their children might study industry and their grandchildren the arts, it is amusing to note that while Corliss's grandfather fought in the Revolutionary Army, his daughter, who died unmarried in 1929, lived comfortably, free of the necessity of labor in the Providence mansion her father built, while his son lived as a gentleman of leisure in Europe for fifty years, mostly in Nice and on the Riviera, and never married. The only biography, written

by a niece who lived with Corliss's daughter as a companion, is not very informative, though it does mention that the family were descended from stock that came from England in the great migration.

9. Diana Karter Appelbaum, *The Glorious Fourth: An American Holiday, an American History* (New York: Facts on File, 1989).

10. Hunter, *A History of Industrial Power*, 2:266.

11. Henry H. Earl, *A Centennial History of Fall River, Massachusetts, Comprising a Record of its Corporate Progress from 1656 to 1876, with Sketches of its Manufacturing Industries, Local and General Characteristics, Valuable Statistical Tables, Etc.* (New York: Atlantic Publishing and Engraving, 1877).

12. Thomas Russell Smith, *The Cotton Textile Industry of Fall River, Massachusetts: A Study of Industrial Localization* (New York: King's Crown Press, 1944), 28.

13. Smith, *Cotton Textile Industry, 45;* Hunter, *A History of Industrial Power*, vol. 2; Peter J. Coleman, *The Transformation of Rhode Island, 1790–1860* (Providence: Brown University Press, 1963), 130.

14. Earl, *A Centennial History;* Smith, *Cotton Textile Industry.*

15. William F. Adams, *Ireland and the Irish Immigration to the New World from 1815 to the Famine* (New Haven: Yale University Press, 1932), 403–409.

16. Oscar Handlin, *Boston's Immigrants, 1790–1880* (Cambridge: Harvard University Press, 1941, 1991), 48–50.

17. Stephan Thernstrom, *Poverty and Progress: Social Mobility in a Nineteenth Century City* (Cambridge: Harvard University Press, 1964); Anthony Coelho, "A Row of Nationalities: Life in a Working Class Community: The Irish, English and French Canadians of Fall River, Massachusetts, 1850–1890," Ph.D. diss., Brown University, 1980; William Hartford, "Paper City: Class Development in Holyoke, Massachusetts, 1850–1920," Ph.D. Diss., University of Massachusetts, Boston, Mass., 1983; William Millett, "The Irish and Mobility Patterns in Northampton, Mass. 1846–1883," Ph.D. diss., University of Iowa, 1980; Frances Early, "French-Canadian Beginnings in an American Community: Lowell, Massachusetts, 1868–1886," Ph.D. diss., Concordia University, 1980; Gerard Brault, *The French-Canadian Heritage in New England* (Hanover, N.H.: University Press of New England, 1986); Bernard C. Rosen, "Race, Ethnicity, and the Achievement Syndrome," *American Sociological Review* 24 (1959)(1):47–60.

18. Famine-era caricatures do, of course, portray the stupid paddy. Prejudice against the first large, foreign immigration to reach New England since English settlement was extreme, and the Irish spoke English in accents that struck Yankee ears as outlandish. Peasant immigrants always strike sophisticated urbanites as stupid, partly because rural ignorance of how to operate indoor plumbing or negotiate urban traffic will look like stupidity to those who take such things for granted, but also because intelligence is a faculty that can be developed. People forced from infancy to encounter novel and complex situations and concepts on a daily basis will develop more intelligence than those whose daily experience is simple and monotonous, as peasant life is. This developed intelligence is independent of natural endowment. It is also a distinct possibility that the immigrants of the famine era, many of whom were severely malnourished in childhood, were actually less intelligent than earlier or later Irish populations.

The stereotype of the stupid paddy faded with the initial immigrant generation. After that we had stereotype of the charming but shiftless, silver-tongued but improvident Irish ne'er-do-well with the gift of blarney.

19. Population was not quite evenly spread. Massachusetts population concentrations were heavier in the coastal counties. Rhode Island and New Hampshire tilted slightly toward the coast. Connecticut, on the other hand, spread its population over the map with an almost perfect evenness. Robert V. Wells, *The Population of the British Colonies in America before 1776* (Princeton: Princeton University Press, 1975). Despite the slight tilt toward the littoral, it is the evenness of population distribution that impresses by contrast with the industrial era.

20. In 1840, when 11 percent of the population of the United States lived in cities, 44 percent of the population of Rhode Island did. Fifty years later, in 1890, 85 percent of Rhode Islanders were city dwellers, but only 35 percent of Americans were. In 1920, 92 percent of Rhode Islanders were living in cities; for New England, this was the peak; after 1920, America fell in love with the automobile and began to move to the suburbs. The nation as a whole lagged New England in urbanization by such a wide gap that in 1920, only 51 percent of Americans lived in cities. That number would continue to grow until in 1970, when 74 percent of the nation lived in cities. But by that date only 87 percent of Rhode Islanders were city dwellers. This example is taken from Marion Wright and Robert Sullivan, *The Rhode Island Atlas* (Providence: Rhode Island Publications Society, 1982), 192. Census Bureau changes in the definition of an urban place make comparisons across time tricky, but do not obscure the trend.

14. The Maine Woods (pp. 189–206)

1. Charles S. Sargent, Arnold Professor of Arboriculture in Harvard College, Special Agent Tenth Census, *Report on the Forests of North America (Exclusive of Mexico)*, Department of the Interior, Census Office (Washington, D.C.: Government Printing Office, 1884), 494.

2. Dard Hunter, *Papermaking: The History and Technique of an Ancient Craft* (New York: Alfred A. Knopf, 1957), 139–169.

3. Judith A. McGaw, *Most Wonderful Machine: Mechanization and Social Change in Berkshire Papermaking, 1801–1885* (Princeton: Princeton University Press, 1987), 66.

4. Hunter, *Papermaking*, 382.

5. Hunter, *Papermaking*, .394–396; McGaw, *Most Wonderful Machine*, 198.

6. McGaw, *Most Wonderful Machine*, 118.

7. Hunter, *Papermaking*, 376.

8. Hunter, *Papermaking*, 378; McGaw, *Most Wonderful Machine*, 201.

9. The *Staats-Zeitung* regular editions of January 6, 8, and 9, 1868, were printed on wood, as were all issues after 1870. Hunter, *Papermaking*, 381.

10. Hunter, *Papermaking*, 391.

11. Ibid., 392

12. Sargent, *Report*, 494–496; James Elliott Defebaugh, *History of the Lumber Industry in America* (Chicago: American Lumberman, 1907).

13. David C. Smith, *History of Papermaking in the United States, 1691–1969* (New York: Lockwood 1970), 153–218.

14. Neil Jorgenson, *A Guide to New England's Landscape* (Chester, Conn.: Globe Pequot, 1977), 142–156, 179–183; Craig Lorimer, "The Presettlement Forest and Natural Disturbance Cycle of Northeastern Maine," *Ecology* 58 (1):139–148 (1977).

15. United States Forest Service, "Results of Recent Research Related to Whole-Tree Harvesting for the Northeast Forest Experiment Station" (Orono, Maine: USFS, USDA, November 26, 1985); M. P. Amaranthus, "Soil Compaction and Organic Matter Removal Affect Conifer Seedling Nonmycorrhizal and Ecthmycorrhizal Root Tip Abundance and Diversity," U.S. Forest Service Research Paper 1996 (494), I–II, 1–12.

16. A. R. Moldenke and J. D. Lattin, "Dispersal Characteristics of Old-Growth Arthropods and the Potential for Loss of Diversity and Biological Function," *Northwest Environmental Journal*, 6 (2): 408–409 (1990); D. C. Duffy and A. J. Meier, "Do Appalachian Herbaceous Understories Ever Recover from Clearcutting?" *Conservation Biology*, 6 (2):196–201 (1992); D. Pilz, R. Molina, M. Amaranthus, M. Castellano, N. S. Weber, "Forest Fungi and Ecosystem Management," U.S. Forest Service General Technical Report 1996 (371), 86–103; Nedavia Bethahmy, "Effects of Exposure and Logging on Runoff and Erosion," Research Note INT-61, USFS, USDA, 1967.

17. C. T. Smith, M. C. McCormack, J. W. Hornbeck, and C. W. Martin, "Nutrient and Biomass Removal from a Red Spruce-Balsam Fir Whole-Tree Harvest," *Canadian Journal of Forestry Research*, 16 (1986); Gordon Robinson, *The Forest and The Trees: A Guide to Excellent Forestry* (Washington, D.C.: Island Press, 1988).

18. David Cameron Duffy and Albert J. Meier, "Do Appalachian Herbaceous Understories Ever Recover from Clearcutting?" *Conservation Biology* 6 (2):196–201 (June 1992).

19. Pelisek, "Conifer Plantations and Soil Deterioration," *The Ecologist* (November, 1975); Mitch Lansky, *Beyond the Beauty Strip: Saving What's Left of our Forest* (Gardiner, Maine: Tilbury House, 1992).

20. The term *paper plantation* was coined by William C. Osborn, *The Paper Plantation: Ralph Nader's Study Group Report on the Pulp and Paper Industry in Maine* (New York: Viking, 1974), an exposé of both exploitative forestry and of the paper company's domination of Maine state government.

21. D. S. Powell and D. R. Dickson, *Forest Statistics for Maine—1971 and 1982* (Washington, D.C.: USDA Forest Service Resource Bulletin NE-81, USFS, 1984), 16.

21. My grandfather, the manager of a mill that knit woolen longjohns and cashmere sweaters in New Britain, Conn., a former officer in World War I, was recalled from the Army Reserve to active duty when the military buildup began. He was breveted to Colonel in the Quartermaster Corps. He once took one of the first production jeeps home on leave. Always a showman, he drove the vehicle that was the marvel of the hour up Fifth Avenue to the admiration of bystanders who wanted to know if it could really do everything they'd heard it could do. He answered them by driving it up the steps of the Metropolitan Museum.

23. Lloyd Irland, *Wildlands and Woodlots* (Hanover, N.H.: University Press of New England, 1982).

24. F. Herbert Bormann and Gene E. Likens, *Pattern and Process in a Forested Ecosystem* (New York: Springer-Verlag, 1979); Gene E. Likens and F. Herbert Bormann, *Biogeochemistry of a Forested Ecosystem* (New York: Springer-Verlag, 1977, 1995); Lloyd Irland, *Wildlands and Woodlots;* Lansky, *Beyond the Beauty Strip; Northern Forest Lands Study* (Washington, D.C.: USDA, USFA, April 1990).

25. A. Asquith, J. D. Moldenke, and J. D. Lattin, "Arthropods: The Invisible Diversity," *Northwest Environmental Journal* 6 (2):404–405 (1990).

26. Gordon Robinson, *The Forest and the Trees: A Guide to Excellent Forestry* (Covelo, Calif.: Island Press, 1988).

27. Ray Raphael, *More Tree Talk: The People, Politics and Economics of Timber* (Covelo, Calif.: Island Press 1994), 161–170; James A. Rinehart and Paul Saint-Pierre, *Timberland: An Industry, Investment and Business Overview* (Boston: Hancock Timber Resource Group, 1991).

28. Large acreages in Maine are held by timberland proprietors unrelated to the pulp mills. Some of these are heirs of logging barons or of speculators who bought the land in the early nineteenth century. Such families may own large blocks of land managed for the benefit of many heirs. Such land is held in what is known as "undivided" ownership, a corporate-type ownership in which several parties hold shares in the forests of a township, which is managed by forestry professionals who share out the profits to the various owners. In many townships, the State of Maine still owns that portion of land once set aside to support town schools that never came into existence. Among these owners are some families who treat their investments as permanent endowments and manage the land for long-term, sustainable yield. Notable among them is the Baskahegan Company, owned by Roger Milliken, Jr.

29. J. H. Beuter and K. N. Johnson, "Economic Perspectives on Maintaining the Long-Term Productivity of Forest Ecosystems," in *Maintaining the Long-Term Productivity of Pacific Northwest Ecosystems*, ed. D. A. Perry (Portland, Ore.: Timber Press, 1989).

15. *Pure Water (pp. 207–221)*

1. L. Frederick Rice, "Engineer's Report," *Report on Proposed Water Works at Lawrence, Mass.* (Lawrence, 1872), 25.

2. The literature on oyster cultivation is voluminous; oyster farming has been a major industry for two centuries on this continent—two millennia in the Mediterranean. Paul S. Galtsoff, *The American Oyster,* U.S. Department of the Interior, Fishery Bulletin of the Fish and Wildlife Service, vol. 64 (Washington, D.C.: Government Printing Office, 1964), is a standard reference work; Mervin Roberts, *Pearl Makers* Old Saybrook, Conn.: Saybrook Press, 1984).

3. Gordon Sweet, "Oyster Conservation in Connecticut Past and Present," *Geographical Review* 31 (4): 591 (1941); John M. Kochiss, *Oystering from New York to Boston* (Middletown, Conn.: Wesleyan University Press, 1974), 42.

4. Ernest Ingersoll, *The Oyster Industry: Tenth Census of the United States* (Washington, D.C.: Government Printing Office, 1881).

5. Ingersoll, *Oyster Industry*, 30; Gordon Sweet, "Oyster Conservation," 593.

6. John M. Kochiss, *Oystering*, 177.

7. Joseph Anderson, ed., *The Town and City of Waterbury, Connecticut from the Aboriginal Period to the Year Eighteen Hundred and Ninety-Five* (New Haven, Conn.: The Price and Lee Co., 1895), 93, 278.

8. Board of Sewer Commissioners, *Contract for Brick Sewers and Specifications* (Waterbury, Conn.: King Publications, 1883).

9. The 1880 Census, "Social Statistics of Cities," records extensive profiles of the sanitary habits of cities as small as Middletown, Connecticut (population 7,000), although cities varied in the detail they reported. We know, for example, that three-fourths of New London's citizens used privy vaults, one-eighth used water closets draining into cesspools, and one-eighth water closets draining into private sewers, and that all of the solid cesspool and privy vault waste was composted. About New Haven, while we know that that proportion of its sixty-three thousand citizens living in the seventh-tenths of its dwellings relying on privy vaults had their waste composted for fertilizer, we know only that of the three-tenths of dwellings enjoying the use of water closets, some had access to private sewers, and some to cesspools that were later emptied and composted, but we have not even a guess at the percentages. Even in cities like Norwich, where we are told that of the one-third of homes with waterclosets, half drained into private sewers and half into cesspools, there is no particular reason to believe that anyone actually counted.

"Social Statistics of Cities," Census Bulletin 100, July 22, 1891, gave figures for the length of sewer lines in miles for the fifty largest cities in the nation. Cities in the Narraganset Bay and Long Island Sound drainage basin range from Taunton, with no sewers, to New York, with 464 miles, not including Brooklyn, still a separate municipality with 380 miles draining into Jamaica Bay and the Atlantic. Of course, only part of the sewage pouring into the Harlem and East rivers flowed toward Long Island Sound. New Haven had 58.41 miles of public sewers in 1890.

In 1905 the Census Bureau responded to greatly increased public interest in sewers by printing as table 12 in Bulletin 20, "Statistics of Cities Having a Population of Over 25,000," a list of cities and the miles of public sewers they boasted in 1902–1903. New Haven now had 101 miles, Waterbury, 37.8, Taunton, 23.8, and New York, having absorbed Brooklyn, 1,517.2. Every city of over twenty-five thousand in the Long Island Sound or Narragansett Bay drainage basin had public sewers, down to the smallest listed city, Meriden, Connecticut, with 33.7 miles. Full of praise for Worcester, where city officials had built a plant that filtered out solids for burial before pouring its effluent into the Blackstone, census officials noted that other cities queried simply poured domestic sewage, storm runoff, and liquid industrial waste into the handiest river or bay. Many industrial plants did cull solid waste for sale as fertilizer. Other attempts at amelioration consisted of building outflow pipes far enough into the harbor that there was some hope the tide would carry it out to sea.

While no accurate figures can be drawn from such sources, it is vividly clear that the rush to build public sewers that began with the coming of waterworks in the

1870s accelerated at the turn of the century, when public sewers, measured in linear miles, seem to have approximately doubled in the region. Population and industrial plants also grew, presumably increasing the amount of sewage flowing through existing pipes.

See Joel Tarr, "Water and Wastes: A Retrospective Assessment of Wastewater Technology in the United States, 1800–1932," *Technology and Culture* 25 (2):226–263 (April 1984).

10. J. S. Gutsell, "Oyster-Cultural Problems of Connecticut," Bureau of Fisheries, Document 960, May 22, 1924. Gutsell believed that set failure was caused principally by chemical pollution, particularly copper discharged by the brass industry. He may have been correct. But his own figures indicate copper in Long Island Sound waters on the site of historic oyster beds in solutions of 0.5 parts per million, not lethal levels. The set failed, moreover, in Greenwich and Stamford, not only at the mouth of the Housatonic, where copper concentrations ought to have been highest.

11. William Firth Wells, "Studies in Oyster Culture" (Albany: State of New York Conservation Commission, 1922), 30.

12. Charles M. Weiss and Frank G. Wilkes, "Estuarine Ecosystems that Receive Sewage Wastes," in *Coastal Ecological Systems of the United States*, vol. 3, ed. H. T. Odum, The Conservation Foundation, Washington, D.C. (June 1974), 71 ff.; John H. Ryther, "The Ecology of Phytoplankton Blooms in Moriches Bay and Great South Bay, Long Island, New York," *Biological Bulletin* (Woods Hole) 106 (2):198–209 (1954).

13. M. W. Luckenbach, "Effects of Two Bloom-Forming Dinoflagellates, Prorocentrum Minimum and Gyrodinium Uncatenum, on the Growth and Survival of the Eastern Oyster, Crassostrea Virginica," *Journal of Shellfish Research* 12 (2):411–415 (1993).

14. R. W. Pierce, "Plankton Studies in Buzzards Bay, Massachusetts, U.S.A. III., Dinoflagellates, 1987 to 1988." *Marine Ecology Progress Series* 112 (3):225–234 (1994).

15. More detail in Diana Muir, "How to Murder an Oyster: Indoor Plumbing, City Sewers and the Decline of Long Island Sound Oyster Farming," *Environmental History* journal, forthcoming.

16. Kochiss, *Oystering*, 178.

17. "Whatever truth there may be in the germ theory of disease, there is no doubt that designing persons impose on the credulity and fears of the public by representing as germs of disease microscopic plants which could not possibly have caused any of the diseases which have been supposed by scientific men to be produced by germs of a vegetable nature. The public should receive with very great caution any statements about the dangerous effects of bacteria in our waters, and, instead of worrying over the subject, had better leave the matter entirely in the hands of scientific people, who, at the present day, are the only persons who can be expected to follow the complicated and obscure relations of this difficult question." W. G. Farlow, of Harvard University "On Some Impurities in Drinking Water Caused by Vegetable Growth," *First Annual Report* (Massachusetts State Board of Health, Lunacy and Charity, 1880), quoted in Barbara Gutmann Rosenkrantz, *Public Health and the State: Changing Views in Massachusetts, 1842–1963* (Cambridge: Harvard University Press, 1972), 82.

18. Theodore Steinberg, *Nature Incorporated: Industrialization and the Waters of New England* (New York: Cambridge University Press, 1991), chapter 6.

19. *Second Annual Report* (Concord, N.H.: Board of Water Commissioners, 1873); *Third Annual Report* (Manchester, N.H.: Board of Water Commissioners, 1874).

20. Steinberg, *Nature;* Louis P. Cain, "An Economic History of Urban Location and Sanitation," *Research in Economic History* 2:337–389 (1977).

21. Rosenkranz, *Public Health and the State*, 81.

22. Steinberg, *Nature.*

23. Charles Folsom, "The Pollution of Streams," *Eighth Annual Report* (Boston: Massachusetts State Board of Health, 1877), 62.

24. Rosenkranz, *Public Health;* Steinberg, *Nature;* William T. Sedgwick, "An Epidemic of Typhoid in Lowell, Mass." *Boston Medical and Surgical Journal* 124 (April 23 and 30, 1891): 397–402, 426–430; William T. Sedgwick, "On Recent Epidemics of Typhoid Fever in the Cities of Lowell and Lawrence Due to Infected Water Supply; With Observations on Typhoid Fever in Other Cities and Towns of the Merrimack Valley, Especially Newburyport," *Twenty-Fourth Annual Report* (Boston: Massachusetts State Board of Health, 1893).

25. Jeff C. Michaelson, "Aniline in History and Technology," *Endeavor*, new ser., vol. 17 (3):121–126 (1993).

26. Jonathan Harr, *A Civil Action* (New York: Random House, 1995), 176–179.

27. V. S. Byers, A. S. Levin, D. Ozonoff, and R. W. Baldwin, "Association between Clinical Symptoms and Lymphocyte Abnormalities in a Population with Chronic Domestic Exposure to Industrial Solvent-Contaminated Domestic Water Supply and High Incidence of Leukemia," *Cancer Immunology and Immunotherapy* 27:77–81 (1988); see also, bibliography in Harr, *A Civil Action.*

28. Theo Colborn, Dianne Dumanoski, and John Peterson Myers, *Our Stolen Future* (New York: Dutton 1996).

29. In most of the world, raw sewage does continue to flow directly into oceans, lakes, and rivers. In New England, the contemporary problem is two-fold. First, the outfall of sewage treatment plants continues to add significant quantities of nutrients, particularly nitrogen, to waters, distorting the balance of species in a waterway and even causing anoxia. Second, dense development relying on poorly designed or ill-maintained septic systems continues to pour raw sewage into ground and surface water.

16. *Fishing for Profits (pp. 222–234)*

1. William Foster Lloyd, *Two Lectures on the Check to Population* (1833; reprint, New York: Augustus Kelly, 1968). The classic, original description of the Tragedy of the Commons, brought to contemporary prominence by Garrett Hardin in "The Tragedy of the Commons," *Science* 162 (1968); 1243–1248.

2. Andrew German, "History of the Early Fisheries: 1720–1930," in *George's Bank*, ed. Richard Backus and Donald Bourne (Cambridge: MIT Press, 1987), 409 ff.

3. Richard Hennemuth and Susan Rockwell, "History of Fisheries Conservation and Management," in *George's Bank,* 430 ff.

4. Bradford Brown, "The Fisheries Resources," and Michael Fogarty, Michael Sissenwine, and Marvin Grosslein, "Fish Population Dynamics," in *George's Bank*, 480 ff., 494 ff.

5. Thomas E. Dahl, *Wetlands Losses in the United States, 1780's to 1980's* (Washington, D.C.: U.S. Department of the Interior, Fish and Wildlife Service, 1990).

6. Figures provided by Tom Decker, Massachusetts Bureau of Fisheries and Wildlife. Since the November 1996 elections, beaver trapping has been reduced by legislation outlawing most kinds of traps as inhumane. The state has had to increase expenditure for animal control officers hired to trap nuisance beavers, which have to be killed because the beaver have already reinhabited all suitable territory and there is therefore nowhere to release them even if nonlethal traps are used.

7. West Point, founded in 1802, was the nation's only engineering school. It trained civil engineers and many of its graduates went on to civilian careers building canals or laying out railroads. Industrial machinery and processes were designed by men who had come up through the shop door.

8. S. C. Prescott, *When M.I.T. Was Boston Tech, 1861–1915* (Cambridge, Mass.: Technology Press, 1954).

9. Peter Hall and Paschal Preston, *The Carrier Wave: New Information Technology and the Geography of Innovation, 1846–2003* (London: Unwin Hyman, 1988); Ann Markusen, Peter Hall, Scott Campbell, and Sabrina Deitrick, *The Rise of the Gunbelt: The Military Remapping of Industrial America* (New York: Oxford, 1991).

10. David L. Warsh, "War Stories: Defense Spending and the Growth of the Massachusetts Economy," *New England Journal of Public Policy* 2 (1): winter/spring 1986, reprinted in *The Massachusetts Miracle: High Technology and Economic Revitalization*, ed. David Lampe (Cambridge: MIT Press, 1988).

11. Ibid., 325.

12. Otto Scott, *The Creative Ordeal: The Story of Raytheon* (New York: Atheneum, 1974).

13. Markusen, et al., *The Rise of the Gunbelt, 127 ff.*

17. Terrarium Earth *(pp. 236–247)*

1. Paul R. and Anne H. Ehrlich, *The Population Explosion* (New York: Simon and Schuster, 1990) 13.

2. The appropriation was formally named the Laundry Brook Drainage Project, Laundry and Smelt being alternative names for the brook that drains Bullough's Pond. When rain is predicted, the Department of Public Works sometimes draws the pond down to enable it to act as a catchment basin. In unpredicted heavy rainstorms, however, the neighborhood streets still flood, since when the pond is full to the lip of its dam it can absorb no more runoff now that it is eight feet deep than it could when it was eight inches deep.

3. Carl Reidel, *The Yankee Forest: A Prospectus* (New Haven: Yale University School of Forestry and Environmental Studies, 1978). In that year, Maine, the most heavily forested state in the region, was 90 percent woodland while even Rhode Island, the

least forested state, was 60 percent woodland. See also Charles H. W. Foster, ed., *Stepping Back to Look Forward: A History of the Massachusetts Forest* (Petersham, Massachusetts: Harvard University Press for Harvard Forest, 1998).

4. National Acid Precipitation Assessment Program, *Interim Assessment; The Causes and Effects of Acid Deposition, Vol. 2, Emissions and Control* (Washington, D.C.: Government Printing Office, 1987). NAPAP was set up by the Reagan administration to evade demands that something be done about the acid rain problem. Study was seen as a politically preferable alternative to action. NAPAP reports merely restated what was already known, but they were a fairly thorough restatement of the problem.

5. G. H. Tomlinson, "Dieback of Red Spruce; Acid Deposition, and Changes in Soil Nutrient Status—A Review," in *Effects of Accumulation of Air Pollutants in Forest Ecology,* ed. B. Ulrich and J. Pankrath; R. G. Pearson and K. E. Percy, *The 1990 Canadian Long-Range Transport of Air Pollution and Acid Deposition Report , Part V, Terrestrial Effects* (Ottowa: Federal/Provincial Research and Monitoring Coordinating Committee, 1990), 42.

6. Arthur Johnson and Thomas Siccama, "Decline of Red Spruce in the High-Elevation Forests of the Northeastern United States," in *Air Pollution's Toll on Forests and Crops,* ed. James MacKenzie and Mohamed El-Ashry (New Haven: Yale University Press, 1989).

7. Reducing ambient ozone to 0.025 ppm would boost wheat production by 8 percent, soybeans by 17 percent, corn by 3 perecent and peanuts by 30 percent. These four crops account for 64 percent of U.S. agricultural output, measured by cash value. The effect of such improvement in air quality would be to increase the value of these four crops by $3.1 billion in 1978 dollars. W. W. Heck, et al., "Ozone Impacts on the Productivity of Selected Crops," in *Effects of Air Pollution on Farm Commodities* (Washington, D.C.: Izaak Walton League of America, 1982).

8. M. Trainer, et al., "Models and Observations of the Impact of Natural Hydrocarbons on Rural Ozone," *Nature* 329 (October 22, 1987): 705–707.

9. The first paved roads leading out of downtown areas were actually built in response to the bicycle craze of the 1890s, a romance dwarfed by the twentieth century's love affair with the automobile.

10. Bradford C. Snell, *American Ground Transport,* presented to the Subcommittee on Anti-trust and Monopoly of the Committee on the Judiciary, U.S. Senate, February 26, 1974, 27–34.

11. Kenneth Jackson, *Crabgrass Frontier: The Suburbanization of the United States* (New York: Oxford University Press, 1985), chapter 11.

12. Fekri Hassan, *Demographic Archaeology* (New York: Academic Press, 1981).

18. The Third Revolution (pp. 248–254)

1. George Perkins Marsh, *Man and Nature; or, Physical Geography as Modified by Human Action* (1864; reprint, Cambridge: Harvard University Press, 1965) 36.

2. By some accountings, there have already been three important revolutions: tool-making, Neolithic (agricultural), and industrial. So little is known about

the invention of tools that we cannot even make a very good guess at a date. We do know that a number of species not in the ape family use tools and that chimpanzees make tools. Neanderthals made tools, as did Homo erectus. Homo sapiens was born in a family of tool makers. Whosoever chooses may begin with the tool-making revolution, number the Neolithic Revolution second, and the Industrial third in the major upheavals in the history of technology.

3. Thomas M. Hoban and Richard O. Brooks, *Green Justice: The Environment and the Courts* (Boulder: Westview Press, 1996).

4. Maureen Smith, *The United States Paper Industry and Sustainable Production: An Argument for Restructuring* (Cambridge: MIT Press, 1997), 130.

INDEX